FRANÇOIS TRUFFAUT

FRANÇOIS TRUFFAUT

THE LOST SECRET

Anne Gillain Translated by Alistair Fox

with a new preface by the author

INDIANA UNIVERSITY PRESS *Bloomington & Indianapolis*

This book is a publication of

INDIANA UNIVERSITY PRESS
Herman B Wells Library 350
1320 East 10th Street
Bloomington, Indiana 47405 USA

iupress.indiana.edu

Telephone orders 800-842-6796
Fax orders 812-855-7931

∞ The paper used in this publication meets the minimum requirements of the American National Standard for Information Sciences–Permanence of Paper for Printed Library Materials, ANSI Z39.48–1992.

Manufactured in the United States of America

Cataloging information is available from the Library of Congress.
ISBN 978-0-253-00834-3 (cloth)
ISBN 978-0-253-00839-8 (paper)
ISBN 978-0-253-00845-9 (eb)

1 2 3 4 5 18 17 16 15 14 13

He used to say that he wished he could have been able to make films during the years between 1924 and 1925. He said: "That time was a truly extraordinary period – It would have been a real experience." He would like to have been a member of Hitchcock's generation, to be able to rediscover the lost secret.

JEAN GRUAULT

Contents

Preface to the English Edition of *François Truffaut: The Lost Secret*

ANNE GILLAIN

IT IS A GREAT PLEASURE TO SEE THE PUBLICATION IN ENGLISH of *François Truffaut: le secret perdu* twenty years after it came out in France. I am most grateful to Alistair Fox for his impeccable work as a translator and for his presentation of my book in a most illuminating introduction. I would like to add a few words, first to explain what prompted me to write this book at the time and also briefly to account for the additional insights time has brought to my understanding of Truffaut's films.

Over the past fifteen years, a number of important books have been published about Truffaut. Two French publications are particularly noteworthy: one is a 400-page biography by Antoine de Baecque and Serge Toubiana that constitutes an essential source of information about the director's life.[1] Since Truffaut's films are profoundly autobiographical, this volume of documented and quotable data is invaluable. The other book, by Carole Le Berre, entitled *Truffaut au travail,* analyzes in depth the genesis of each film from beginning to end.[2] Carole Le Berre has interviewed many of Truffaut's artistic collaborators – scriptwriters, photographers, editors, and actors – and discloses significant information about the conception of each film and its progressive elaboration. When these books came out, I was of course interested in the ways they might support my reading of the films. My goal, when I wrote *François Truffaut: le secret perdu,* was to follow the transformation of experience into fiction through a series of recurring thematic and structural figures. Twenty years later, the analyses of the films have, in my opinion, stood the test of time; they are in fact documented and contextualized by new knowledge in a most stimulating way.

As most viewers did worldwide, I had unconditionally loved all of Truffaut's films in the sixties. The early seventies, however, marked the beginning of some difficult times for the celebrated New Wave director. Between 1969 and 1973, Truffaut only had one international success with *The Wild Child*. The first discordant note was struck in 1969 with *The Mississippi Mermaid*. The critical reception of the film was harsh and started the legend that Truffaut, shooting with big stars and a big budget, had betrayed the ideals he had brilliantly helped to formulate, disseminate, and illustrate in the early sixties. *Bed and Board* (1970), *Two English Girls* (1971) and *A Gorgeous Girl Like Me* (1972) reinforced the downhill spiral with acerbic critics, dwindling audiences, and little financial rewards. While success came back in 1973 with *Day for Night* and its Oscar for best foreign film, it also fed and reinforced a prejudice: Truffaut was a seasoned director who worked well with actors and made charming old-fashioned movies, but his films lacked scope, substance, and depth. In the seventies, I was so convinced of the truth of this cliché that I had more or less stopped seeing his films altogether, or had, at least, missed several of them.

As it happens, on a hot day in the summer of 1976, quite by chance and partly motivated by the prospect of spending a couple of hours in an air-conditioned theater, I decided to go and see for the first time *Two English Girls* in an art-house theater – the Orson Welles – that was close to my place in Cambridge, Massachusetts. When I came out of the theater two hours later, my state resembled that evoked by Truffaut in his description of his goal as a director:

> I want my audience to be constantly captivated, bewitched. So that it leaves the theater dazed, stunned to be back on the sidewalk. I would like my audience to forget the place and time in which it finds itself, like Proust immersed in reading at Combray. I want above all emotion.[3]

Emotion had certainly occurred. *Two English Girls* had hit me full in the face. The depth and poignant accuracy the film displayed in his depiction of physical passion; its Proustian evocation of the flow of time through the flesh of the characters; its masterful use of voices, spaces, colors; and its distinctive weaving of text and images all deeply affected me. The scales had literally fallen from my eyes. I now knew two things: the recent critics who had condemned Truffaut's films were unfair, and the appreciation of his work as a whole was well worth reassessing. Truffaut was not a traditional and superficial director. His work captured an eternal truth about human nature and was endowed with timeless beauty. I think that my own experience is not exceptional. While preparing an edited volume on Truffaut,[4] I had the privilege to conduct, with my co-editor, Dudley Andrew, an interview with French director Arnaud Desplechin, who has an exceptional understanding of Truffaut's films.[5] One of the leitmotifs of his interview was to stress how wrong ("foolish" was the word he used to describe himself) he had been in his appreciation of Truffaut when he was young and how much he had underestimated the latter's work. It could, however, be said that Truffaut himself is responsible for the misreading of his films given his famous "ivory eggs" motto: films should be beautiful objects that can be looked at and touched, but not broken into. In other words, Truffaut's films are specifically designed to be enjoyed, not to be "understood." The contrast with Jean-Luc Godard, who forbids enjoyment but invites deconstructing, comes to mind. This may explain the abundance of scholarly work on the latter and the scarcity on the former. While admiring *Two English Girls* on the screen as a spectator, I also knew that it would be most difficult to account for its powerful spell as a critic.

A couple of years later, I used a sabbatical leave to go to Paris and take a French doctoral degree in film studies. There I had the privilege to study with world-renowned film theoreticians Christian Metz, Raymond Bellour, Michel Marie, Marc Vernet. It was a fascinating time when I also plunged into psychoanalytical theory and read Freud, Melanie Klein, Winnicott, and Guy Rosolato. I was supposed to write a short thesis and had already decided it would be on Truffaut's recent film *The Man who Loved Women.* Several of my colleagues were critical of this choice and told me I was making a serious mistake. Films by Marguerite Duras and Alain Robbe-Grillet, which seemed designed to illustrate the prevalent critical theories, were among the favorite thesis topics. In contrast to these works, Truffaut's films were considered "popular" art designed to please a wide audience and not highly regarded in academic circles.

The time was 1979 before videos or DVDs made films readily accessible. It was very difficult to gain material access to movies. Film remained, as the famous article by Raymond Bellour describes it, "Le texte introuvable." For this reason, I wrote a note to Truffaut's office asking for support. The following morning, I was awakened by a phone call from Joelle Couëdel, Truffaut's secretary, telling me: "Je vous passe François Truffaut." After a minute of shock, I adjusted and gratefully accepted his invitation to come and meet him at the office of Les Films du Carrosse in a small cul de sac near the Champs Elysées. I remember well this first encounter, which took place on the day in February when the radio was announcing Jean Renoir's death in Hollywood. My main impression when I left after an hour was one of contrasts. First, a contrast between his small, vivacious, and mobile person and the solemnity of an imposing mahogany-lined office that was filled in all directions by books. Books from the floor to the high ceiling on the shelves, books carefully piled up on his oversized desk. The most striking contrast, though, was between Truffaut's extreme kindness and generosity and a distant air that, in flashes, passed over his face, as if part of him were anchored in a different reality and engaged in thoughts lost for the rest of us. It was an uncanny feeling. His collaborators have often said that he was both shy and intimidating at the same time. One thing is sure: his eyes were extraordinarily intense and piercing. One of his favorite sentences was "J'ai tout de suite repéré ça" ("I immediately spotted that").

Truffaut took care of my problem in a regal way. First, he organized a private screening in a Champs Elysées theater so that I could see his most recent film: *The Green Room*. Then, from February to June, every Saturday morning, a motorcyclist brought one film in 35mm from Truffaut's personal collection to the Sorbonne-Paris III small viewing room, where I spent every Saturday afternoon handling the heavy rolls of films and watching them. In July of that year, Truffaut granted me an interview that was published in the United States.[6] My degree completed, I returned to Boston with an intention to write about his whole body of films sometime in the future. I still had the impression that accounting for the powerful vision his films created would be a challenge. It seemed to me that he was, by a long shot, the New Wave director about whom it was the most difficult to write.

When *The Last Metro* came out in 1980, I was directly confronted with this challenge. I loved the film but could not find any way to break inside it. *The Last Metro* was among the most perfect of these "ivory eggs" Truffaut prided himself on creating. Convinced that the fabric of cinema is time, I took a stopwatch and started to time each scene and, within the scenes, each shot. Shortly, beautiful patterns appeared under my eyes, a wonderful network of hidden forms and figures that I attempted to analyze in an article. I was fairly pleased with the result and sent it to Truffaut. When I came back to France that summer, Truffaut invited me to dinner. The evening went by without him ever mentioning my article. He offered to drive me back to my place and, in the car, just before arriving, I made a slightly peeved remark about my article. I can still remember his little smile. He stopped the car and turned off the ignition as if he was going to have a conversation. Then he said, without looking at me: "J'ai été estomaqué" ("It knocked the wind out of me"). I was so surprised by this unexpected reaction that I probably remained silent. In any case, I don't remember anything else about the conversation. He was "estomaqué," but I was puzzled. I could not understand why he had used this word. I am now convinced that if I had simply said "Why?" he would have explained his reaction, even though it concerned a most personal matter. As things stood, it took me almost ten years to understand this exchange.

Truffaut died at 52 in 1984, and I first edited a volume gathering his interviews in French and in English in 1988. For each film I created a montage of his most significant remarks at the time the film had come out and added a section with his subsequent comments over the years. The book was published by Flammarion in France under the title *Le Cinéma selon François Truffaut.*[7] This work completed, I undertook to do research for a critical book on all of his films. Truffaut had named his ex-wife, Madeleine Morgenstern, as legal representative for his estate, and she generously welcomed scholars to Les Films du Carrosse, which from then on exclusively handled the distribution and rights of Truffaut's films. Madame Morgenstern came daily to the office, a warm and discreet presence, and worked with one of the director's former secretaries, Monique Holveck. Everything had been left as it was before Truffaut's death, and his vast office with its high ceilings was kept unoccupied, a silent space with its bookshelves filled with the books he loved. Les Films du Carrosse was still inhabited by its organizer, but now it seemed sadly quiet in contrast to my memory of its feverish activity on a day when I had visited it in January 1980. On that occasion, *The Last Metro* had been about to go into full production, and people were coming and going, doors slamming, and all the rooms were filled with busy professionals. Suzanne Schiffman, who had a small office next to Truffaut's, was present, overseeing many different tasks, while the director himself seemed all over the place, dashing along the sinuous corridors, the *genius loci.*

In the late eighties, I worked there for many months side by side with Carole Le Berre, who was preparing her first book on Truffaut, consulting the wonderful archives Truffaut had so carefully accumulated and preserved over the years. For each film there were folders with countless precious documents: the different versions of the scripts (one of the largest was *Adèle H,* which Gruault rewrote eight times). Letters, photographs, and production documents were also available.[8] Sometimes a former collaborator or actor would come for a visit. I remember seeing Marcel Berbert, Truffaut's faithful producer, who played small parts in several of his films,[9] and a few actors, but I would like to evoke here what was for me the most moving of these encounters. While doing my research at Les Films du Carosse, I met the real-life René, Antoine Doinel's inseparable friend in *The 400 Blows.* His name was Robert Lachenay, and he was now a fragile older gentleman with white hair. He had met Truffaut in 1943, as a schoolboy, and remained in close contact with him throughout a life that had been much less successful than that of his illustrious friend. At the time, Truffaut's correspondence had just come out, and I had noticed that the first sixteen letters of the book were all addressed to Robert Lachenay between 1945 and 1950. I took this encounter as a chance to ask him a question that had intrigued me: why he had kept, as a youngster, the letters from a 13-year-old school friend. He looked at me and said in a contained voice: "Parce que j'ai toujours su qu'il serait quelqu'un" ("Because I always knew he would be somebody").

When I finally wrote *François Truffaut: le secret perdu,* I had no knowledge of Truffaut's life except for the few facts of his official biography. The recurrent presence of a seductive and awe-inspiring maternal figure was obvious in his work, and I chose to organize my book around it. I wasn't especially concerned with knowing anything more. I was interested in the system the films represented and the way they reflected a powerful and highly structured imaginary world. I knew – because he had said so – that his childhood was the most central part of his life, and I trusted what Truffaut had declared in an interview from the sixties: "*The 400 Blows* is not my autobiography." It so happened that in 1990, shortly before I turned in the manuscript of my book, Truffaut's father, Roland Truffaut, died. I had never met him, but I remembered the way Truffaut used to refer to him in a rather touching way as "mon papa." This is why I was most surprised to learn from Madeleine Morgenstern after his death that he wasn't Truffaut's father. He was the man who had married his mother and given the child a name, exactly as in *The 400 Blows*. I was told that Truffaut did not want this fact to become public knowledge as long as Roland Truffaut was alive, but that it could be disclosed now that the latter had passed away. I also came to hear the story everyone knows now: while shooting *Stolen Kisses,* a narrative that centers on a detective agency, Truffaut hired one of the detectives he had used for his documentation to find out the truth about his origins. He was told his father was Jewish and had become a dentist who lived in eastern France. Truffaut never contacted him, but legend has it that he made the trip to go and observe him in secret at night. I added a few sentences to mention this information in the preface of my book. At the time, *François Truffaut: le secret perdu* was completed, and I didn't see any connection between this newly revealed fact and the reading of the films I had presented in it. It took me a while to relate all of this to Truffaut's reaction in 1982 and finally to understand why he had been "estomaqué."

The reader will find the text I wrote in 1982 in this book, but I must briefly summarize my conclusions in order to lay out my surmise. In a nutshell, following the network of repetitions in the film, in particular the images of hands, forbidden spaces, and the recurring theme of undisclosed secrets, I concluded that the whole film was a vast metaphor evoking a hidden father inside the mysterious maternal body represented by the space of theater. The subject of this exploration is Depardieu, who is, from the start of the film, associated in a shot with the young son of the concierge, a boy of 10, the age Truffaut was during the German occupation of France. Lucas Steiner, the hidden figure, is of course Jewish. The reason Truffaut had said he was "estomaqué" when he read my analysis was simply because it made him realize that in *The Last Metro* he had staged the central mystery of his destiny: the unknown Jewish father. He had staged it unknowingly.

This anecdote, I think, calls for a couple of remarks. First, it proves that the application of psychoanalytical theories may lead straight to the truth; I like to make a note of it since, when my book came out, it was occasionally criticized for its use of psychoanalysis. Second, and more importantly, the anecdote proves that autobiography is indeed at the root of Truffaut's work in an intimate, profound, but largely occult way. Truffaut had no idea when he wrote the script and shot the film that he was weaving in its fabric the most central component of his biography, a fact that largely informs the structure of his imaginary world. A very private person, he would obviously never have devised a plot that was so blatantly indiscreet.

The place of autobiography is, to say the least, a thorny matter when it comes to discussing Truffaut's work as a director and often raises a fair amount of critical irritation. The concept is decried by film critics, and rightly so. It would be doing a terrible disfavor to Truffaut's artistic genius to reduce the interest of his work to autobiography. Autobiography has nothing to do with the lasting beauty of the films; this depends on their audacious, robust, and infinitely graceful constructions. At the same time, it is undeniable that experience is the stuff imagination processes to create fictions, and since the exercise of the creative imagination is indeed the topic of my research, I would like to review briefly the different modes through which this exchange between experience and imagination takes place.

Truffaut was not naïve and knew perfectly well he was using his life to create his films. He was also using the life of his entourage or the life of unknown persons when he clipped interesting "faits divers" from newspapers with the intention of archiving them for future use. Fiction is a vampire and constantly needs fresh blood. All the persons close to creators know it. *The Last Metro* was, with *The 400 Blows,* the largest financial success of Truffaut's career; both films are packed with personal references. *The Last Metro* presented for the first time a historical reconstitution of the actual time period of Truffaut's childhood (the German

Occupation), which had been transposed to the late fifties in *The 400 Blows*. *The Last Metro* was also explicitly designed around a beautiful feminine figure played by Catherine Deneuve, who, as Truffaut's biographers have disclosed, played a central role in Truffaut's personal life. Their encounter in 1969 on the set of *The Mississippi Mermaid* marked the beginning of a momentous two-year relationship in the director's life. When she left him, Truffaut suffered a nervous breakdown that required time in a clinic and a sleeping cure. *The Mississippi Mermaid* marks a turning point in the thematic components of Truffaut's films. The last shot, where the two lovers walk away in the snow looking for happiness, represents indeed the last representation in Truffaut's work of a passionate couple hoping for a shared future. From then on, love would only be represented as a painful and hopeless quest. *Two English Girls* would depict the failed love of a man for two sisters, inspired by Truffaut's relationship with Catherine Deneuve and her sister Françoise Dorleac, who had died in 1965. *Adèle H* and *The Green Room* would center on two forms of lost love. Either as unrequited or ripped away by death, love would be depicted as leading to madness or annihilation. After *The Mississippi Mermaid,* artistic creation would become the only locus for comfort and self-realization, as Truffaut's big comeback with *Day for Night* vibrantly celebrated. Unlike what happens in *Jules and Jim,* the exercise of creativity would protect the triangular love relationship in *The Last Metro*. The lovely exchanges between Lucas Steiner and his wife, played by Catherine Deneuve, may represent the idealized projection by Truffaut of the couple he would have formed with the actress had their relationship survived. There are, of course, the famous echoes from *The Mississippi Mermaid* in *The Last Metro* with "L'amour fait mal" and the heroine's first name, Marion, being the same in both films. *The Mississippi Mermaid* also finds an echo in *The Man who Loved Women* with the character of Vera, the lost great love, played by Leslie Caron. Carole Le Berre notes that the feather boa Vera wears when she runs into Bertrand in a hotel lobby was a deliberate replica of the one that adorned the Yves Saint-Laurent coat in *The Mississippi Mermaid.*[10] *The Woman Next Door,* as a whole, can be seen as a development of the Vera episode, centering on a passionate and destructive passion: "Neither with you nor without you." The biographers note that Truffaut said, half-jokingly, that he could have paid royalties to Deneuve for the dialogue of *The Woman Next Door.*[11]

These biographical references are clear and quite conscious on Truffaut's part. They are a wink to those who are in the know, and Truffaut mentioned that he sometimes made a film just to tell someone something instead of writing a letter. They also belong to the Balzaco-Proustian dimension of Truffaut's work as a global construction. His films can be enjoyed on their own, but contain as a whole countless intertextual references, rhymes, and correspondences. The biographical element belongs to this echo-chamber effect that lends continuity and coherence to his creation.

I will address now a much more complex side of autobiography. Truffaut has often said that he understood the personal ramifications of his films long after they had been completed. For instance, he realized that *The Wild Child* was not, as he had thought, about his encounter with Jean-Pierre Léaud, but about his relationship with André Bazin. His reaction to my essay on *The Last Metro* gave me an essential clue as to how the creative imagination worked and stealthily snatched away from its owner buried fragments of experience. "Estomaqué" illustrates a mental mode of perception that plays an essential role in the conception and reception of fiction. It has been studied by Christopher Bollas under the label of "unthought known" and by Daniel Stern as "implicit knowing." To account for this perceptual mode, we have to go back to the affect Truffaut placed at the center of his aesthetics: emotion.[12]

Recent research by the famous film theoretician Raymond Bellour – on cinema and hypnosis – and by the psychoanalyst Daniel Stern – on the pre-linguistic infant – casts a fascinating light on this issue.[13] Bellour, at the end of an extensive review of the interactions between cinema and hypnosis, concludes baldly: "Emotion . . . amounts to hypnosis."[14] If we remember Truffaut's eloquent description of his ideal spectator leaving the movie theater "bewitched . . . dazed, stunned to be back on the sidewalk," the evocation of a hypnotized subject does come to mind. This connection between emotion and hypnosis allows Bellour to engage in an in-depth exploration of the complex network of perceptions that fiction activates for the spectator. The hypnotic state has been compared to the pre-linguistic child's reception of reality, in which the body fully participates. This is where the research conducted by Daniel Stern becomes central to Bellour's argument. Stern's book offers a riveting account of the child's first reactions to his environment and the modalities of a perceptual mode that the acquisition of language will either repress or fracture. His views sharply differ from previous descriptions, in particular those of Piaget. Unlike Piaget, who considers the child's development as a series of successive stages, each replacing the previous one, Stern asserts that both systems, pre- and post-linguistic, remain active and develop in parallel throughout life without ever meeting each other. Language cannot and will not "translate" the pre-linguistic system that will be reactivated throughout life in a variety of human contexts, such as intersubjective, analytical, or religious or aesthetic experiences. In art, the formal components are for the adult subject the vectors of this experience, and style will trigger the pre-linguistic perceptual mode. Aesthetic emotion that involves, as it does in the infant's perceptions, a physical component promotes, as hypnosis does in the field of psychotherapy, a reordering of memories and a realignment of past and present that endows the experience with healing properties.

I will not attempt to summarize here Raymond Bellour's brilliant use of Stern's theories but will simply offer a glimpse of it by quoting the key statement of his demonstration: "Daniel Stern's *infant is* the cinema spectator."[15] Following this central insight, Bellour uses several of Stern's concepts to account for filmic reception. Among them, "vitality affects" is the most central.[16] According to Stern, the infant's first reading of reality is conducted through global perceptions of intensities and rhythms rather than by perceptions channeled through separate senses.

> Like dance for the adult, the social world experienced by the infant is primarily one of vitality affects before it is a world of formal acts. It is also analogous to the physical world of amodal perception, which is primarily one of abstractable qualities of shape, number, intensity level, and so on, not a world of things seen, heard, or touched.[17]

Vitality affects, contrarily to categorical affects such as joy, sadness, fear, et cetera, are best captured by dynamic and kinetic terms such as "surging," "fading away," fleeting," "explosive," or "crescendo." Stern considers that dance and music are, par excellence, examples of the expressiveness of vitality affects, while Bellour is prompt to declare that cinema, much more than dance or music, is the art form that fully captures the whole spectrum of exchanges between spaces and bodies. In this context, mise-en-scène can be viewed as an inscription of vitality affects in the shots and Bellour establishes "a frontal equivalence between the vitality affects in spontaneous behavior and style in art."[18]

Carole Le Berre was the first critic to highlight Truffaut's extreme care in his use of bodies and spaces in mise-en-scène. His characters, she noted, are rarely immobile in the frame, and only in scenes of extreme tension. Truffaut considered that while most shooting mistakes could be rectified on the editing table, an error of casting was irreparable. The wrong body would forever remain as a fatal flaw in a film. For instance, Truffaut always thought that Jean Desailly was miscast in *The Soft Skin* since, as Michel Chion writes: "His sluggish gait did not drive the film forward in space."[19]

One should also note that Truffaut's desire to make a film could originate in silent visuals that involved motions, as in the two following evocations of *Shoot the Piano Player* and *The Soft Skin:*

> As far as *The Piano Player* is concerned, I think that I made it on account of a single image. In Goodis's book, at the end, there is a little house in the snow, with fir trees, and a small sloping road, and a car glides along it silently, without one being able to hear the noise of the motor. I wanted to re-create this image.[20]

> *The Soft Skin* originated from an image . . . of a couple in a taxi. I could see it as taking place around 7:30 pm. They are intending to have dinner. They are not married or, if they are married, they are married, with children, to someone else, an incredibly carnal kiss takes place in this taxi, in the midst of a big city.[21]

These two primal images of cars moving along in well-defined settings highlight the non-verbal nature of inspiration. Truffaut loved wordless scenes where, as in silent movies, mise-en-scène produced meaning through the use of bodies and spaces. A kinetic reading of Truffaut's films is particularly rewarding, starting with Antoine Doinel's long run to the sea, or the trio on bicycles in *Jules and Jim,* or the women's legs in *The Man who loved Women.* One might also recall the opening scene of *Day for Night,* in which the director orchestrates the motion of the actors in the street scene as a conductor would with his musicians, imposing his own internal cadence to the moving bodies. I would like to suggest that this is where the real autobiographical impulse lies. Imagination invests visual configurations and formal structures that define the artist's style. I will take, as one example among many, the prevalence of the vertical space in Truffaut's mise-en-scène. Verticality functions in his films as a fundamental vector of subjectivity, and most of his characters are defined according to this spatial component: *The Soft Skin* is entirely organized between the initial subway ride underground to the flight in planes or the elevator rides. *The Wild Child* begins with the ascension of a tree and ends with Victor climbing a stair. Truffaut loved aerial shots, and we can find them in *Jules and Jim, The Bride Wore Black,* and the opening of *Stolen Kisses.* Let us also remember the rotor in which Antoine Doinel escapes the pull of gravity and exults with happiness. In contrast, underground spaces are always confining and claustrophobic: the cellar in *The Last Metro* or in *Confidentially Yours.*

The pre-linguistic language that Bellour identifies in the film of fiction is not only present in the form of spatial mise-en-scène in Truffaut's films, but also in the form of elegant and powerful metaphors, a stylistic figure that Daniel Stern defines in the following terms:

> Metaphor is a major form of linkage between unconscious autobiographical memory and conscious experience . . . metaphor is not just a figure of speech but a primary form of cognition (prior to symbol formation and language) that links different domains of experience including past and present. Language can later use these linkages and turn them into linguistic metaphors, but it does not start with language.[22]

This quotation could have been made with the "unknown Jewish father" in *The Last Metro* in mind. What better example could there be of "unconscious autobiographical" memory as metaphoric figure? Imagination is the key operator in the metamorphosis of experience into metaphors that Stern's statement identifies as being an integral part of the pre-linguistic system. Metaphors represent the mind's fundamental way of structuring reality and establishing a signifying network of "correspondences."

This process seems highly operational in Truffaut's work, and I will give a few examples of the way it structures the narrative flow. At the beginning of *The Last Metro,* the film displays a prohibition on touching with hands, while the last shots present a close-up of hands clutching each other in a glorious reconciliation. Metaphoric figures also create an intertextual network from film to film. Within *Jules and Jim,* the initial fire that catches Catherine's nightgown forms an internal rhyme with the cremation fire at the end, but the close shot of Catherine's foot under the table creates another rhyme with the close-up of her foot on the accelerator of the car in the murder/suicide scene. Both images recur through all of Truffaut's films: the reader will recall the many shots of fire and women's shoes in his oeuvre.

I remember students asking if Truffaut "knew" he was inserting these rhymes. When I conducted my interview with him, I wanted Truffaut to comment on formal constructions in his films – for instance, the numerous windows in *The Wild Child.* His answer was: "I needed them. Decisions in mise-en-scène are instinctive."[23] Imagination, to use a word Truffaut was fond of, invests formal constructions in an "indirect" way, and the whole process could be summarized, in a terse but accurate manner, as follows: autobiography gets imbedded in vitality affects (and other components of the pre-linguistic system that Daniel Stern studies at length); in turn, vitality affects inform and determine style; style generates a slight hypnosis that modifies the viewer's perceptual system and triggers emotion. Most of this process is indeed instinctive for the artist. Its vector is imagination, and it does not go through the regular cognitive channels of conscious thought. Along the same line of inquiry, another question can be raised that is much more important for the critic: does the spectator "see" these formal constructions when he watches the films? Yes and no. They belong to the slight hypnosis the film generates. These constructions both induce hypnosis, expanding the range of our perceptual system that normal activity purposefully restricts, and allow for the reading of the network of correspondences. The best way to define this perceptual mode is to compare it to unfocused vision as contrasted to focused vision. We see these forms, but we don't consciously "know" we are seeing them. While our attention is focused on plot development, our peripheral vision absorbs the multiple parameters of mise-en-scène (for instance, the vertical organization of space, visual rhymes, motions of bodies, objects) as well as metaphoric figures. This ensemble constitutes the texture of shots that are packed with indirect signals. It frontally affects our reading of the film and triggers emotion, but nevertheless belongs to implicit knowing as Stern defines it: "Most simply, implicit knowledge is nonsymbolic, nonverbal, procedural, and unconscious in the sense of not being reflexively conscious."[24] Truffaut's films are rich in a nonconscious subtext that relentlessly stimulates the spectator's perception. His style presents a tight codification of reality (Truffaut called it "stylization") that is not meant to be readily deciphered but deeply impacts the viewer in a subliminal way. Truffaut's evolution can be defined as a progressive simplification of his code of representation. Selecting some highly charged signs (photographs, fire, scissors, key sentences), Truffaut cultivates in his latter films a Spartan style that evokes the simplified lines of Matisse's drawings at the end of his life. Retrospectively, I understand that *François Truffaut: The Lost Secret* offers a decoding of the peripheral vision present in the films. The book weaves back and forth between the main thrust of the narrative and the innumerable signals embedded in the shots. I received a few letters after the publication of my book, and one correspondent explained that after seeing a Truffaut film, he would rush home to read the relevant chapter and thus know what he had seen. This is, of course, exactly what I hope this book could accomplish for each viewer: open up the beautiful ivory eggs and reveal their secret constructions.

One reason I am especially gratified to see this book published in English is that Truffaut had a deep attachment to the United States. It was not only the land where the film industry was born, but also where his two mentors, Jean Renoir and Alfred Hitchcock, lived. Until their deaths, which occurred a few months apart, he came every year to visit them in Hollywood. Truffaut was most sensitive to the critical reception of his films in this country, and I remember a little anecdote he had told me. When he stayed at the Plaza Hotel in New York, he could see from the window of his room the entrance of the Paris Theater down below across 58th Street. If, by chance, one of his films was playing there, he would watch the line forming in front of the cinema and rejoice when it was long: "Bon. Ils viennent" (Good. They are coming). He laughed telling the story, and his laughter was, I remember, infectious. I feel especially gratified that my book will come out in the country he loved so much and hope it will contribute to the appreciation of his films. I want to express once again all my grateful thanks to Alistair Fox for translating it and to Indiana University Press for publishing it.

Emotion and the Authorial Fantasmatic
An Introduction to the English Edition of Anne Gillain's *François Truffaut: The Lost Secret*

ALISTAIR FOX

1

Few would dispute the view that François Truffaut was one of the most important influences on cinema in the twentieth century, both as a filmmaker in his own right and as a critic. As one of the young "firebrands" associated with the journal *Cahiers du cinéma* in the 1950s, he attacked the conventional practices of the so-called "cinema of quality" in France, which he considered clichéd and unimaginative, and, in the course of doing so, propounded the "auteur theory," which asserted that "a work is good to the degree that it expresses the man who created it."[1] As a filmmaker, he established the model for "personal cinema," consisting of low-budget productions that serve as vehicles for the exploration of personal issues through imaginative representations that are depicted in a style that is recognizably distinctive to the filmmaker. Not only was Truffaut a formative influence on the films of the French New Wave, but he also paved the way for the independent films in the 1960s and beyond that constitute the New American Cinema, as well as providing a model for auteur filmmakers in any number of national cinemas (one thinks of Jane Campion in Australia, Wong Kar Wai in Hong Kong, or Tsai Ming Liang in Taiwan, for example).[2]

Despite Truffaut's importance as an influence on subsequent filmmaking, his own films have not received as much critical attention as they deserve, with the majority of studies being descriptive rather than analytical. Anne Gillain's *François Truffaut: le secret perdu,* published in French in 1991, is a notable exception, and a number of scholars and critics have recognized that this extraordinary book is one of the best and most important interpretive works on Truffaut ever written. For those fortunate enough to have encountered her work, this volume needs no introduction. For those as yet unfamiliar with her analyses, it may come as a surprise to find how highly regarded this undeservedly neglected project has been among the world's foremost experts on the French New Wave. Michel Marie, a leading authority on the New Wave, describes it as "a brilliant psycho-biographical analysis,"[3] while David Kehr, in appraising a retrospective of Truffaut's films in 1999, adduced Gillain's book in support of his contention that Truffaut was "a thornier, more complex filmmaker than we [have] thought, and perhaps a greater one."[4] Given its manifest importance, it is all the more striking, then, that Gillain's study has remained largely overlooked in the Anglophone world.

This strange neglect can be explained by the fact that, at the time Gillain's book was first published, neither her subject matter nor her approach was in vogue: in short, she was ahead of her time. By the 1990s, Truffaut had come to be regarded with some degree of condescension by those who preferred the allegedly greater complexity of Jean-Luc Godard, one of the leading lights of the New Wave.[5] Whereas Godard was widely considered to be intellectual, innovative, and politically engaged, there was a tendency to think of Truffaut as a rather lightweight filmmaker associated, as Kehr puts it, with "a life-loving, lightly romantic view of the world as a place filled with pretty girls, adorable children and heroes illuminated by a wise, warm understanding of the fleeting nature of love."[6] Gillain's achievement in *François Truffaut: le secret perdu* was to demonstrate beyond question that this view of Truffaut was very far from the truth, but few scholars seemed predisposed to register this fact. She was not the only one to have suggested the existence of a deeper complexity in Truffaut's work. Earlier, Serge Daney had detected two creators at work simultaneously: "a 'Truffaut-Jekyll,' respectable and ordered, who pleases families, and a 'Truffaut-Hyde,'" who was "asocial, solitary, spontaneously passionate, a fetishist."[7] Gillain, however, has been the only scholar able to provide at length convincing evidence to support Daney's intuition. Drawing upon the psychoanalytic theories of D. W. Winnicott, she was able to establish the coexistence in all of Truffaut's films of a fantasmatic script that the filmmaker elaborates in conjunction with the superficial literal narrative. More than that, she was able to demonstrate the coherence and continuity of a unified personal vision that spans Truffaut's entire oeuvre, a vision that informed every aspect of his mise-en-scène at the same time as it ensured that each work would relate to all the others as variants on a common theme.

In pursuing a study of this sort, Gillain was extending the work of earlier scholars who had begun to interpret cinema in the light of psychoanalytic theory. The idea that a film could function like a dream, or a form of play, was proposed as early as the 1920s, later receiving serious critical attention from scholars such as Jean-Louis Baudry and Christian Metz (in his influential book, *The Imaginary Signifier: Psychoanalysis and the Cinema* [1977]).[8] At the level of textual analysis, Raymond Bellour had also demonstrated how useful a psychoanalytic framework could be for the interpretation of cinema in his groundbreaking study of the films of Alfred Hitchcock, while feminist scholars with a psychoanalytic orientation, such as Laura Mulvey, Teresa de Lauretis, and Mary Ann Doane, had drawn upon psychoanalytic ideas in their exploration of such issues as gender stereotyping, and the role of women as fetishes and the objects of the male voyeuristic gaze.[9] Despite these earlier explorations, however, the potential for a psychoanalytic approach to reveal the dynamics of the creative process that links an auteur filmmaker to his or her work had hardly begun to be explored. It was only when Anne Gillain invoked Winnicott's theories in order to consider cinema as a transitional space enabling a filmmaker, in this case Truffaut, to engage in a form of unconscious therapeutic "play," that the full extent of these links became apparent for the first time.

A further reason for the initial neglect of Gillain's study when it first appeared is likely to have been her choice of a psychoanalytic approach that privileged the author/auteur as a primary, originating source of meaning. *François Truffaut: le secret perdu* was written at a time when enthusiasm for poststructuralist theory was at its height. According to such theory, the author, following Roland Barthes, was presumed "dead."[10] Similarly, Michel Foucault had replaced the idea of an actual author with that of an "author function," in which "the author" was merely the product of a network of relationships and discourses rather than an individual originating genius.[11] Under the influence of this assumption (that is to say, that texts are culturally written, rather than personally written), scholars writing on Truffaut since the 1980s have tended to distance themselves from any suggestion that a director's films embody a "coherent set of themes and motifs which correspond to the particular genius of the individual," focusing instead on the idea that filmmaking involves "a complex process of film production and reception which includes socio-economic and political determinants, the work of a large and highly skilled team of artists and technicians, the mechanisms of production and distribution, and the complex and multiply determined responses of spectators."[12] The result has been a series of studies that concentrate on the sociopolitical contexts of the creation and reception of Truffaut's films;[13] their thematic and generic categorization;[14] the strategies of Truffaut the craftsman;[15] and their imbrication "in a broader intertext of a proliferation and variegated spectrum of texts."[16]

By opting for a psychoanalytic approach grounded in object-relations theory and D. W. Winnicott's theories concerning the purposive role of play involving the use of transitional objects, Anne Gillain set herself on a trajectory that was independent of the dominant intellectual trends at the time when her book was written. Not only was the idea of an author with originating agency out of fashion, but what psychoanalytic criticism did exist tended to be heavily influenced by the differential theory of Lacan, which, being based on an assumption that any entry into subjectivity depends upon a specular illusion, because of the inescapable indeterminacy resulting from the differential process, also tended to deprive the author of creative agency. Instead of focusing on the author, therefore, Lacanian approaches concentrated on the deep structures underlying the production of meaning in films.[17] The novelty of Gillain's approach meant that she could not be categorized within this kind of poststructurally inflected approach, just as Truffaut had been out of step with his times because of his distance from contemporary intellectual movements, including poststructuralism.

Recently, however, there have been signs that the pendulum has begun to swing in the opposite direction, providing circumstances that are propitious for the reappearance of Gillain's pioneering work. Andrea Sabbadini has noted a new pluralistic orientation in psychoanalytic approaches to the study of cinema that has produced "interpretations of films in the light of unconscious defensive mechanisms, internal objects and their relationships, developmental stages and positions, modalities of attachment and separation-individuation, transitional phenomena, Oedipal predicaments, [and] psychodynamic understandings of mental pathology."[18] The advent of studies of this sort signals a shift away from what Sabbadini calls the "Lacanian matrix," allowing "significant light" to be shed on "the emotionally charged interrelationships between filmmakers, their artistic products and their audiences."[19] Building on his perception of this shift, Sabbadini has recently drawn upon Winnicott's ideas to formulate his own Winnicottian concept of cinema as "a bridge space connecting external reality to its filmed representation, as well as the latter to reality as perceived by the viewer's gaze."[20] Filmmakers themselves have contributed to this process. Bernardo Bertolucci, for example, has talked very frankly about how cinema provides a transitional space for him, in which the material he unconsciously elaborates in films serves the same function as the material he takes to a psychoanalytic session.[21] In words that echo what Truffaut had said several decades earlier,[22] Bertolucci has admitted that "Very often, I think that I understand my movies after I've done them."[23] The arrival of a wider range of psychoanalytic theoretical parameters makes the time ripe for the reappearance of Gillain's investigation of the processes with which they are concerned.

Commensurately, the idea that the author is dead seems largely to have run its course, as attested by a renewed scholarly interest in the question of authorship. The plethora of recent books on auteurism and authorship that have appeared since the turn of the millennium suggests a degree of dissatisfaction with the extent to which the auteur role was downplayed as a result of the poststructuralist privileging of discursive processes and contextual circumstances over the input of the filmmaker.[24] It is significant, for example, that in the most recent book devoted to the study of literary adaptation, Francis Vanoye's *L'Adaptation littéraire au cinéma* (2011), Vanoye appeals to exactly the same Winnicottian framework that Gillain had applied twenty years earlier, affirming that cinema provides a powerful form of "transitional space" in which the imaginative filmmaker, through strategies of identification and projection, can engage in a form of creative play that allows him or her to gain access to reality in terms that allow a fruitful participation in it.[25] Such a view reflects a reaction against the kind of "post-auteurism" that assumes that the auteur is nothing more than "an intricate set of industrial processes."[26]

Finally, the two trends identified above are reinforced by a further trend: namely, a new interest in the sources, role, and effects of emotion, evident in both the humanities and the social sciences, which Patricia Ticineto Clough has identified as "the affective turn."[27] One of the most influential figures in this regard has been the neurobiologist Antonio Damasio, whose revolutionary findings and hypotheses have led to a revised concept of consciousness itself. Damasio argues that consciousness resides in "the ability to create representations of the world within, and of the world around an organism," and then "the ability, in turn, to make those representations felt," which is a consequence of the brain's capacity to generate a "feeling aspect" to any thought one has, as a result of the body's reaction to the stimuli of the senses.[28] The central role that emotions and feeling have in allowing the brain to manage our strategies for operating in the external world obviously has huge implications for the way in which we construe the purpose and effects of fictive representations such as those Truffaut creates. As Michael Hardt points out, affects illuminate "both our power to affect the world around us and our power to be affected by it, along with the relationship between these two powers."[29] Cinematic representation, as Gillain recognized, is at the intersection of these two powers, and her deep understanding of the importance of emotion for Truffaut makes her study of this filmmaker an important source of evidence for the processes that are involved.[30] Speaking in 1976, Truffaut himself admitted that "I've had to come to terms with the fact that the affective domain is the only thing I care about, and the only thing that interests me."[31] Such a preoccupation on the part of the filmmaker means that he is an ideal subject for anyone studying the workings of affect. For many reasons, then, the reappearance of Gillain's *François Truffaut: le secret perdu* is unusually timely given the current conversations that are being conducted within cinema studies.

2

Apart from offering unique insights into the work of a master filmmaker, Gillain's book also illuminates the very nature of the creative process, thus making a significant contribution to the emerging debates concerning authorship, the role and nature of fictive invention, and the wellsprings of creativity itself.

Gillain argues that the creation of emotion was the structuring principle of Truffaut's work, and that this creative impulse was anchored in his personal experience of a traumatic childhood. She demonstrates how, for Truffaut, the representational strategies of cinematic fiction-making enabled him to gain access to his unconscious, and how necessary such access was for the restoration and maintenance of his personal equilibrium. For Truffaut, she argues, the imaginative outlet provided by cinematic creation was the only way that the nature of things could be comprehended, owing to the ability of fictive representation to provide a symbolic order capable of providing a safeguard against the threat of an undifferentiated chaos in the outside world, the experience of which was potentially terrifying. In her analyses of the individual films, Gillain shows how involuntary memories arising from Truffaut' childhood furnish a succession of motifs that are repeated from film to film. All of them involve a single, unique, fantasmatic scenario that centers on a maternal figure who is distant, ambiguous, and inaccessible, causing the filmmaker, via his avatars, to be engaged in an endless search for a security and satisfaction that eludes them and, by extension, Truffaut himself.

To show the consistency and continuity of Truffaut's imaginative (and often unconscious) practices, Gillain discusses his films in pairs, often selecting them from different periods in his filmmaking career or combining apparently disparate films that diverge in tone or mode. Thus she shows how an early and a late film that superficially seem to be diametrically opposed – *The Woman Next Door* (1981), which explores a compulsive, adulterous, death-dealing erotic attraction between two adults, and *The 400 Blows* (1959), which depicts the rites of passage of an adolescent boy – are in fact preoccupied with the same thing: a desire for fusion with a maternal figure that dissolves the differentiation between the world of adults and that of children through an irresistible Oedipal regression (see Chapter 1). Similarly, the pairing of *The Bride Wore Black* (1967), a dark, tragic tale of revenge and murder involving a virgin, with *A Gorgeous Girl Like Me* (1972), a lighthearted comedy involving a prostitute, might seem unlikely until one encounters Gillain's compelling elucidation of the common obsession that drives both of their heroines, arising from the theme of a murdered childhood (see Chapter 5).

Gillain's unequaled sense of the relationship between Truffaut's unconscious fantasmatic preoccupations and his mise-en-scène enables her to identify and interpret the meaning of visual motifs that are laden with a latent signification that less-attentive spectators might not consciously register. Thus she points to the recurrence of incidents in which people or things fall, representing a fear of psychic dissolution – the falls of Thérésa in *Shoot the Piano Player* and Madame Jouve in *The Woman Next Door;* the association of hope with aerial movement – Lachenay taking off in a plane for Lisbon in *The Soft Skin,* Louis Mahé climbing up the facade of the hotel in *Mississippi Mermaid;* the motif of books and reading as a transitional object symbolizing attachment to the mother – the books in *Fahrenheit 451* and the book that Bertrand Morane is writing in *The Man Who Loved Women;* and so on. Locations, too, are seen to have symbolic resonance in Gillain's readings. She points, for example, to the function in *Jules and Jim* of timeless natural landscapes and moist places as an extension of the female body, as in the lake shrouded with mist that Catherine and her lovers visit during their stay in a chalet near the Rhine. The female body is again symbolically evoked through the use of space, in Gillain's account, in the labyrinthine corridors and stairways of *The Last Metro,* just as it is in the dark recesses of the sewer into which Antoine pushes a milk bottle in *The 400 Blows.*

Equally revelatory is the connection she is able to make between Truffaut's stylistic practices and the nature of the fantasmatic script they are designed to articulate. In *The Soft Skin,* for instance, she shows how Pierre Lachenay's attempt to live through the maintenance of a false self is reflected in a larger-than-usual (for Truffaut) number of shots that focus on close-ups of impersonal objects. Whereas his standard films consist of around 500 shots, this one contains nearly 900. As Gillain demonstrates, Truffaut's strategy serves to emphasize how Lachenay's attempt to create a false self lead to a life that is like an empty shell. At the other end of the spectrum is *The Bride Wore Black,* containing only 400 shots, among which are many long sequence-shots. This strategy, Gillain shows, is designed to reinforce the mythic, fairytale quality of the narrative and its rigorous stylization and simplification, in order to underscore the function of the film as a fantasy concerning the avenging of a murdered childhood and the arrest of a dream of unfulfilled love.

Gillain also establishes how even the framing in Truffaut's movies is governed by the fantasmatic scenario that is driving each film. We see this in *The Man Who Loved Women,* in which the constant fragmentation of the female body, through the alternation of shots that isolate the busts and legs of women, intimates the fantasmal presence of a maternal figure who is as unknown and inaccessible as she is desirable, to the son who longs for fusion with her at the same time as he fears the consequences of that fusion. Another striking example occurs in *Fahrenheit 451,* where the recurrent framing of books as they fall to the ground is realized through tracking shots that ensure that no books are allowed to fall outside of the frame. The effect is to underline the function of the book-object as a metonym for a sentimental attachment that is associated with the maternal presence (see Chapter 6). By drawing attention to countless instances such as these, in which technique is determined by an unconscious fantasmatic intention, Gillain provides startling new insights into the nature and workings of Truffaut's creative imagination and the unconscious motivations that fuel and shape his practices as a filmmaker. In so doing, she displays an interpretive acuity that is almost unique in Truffaut criticism, at the same time as she confirms the depth and complexity of his filmmaking.

3

What, then, does Gillain's analysis reveal about the creative process? In the first place, it confirms the parallel between fictive creation and the mechanisms of a dream as posited by Freud. The type of representation to be found in Truffaut's films constitutes an indirect response to the world that is formulated at a displaced remove from the filmmaker's actual experience in a highly condensed metaphoric language. The aim of such a strategy is to attain a state of psychic well-being as a result of the experience of emotion generated by the strategies of the representation. Emotion enables the author's repressive and censoring mechanisms to be bypassed, which in turn allows access to the unconscious, so that the real issues besetting the subject who is engaged with the creative work can be addressed.

Normally, Gillain surmises (following Freud), the psychic apparatus is set up to impose a "blocking procedure" that protects the individual subject against the primal fear aroused by archaic perturbation. She demonstrates how Truffaut used cinematic creation as a means of achieving liberation from this psychic blocking by exploiting ellipsis created through techniques such as voice-over (to create a tension between what is said and what is shown), superimposition (to mix iconic referents), and the multiplication of micro-stories (to delay the constitution of the representation as a story). She also shows how Truffaut uses repetition to create a system of rhymes and parallels forming a network of overdetermined images, actions, and motifs that encompasses his whole oeuvre, providing a subterranean unity. The repetition of such overdetermined material not only allows the filmmaker access to his or her unconscious, but also activates the imagination of the spectator in order to achieve the same purpose by allowing his or her perceptual apparatus to evade the vigilance of the rational. Paradoxically, on the filmmaker's part, such a process allows simultaneously for the expression of repressed content and also for the maintenance of a protection against the potential effects of its expression. Although Truffaut himself did not articulate the self-protective dimension of this representational strategy, its ambivalent motivations have been succinctly identified by another auteur director, Jane Campion; commenting on her film *Sweetie* (1989), she says:

> I can't let myself know things in a direct way, so I've always understood and known more than I can know directly through metaphor. Like, it's the same as going to see a psychic – part of me already knows something's doomed, but I can only read it in signs . . . all the good ideas just arrive, you don't figure them out, they just arrive. You don't know how they come. A lot of the time you're trying to block that instinct because it's more than you want to know about.[32]

As Gillain demonstrates, Truffaut might have said exactly the same thing with regard to his own creative impulses.

Gillain again follows Freud in supposing that the creativity involved in this kind of fiction-making activity relates to universal originary fantasies. In Truffaut's case, such fantasies, she shows, are associated with the great staging posts of human development: the acquisition of language, separation from parental figures, the quest for identity, integration into society, the discovery of the other, emotional relationships, sexuality, initiation into culture, the expression of creativity. Using Truffaut as a case study, she demonstrates the capacity of creativity to transform the undifferentiated aspects of experience into the order of a comprehensive vision by reactivating a syncretic mode of perception that transcends the limitations of rational perception. The result is a double reading encoded in the fiction that involves an opposition between two different modes of thought: a logical mode that is continually suspended by the detours in the story and a fantasmatic mode elicited by the repetitions that organize the coherence of the overall vision. The end purpose of such a strategy, and of the mechanisms to be found in fiction films generally, is, in Gillain's view, to enable a form of psychic regulation that allows us to situate ourselves in the world, and thus achieve or maintain a degree of equilibrium and psychic health. Significantly, a distinguished practicing psychoanalyst, Simona Argentieri has independently corroborated Gillain's findings concerning the functions of the creative process, basing her hypotheses similarly on a study of Truffaut's films. Recognizing that Truffaut "describes for us and for himself his childhood drama of not having had a symbolic space in the internal world of his mother or – in symmetry with this – the possibility of constructing within himself a safe and stable image of the female figure," Argentieri argues that "by vocation and unconscious motivations [he] is able to capture, evoke, create and re-create by means of the camera all the images of his own internal reality." On the evidence of Truffaut's practice, she concludes that "art – for those who create it as well as for those who enjoy it – is not only 'consolation' but also 'reparation'; it is an attempt to repair what, in the past, has been lost or damaged in our internal world."[33] Argentieri thus, from a psychoanalyst's point of view, arrives at the same point Gillain had reached twenty years earlier.[34]

Gillain's view of the creative process has significant implications for an understanding of the nature of cinematic authorship (and the authorship of any other kind of fictive representation, for that matter). Obviously, the author is far more than merely a set of industrial processes, even though his or her motivations inevitably have a social and institutional component. Despite the presence of these extrinsic factors, rather than simply being culturally written as an effect of socially produced discourses, the fiction he or she creates is the consequence of a conscious choice to give form and expression to a creative impulse arising from a complex nexus of intrapsychic desires and emotions, both manifest and latent. Furthermore, the work of art that results from this impulse is produced by a personal affective investment in the medium and its forms that is reflected in the nature of its enunciation. By establishing the integral relationship, in the case of Truffaut, between the nature of these investments and the circumstance of his biography on the one hand, and the nature of his thematic and stylistic choices on the other, Gillain does indeed demonstrate how the author as agent is personally responsible for the enunciation of his own work, although the extent of this responsibility is likely to vary to a greater or lesser degree depending upon the extent of the filmmaker's personal investment. In doing so, Gillain's study constitutes a major intervention into the current debates about authorship, which means that the appearance of this new edition in English is truly timely.

FRANÇOIS TRUFFAUT

Preface to the Original French Edition
One Secret Can Hide Another

JEAN GRUAULT[1]

I CAN STILL SEE AND HEAR FRANÇOIS IN THE SPRING OF 1983. We were sharing a light lunch, settled in a corner of his sitting room at la rue Pierre 1er-de-Serbie, which reminded me of that of Mila Parély in *The Rules of the Game,* surrounded by small-scale models of the Eiffel Tower and large windows, through which one could see the tower itself, served by Ahmed, his severe major-domo, who, in spite of our gross jokes, we could never get to crack a grin. François had hired him because he had formerly been the *maître d'hotel* of Marie-France Garaud, one of the two female politicians for whom he professed great admiration, the second being Mrs. Thatcher. He confessed his regret that he had not been born sufficiently early to start off as a filmmaker during the last years of the silent era and the very beginning of the talkies. He had a feeling that he had missed something, an experience that had been unique and irreplaceable, because although the language of cinema had been developed around 1912, it had only attained its perfection at the end of the 1920s. During the five or six years that had immediately preceded the appearance of movies with sound, exceptional conditions, which have never been replicated since, allowed the flowering of a surprisingly large number of first-rate works, considering such a short time span, and François would have liked to have been there, with Chaplin, Lubitsch, Hawks, Dwan, Walsh, Ford, Hitchcock, Gance, Duvivier, Renoir, and several others. Nevertheless, apart from a fascination with turn-of-the-century feminine underwear, he was not all that carried away by nostalgia. What he regretted was not so much the cinema of this period as its audience, to which he attributed virtues that it had possibly never had: a freshness of spirit, a mental agility that stimulated the imagination of directors, leading them to refine their style, to perfect their narrative strategies "by using images," to the point where, as with Murnau, they could communicate what was happening without using any intertitles at all. While he thought that spectators of his time were less naive, better informed, more cultivated, and also more intellectual, in many cases (which for François was not far away from being a defect), he also found them lazier and, according to him, through a boomerang effect, this laziness was communicated to filmmakers, who sent it back to the spectators – and so on . . .

The spectator of the 1930s, once he had recovered from his astonished amazement at hearing revolver shots, the wind howling, bells ringing, motors revving, floors creaking, and Greta Garbo speaking (just as thirty years earlier viewers had been amazed to see a train arrive at the station at La Ciotat), quickly fell into the habit inherited from silent cinema of interpreting what was presented to him, of resolving the riddle presented to him, in full complicity, at every moment, by clever young (and not-so-young) directors, most of whom had learnt their ropes, or had already had a career, in silent cinema.

Stories are always the same, whatever one might pretend. The problem, already faced by Scheherazade, is to keep the audience's attention to the end, of constantly awakening interest in what you are telling, *in images:* "Don't ever *tell* but *show*" (I am quoting François). That is why the word "image" annoys me. I do not want to refer to a "beautiful image," but an image that invites you to play with it, or rather with what it makes you see (the true filmmaker never plays on the spectator; he plays with him). That, it seemed to François, was what "the lost secret" was – for lack of other words, *gags.* As a group, these gags are linked together, reacting to each other in such a way as to form a story with a beginning, a middle, and an end. "I make normal films for normal people," François would always say.

In order to explain better what I mean, I am going to offer several examples. How does one show a young woman trying to decide between two lovers, while letting it be understood that her whole fate is going to depend on the nature of her choice? One could spell it out in intertitles (the solution of lazy silent cinema), or by an interminable dialogue between the girl and a bosom friend who gives her good or bad advice that she follows or does not follow (the solution in television dramas), or by a voice-over that reveals to us the dilemma that is tormenting the young woman while one watches her in front of her mirror doing nothing (the solution of the later New Wave movies).

What does Lubitsch do? It is Sunday. The petite milliner Pola Negri has two meetings: one with Armand, the honest young man she loves, and who loves her in return; the other with the noble libertine, Don Diego, the Spanish ambassador. Perplexity. She plucks the petals off of a daisy (figuratively speaking), by pointing successively to the five bows that adorn her bodice from top to bottom, from her breasts to her pubis, pronouncing alternatively with each ribbon the name of one of these two aspiring lovers – this starts with: "Armand, Don Diego, Armand . . . " and at the fifth and last ribbon she falls on Armand. She looks disappointed. After hesitating for a moment, she tries again, this time beginning with Don Diego, and, sure enough, she ends on Don Diego. What she wished for most deeply in her heart of hearts, but did not dare to admit, is thus justified by fate, a fate that she has, to our great amusement, somewhat contrived; she is going to become "la Du Barry." On the screen, all that merely lasts a few seconds: a single shot cut by two intertitles that create the image. You see, nonetheless, that I am not succeeding. Words are made for something else – something other than things.

Do I need to cite the very well-known episode in Charlie Chaplin's *A Woman of Paris: A Drama of Fate*? Marie and her rich protector Pierre Revel are arguing over the marriage that Marie is contemplating with her lover, a young penniless painter. Revel has a good laugh and tells her that she could never tolerate poverty. She replies to him: "What do I have in life? Nothing!" – "And what about that?" he replies to her, pointing to the magnificent pearl necklace she is wearing around her neck. Then in a grand theatrical gesture, she rips the necklace off and throws it out the window. In the street, a tramp picks it up. Suddenly changing her mind, she rushes outside, runs after the tramp, brutally snatches the necklace out of his hands, and returns into her apartment, but not without having broken the heel of her shoe. Revel is doubled over with laughter. We are too. And we have learned a lot more about Marie's character.

Other examples? A shy young man is sitting next to a young woman engaged in sewing. He loves her, she well knows, and she would like him to declare himself, but he does not dare to do this . . . and, for her part, she does not dare to take the first steps. A stalemate. She accidentally pricks herself with her needle. Motivated by gallantry as well as a concern for hygiene, he rushes forward to suck the blood that is welling from her finger. Then he quietly resumes his seat. The young woman is very impatient: is he finally going to take the plunge and kiss her? Then, deliberately, she pricks her lip . . . (*La Jeune Fille au carton à chapeau* [Boris Barnet, 1927]).

Need one recall sequences like the one with the pajamas that opens *Bluebeard's Eighth Wife,* that of the gondola-ashtray in *Trouble in Paradise,* the Laughton episode in *If I Had a Million,* – and let us go on, why scrimp? *To Be or Not to Be* in its totality? I invite you rather to go and see these films, or see them again. As Bach (the outrageous comedian, not the composer) said in one of his monologues: "to say what happened is not funny, but if you had only seen the picture!" Go, then, and see the picture!

What does this have to do, you ask me, with the secret that the book you are about to read explores? One secret can hide another.

François wondered who his father was (we considered many projects that would have dealt with this theme). I know only too well who mine was. But our true fathers, those that we would have chosen for ourselves, were the same, and we tried to be sons that were not too unworthy of them. François had their photos on his desk at the "Carosse"[2] they were Lubitsch and Chaplin, the guardians, if not of *the* lost secret, at least of *a* lost secret, one of those he was searching to find all through his life, and perhaps the only one (as his final films attest) that he succeeded in finding.

Jean Gruault
Sunday, 3 February 1991

Introduction
The Secret of the Art

FRANÇOIS TRUFFAUT BELIEVED THAT FILMMAKERS FROM THE past were the guardians of a lost secret, a nostalgia which haunted him. His achievement, having studied the art of his predecessors, was to know how to replicate this secret in his films. Since the appearance of his first film, *The 400 Blows,* Truffaut's work has moved audiences of all nationalities, ages, and cultures around the world. Thirty years after its creation, however, his oeuvre remains mysterious in terms of its dynamics, strategies, and aims. The qualities for which he is generally known (clarity, intelligence, sensitivity, humor), unremarkable in themselves, are not sufficient to explain fully the strange hold that his films have exercised over the imagination of spectators. The aim of this book, therefore, is to explore this phenomenon and respond to the three main questions that it prompts: What does Truffaut say in his films? How does he say it? Why do people everywhere listen to it?

Truffaut himself answered the first question:

> I have always thought that if *one has something to say,* then one should either say it or write it, but not make a film. A film does not say anything, a film conveys emotional information that is too shattering, too sensual, too dislocating for it to be capable of eventuating in a cold-blooded message.[1]

Accordingly, his films do not aim to convey a message. For a French artist active during the period between 1959 and 1983, the issues surrounding knowledge and its transmission were far from inconsequential. At the height of his fame and international success, Truffaut was subject to accusations that he had nothing important to say, and nothing that he stood for, even though, in actuality, he was highly attuned to what was taking place in his own times. Anticipating the needs of the collective imagination with an uncanny instinct, he was able to derive insights from his observations that informed his artistic creativity. The pattern of his development as an artist confirms this; the fact that his works are still being shown long after his death also confirms it. Nevertheless, he inhabited an internal time of his own, in which he drifted in a no-man's land, making him the contemporary of Proust, of James, of Léautaud, even though he remained firmly rooted in the pre-war years of his childhood – the epoch of his parents and the films of his early years, by Renoir, Guitry, and Carné – because of the effect of emotional memories that could be triggered by such things as social and linguistic habits, feminine fashions, and songs. He was never close to his contemporaries and remained at odds with the France of the 1960s, then undergoing one of the most powerful ideological convulsions in its history. This was a France in which intellectual life was dominated by a spectacular expansion of the human sciences – psychoanalysis, anthropology, sociology – and that displayed, in the fields of literature and cinema, an acute interest in the formal structures of artistic creation. This was a France marked by a rather striking absence of imaginative works, and in which, for a span of more than twenty years, a preoccupation with ideas was going to reign supreme. In short, this was a cerebral France in which the sciences were elevated over the arts and in which the rallying cries were: "understand," "learn," "instruct," "reform." The chasm between Truffaut and these contemporary intellectual movements opened up very quickly. From the time of *Shoot the Piano Player,* he was accused of not being interested in the Algerian War (even though he signed the Manifesto of the 121) and of ignoring May 1968 with *Stolen Kisses* (even though he was beaten up for seeking to protect Henri Langlois's cinémathèque). More seriously, his art was denounced as bourgeois, reactionary, and academic, reproaches that were used as critical clichés to justify the neglect of any in-depth analysis of Truffaut's films, and which would dog Truffaut right up until he made *The Last Metro.*

A man of imagination in an age that privileged intellectual reflection, Truffaut was destined to create his films in relative isolation, and he would see his work suffer a certain incomprehension, tinged with a degree of disdain. This contrasts with the success of his films overseas – in the United States, for example, where no such reservations dampened the enthusiasm with which they were received. The reticence in France was prompted not merely by the era itself, but also by a long tradition that has often prompted members of the French elite to be suspicious of works of fictive imagination, especially if they are received favorably by the general public. Such a predisposition is seen in Sainte-Beuve's criticism of Balzac, or in Gide's laying down of a resounding "Alas" at the feet of Victor Hugo's glory. For a long time, Truffaut was dismissed as a "commercial" auteur, prompting him to retort: "The word 'commercial' almost always gets us nowhere, since the most commercial *metteur en scène* in the history of cinema was also the greatest, Charlie Chaplin."[2]

One of the major causes of Truffaut's admiration for Chaplin was the latter's achievement in appealing to the largest audience in the history of cinema:

> It is difficult today, probably because of the trivialization of personalities by television, to imagine the celebrity of Chaplin. One photo from *L'Illustration*, taken in the 1920s, shows him from behind, on a balcony of the Hôtel Gillon, greeting a crowd that had assembled in the Place de la Concord, not only to acclaim him, but also to thank him for his very existence.[3]

Chaplin's popularity fascinated Truffaut because of its universality, a quality, as we shall see, that was an essential aspect of his aesthetic system. Silent cinema always remained that of the "Great Secret" – as he entitled the section in *Films de ma vie* devoted to his masters – because it constituted, by its very nature, a universal language.

One film aptly sums up his attitude to the attacks that were launched against him in the sixties. After the only critical setback that really wounded him – the reaction to *Two English Girls*, which left him feeling abandoned because his work was not understood – Truffaut made a film designed to vindicate himself, a pure product of his rebelliousness: *A Gorgeous Girl Like Me*. It deals with a sociologist who confronts a feisty, pragmatic female criminal, knowing her to have been conditioned by experience, a desire to understand, and a determination to survive. This beautiful girl ends up not only muzzling the impudent upstart who had made her the object of study, but also attracts media coverage and becomes a celebrity.

Even though this film is manifestly polemical, its aim is not to put intellectuals on trial but to suggest the existence of another value system, of a different mode of communication. Going against the spirit of his times, Truffaut defends a form of expression that mobilizes the collective imagination. Apart from this isolated outburst, he always maintained his reserve, displaying little concern with trying to clear up what he saw as misconceptions regarding his work. It seems, moreover, that even though Truffaut may in certain respects have suffered from the gap between his art and the era in which he lived, he also greatly benefited from it in others. He was consistently driven by a rebellious impulse – by a pleasure he took in creating *against* something, and in pitting himself against prevailing ideas. One thing is certain: he doggedly pursued his own project, which, in contrast to those of Godard and Rivette, did not involve questioning conventional ways of reading film, but rather a desire to continue the tradition of fiction-filmmaking.

For Truffaut, to make works that obeyed the laws of the imagination meant, above all, concealing, masking, dissimulating, and rendering inaccessible the mechanisms of creation:

> During the past decade of ideological terrorism, people have tried to convince us that films must be "open," and that they have to conduct "dialogues" with the public. Well, I've watched my favourite films again, I've scrolled through them in my head, and I've noticed that almost all of these films are "closed," and that they function like monologues. My distaste for what is fashionable, and my impulse to contradict have prompted me to make *The Wild Child, The Story of Adele H.,* and *The Green Room* as if they were objects, and even, if I am to be truthful, like ivory eggs that one can see and touch, but not break into.[4]

If there is a secret in the work of Truffaut, one can detect its origins here. Truffaut's works are constructed like a beautiful smooth vessel that he has launched on the current of time, upon which the spectator, once he has embarked, need only let himself be carried away by the scenery without knowing anything about the activities taking place in the engine room. This habit, of creating a mise-en-scène that is contrived to conceal its art, is one of the major practices observable in Truffaut's aesthetic evolution. It also explains the misunderstanding that surrounds his films. Whereas his work has been considered as realistic, in fact it offers the image of a world deformed by the violence of desire. It is also psychological, tracing the routes taken by impulsive energies that elude the organizing structures imposed by thought. Moreover, it can be lighthearted and comical, even when its actions are being played out against a backdrop of psychic destruction.

As far as cinematic form is concerned, the accusation of academicism, often leveled at Truffaut during the 1970s, corresponds paradoxically to an artistic control that became ever stricter on his part. The development of his narrative style consisted of skillfully disguising his work through the use of classical techniques, employed with an increasing economy of means, in order to close off his films against analysis.

Nevertheless, even though he closed his films in this way, Truffaut did not operate as the guardian of a secret that he refused to reveal. To the contrary, many of his statements suggest there was a dimension of his work that remained opaque to him, and that he did not want to have explained:

> Because I work in a way that is more instinctive than intellectual, I only understand my films several years after their release. This delayed insight is a help rather than a hindrance, as I think that I would lack the incentive to get up each morning to go and shoot a film if the meaning of that film was already pre-established.[5]

He even went as far as to say that he preferred not to read analytical studies of his films because if he were to discover the internal mechanisms of his works, he would run the risk of losing the ability to create them. One can see how far this method of working differed from that adopted by other contemporary creative artists – the authors of the Nouveau Roman, for example. Whereas the latter consciously tried to devise formal structures that mirrored the processes cultural theorists during the 1960s postulated in the functioning of works of art, Truffaut preferred to let these structures emerge in his films without consciously registering them. If there is a secret art involved in mise-en-scène, it is because it results from a structuring process that is unconscious. To invoke the formula that Lévi-Strauss applied to mythic thought,[6] one could say that it is not only the experience of fictive cinema that requires its workings to "remain hidden," but also its creation. Why? Because of emotion – a magical word, a word that Truffaut fetishized because it summed up the reason for all his preoccupations and efforts. As far as the creation of emotion was concerned, he only ever acknowledged one master, Hitchcock, whose influence on his filmmaking grew as the years progressed. As Truffaut himself put it:

> Hitchcock, from the outset of his career, understood that whereas one reads a newspaper with one's eyes and head, one reads a novel with one's eyes and one's heart beating, and that a film must be viewed in the same way that one reads a novel . . . For Hitchcock, it was not a question of teaching us something, of instructing us in order to reform us, but of arousing our curiosity, of grabbing us, of captivating us, of taking our breath away, and above all, of making us participate emotionally in the story that he has chosen to present . . . The filmmakers of the New American cinema are almost all the children of Hitchcock, but in spite of their commitment to a dramatic use of the camera, we notice that they are lacking an essential ingredient of Hitchcock's cinema: deep feeling, the experience of fear, the ability to register emotion, an intimate and profound understanding of the emotions that one is filming . . . There is nothing that can't be learnt, but that doesn't mean it can be acquired, and even though his disciples may claim, from time to time, to have equaled the technical skill and virtuosity of the master, they still lack the emotional power of the artist, beyond a doubt. Alfred Hitchcock remains, even today, in 1980, even though his state of health is preventing him from shooting his eightieth film, not only the man who knows the most about it, but also the filmmaker who moves us the most.[7]

This tribute, vibrant with emotion, which was written for a retrospective of Hitchcock's films mounted in 1980 – in other words, at the time of *The Last Metro* – summarizes in a nutshell all the experience of a filmmaker at the height of his art. One cannot hope to understand the lost secret without conducting an anatomy of emotion.

If the films of Truffaut hide their secret, it is because it is probably impossible for someone to understand and move, and, definitely, to understand and be moved. Emotion involves laughter as much as grief and is, by definition, a force that conditions one's understanding – surprising it, overturning it, paralyzing it, and, in a word, short-circuiting it. Emotion momentarily allows an investment to manifest itself through the economy of consciousness. With lightning speed, it connects the mind to a system that makes it possible for the mind to traverse in a flash the links of a logical chain that can normally only be reconstituted through a long and patient process of reasoning. In contrast to what happens in real life, the emotion aroused by art also guarantees that the affective experience to which it subjects us, in the course of redirecting the logical destination of thought, will be rewarded. Instead of generating the disorder that an absence of the rational usually induces, aesthetic emotion, to the contrary, promises us that a hidden order will become manifest in the process of the journey. Cinematic emotion, therefore, both provides a marvelous way of managing psychic energy and also leads to the registration of an interior harmony that we seldom have the luxury of attaining in real life. For this reason, in the case of a young spectator oppressed by an existence that overwhelms him, films can act like a drug that becomes difficult to give up. Indeed, cinephilia, together with friendship, was the only refuge the young Truffaut had during his adolescence: "It would hardly be an exaggeration to say that cinema saved my life. That's the reason why I can't talk about it intellectually. It occurred to me to use the word 'drug' in this regard, before the word became fashionable."[8]

Above all, emotion, for Truffaut, was what he found in the films of his youth, an emotion that was the earliest and sole shaping influence on his sensibility. His evolution as an artist consisted first of studying, when he was writing as a critic, the techniques used by filmmakers he admired to create emotion, and then of making it the structuring principle of his own work after he had become a filmmaker. Given that emotion, for Truffaut, related to the legacy of a childhood in which it was his only means of maintaining equilibrium, one can understand how, for him, the process of creation was related, more closely than for most filmmakers, to the operations of the unconscious. A child gripped by the impact of images, Truffaut, at the very moment when he was playing truant with regard to the long process of acquiring knowledge through rational learning, and of becoming integrated into society through schooling, was being conditioned by a mode of representing the sensible world that transcended the categories of Cartesian thought. As far as he was concerned, the representational strategies of fiction did not have to assert themselves at the expense of other competing models of knowledge and organization; they imposed themselves as the only means by which the nature of things could be understood, the only safeguard against incoherence. This gives his films an instinctive tone that relates them to the most ancient and traditional forms of storytelling found in fairy tales and myths – that is, narrative forms that directly bring into play the deep structures of the collective unconscious.

As another great storyteller, Isaac Bashevis Singer, has said, "the deeper the roots of a writer in his environment, the more he is understood by all. And the more he is national, the more he becomes international."[9] One could add: the more he is personal, the more he attains the universal. One does not have to investigate the works of Truffaut for very long before realizing that they emanate from an irresistible interior necessity. The succession of films seems to answer to a hunger in him that is never appeased. Truffaut could not stop making his stories – one after another, one at the same time as another, because the various scenarios were often overlapping in his head – as if his psychic survival depended on it. This necessity determines their unity. The films seem to burst out of a single center, a point of emotional anchorage in his personal experience. The most distinctive characteristic of his oeuvre is its continuity: its logic and its exceptional coherence that is reflected in a complex network of rhymes and repetitions. In spite of the diversity of themes, genres, and narrative structures, his films give the impression of an uninterrupted tapestry that reminds one of the Proustian search, given that, with Truffaut, involuntary memories also produce a succession of motifs. But instead of unfolding as if in accordance with a planned and knowledgeable scheme, memory, in Truffaut's case, seems to embody a reworking, from film to film, of a single, unique scenario, with each version picking up, refining, contradicting, or deepening the preceding one.

To what psychic reality, without knowing it, was Truffaut endlessly trying to give form? In various ways, his stories all describe heroes who suffer from an emotional deficiency, sometimes so profound that it leads them to the verge of madness and death. It is not so much the visible hero that one needs to examine, but rather the invisible truth that the story tries to outline through him by means of its narrative riddles. Each of his films represents an unconscious questioning of a maternal figure who is distant, ambiguous, inaccessible. She is responsible for the emptiness that calls into being the ceaselessly repeated scenarios that Truffaut constructs. The stories succeed one another like a sequence of Oedipal hypotheses concerning this figure who eludes definition and holds the secret of the hero's identity. No matter how many films he makes, nor how many responses to the enigma she embodies, she always remains the source of Truffaut's creative dynamic. Thanks to cinema, the maternal space, that in which the infant's future relationship to the world is mapped out, is rendered for a moment through the dynamic of exchanges and communication. An interior winter landscape, icy, lacking in hope, suddenly takes on movement, life, and colors. A happy ending is unlikely, but emotion flows, and that is the essential thing.

The known facts of Truffaut's biography shed light on this constant preoccupation one finds in his films. While we know that *The 400 Blows* re-creates the salient events in his childhood, how close the representation is to the actual reality of his life is less certain. Truffaut, like Antoine Doinel, was an illegitimate child who never knew his father. Janine de Montferrand, his mother, was only 18 years old when she gave birth on February 6, 1932, in a religious institution reserved for unmarried teenage mothers. Her family, who had arranged for this hushed-up confinement, also made the necessary arrangements for the infant to be cared for by a wet nurse in one of the suburbs of Paris. It is there that Truffaut passed the first year of his life. His mother, who was working in Paris as a secretary at *L'Illustration,* subsequently met Roland Truffaut, who married her on November 9, 1933, and adopted the child. The young François lived with one or another of his grandmothers until 1942 and then went to live with his parents, in whose household he learned the truth when he was about 12. Roland Truffaut kept a journal, and one day, while rummaging in a wardrobe when he was alone, the young Truffaut accidentally stumbled on the diary with its revelations. He did not tell anyone about it. His father only discovered that his son knew the truth when he took him, as in *The 400 Blows,* to a police station because he had stolen a typewriter. While sitting in a corridor, he overheard the adolescent inform the police commissioner in his deposition that Roland Truffaut was not his real father. Truffaut never met the latter, but in 1968 he made an inquiry through the agency that had advised him on the shooting of *Stolen Kisses* and learned, without ever being able to confirm the information, that his real father was a dentist who lived in the east of France. He was also Jewish, which would explain why, at a time when anti-Semitism was rife, Janine de Montferrand's family opposed the marriage. For Truffaut, that was the end of the matter.

These facts explain both the complexity of the relationship between Truffaut and his mother and also why the idea of a secret was so important to him in relation to childhood. It is understandable that the young woman might have experienced ambivalent feelings toward this child, whose arrival had exposed her to shame and had tragically turned her life upside down. Separated from his mother during these years, Truffaut, when he caught up with her again, not only discovered, like Antoine Doinel, that she was unfaithful to her husband, but also the nature of the mystery surrounding his birth. He was all the more fixated on this mother who had abandoned him because she alone knew the identity of his unknown father, and thus the secret of his origins. The fact that he also found her very beautiful, and felt the allure of her seductiveness, added to the power she exerted over him. For many reasons, the child experienced her as someone who was formidable, fascinating, and inaccessible. Her secret became his. It was not simply the mystery of his birth that weighed upon the young Truffaut, but also the unsaid that existed between him and his mother – as is demonstrated by his unwillingness to discuss the matter with his parents once he had discovered the truth. It is certainly no exaggeration to say that this secret haunted him all his life. He was fascinated by characters, both real and fictional, whose circumstances resembled his own: David Copperfield, D'Alembert, Léautaud, the Child of Aveyron . . . His preoccupation with the idea of information – which plays such an important role in his aesthetic system – derives from this personal, private problematic. Significantly, the secret of his mother also merges with that of cinema. It is thanks to films that Truffaut discovered an answer to the questions that perturbed him in his childhood, and a system of representation that was capable of organizing the troubled reality of his life. His whole oeuvre deals with this material in a manner that is indirect, clandestine, and hidden.

In Truffaut's voluminous *Correspondence* there is almost no mention of his mother, but in reply to a journalist who asked him in 1979 "why have you never spoken about your mother," he made this surprising statement:

> I classify my books by author. But I would like to reserve a shelf in my library for books about mothers. They comprise the best work by each writer. Think of Simenon, Roger Peyrefitte, Bataille, Pagnol, Albert Cohen. If one were allowed to have only one subject, it would have to be that one. For me, it is perhaps too soon.[10]

This response functions like a slip of the tongue, in which Truffaut is saying "yes," but without revealing all that is in his mind. It is as if he were saying: "No, I don't talk about it; yes, it's my only subject." Certainly, after *The 400 Blows,* which established a paradigm for all the films to come, Truffaut concealed all references that were too explicit to this aspect of his personal experience. Moreover, he did not like it when people emphasized the autobiographical dimension of his works. Even though autobiography may be an incontrovertible given in his creations, Truffaut believed it needed to be presented subtly, in an instinctive form that he felt did justice to its full complexity. His films are not instruments of revelation or regression, but of communication.

For Truffaut, it was never a question of lifting the veils from his own life; to the contrary, more than most people, he was determined to keep it private. He constructed his stories from bits and pieces of real life, borrowed not only from his own experience but also from that of his friends, from newspapers, and from books. In this regard, he was in the habit of making a fire from all kinds of wood, as all the evidence relating to his method of working confirms. For him, the process of creation involved a conscious effort to conceal the autobiographical wellsprings of his inspiration. Nevertheless, the unconscious is constantly at work within these carefully contrived constructions. His films, like dreams, say more than he intended, and ceaselessly decode, without him knowing it, the elements comprising the maternal enigma. Each of them is susceptible to a double interpretation, and projects simultaneously two stories: the first one is realistic, shaped in accordance with the ordering logic of a classical narrative sequence (a love story, a coming-of-age story, or the intrigue of a crime thriller); the second one is fantasmal, the projection of a personal lived experience in which the son tries to comprehend his relationship with his mother and to restore the possibility of having a relationship and communication with her. Of these two stories, only the second is autobiographical, but it concerns an unconscious expression that is directly linked to the process of creation itself. It is the unfolding of this second story that this book is going to follow. The purpose of this fantasmatic projection is not simply to reproduce the unresolved conflicts in Truffaut's life, but rather to resolve them. Truffaut, like all creators, made films in order to move beyond childhood and become an adult. This motive explains his compulsive need to construct stories, one after another, that are able to play an essential role for him as psychic regulators. Unlike dreams and fantasies, a film faces toward the future and not toward the past, and the unconscious in the work is no longer solely that of the artist. An analysis of the work requires one to identify the archaic, regressive figures in whom the same energy was originally invested that, set free by the act of creation, allows new meanings to be inscribed in the film. It is not enough merely to unmask repressed content; one must also trace the dynamic that gives shape to the work, given that a film is only able to constitute itself as an artistic reality, and become a cultural object, as a result of its formal attributes.

In his writings on cinema, Truffaut never theorizes about the message of his films, but focuses on the "receiver" – that is, the spectator. Constituting a veritable laboratory for Truffaut's aesthetic experimentation, the spectator is the one who must be intrigued, stunned, fascinated . . . moved. The film must, with the precision of clockwork, stimulate the perceptual system of the spectator – that is, a psycho-physiological process in which memory is the chief agent. Just as in cinema the illusion of movement depends upon the capacity of the retina to retain the impression of the image after it has disappeared, narrative schemes play on the ability of the mind to retain a certain amount of information and to order its contents. An essential characteristic of cinema is that it takes place, like music, during the span of a finite length of time, without the possibility of a return to the moment before it began. The work of mise-en-scène, then, consists of deploying – and this applies equally to style – a perceptual field that the mind of the spectator can scan without losing its bearings during the course of the screening. The stylistic effectiveness of Truffaut's films depends upon the implantation within his stories of a double system of perception. As they unfold, the mind of the spectator is solicited through two different and complementary means: at the same time as one's attention is engaged by the complex structure of a story that, because of ellipses, twists and turns, and mysteries in the narrative, retains all of its energy, an unconscious reading, aroused by a series of rhymes, repetitions, returns, and parallels, allows one to ignite the slow-moving stages of rational process in order to organize the elements of the image into a coherent and harmonious vision. The goal of narrative is to paralyze the conscious mind – resulting in the experience of emotion – while feeding the unconscious, resulting in the experience of pleasure. All of Truffaut's efforts are geared toward bringing into being this process of unconscious structuring. When he would revise his screenplays continuously, in order to add a silent sequence to his films at the last moment, this work would always move in the direction of a growing economy of means, of an ellipsis, of an indirect vision of things. It is aimed at intercepting the spectator's conscious mind in order to force him or her to move into a mode of unconscious perception. If Truffaut was obsessed with issues of narrative construction, declaring more and more frequently as the years went by that he was indifferent to the content of stories, and was only interested in their form, it was because he glimpsed with growing clarity what his art was all about. In order to be effective, the structures of the story needed to stimulate the deep recesses of the mind of the spectator, those that lie beyond the accidental variations that are determined by one's nationality, one's cultural development, or one's context in a historically determined era. While the components of emotion may vary from individual to individual, the mechanisms that provoke it are the same for everyone, given that they operate in accordance with the universal attributes of human nature. A successful film will be able to reach these permanent psychic zones that only the functioning of the human mind can determine. Narrative structures that are sufficiently dynamic to be able to stimulate them will unfailingly create emotion, and, in the process, the storyteller will have activated a mechanism that has an assured effectiveness and durability.

Works of fiction are just as necessary to the psychic life of human beings as food is to the body. All societies have created stories; every child, from his earliest years, asks to be told stories. Truffaut plays on this need, which was even more fundamental in him, and his work has no other purpose than to satisfy it. That is seldom true of works of fiction. While all novelists and filmmakers, to varying degrees, put in place in their creations an affective system similar to the one being studied here, most of them also incorporate elements that are the product of intellectual reflection: reports, documentaries, social, political, philosophical, or religious theories. In such instances, the work of the imagination is often obscured by the explicit message that the author is seeking to convey – Émile Zola's practice is typical in this regard. In short, even though emotion may always be the wellspring of fiction, most works rely heavily on an appeal to ideas. Truffaut's originality consists in having deliberately eliminated from his work everything that does not arise directly from the perceptual processes activated by the representation itself. His films, then, along with those of Hitchcock, are among the only ones that could be described as representing fiction in a pure state. In contrast to the master of suspense, however, there is not a trace of sadism in Truffaut's relationship with his audience. To the contrary, everything takes place as if Truffaut, who was acquainted with all the great works of fiction, including both novels and films, were adhering to the following rationale: "These works make me think, and they teach me something about the world, but above all they are beneficial for me, they calm me, they reconcile me to myself, why?" It is as if his films served as a laboratory in which he could answer this question by producing the same result.

The study of his films allows one to explore the larger issues that they raise. Why do we need works of fiction? What fundamental function to they fulfill in our psychic economy? Why does one experience, in the presence of a great storyteller (as Truffaut suggested with regard to Chaplin), a feeling of gratitude? This feeling touches on something deeply embedded in human nature and brings into play our relationship with the world, with experience, and with the prospect of death. From Truffaut's films, we can learn how and why.

1

Family Secrets
The 400 Blows (1959)
The Woman Next Door (1981)

TRUFFAUT'S FILMS ARE PARTICULARLY SUSCEPTIBLE TO PSYCHO-analytical interpretation. It would be a mistake to view this as merely accidental. Emanating from the unconscious experience of the filmmaker, they manifest, as naturally as a patient on an analyst's couch, the grand Freudian scenarios – in particular, the fundamental Oedipal one.

One can compare this scenario to a play in three acts. The first begins with the birth of the infant who enjoys, for a certain length of time, a state of symbiotic fusion with the mother. During this stage, if it is experienced harmoniously, all of the child's desires are gratified. For the infant, who as yet has no awareness of having a separate identity, the mother represents the only reality and meets all of his or her needs. The second act marks the intervention of the father into this Eden-like tableau, and the child's movement out of a dyadic relationship into a triadic one. By demanding a separation of mother and child, the father imposes a limitation on the desires of the latter. At this stage, the infant displays feelings of hostility and jealousy toward the father and feelings of love for the mother, who has now assumed an autonomous reality. If they were to be pushed to the limit, the logic of these drives would require, as in the myth, that the child kill his father and marry his mother. The resolution of the Oedipus complex occurs in the third act, when the child, acknowledging the law of the father, identifies himself with it and thus becomes integrated into the world of culture that regulates social behavior. Renouncing the possibility of a limitless desire, he accepts that words replace things – the learning of language – and that woman replaces the mother – the institution of marriage, which sanctions the integration of desire within the law. The fundamental role that this scenario plays in shaping personality, together with the dynamic of desire, constitutes a psychic reality that is never brought to a definitive conclusion.

With François Truffaut, as this examination of *The 400 Blows* will demonstrate, this schema quickly becomes arrested, never passing beyond the first two stages. It is the first stage that one finds endlessly represented, but in disastrous forms, which explains why the writings of D. W. Winnicott, a psychoanalyst who devoted his research to the study of young children, are best able to shed light on the troubled relationship to the mother that one finds in Truffaut and the dire consequences for the emotional well-being of his heroes that result from its failure.

The Freudian model has been refined and extended by the findings of anthropology, which have challenged its assumption of universality by demonstrating that the father does not always play the role described by Freud in all societies. Lévi-Strauss has shown in *Elementary Structures of Kinship* that if there is one phenomenon that is universal, it is the prohibition against incest – that is, an interdiction against allowing a marital alliance to coincide with a parental one. Human society is founded upon this interdiction; because it creates different types of relationships between individuals, it imposes a differentiation between a natural state and a cultural state. The Oedipal myth is thus always played out in the space between nature and culture.

THE 400 BLOWS (1959)

Visually, *The 400 Blows*[1] is organized according to a neat binary opposition that operates throughout the film: in the interior scenes, the story is shot in fixed close-ups, while in exterior scenes, tracking, traveling, and long shots dominate. This alternation invests the film with a powerful rhythm between tension and relaxation. Whereas in the interior scenes Antoine (Jean-Pierre Léaud) is a prisoner, when he is outside, he becomes a child who is free to roam and play. Accompanied by René (Patrick Auffay), he escapes from solitude, and when he is alone, he experiences magical encounters: with Jeanne Moreau, the sea. The uninterrupted series of disasters that oppress him in the house, at school, and in the penitentiary are suddenly arrested and suspended. Two types of temporality correspond to these two spaces. In the interior, a leaden, oppressive time holds sway, a linear, irreversible time in which consequences ensue from actions with an implacable rigor. Outside, the world is governed by cyclical time, marked by a return of the same things and a playful weightlessness. Inside, Madame Doinel (Claire Maurier) screams, threatens, punishes; outside, she remains silent, and is scared when her son surprises her in the arms of her lover.

One of the most striking examples of this system of contrasts occurs between the time Antoine discovers this infidelity and the first time he runs away, on the following morning. After he has been brought back to the house and given a bath, Madame Doinel tries to regain his affection – in an attempt to ensure his silence – by reminiscing about her own childhood. She also proposes to make him a deal: she will give him some money if he does his schoolwork dutifully. This tense exchange between mother and son is filmed in a series of shots/reverse shots in close-up that capture the sullen reserve of the two interlocutors. The shot that follows abruptly presents an outdoor scene in which a gym teacher is leading a group of children in the streets. In the course of this exercise, they all disperse, several at a time, giving their instructor the slip. At first presented from a normal angle, with the camera at eye level, this scene is suddenly filmed in a high-angle shot, from the rooftops. This unusual visual effect reinforces the contrast with the preceding segment and invests the episode with a mythical quality. Paying tribute to a similar scene from Jean Vigo's *Zéro de conduite,* the scene depicts the irrepressible energy of childhood, serving as an allegory of its dispersion through the pathways of life. The credit sequence of *Small Change* offers a similar vision, with hordes of children flowing endlessly down the sloping alleys of Thiers.

There seems to be a sharp division in the narrative between Antoine's conversation with his mother and this outdoor scene. But by proposing such a bargain, it was as if Madame Doinel were saying to her son: "We can both have little secrets, so long as you don't say anything to your father." The gym instructor who is so blithely ridiculed evokes this derided paternal authority. As Georges Franju aptly notes about Antoine's father: "Here is a man who is a cuckold, and who does not notice it. Only one thing matters to him: someone has taken his Michelin guide."[2] Significantly, this is the only emphatic, clear demand he makes in the entire film. Antoine thus carries the weight of responsibility for the secret of his mother's adultery without any support. This perturbing experience is compounded by another one – the revelation of Antoine's illegitimate birth. At first, Truffaut had thought of replacing this discovery of the child's illegitimacy with that of his mother's infidelity: "To get the action underway more powerfully, I considered giving up the revelation of illegitimacy in order to replace it with another: in the course of playing truant, Antoine would meet his mother with a young guy, her lover."[3] In any case, this confirms that from the outset Truffaut's intention in the script was to bind mother and son in the sharing of a secret from which the father is excluded.

Representations of space and the maternal figure are closely linked in the logic of the imaginary that shapes *The 400 Blows.* Winnicott's writings on the behaviors associated with delinquency, and, in particular, his theory of transitional space shed a remarkable light on this association. Transitional space is a potential space situated between the internal world and the external world, the constitution of which determines our future relationship with the real. In the first months of life, the nursling is incapable of distinguishing between the subjective and the objective. In creating a world that conforms to his desires, the mother gives him the confidence that is necessary for him to come to terms with external reality. For the experience to be a good one, this first discovery must occur as the result of an illusion – which involves, when the process is normal and healthy, the subject finding an expression of his own subjectivity in that which he perceives objectively: "This early stage of development is made possible by the mother's special capacity for making adaptation to the needs of her infant, thus allowing the infant the illusion that what the infant creates really exists."[4]

The first product of this creative capacity is what Winnicott calls the transitional object, a toy, or a favorite object, that comes to be identified with all the positive elements that can be brought together in transitional space. As a result, the infant is able to bear the absence of the mother, and hence to be separated from her – that is, to cross the inevitable watershed necessitated by disillusionment. The transitional object marks the "transition" of the child from a state of union with the mother to a state of relation with her as a separate being. The paradox of this object is that before it can be *created,* it needs to be *found* in the external world. It is a phenomenon that is simultaneously objective and subjective, in order to fill in the gap between the inner world and the outer world. Later, transitional space will become the area in which play and creativity take place, with the transitional object becoming replaced by cultural experience. If a child is deprived of maternal care for too long during these first years of life, he or she will lose the ability to tolerate contact with external reality and will experience what Winnicott calls an "unthinkable anxiety." Confidence is replaced by fear, and the transitional space becomes filled with persecuting objects. It transforms itself into an imprisoning space. Delinquency is one of the least catastrophic consequences of an experience of this sort, which, in the most severe cases, can lead to outright withdrawal from the world, and autism, as in shown in *The Wild Child.* Most of Truffaut's films are organized around a problematic that closely resembles the processes described by Winnicott. The personal itinerary of Truffaut's antisocial heroes consists of an attempt to recover this space of communication, of creativity, and of shared experience that constitutes the transitional zone. *The 400 Blows* addresses these issues with a particular clarity.

By setting the first scene in a school classroom, Truffaut immediately foregrounds the failure of an institution that is meant to help a child adapt to social reality. He also highlights the initiative and creative ability of Antoine, whose behavior distinguishes him from the other children. The ill-fated photo of the pin-up girl circulates quietly around the class until it lands on his desk. With a vengeful stroke of his pen, Antoine adds a moustache to her face. For him, being able to accomplish this aggressive act directed against the feminine is worth being stood in the corner – the first representation of an imprisoning space that progressively narrows in around him. Far from remaining passive in it, he immediately composes a poem, the autobiographical freshness of which contrasts sharply with the gloomy caricature of literature embodied in "Le Lièvre," a poem that the teacher copies onto the blackboard.

In the decline and fall of Antoine Doinel, writing plays the part of original sin: as soon as Antoine picks up a pen, disasters descend upon him. In this context, his foolish decision to steal a typewriter is quite logical, if one recalls how important language was in Truffaut's view of things. In the sphere of transitional activities, writing is one of the most effective ways of affirming one's identity and of gaining mastery over the external world, in which, to use Lacanian terminology, language represents the passage from the imaginary to the symbolic, from the past to the present, and from a dyadic relationship dominated by the mother to a reality in which the mediation of the father has intervened.

As Antoine is writing his poem on the wall, two shots are inserted that show the other children playing in the playground. This filmic construction, in which writing and playing alternate, suggests the existence of a similarity between the two activities. Like writing, playing brings the internal world into relation with external reality. In play, the child projects his dreams and fantasies onto the world, and "there is a direct development between transitional phenomena to playing, and from playing to shared playing, and from this to cultural experiences."[5] In *The 400 Blows*, even though writing always ends in failure, play is repeatedly used to represent the energy and indomitable health of childhood. The playful approach to reality adopted by Antoine and René is manifest in play of many different sorts – pinball machines, backgammon games, riding in a rotor, a puppet show. But truancy, the very notion of which inscribes play within the context of delinquency, marks a limit to what is permissible during these schoolboy years.

The incarceration of Antoine signals his crossing of this boundary. Nevertheless, the redemptive nature of play is apparent even beyond this point of rupture. When, following his arrest, Antoine spends the night at a police station, long tracking shots – not usually found in an interior scene – reinforce the representation of the nighttime activities that take place in this confining space. Two panoramic shots, the first of which is filmed from Antoine's point of view, show the police officers absorbed in a game of *petits chevaux*. This sequence, possibly the episode that shows the social exclusion of Antoine at its most painful, is alleviated by the presence of this transitional activity. With play, hope seems to be reborn.

The vitality that Antoine displays in adversity is demonstrated in a third activity – theft. It is first mentioned when the children come out of school, at the moment when René asks a distressed Moricet where he has stolen the money from to buy the goggles that he is sporting so proudly. Theft, in *The 400 Blows* as in all of Truffaut's films, becomes an obsession.

Antoine and René devote most of their energy to it, pilfering pens, an alarm clock, photos of actresses, and, indeed, the inevitable Michelin guide.[6] Their respective mothers also show themselves to be experts at it. An anonymous child at school and the receiver of stolen goods, loaded with the typewriter, will be caught in the act.

In numerous writings on delinquency and its associated behaviors, Winnicott defined theft as an act of hope on the part of a child who feels deprived of love and the care to which he is fully entitled:

> *The thief is not looking for the object that he takes. He is looking for a person. He is looking for his own mother, only he does not know this.* A child who is ill in this way is incapable of enjoying the possession of things stolen. He is only acting out a fantasy which belongs to his primitive love impulses . . . The fact is that he has lost touch with his mother in some sense or other.[7]

In this sense, theft and delinquency constitute behaviors that are positive and therapeutic. Instead of renouncing the tie with the mother, the child demands compensation: he attempts, by stealing, to avoid a retreat from the real and to rediscover a transitional space. In the film, a superb elliptical scene illustrates this phenomenon. In a way that is fairly surprising, Antoine and René make the decision to steal a typewriter while they are watching a puppet show in the Luxembourg Gardens. Their conversation is framed by shots in which one sees much younger children engrossed in the performance. This strange juxtaposition suggests the symbolic relationship that unites these two activities. Thieving represents a determination to recover in a violent and destruction way the passionate communion with the real that transitional experiences generate. But the regressive nature of theft is clearly indicated by the difference in age between the two adolescents and the young spectators who are surrounding them. At a time when school studies and the first manifestations of creativity should be absorbing their energies, Antoine and René are reduced to expressing them in a theft that reflects a regression to the condition in which the young children are listening, with gaping mouths, to the story of Red Riding Hood.

After this masterful opening, which reveals all the symptoms of Antoine's emotional disturbance, the second sequence proceeds to unveil the origins of his perturbation. His first three actions in the empty apartment of his parents are gestures of anger and destructiveness: opening

1.1. Antoine (Jean-Pierre Léaud) at his mother's dressing table.
The 400 Blows, dir. François Truffaut, 1959.

the lid of the stove, he lets high flames leap into the room; wiping his dirty hands on the curtain, he soils them; finally, he steals money. After these displays of belligerence, the following scene, which takes place in his parents' room, expresses a wistful nostalgia for an absent mother. Antoine sniffs her perfumes and plays with the strange implements she uses to enhance her beauty. The reflection of his lonely image in three mirrors suggests a painful fragmentation of his personality that has occurred in his quest for a stable identity. In his commentary on the Lacanian mirror stage, Winnicott observes: "In individual emotional development *the precursor of the mirror is the mother's face.*"[8] The child, in looking at his own image, tries to find the maternal gaze in his reflection. Antoine is a child who wishes to be seen, to be the object of attention. Gazes play an essential part in the visual dynamic of this film, but they are only ever hostile, serving merely to convey reprimands, slaps in the face, and punishments. The only gaze that Antoine succeeds in attracting to himself is that of the law. When Madame Doinel arrives home, she does not even glance at her son, but displays, with an egregious disregard for his budding sexuality, her silk-clad legs. This image persists throughout Truffaut's oeuvre, with similar shots recurring each time a maternal figure appears in his films. The feminine limbs of the mother both scare the child and, at the same time, fascinate him. Whereas Antoine is looking to find confirmation of his identity in his mother's glance, all he receives back is an indifferent display of aggressive femininity, leaving him subject to the disturbing power of desire and seduction.

Madame Doinel, throughout the story, is the main source of textual energy: whether Antoine pronounces her dead, after having seen her with her lover, or sets fire to the house, his actions are always determined by Oedipal impulses focused on his mother. The only manifestation of his creativity, which might otherwise have been channeled into social integration or success at school, is thus directly linked with the kind of attention his mother pays him. As I have noted above, after Antoine runs away the first time, Madame Doinel proposes a bargain with him. This scene is followed by an evening at the movies, an episode that provides the only suggestion of a happy family life in the film. For one brief moment, harmony exists between the three family members, and desire is communicated between husband and wife: one sees Monsieur Doinel lay claim to his wife as a physical being when he takes hold of her leg on the staircase in order to show his son its shapeliness. But the dice are loaded against the possibility of happiness in this family, because the secret contract between mother and son makes a mockery of paternal authority. We see Antoine come to grief when he unintentionally plagiarizes Balzac. This occurs because the novelist clearly fulfills the function of a transitional object for the adolescent, who develops a cult of hero-worship by installing a little altar and candle in front of Balzac's image. Antoine's regressive behavior – his action belongs to early childhood – results in the house being set alight, which provokes great rage in his father, because he briefly senses the boy's disloyalty. Antoine's unconscious plagiarism of Balzac demonstrates the inherent confusion in the transitional object between the inside and the outside. The boy believes that he has *created* the text, whereas in actual fact he has *found* it. Because his efforts to come to terms with external reality are misunderstood, delinquency is the only avenue that is left for him to follow.

The 400 Blows would not have had the success it enjoyed, however, if it were only a simple story of failure and despair. Underneath the realistic story, another more complex and ambiguous one can be discerned. This fantasmatic script in *The 400 Blows* manifests, in the first place, a passionate desire for fusion with a maternal figure. This desire is not presented in a literal way – Madame Doinel will never satisfy it – but as the expression of an obsessive nostalgia. Nostalgia is a feeling that is often encountered in Truffaut's films: it always corresponds to the precarious hold that the hero is able to maintain over the internal representations of a lost object. Such nostalgia relates to an archaic past, and Antoine, like Truffaut's other characters, seeks to fulfill his desires by reproducing indestructible forms of infantile satisfaction.

Antoine's wish for fusion with a maternal figure is conveyed, in the introduction and conclusion of the film, through natural images that serve a symbolic purpose. The opening credit sequence consists of a series of shots that suggest the quest of an impatient camera seeking to be reunited with the Eiffel Tower. In a similar manner, at the end of the film, a long traveling shot accompanies the boy to the exact spot on a beach at which waves touch the sand. Poets have long seen the shore as a symbol of the maternal body, the site where a child arrives into the world: "On the seashore of endless worlds, children play."[9] Within the film itself, however, the desire for fusion is seen in the passionate relationship between Antoine and Paris. The city is a maternal space, a mother environment, that shelters the child, protects his games, hides him, washes him, and feeds him. The striking sequence in which Antoine wanders through Paris at night shows him in the act of stealing a bottle of milk, and of drinking its contents furtively in the deserted streets. In the morning, he wipes his face with a little water from the Fontaine de la Trinité. The only time he is seen showing signs of unhappiness or weeping is when, being carried off by the prison van, he finds himself separated from this great maternal body.

We can also associate the famous scene involving the rotor with this desire for fusion with the maternal body. As many critics have said, the rotor resembles early machines that allowed an illusion of movement to be created from a rapid succession of fixed images; in this way, it evokes cinema itself. The rotor, however, is also presented as a round, enclosed space in which Antoine playfully folds himself into a fetal position. Such an interpretation does not exclude the former one, but completes it. Cinema plays an important role in Antoine's life: it is a space that offers him the security and the illusion of a harmonious relationship with reality; it is, for Truffaut, a transitional space par excellence. For the child, cinema

1.2. Antoine (Jean-Pierre Léaud) in the rotor.
The 400 Blows, dir. François Truffaut, 1959.

fulfills the essential function of providing a substitute form of emotional mothering; the episode involving the rotor pays a tribute to the former by evoking the latter. But it is obviously the scene with the psychologist that most explicitly actualizes this nostalgic wish for reunion with a maternal figure. Looking into the camera during this interview, Antoine appears natural, relaxed, and confident with an adult for the first time. He displays a remarkable understanding of his "case," and is able to painstakingly itemize the things in his situation that perturb him. But he speaks in a disembodied voice. The fact that the female psychologist is outside the field of vision imparts an unreal effect to the scene, reinforcing its nostalgic character. Most importantly, it leaves little doubt about Antoine's ability to communicate with a positive maternal figure, provided she remains unknown, idealized, and inaccessible. Antoine Doinel's future choices in love will show the cruel effects of these three prerequisites.

In contrast to these nostalgic images suggesting reunion, the film also presents the spectator with a second, fantasmal interpretation that conveys the profound ambivalence Antoine feels toward his real mother. Truffaut achieves this effect by employing a narrative style that is deliberately elliptical and fragmented. Certain scenes seem to be unrelated to the central preoccupation of the film and slow down the story. One sees, however, that their function is to foster the fantasy element, and that between them they link up to form a coherently structured network. Two examples of these underlying chains of signification show that what they share in common is a questioning of Madame Doinel's character.

During the first scene at school, one ironic vignette shows a small schoolboy desperately trying to copy a poem. He ends up in surrounded by an ocean of ink and screwed-up sheets of paper. Through metonymical displacement, this episode suggests Antoine's own difficulties with writing. In addition, however, it also introduces, metaphorically, the constantly repeated themes of disorder, dirt, and trash. Antoine soils the curtains and, throughout the film, seems to find it difficult to wash himself. Moreover, it is his job to empty the household's rubbish. One scene depicts him coming down the stairway, to the strains of the Marseillaise, and upending the contents of a foul rubbish tin into the collective trash bin, with obvious distaste. The staircase, an important image with Truffaut, is often associated with the legs of women. As we have seen, Monsieur Doinel invites his son to admire the legs of his wife as they climb the stairs after the cinema. In typical fashion, Truffaut cut a scene from the commercially released version of the film that might have shed light on these associations. In the second sequence of the original narrative, the young boy is shown arriving at a grocery shop to buy flour in response to his mother's nagging. He finds himself in a queue behind two tattletales who are describing in minute detail a difficult, messy labor that ended up with the patient having to have "everything removed." Antoine listens with a distraught expression and seems about to faint in the final shot of the sequence. Truffaut probably removed this episode because it revealed too explicitly the submerged fantasmatic content of the film. For a fantasy to be able to work on the imagination, its content must remain latent so that it does not trigger a censoring reaction in the spectator. As part of this process of indirect revelation, repetition, working through displacement or condensation, plays a crucial role in the filmic representation. The network of repetitions in which stairs, women's legs, and trash are associatively linked together reveals the deep anxiety that the female body arouses in Antoine. For him, this body represents a frightening mystery, generating visions of chaos, dirt, and blood. In her analysis of epistemological disorders in adolescents,

Melanie Klein observes that learning difficulties at school often originate in a child's inability to form a mental representation of the inside of the feminine body, and, in particular, to understand its specific functions, such as conception, pregnancy, and giving birth.[10] In the film, the network of repetitions outlined above evokes fears that are tied to the difference between the sexes, and the consequences of these fears – but it does so in an indirect way, without threatening the psychic apparatus of the spectator with brutal images of violence. During his nocturnal wanderings through the streets of Paris, Antoine pushes an empty milk bottle into a sewer. This image is encountered again in *Small Change* and *The Man Who Loved Women.* In committing such an unusual act, the child seems to be wanting to probe the insides of the city. In *Stolen Kisses,* the famous scene involving the *pneumatique,* in which one follows the underground trajectory of a letter across the town, reflects the same curiosity tinged with aggressiveness. One can detect in such images a metaphorically expressed fascination – present in all of Truffaut's films – with the mother's body. These representations of space suggest how the feminine body, in the child's imagination, is perceived as a secret labyrinth containing unfathomable mysteries.

The second example concerns one of the most enigmatic scenes in the film. Set in the Centre for Delinquent Minors, it presents three little girls being shut up in a cage constructed of wire netting. To understand it, one needs to recall two complementary scenes. In the first, Madame Doinel returns to the family home late at night. Antoine, who is in his bed asleep, is woken up by the car that brings her back. During the animated fight between his parents that follows, the father accuses his wife of sleeping with her boss. At the police station, Antoine is similarly woken up by the sound of a vehicle engine. This time, it is the sound of a prison van conveying three prostitutes who are going to be shut up in the cell next to his. In an interview, Truffaut revealed that he deliberately adopted a style found in children's stories for this sequence:

> The three prostitutes who come into the police station speak in a way that exactly replicates what one would find in a fairy tale. One of them says, "As for me, I've seen a police station in a film; it was really clean." The next one says, "As for me, I have seen ones that are dirtier." The third one says, "Well then, I've seen ones that are prettier."[11]

1.3. Antoine sees his mother, Gilberte Doinel (Claire Maurier) with her lover. *The 400 Blows,* dir. François Truffaut, 1959.

The image of the three little girls in their cage relates directly to that of the three prostitutes in their meshed cell. Antoine's ambivalent feeling toward his mother is unerringly inscribed within this signifying chain. The noise of an engine says that she is a whore; the prostitutes, three in number, say that she is a fairy; in addition, the shot of the three little girls proclaims that, like her son, she is an imprisoned child who acts the truant with her lover in the streets of Paris. The whole of Truffaut's art is encompassed within this insight.

THE WOMAN NEXT DOOR (1981)

The credit sequence has scarcely ended when *The Woman Next Door* presents the image of a divided space: on one side, we have a close-up shot of the face of the narrator, Odile Jouve (Véronique Silver); on the other side, behind a high wire fence, tennis players are shown in a long shot. From the outset, a rupture is established between the space of social exchange, in which rules and propriety are observed, and an imprisoning space of emotional disorders in which the mutilations of the spirit are inscribed on the body. Madame Jouve does not play – she is disabled. From the first images, the camera installs itself without hesitation in the space of lack and exclusion; that is, at the heart of the experience that Winnicott describes as "unthinkable anxiety." It will explore all the nooks and crannies of this space with a dispassionate relentlessness right until the final moment of the film. There is also another sign of our incursion into the domain of the pathological, of the monstrous, of the transgressive that is less immediately visible: the proliferation of doubles, seen in the two vehicles shown during the credits (ambulance and police car), the two temporalities ("This affair commenced six months ago. One might say that it really began ten years ago"), the two houses, the two young boys who, to leave no possibility of doubt, are both called Thomas. The scene is set up for the reunion of the two lovers.

For Truffaut, *The Woman Next Door* was "a film as simple as pie" (*un film simple comme bonjour*).[12] Its effectiveness lies in its clarity, its coherence, and its classicism. Chronology is respected, the narrative is divided neatly into three parts, and the subject is crystal-clear: "A story of modern love-passion" (*Une histoire d'amour-passion moderne*).[13] Nevertheless, as the story unfolds, the spectator's discomfort progressively increases. Something terrifying seems to intrude itself into these scenes of provincial life. A savage force is unleashed. Signs accumulate that a fundamental disorder is being uncovered, the existence of which will be confirmed by the final tragedy, but without the origin ever being explicitly revealed. The presence of this disorder is conveyed in a veiled, indirect way, but it always involves the breakdown of a system of compartmentalization. While conventional boundaries are ignored or transgressed, others are erected in places where their presence defies logic.[14]

The first of these transgressions involves a double disruption of the normal cinematic system. In the film's prologue, Madame Jouve speaks directly to the spectator – a unique instance in Truffaut's practice as a filmmaker – thus breaching the hallowed principle in fiction-cinema that the distinction between these spaces should be observed. But that is not all. Interrupting her story, she suddenly addresses the camera to order it to move back so that the prosthesis she wears on her right leg can be included within the frame. The boundaries between the character and the audience, and between the actor and the cameraman, are thus done away with. That which should be separate is reunited; that which should obey imposes its own law. The normal order of things is unsettled.

Another narrative element contributes to the creation of unease in the spectator: the unusual length of certain scenes, or a brutal disruption of tone in their conclusion. Again, a separation between narrative elements, normally required by generic conventions, is no longer practiced. In several other instances, when all of the indicators (music, lighting, dialogue, action) lead one to think that a scene has finished, against expectations it is protracted and goes on to reveal something disturbing and unusual. Thus, when, at the beginning of the movie, Arlette (Michéle Baumgartner) surprises Bernard (Gérard Depardieu) in the act of eating in the kitchen during the night, they speak for a moment, go out of the room, and head toward the staircase leading to their bedroom. But instead of the anticipated transition into the following scene, one hears a meowing outside. Bernard says: "Those are cats . . . They're fighting." Arlette replies: "No, no, they are making love . . . like savages," throwing him a glance loaded with veiled meaning. It is the first indication in the film of an analogy between the act of love and an act of violence, between sexuality and destruction. In the darkness, beyond the protective walls of the house, bestial, primitive, instinctual things are happening.

A further example of this narrative procedure also takes place during a night scene. After having dined with Arlette, with Bernard having slipped away at the last moment, Mathilde (Fanny Ardant) and her husband (Henri Garcin) return to their house. A single long shot follows them outside as far as their doorstep, to the accompaniment of gentle, soft music. They enter, turn off the lights, and, through the window, are seen climbing the stairs until they go out of sight. Instead of ending there, the scene, again, is prolonged. As the music grows more mysterious, the camera turns slowly and reveals Bernard, hidden in the shadows. One follows him while he, in turn, re-enters his own house, shuts the door, and climbs the stairs. Yet again, irrationality is shown to reign outside, in the darkness.

Furthermore, it frequently happens, in the course of the narrative, that the tone of a scene abruptly switches from trite to tragic. In the episode in the parking lot, Bernard and Mathilde, who have met by chance in the supermarket, advance together toward the young woman's vehicle. Up until this moment, Bernard has refused to have any contact with her; now, he agrees to become her friend. Their conversation is open,

1.4. A couple without house or home. Bernard (Gérard Depardieu) and Mathilde (Fanny Ardant) in *The Woman Next Door,* dir. François Truffaut, 1981.

cheerful, and they say goodbye by kissing each other on the cheeks. But then Mathilde, suddenly serious, asks him to say her name. Bernard steps around the car door that is separating them, caresses her face, and says: "Mathilde." They kiss passionately; the young woman sinks to the ground in a faint.

In terms of the chronological level of this story, a second boundary is dangerously removed: that which separates past and present. The temporal unity of the film is disrupted on several occasions by a double subversion. Mathilde and Bernard, in resuming their affair, are toppled by a tragic past that they believed they had exorcized. But the past also reasserts itself in the present with the unexpected return of Odile Jouve's former lover, because of whom, twenty years earlier, she had wanted to die by throwing herself from a building.

The world of adults in *The Woman Next Door* ceases to be clearly differentiated from that of children. The most egregious example of this confusion is seen in the images of Bernard at his place of work. Charged with retraining the helmsmen of marine tankers by having them practice on scale models, Bernard seems to spend his days drifting, seated on a miniature ship, in the middle of a little reservoir. One never sees him being active, productive, or responsible. The two Thomases, with their games and their discreet presence, also constantly invade the space of the adults. One scene shows a child playing a crucial symbolic role. At the moment when he is about to depart one morning for work, Bernard, troubled by the presence of Mathilde at her window, slams shut the door of his car, while the engine is left on. All the doors are now locked, and the only way of opening them is to get in through the hatchback. Bernard goes to climb in, but his son, more agile than he is, takes over and does it for him. This scene is simultaneously comic and perturbing. Should the child make a false move, the car could leap forward out of control. In the passionate relationship between the two lovers, cars occupy an important place throughout the film: they are used for the purpose of going to places of assignation, for checking whether the other is in the marital home, or, simply, as a place in which to make love. The car, then, which is primed to hurtle forward, with Bernard having lost control, symbolically suggests the idea of the savage power of passion. This disturbing scene suggests that, in order to defuse the infernal engine, one must pass through childhood. Bernard, with his massive adult stature, does not have the slightest chance of succeeding at that.

But the barrier that most notably disintegrates in the course of the film is that which separates the lovers from social norms, and private disorder from collective order. As I have suggested, the film is divided into three main parts, punctuated by three long scenes that depict collective relaxation and partying. The first is the most reassuring. Bernard and Mathilde, dressed in white, mingle with other middle-class citizens from Grenoble who are members of a sports club. Crossing each other's paths several times in front of the mesh-covered gates of the tennis courts, the lovers move without difficulty in the space of this game and participate in its pleasures. A minor disagreement between them at the end of the scene remains private and benign. The only untoward event in this comforting scene is the unexpected arrival of a telegraph operator whom the camera follows, with a sense of irony, as he tries to find Odile Jouve. When he finally catches up with her, Madame Jouve momentarily seems worried by the message he gives her. Bernard arrives solicitously to offer his assistance. She sends him back to his game without explaining what has perturbed her. We learn later that the message was announcing the return of her former lover.

The second large social gathering takes place in the Bauchards' garden, to which many guests have been invited. In the course of this garden party, in which good humor prevails, Bernard gradually loses his composure until finally he loses his head completely. Two incidents serve to ignite the gunpowder. The first is Philippe's announcement that he and Mathilde will be leaving that night to go on a honeymoon trip. Soon after, Mathilde's dress catches on a chair and comes undone, revealing the body of the young woman in flimsy underwear. Laughing, she runs inside to change. Bernard, with a grim expression, follows her inside, momentarily prowls around looking at their suitcases, and finally goes to seek her out in her bedroom in order to confront her with a violence of passion we have not seen before. He pursues her, hitting out at her, into the midst of the guests, who look on, stunned. Their secret is now exposed. Eventually, Bernard is able to confide in Arlette and succeeds in calming himself down.

From this point onward, the burden of their passion rests solely on the shoulders of Mathilde, who, in the course of a reception at the tennis club, is herself going to lose all emotional self-control. The occasion on which this occurs involves a celebration for the launching of her book for children, and the scene begins in a mood of calm and relaxation. As with Bernard, a twofold incident has the effect of transforming the festivities into high drama. A small fire suddenly breaks forth in Madame Jouve's kitchen. As everyone moves out of the way, Mathilde rushes forward and, seizing a fire extinguisher, puts out the blaze. Then, in the bathroom where she goes to wash her hands, Mathilde overhears a ribald conversation between two men talking about one of their friends who is trying to extricate himself from an amorous entanglement with a woman who lives on the same floor. As one of them comes out of the room, he concludes: "He's in the process of learning that the only person he mustn't sleep with is the woman next door." From that moment on, Mathilde's expression closes up. Instead of going to rejoin the guests, she draws away toward the shrubbery and collapses to the ground, wracked with sobs, her face pressed against the earth. Philippe, who has gone looking for her with a group of friends, finds her there a few moments later.

These three occasions when uncontrollable passion breaks out in the midst of social order are structured in accordance with a meticulous dramatic progression. The first is soon resolved by the departure of Madame Jouve for Paris; the second is eased thanks to the kind understanding of Arlette; the third results in the removal of Mathilde to a psychiatric hospital. But the impression remains that nothing is capable of controlling or appeasing the strength of these passions. The wise thing – as demonstrated by Madame Jouve, who, even twenty years later, dare not risk confronting her own passion – is to flee from it. The two lovers, however, constantly try to understand the violent emotions that possess them, seeking to disable them through language – which, for Truffaut, was the best way of gaining mastery over irrational impulses. Expressions such as "I've got to speak with you" or "we never have time to talk to one another" recur like gloomy leitmotifs throughout the film. Indeed, their conversations always end in failure – or rather the order of language, even when it seems to be triumphing, is seen to be destroyed on each occasion by the disorder generated by passion. Toward the middle of the film, Mathilde refuses to enter a hotel room with Bernard. She does not want to succumb to the sexual attraction between them, but instead wants to "talk about it," so that they can end their affair. Their ensuing conversation, which takes place in a cafeteria, though sad, seems to mark the triumph of reason. Mathilde wants to break up, and she asks Bernard to take her home to her house. The following scene, however, shows them making love, in Bernard's car, with a violence of passion that is more intense than anything shown up until this point.

The use of the telephone in the film demonstrates the limitations of spoken language. From the very beginning, the telephone, by definition an instrument for communication, has the effect of compounding misunderstandings, intensifying conflicts, and separating the couple. A barrier arises where one should not exist. Having discovered that they are neighbors, Mathilde decides to call Bernard while Arlette is out. During this exchange, a parallel montage presents the lovers in exactly symmetrical positions. Both look out of their window at the other. Mathilde is to the right of the image and holds the telephone in her left hand; Bernard is to the left and holds the telephone in his right hand. While the image gives the illusion of a face-to-face conversation, their words belie the impression of proximity. Indeed, Bernard, who is overtly hostile, refuses to speak or take Mathilde's number, and hangs up without saying goodbye. However, the long look that he then directs out the window suggests that his indifference is feigned, and that his words were not reflecting what he was really feeling. Subsequently, the telephone serves alternately to convey a lie (during the dinner that Bernard misses); to prevent the lovers from speaking to one another (by giving an engaged signal when, in their eagerness to see one another, they call at exactly the same moment); to interrupt contact between them (when Mathilde hangs up on Bernard, saying that he is scaring her); and, finally, to draw Mathilde into a trap (when, in the course of the garden party, Bernard pretends that someone has called in order to make her come out of her bedroom so he can attack her).

What is the cause of this disorder? What could motivate a transgression that each image in the film shows to be so violent? Is it merely an example of the kind of adultery that typifies contemporary behavior? The respective spouses of the two lovers display remarkable tolerance following the unmasking of the affair. As for the dull, charming society that surrounds them, its members react with a polite surprise that is silent and fleeting. From the outset, the passion that binds Mathilde and Bernard to each other seems inexplicable, and both complain until the very end that they do not understand it. Bernard says to Arlette, after the garden party: "There are plenty of things about her that I have hated from the beginning. I don't understand . . . I don't understand . . . no, I don't understand!" And Mathilde, lying in her hospital bed, says: "I would like to understand . . . I would so much like to understand." While the narrative never provides an explicit explanation for this passion, it nevertheless shows it implicitly. Indeed, when all the indications are brought together, we can interpret the sequence of events in *The Woman Next Door* as the relentless unfolding of an Oedipal regression.

At the beginning of the film, Bernard Coudray appears to be an adult man, perfectly integrated into society, with house, wife, child, and occupation. From the first scenes, we are shown that his marriage is happy, his sex life fulfilling, and his existence unmarred by problems. Then the woman from the past emerges on the scene, Mathilde, whose appearance is announced in a memorable way by her legs – that is, by the instrument of maternal seduction, as was shown in *The 400 Blows.* Philippe has invited the Coudrays into his house, and calls for Mathilde, who is upstairs, to come and meet them. The camera, placed behind a set of open-work stairs, frames the legs of the young woman as she comes down the steps. From the outset, Mathilde is actively possessive of Bernard. It is she who calls him, and, when they finally decide to meet, we are not presented with an image of a mutual telephone conversation, but simply of Bernard, in his car, looking for the address of the hotel that we hear Mathilde giving him in a voice-over. He seems to respond, incapable of resisting it, to the call that she directs at him.

The whole film follows the course of a regressive movement in which Mathilde, a stand-in for the possessive, archaic mother, arrives to reclaim her son, to tear him away from the order of society so as to re-create a dyadic relationship with him that will lead them to death. At the end of the film, she kills Bernard by putting a bullet through his head while they are having sex. Bernard's lifeless body literally sinks between the legs of Mathilde, suggesting the return of this adult man to the maternal womb, and extinction.

The particular nature of the love that unites the two lovers confirms this reading of the film. Instead of being based on the difference between the masculine and feminine, love in *The Woman Next Door* is represented as a process of fusion, a mirror game, a terrifying movement toward the obliteration of sexual differentiation.[15] The emotions of the two lovers, far from being complementary in their alterity, are replicated, creating a suffocating network of narrative and visual parallels, several examples of which I have already highlighted. As if through the effects of contagion, barriers collapse around them, and little by little their absence comes to undermine the very foundations of the entire social structure. Separate, distinct, identifiable at the beginning of the story, Bernard and Mathilde let themselves be drawn by degrees into a vertiginous whirlwind that leads to their deadly fusion in the final image. Twins, monstrous doubles, the lovers project at the heart of a peaceful society the intolerable image of a symbiotic relationship in which identities are inextricably merged, in which mutual dependence, need, and manipulation are uppermost. This regressive relationship is modeled on that of a child with its mother. Placed under the sign of their limitless desire, such a relationship encloses the couple in an infernal cycle involving a lack that nothing can ever satisfy. The real transgression, which the mise-en-scène ceaselessly inscribes in the narrative at a displaced remove, is incest.

No prohibition, no law, is able, in this instance, to restrain this desire. Philippe, with his "British stolidity," and the vague suggestion of a latent homosexuality that surrounds him,[16] shows himself incapable of separating the couple. His only attempt to take back possession of Mathilde and separate Bernard from the maternal body, on the occasion of the garden party, ends in an unleashing of violence. Observing the logic of their unconscious roles, the story removes any signs of a sexual difference between them, but suggests instead, through the way each lives out his or her conflicts, a generational difference. More of an adult than Bernard is, Mathilde suffers more. Already, eight years earlier, she had needed to leave him, because, as she explains, "it was either that or go mad." We are led to believe that she even attempted suicide. In the course of the adultery, she shows courage in assuming responsibility for her actions. She suffers remorse at deceiving Philippe and lying to him. She is fully aware of the contradictory impulses that are driving her. For his part, Bernard allows himself to be guided by blind instinct. He surrenders to passion without reflection, and abandons himself to it with the recklessness of a child who gets carried away. Not caring about the effect on his family, he impulsively urges Mathilde to abandon everything and go away with him so they can build a new life together. Following the garden party, he seeks refuge with another maternal figure – the discovery of his wife's pregnancy occurs immediately after that of the adultery – and seems to have found peace. Mathilde, for her part, suffers a nervous breakdown.

Like *The 400 Blows, The Woman Next Door* questions the character of the mother: "What's that woman doing here?" says Bernard at the beginning of the film, referring to Mathilde. But, whereas Antoine tries to affirm a separate identity in the context of a nostalgic dream of fusion, in this instance such a fusion is actually achieved, with all its disastrous consequences. If *The 400 Blows* depicts a rising movement toward an affirmation of the self, *The Woman Next Door* shows a movement that descends toward the obliteration of differentiation. In the first film, one can identify several activities that suggest an attempt to symbolize desire: writing, play, and, in a regressive form, theft. In the second, the symbolic loses a little more ground with each successive scene. The internal psychic structures that – owing to the process whereby maternal love comes to be symbolized – allow the individual to confront external reality and adapt to it seem never to have been securely put in place in Bernard. As for Mathilde, she occupies the place of a mother who refuses to let go of her power to control her son, because of her own psychic fragility. Both of them gradually enclose themselves within a space of emotional dysfunction in which they soon find themselves imprisoned, without any other opening on to the world. There is only the other, and this other can only be experienced as a lack.

Fear of separation becomes intolerable. In Truffaut's films, it often reveals itself, in visual terms, in an obsessive fear of falling into a void – which brings about, dramatically and irreversibly, a rupture of all contact between mother and child. In this film, it is Madame Jouve who represents this horrific realization; speaking of her bungled suicide attempt, she says to Bernard: "I threw myself into a void like a sack of dirty washing." It is also represented by Mathilde's physical collapse onto the ground, and her metaphoric fall into a nervous breakdown. When these catastrophic experiences occur, there is nothing else that is able to support the subject, who becomes overpowered by a feeling of "unthinkable anxiety." If the episode involving the rotor in *The 400 Blows* constitutes a moment of intense euphoria, it is probably because this machine counters the fatal force of gravity that pulls things toward the ground. In it, the body is able to float without ever falling, thus offering a striking visual evocation of what an environment conducive to psychic expansion would be like.

In this film, in which the traces of a regressive movement are repeatedly found, the absence of symbolization is not merely manifest in the failure of spoken language. It is also signaled by the importance accorded another mode of expression: drawings, made for, and by, children. We see Mathilde doing a drawing with Bernard's son when she comes to dinner at the Coudrays' house with her husband, but, in particular, it is her career as an artist who illustrates books for children that is highlighted many times in the film. In contrast to language, drawing represents a form of communication that remains associated with maternal language – of that exchange without words or grammar that takes place between mother and child. Closely linked to the first stages of separation, drawing comes prior to the Oedipal transition and the process of symbolization that marks the acquisition of language. Significantly, when the two lovers recall their first encounter, they describe it as being exactly like taking possession through a glance – a silent visual exchange in which language does not play any part. Mathilde, seeing Bernard brushing aside a lock of hair from his forehead, exclaims: "This is unbelievable. I was hoping you would perform this gesture in front of me. The first time I saw you do it, I said to myself: 'If he asks me to sleep with him, I will say yes.'" Bernard, in turn, remembers having seen Mathilde framed in a window: "You were in the middle of making sandwiches for children, and it is because of that that I fell in love with you." Mathilde's maternal role is confirmed by her professional activity, which puts her in direct contact with the world of childhood. Her talents in this regard are emphasized, moreover, as the film goes on. She becomes an author, but the publication of her book marks the moment of her psychic collapse, as if the logic of the film requires that her mastery of this primitive language coincide with the rupture of her links with the socialized world of adults.

In the film, in which the unconscious imposes its vision with a clinical precision, every detail serves to enhance the fantasmatic dimension of the story. In their futile efforts to escape from the force of passionate regression, on several occasions, the lovers, each in their turn, make plans to go away on vacation. Bernard asks Arlette to go away with him at the beginning of the film; she replies that she cannot get away from work, nor take Thomas out of school. During another attempt to regain a foothold in reality, Bernard takes his wife to the cinema. After the screening, they go to a restaurant, and Bernard once again raises the prospect of going on a vacation. Scarcely has he formulated his proposition than Madame Jouve's leg, cased in metal, is seen coming down the spiral staircase that descends into the hall. Thus, at the very moment when Bernard is trying to place his life back into the context of a normal experience, something obtrudes into the image to reassert the monstrous, the ill, and the symbolic marker of the mutilations brought about by uncontrollable

1.5. Mathilde (Fanny Ardant) attempts to exorcize her passion for Bernard by removing his image from photographs. *The Woman Next Door,* dir. François Truffaut, 1981.

passion. The remainder of this scene confirms this dark portent. From his subsequent conversation with Odile Jouve, who has returned from Paris, we learn that Bernard has actually understood nothing about the movie he has just seen, and is not as relaxed as he pretends to be. By chance, the subject of the film in question was a suicide dressed up as a murder, thus foreshadowing the end of *The Woman Next Door.*

Mathilde herself also attempts to flee. Her honeymoon is a disaster, and on the morning of their return, her husband accuses her of uttering another man's name during her sleep. Filled with desperation by the violent emotion she is unable to master, Mathilde then attempts to exorcize it. We see her, sitting near a chimney in which a fire is burning, cutting up old photos, one by one, and throwing them into the flames in order to make the face of Bernard disappear. In Truffaut's films, photos are always associated with morbid obsessions, or death. At the beginning of the film, the image of the Coudray family in a photo is an ominous sign. At the garden party, Bernard's madness is unleashed just after a photo is taken of him with Mathilde.

During this scene in front of the fireplace, intense, dramatic music accompanies the febrile hand movements of the young woman. Indeed, the use of music in the film is entirely governed by the fantasmatic vision that determines the shape of the story. The moments where music makes its presence felt are all, without exception, those that show the return of the repressed, the uncontrollable resurgence of former passions. Music intervenes ten other times in the course of the narrative.[17] During the house removals that mark the beginning and end of the film, Thomas comes to play random notes on Mathilde's piano. This repetition suggests that, in spite of appearances, the young woman is not cured. Each recurrence of the music serves to emphasize the presence of an interior emptiness caused by emotional deprivation.

The Woman Next Door is wholly preoccupied with regression – not only Oedipal regression, but also regression away from culture toward a nature that is untamed, menacing, murderous, capable of unanticipated violence – exactly what the taboo against incest, the foundation of all human civilization, attempts to ward off. The lovers in the film not only confront this violence in its most elemental forms, but also bear witness to their affinity with it. In an early draft of the screenplay, Arlette says to Madame Jouve, after the scandal at the garden party: "I'm not angry. One doesn't get angry at the rain; one waits until it's not raining anymore." Several details underline the irruption of this natural force that is incommensurable with cultural order. The theme of animality, so rarely encountered in Truffaut's films, makes several appearances here in *The Woman Next Door.* I have already mentioned the episode with the mating cats howling in the night, but, when Madame Jouve comes back from Paris, her dog also goes into a panic when it sees her suitcases. This incident recalls Bernard's instinctive behavior when, before attacking Mathilde in front of the guests, he prowls around the suitcases she is going to take with her on her honeymoon trip. One scene included in the first draft of the script, moreover, anticipates showing a fight between two dogs, the ferocity of which is condoned only by the lovers. The scenes set at night, which Truffaut handles so skillfully in the film, also show the irruption of a subversive force that threatens civilized order. During the dinner that reunites the two couples, "noises, hasty footsteps, barking" are heard outside. Philippe goes to open the door, explaining that it is probably a mad thief at work in an empty house. In the same scene, the appearance of Mathilde in the "indecent" dress that Philippe gave her recalls the incident in the garden party. In both cases, the revelation of the naked female body seems to awaken a savage instinct in the lovers, who react with a brutal change in their behavior. But during the final reception, it is the fire that shows most clearly the elemental force in the story and its affinities with the psyche of the lovers who, right from the start of the film, have abandoned the condition of culture.

This opposition between nature and culture is revealed through another series of powerful images: the doorsteps that characters constantly cross as they pass from the interior to the exterior, and vice versa. The house becomes, in effect, the chief symbolic representation in *The Woman Next Door* of civilized, social, and emotional order. It protects the couples against the dangers outside: night, animals, thieves. Mathilde and Bernard have no private space, no place of their own, no house. They meet in garages, in hotels, and in cars. In the hospital, Mathilde quotes the words of a song to Bernard: "I am an empty house without you." Even the household that each of them believes they have built without the other is only an illusion. Despite doors and shutters, their respective houses constantly open on to an outside that is wild and untamed. In the last scene, Bernard gets up because he hears the door of the house next door, which is meant to be empty, knocking in the night. In this poorly locked-up house, the person he discovers there turns out to be Mathilde, who has come for their final meeting. When she sees him, she says simply: "I have to talk to you." But they do not exchange any words. The sexual act, followed by their death, will consummate the failure of all adult, civilized, spoken communication. Mathilde's final gesture is to take off her pantyhose, which, allowing for the updating that has occurred, seem as if they are a contemporary version of Madame Doinel's stockings in *The 400 Blows.*

The Woman Next Door is perhaps the most accomplished film that Truffaut ever made, with its style attaining an unequaled perfection. Unquestionably, it is his darkest work. In it, even though madness is avoided, the only alternative is death. If one compares *The Woman Next Door* with *The 400 Blows,* one notices that the fantasmatic script is much more remote from the realistic script than was the case in the earlier film. Rather than there being a correspondence between the two scenarios, there is a gap. In *The 400 Blows,* the fantasmatic script simply picks up the elements of the realistic story in order to develop the dynamic of the unconscious representations that it contains. They constitute a clinical commentary that is remarkably precise and accurate: while the realistic story depicts Antoine, the hero, as a passive victim of abuse, the fantasmatic script reveals the formidable vitality with which he conducts an operation that is designed to ensure his psychic survival. In *The Woman Next Door,* adultery and incest have nothing in common apart from being forbidden. The image of the mother remains concealed, submerged. In contrast to the earlier film, we see characters who are apparently adults made prisoners of an interior destiny that nothing seems able to explain. The fantasmatic script takes this destiny into account. All critical studies of the film end up pondering the meaning of a work whose formidable emotional power few would question: *The Woman Next Door* galvanizes, but conceals, its secret.

Between the first and the second film, we see, furthermore, a shifting of the center of interest away from the child and onto the adult. *The 400 Blows* focused on the difficulty experienced by the son in forging an independent identity; *The Woman Next Door* is preoccupied with the suffering of a mother who is shown to be incapable of freeing the child from her maternal influence, or of allowing the normal process of separation to occur so that the child can grow into maturity. Between *The 400 Blows* and *The Woman Next Door,* the representations of the mother undergo a profound change. Whereas Madame Doinel remains a caricature, Mathilde is presented as a courageous woman, moving and tragic, arousing compassion. Despite the fatal outcome of the narrative, it is possible to see in this careful and nuanced story a form of forgiveness.

2

Deceptions
Shoot the Piano Player (1960)
The Soft Skin (1964)

AN ARTIST, AN UPPER-MIDDLE-CLASS PROFESSIONAL MAN, TWO men who are uncomfortable with who they are; a meeting with a new woman, the hope of renewal . . . and, at the end of each story, two gunshots that echo one another. With *Shoot the Piano Player* and *The Soft Skin,* separated by only three years, the filmmaker anatomizes both the faking of success and the faking of a couple's relationship. There is little doubt that autobiography played a role in the genesis of these two works. Each of them was made in the wake of moments of exhilaration that Truffaut, by his own admission, found hard to bear: "I have experienced periods of emptiness and sadness more often after successes than failures: I had violent bouts of depression after *The 400 Blows* and *Jules and Jim,* for example."[1] *Shoot the Piano Player* and *The Soft Skin* are the works that followed, respectively, each of those two films. More specifically, what Truffaut was analyzing through their twin protagonists was the loneliness of men who live a hidden life, closed in upon themselves, and whose deeply concealed self only reveals itself through the interior monologues of Charlie Kohler or the secret activity of Pierre Lachenay: stolen glances, furtive telephone calls, secret rendezvous. The former lives in silence, the latter lives a lie. The first looks for places to hide; the second prepares himself for flight in advance. The dissociation between appearance and reality, both as it pertains to the individual and to the environment, superficial and deep, is conveyed in the case of *Shoot the Piano Player* through narrative fragmentation, and in the case of *The Soft Skin* through visual fragmentation. Both the atomization of the story and that of the images reflect, in this instance, the splitting up of the self, experienced as internal self-mockery or externalized drama, by masculine heroes who are unable to bear their need and desire for women.

SHOOT THE PIANO PLAYER[2] (1960)

As one might expect in an oeuvre that has such a powerful unity, we find the same image in *Shoot the Piano Player* that haunts *The Woman Next Door*: the fall of a woman who, out of despair, throws herself out of a window into the void. Madame Jouve survives it, but Thérésa (Nicole Berger) dies, sealing the inevitability of Charlie Kohler's fate. Her dramatic suicide is filmed from a high-angle perspective by the camera, which follows the body to the street where it lies smashed. This scene is followed by close-up shots of newspaper headlines announcing the death of the wife of the great pianist Edouard Saroyan (Charles Aznavour), and the latter's disappearance. A cross-fade then registers on the screen the desolate landscape of a poor suburb, showing wasteland strewn with rubbish and old cars. It is here that he has come to find refuge. One could find no more eloquent way of signifying the bankruptcy of Edouard's world following the death of Thérésa. Renouncing his name, his art, and his success, he has become Charlie Kohler, who plays nightly in Plyne's dance hall. His daily routine manifests the same mechanical movement as the keys of the piano on which the camera focuses during the credit sequence. Having retreated from all intimacy, he limits his contacts with the world to rituals that are characterized by distance and indifference: he refuses to use the familiar "tu"; he thumps out the same old tunes to accompany the dancing of the locals; he engages in fleeting sexual encounters with Clarisse (Michèle Mercier), the local prostitute, whom he sends away unceremoniously in the early hours of the morning. Who is Charlie Kohler? A man who merely survives from day to day, enclosed in silence and solitude, an automaton. One is also struck by the irony of having the marginal figure of Bobby Lapointe sing in a film in which Charles Aznavour plays the leading role. Suppressing the charisma of the star, whose realist lyrics are famous throughout the world, Truffaut replaces him with a singer who was at that time unknown, someone with an impassive face and jerky gestures, who, to the kind of rhythm that would accompany a zany cartoon, delivers words that are puzzling to

2.1. Charlie Kohler (Charles Aznavour) in *Shoot the Piano Player,* dir. François Truffaut, 1960.

the point of being absurd. Charlie Kohler, at the beginning of the film, is a man in whom there remains only a distant and parodic vision, darkly ironic and shattered, of a world from which he is cut off.

After the film's release, Truffaut confided to Helen Scott: "David Goodis wrote me a letter in which I learned that he was less happy when he saw *The Pianist* with subtitles than when he didn't understand any of the dialogue and had believed the film to be much more faithful to his book."[3] This points to how there seems to be a radical rupture, from the very first scene, between the visual track and the soundtrack. A short, panic-stricken man is pursued by an unidentified vehicle at night. Suddenly, he collides with a lamppost and falls to the ground. Instead of being immediately chased down by his pursuers, he is assisted by a debonair passerby who helps him get up. Strolling calmly through the dark streets, the two men then engage in a conversation on the joys of marriage. The visual track conveys a story about gangsters, the soundtrack a story about love: "The men in it talk only about women, and the women only talk about men; in the midst of brawls, reprisals, kidnapping, pursuits, they only speak about love: sexual, sentimental, physical, moral, social, conjugal, extramarital, etc."[4]

Describing the sources of his inspiration for the unusual style of *The Piano Player,* Truffaut said that he had wanted to recapture the style found in fairy tales:

> One day while I was in a military hospital, someone sent me 10 or 12 *Série Noire* novels that I subsequently read and realized that they were very fairy-like. Moreover, certain aspects of these *Série Noire* books made me think of *The Eagle Has Two Heads* or *Les Enfants Terribles*. *Shoot the Piano Player* probably eventuated from the idea of taking a *Série Noire*–type story[5] – one that was already poetic, given that Goodis isn't just anybody – and push it to the limits of its possibilities in order to make it seem like a fairy story for adults."[6]

In *The Piano Player,* this fairy-like dimension is especially evident in the visual track, whereas the dialogue deals with love in a melancholic, realist tone. In fact, the disjunction between the image and the sound does not constitute a rupture so much as a simple discrepancy in tone. The images illustrate, in a way that is unreal, ludicrous, extravagant, and tragic, problems that the words expose through reason. The offhand, moving charm of *The Piano Player* arises from this double discourse.

The harmony between the two plots is apparent, moreover, from the beginning of the story. On the evening when the tale begins, Charlie is subjected to a double intrusion: that of Chico, who arrives to seek help; and that of Léna (Marie Dubois), who asks him for money, inviting him back to her place. From the outset, gangsters and love are linked together. At the end of the film, it is Momo and Ernest who, by shooting the girl, put an end to Charlie's amorous adventure. Between these two moments, *The Piano Player* analyzes the symptoms of the malaise that grips the hero. The first of these is fear, of which Plyne (Serge Davri) accuses him early on in the film. "Shit, I'm scared," Charlie repeats after him, with a wry face. The story is not content, however, simply to announce this anxiety: it depicts it spatially in a visual form. When Chico (Albert Rémy) comes to find his brother at Plyne's establishment, the camera spends a long time tracking through the labyrinth of corridors that lead to his dressing room. One of the dominant metaphoric images that structures the imaginary of *The Piano Player* is that of a burrow, in the depths of which Charlie seems to conceal himself throughout the film: corridors, elevator cages, courtyards, alleys, roads. Charlie scampers off at each turn in the story without ever finding anything other than temporary refuges: hotel rooms, a cellar, a small house surrounded by snow. A den, an imprisoning space, a visceral space – these symbols constantly reappear up until Truffaut's final films: the cellar in *The Last Metro,* the basement in *Confidentially Yours.*

Fear of the outdoors is confirmed, as in Truffaut's other films, by the way in which every transition from an interior toward an exterior takes on a menacing aspect. When Chico arrives outside of Charlie's dressing room, the latter orders him to stay in the corridor – an act conveying a presentiment that his brother will be associated with all the dangers lurking outside, waiting to burst into his protected universe. Charlie never seems able to go outside without being immediately pursued, attacked, kidnapped, or becoming involved in a violent action of one sort or another. The final time he crosses the doorstep of his hideaway to rejoin Léna, he finds her dead in a field of snow. Doors also play a pivotal narrative role in the story: the one that Charlie opens too late when Thérésa commits suicide; the one in Léna's apartment behind which he discovers the publicity poster for Edouard Saroyan – the future promised by the waitress's invitation opens onto the return of a catastrophic past.

The depiction of Charlie as a man being hunted down is conveyed, however, not only through the use of space: time also closes its vice on him. Built around a long flashback that occupies a third of the film, the story involves the repetition of a time that is cyclical. The story of Charlie, Léna, and Plyne in the present mirrors that of Edouard, Thérésa, and Lars Schmeel in the past. In both cases, another man's desire arrives to destroy the harmony of a couple; in both cases, the woman's death marks the denouement of the story. Because of the way its narrative is constructed, the story eludes the possibility of linear progression, and of any resolution that does not involve a repetition. In the final images of the film, the bar owner introduces Charlie to a new waitress who is going to replace Léna (Thérésa had earlier occupied this job), which allows for the possibility that the same tragedy is going to recur for a third time; for Charlie, unhappiness always arrives through a woman.

Taken as a whole, the film displays, in fact, an underlying fear of the feminine – one, indeed, that verges on deep misogyny. With the exception of the passerby whom Chico meets, who has succeeded in overcoming his ambivalence to find happiness in marriage (at the opening of the story he evokes an unrealizable ideal), the film presents a gallery of men who are incapable of living harmoniously in a relationship with a woman. The libidinal fixations of the gangsters and the pianist's brothers are infantile. Lars Schmeel and Plyne covet women they cannot have. For his part, Charlie is obliged to manage the anxiety that the female body arouses in him through strategies that are as diverse as they are disastrous. As is indicated by the scene in which Clarisse does a striptease behind the dressing screen, and the importance accorded to her lingerie, fetishism is the main solution he leans toward. Both the camera and Charlie's gaze fragment her body, the otherness of which threatens and disturbs him. With Thérésa, he can establish a happy relationship because of a careful ritualization of the interchanges between the couple. At a symbolic level, this ritualization indirectly signifies the institution of marriage. At first, Charlie and Thérésa relate to each other as teacher and student; then they act out the parts of customer and waitress. Such roles allow them to reduce the threat arising from the difference between the sexes, and to harmonize the masculine and the feminine – until the moment when Lars Schmeel takes their game literally. After that, Thérésa herself becomes fetishized, cut in two by the desire of the impresario, and then disarticulated on the pavement. With Léna, the difference between the sexes is initially suppressed. We only need to see the images of the couple, arm in arm, with each of them wearing an identical raincoat, to understand their attempt to construct a dual identity, a reciprocal identification. The salacious remarks of the gangsters in the scene with the car, followed by the revelation of Plyne's desire of her, reassert Léna's sexual difference as a woman, leading inevitably to her death.

The threat represented by the female body – which, as often occurs in fiction, is converted into a threat against the body of the woman – is revealed in a new network of images involving bars through which silhouettes are often glimpsed. When Charlie ascends the stairs to Léna's place for the first time, the camera presents a close-up of the young woman's legs filmed through the banister of the staircase. Clarisse's comings and goings on the landing outside her room are filmed in the same way. During their first walk together, Léna and Charlie, pursued by the gangsters, hide behind a high set of railings, the bars of which throw a shadow on the couple in the foreground. When Léna tries to rejoin the pianist in the snow-surrounded house, he sees her through the gridwork of a window. These images, which form a constantly recurring motif in Truffaut's works, mark the conflation of desire with the forbidden.

The threat that women pose comes from the power they exert, which is both physical and moral. In the film, the feminine is associated with a mobility and restless vigor that contrast with the fearful withdrawal of the hero from exposure to the outside world, and his need to hide himself. At the beginning, it is Léna who, striding briskly and confidently, literally leads Charlie toward the dangers that await him in the outside world. Every time they go on a walk, he ends up encountering deception or some unforeseen event that causes pain. On the first occasion, she leaves him standing alone in the street without warning; on the second, she reveals to him that she knows his true identity. After Plyne has been killed, she demonstrates yet again her energy and determination by carrying the lifeless body of her would-be lover out of the cellar in which it had been hidden, and takes it away to the mountains in a car she has "borrowed" from her landlady. Tragedy will occur at the rendezvous. Being in possession of knowledge, of a secret, women also exert complete control over the way the hero's life unfolds. Charlie owes his international success to Thérésa, who has the courage to maintain a lengthy silence over the ordeal that has broken her. As far as Léna is concerned, it is she who energetically encourages him to resume the path to success for their common good. As in *The 400 Blows,* the exercise of creativity is linked to a female character. During the enigmatic scene involving the audition at Lars Schmeel's establishment, when Charlie is hesitating to ring the bell, gripped by an uncontrollable panic, it is a young, unknown female violinist who opens the door.

This power that women exercise throws the pathological shyness of the piano player into sharp relief, along with his fear. The audition scene provides one of the most ironically detailed examples of these symptoms through its visual presentation: a series of close-up shots, growing bigger with every moment, follows the progress toward Lars Schmeel's bell of Charlie's index finger, until it finally freezes several centimeters away from it. The scene recalls the hesitant ballet performed by the pianist's hands around Léna's waist during their first outing, which is also filmed in close-up. In the soundtrack accompanying these images, Charlie wonders, in an anguished interior monologue conveyed in voice-off, what he should do next. What is happening during these moments of internal disarray, the seriousness of which is deflated in this instance through the use of a mocking style, but which will later take a tragic turn in the episode where Thérésa dies? The interior unity of the character seems to fly to pieces. His body pulls back, paralyzed in the face of a desire – to succeed, to be loved – that nevertheless reflects the profound truth of the man's being.

This dissociation between mind and body reaches its culmination when Charlie achieves fame. After his first major concerts, his manager criticizes his inability to make an impression at press conferences because of his reluctance to speak. In the following scenes, Charlie looks at photos posted on the walls of a street of a man demonstrating poses that illustrate the comportment of a person who is "not shy." He then goes to buy a pile of manuals designed to help victims of stage-fright to overcome their handicap. His reading of this material apparently bears fruit, because in the following scene a series of wordless shots show Charlie engaging with enthusiastic journalists with a supremely confident demeanor. He seems to have completely overcome his impediment. But this saga relating to his shyness is inserted between the two major scenes that depict his tragic misunderstanding with Thérésa. In the first, Charlie reproaches his wife for not being interested in his career. In reply, she denounces the egotistical vanity he has acquired since becoming a famous artist. In the second, she brutally reveals to him that she has slept with Lars Schmeel, as a means of procuring his success. Unable to cope with this confession, Charlie walks out on her in a way that shows the psychic dissociation he experienced during his shyness dramatically reasserting itself. While Charlie's inner voice is telling him: "Yes, look at her, go toward her, bow your head. Get on your knees, quickly, while there is time. Reflect, try to reflect. If you go out that door, she will be left alone. You must not leave her alone," his body slams the door and hastens off down the long hotel corridor. This process of dissociation occurs again at the moment when Charlie separates from Léna, who has taken him to his brothers' house. Whereas in outward action he sends her back to Paris, his interior monologue betrays his desire to have her stay by his side. One can imagine that, had he followed this instinct, Léna would not have fallen prey to the gangsters' bullets.

On several instances during the two scenes in which Charlie fights with Thérésa, the exchanges between the couple are filmed in the mir-

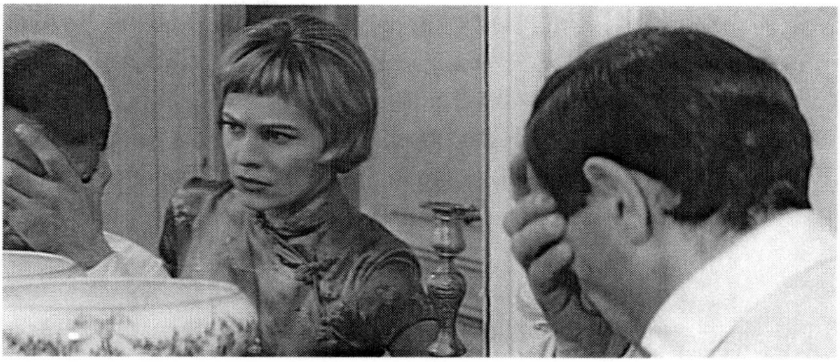

2.2. Charlie Kohler (Charles Aznavour) and Thérésa (Nicole Berger) in *Shoot the Piano Player,* dir. François Truffaut, 1960.

ror that is mounted above the fireplace in their hotel room. Mirrors, in fact, mark out Charlie's itinerary: the mirror before which he is preparing himself when Chico arrives, the mirror above the piano in Plyne's bar, the mirror in which he knots his tie after having spent the night with Léna, the broken mirror at his brothers' place, in which his face is reflected for the last time.

With regard to the relationship between Edouard and Thérésa, Truffaut commented: "In watching this film again, I recalled that there is a whole part of the relationship with Nicole Berger that was influenced by Moravia's *Contempt.* Part of this story dealt with a woman who put her husband's success first; he thought that she despised him."[7] This sub-theme relates directly to the major problem that is explored in the film. Charlie has a need to accept himself as reflected in the mirror that the women who love him hold out on him. His basic fragility derives from the fact that he has been unable to construct, and then internalize, an independent, autonomous image of himself. After he has become successful, Thérésa, with maternal tenderness, accepts a function as his narcissistic supplier, sharing a playful reality with him in which each enacts an agreed role, as we have seen, for the pleasure of the other. With the arrival of his celebrity, for reasons he does not understand, she closes up and withdraws from their intimacy, reflecting back to him an unacceptable image of himself. The continuity of being secured for him by sharing a fantasized reality with Thérésa is broken. Thereafter, he lives in a dissociated way, losing contact with his body.

As we learn from Thérésa's confession, the breaking point occurred precisely at the moment of the audition, thus coinciding in Edouard's life with his first crisis of shyness, and in Thérésa's life with her seduction by Lars Schmeel. Here is how the young woman describes it:

> The following day, he came back, you know, working like a spider. As if he were cutting me in two . . . as if my heart was in one piece and my body in another. It was not Thérésa who went with him, but only the body of Thérésa . . . Only, you know, it's strange, how what you did yesterday stays with you today. I look in the mirror. What is it I see? Thérésa? Your Thérésa? No, not Thérésa . . . not anywhere.

The dissociation that Charlie suffers is, first and foremost, Thérésa's own, which she causes to be reflected in him. In surrendering to Lars Schmeel against her will, Thérésa becomes split. A prisoner of her secret, she is never able to recover her original unity of being thereafter, and becomes enclosed in depression. Charlie's emotional environment then disintegrates. With the removal of her support, he in turn has recourse to dissociation as a means of coping with the emotional deprivation occasioned by the psychic death of his wife. It is these factors that cause him to construct for himself, at the height of his fame, what Winnicott calls a "false self." This concept, which will be encountered again in the exploration of *The Soft Skin,* has its origins in a commonplace phenomenon. The false self, in the case of harmonious personal development, consists of the protective outer layer, determined by education and social norms, that allows an individual to maintain civilized relationships with others. It in no way removes the capacity of the true self to manifest itself in other domains – for example, in the exercise of creativity, or love. In situations of serious emotional deprivation, a cleavage opens up that dissociates the false self from the true self, depriving the latter of the means of expression and satisfaction. Bodily experiences are a constituent part of the true self; it is through the body that an individual acquires a sense of well-being and reality. When the false self takes charge of an individual, the body no longer responds to the deep needs of the psyche: alienated, it betrays its function and retreats.

This is what Charlie's bouts of shyness illustrate, given that in the film they always express themselves in the form of physical dysfunction. It is also what explains the surprising devaluation of artistic experience in the film. Edouard is never seen performing his art as a virtuoso with any joy, and the visual depiction of his first major concerts suggests the bodily oppression of the pianist by his environment: a shot of his strained expression, jammed in behind the open lid of a black piano that fills nine-tenths of the screen; a shot of his lonely silhouette on a gigantic stage surrounded by two enormous, truncated pillars. His talent remains unimpaired, but, because it reinforces his false self, it is incapable of giving him pleasure. For the exercise of creativity to be happy, it needs to be sustained by the elaboration, in fantasy, of an interior unity involving continuity between psyche, body, and environment. It is because of this that an individual is able to acquire the feeling of existing and being real. In contrast, Edouard drifts in a state of unreality and dissociation. The film's narrative discontinuity, its grating, jerky style, and its abrupt shifts of tone are a reflection of the interior universe of its hero.

After the suicide of Thérésa, who, by her own admission, was seeking nothing from her husband other than a restoration of his true self through a gesture of love, Charlie no longer tries to maintain the false appearance he has constructed for himself. Instead, he is content to hide behind an impassive, anonymous façade. As Winnicott puts it, describing this type of situation, "The individual then *exists by not being found.* The true self is hidden, and what we have to deal with clinically is the complex *false self* whose function is to keep this true self hidden."[8]

Charlie hides himself; Léna finds him. The moving love scene in which, following the flashback she has triggered, the girl tells him of her longstanding attraction to him, suggests visually the reconstruction of the fragmented self of the piano player. We see Léna trying to establish a relationship of intimacy with Charlie, who is lying passively and silently beside her. Preceded by a vast panoramic shot around the walls of the room, filmed in a succession of cross-fades, this scene seems to symbolize the return of a continuity and reconciliation between Charlie and Edouard. However, following his euphoria during the early hours of the morning, the process of interior dissociation again makes an appearance during the violent argument that takes place between Léna and Plyne, when the couple comes to the latter's café so that Charlie can give his notice. Resuming his interior monologue, Charlie is critical of the brutality the girl displays toward a man who desires her. In using scurrilous language, Léna loses her "purity" not only in Plyne's eyes, but also in Charlie's. Like Thérésa, she becomes soiled by the desire of another man who is, like Lars Schmeel, superior to the hero in status. Nevertheless, the murder of the father remains thematically insignificant. It is the woman who will pay.

Because Léna will die, and the slow descent of her lifeless body down a snow-covered slope in the Alps at the end of the film picks up the image of Thérésa's suicide: the whiteness of the walls of the hotel room, the fall. Another scene draws the same motifs together in a comic manner. This occurs in the scene in which Fido, Charlie's young brother – a character who does not appear in Goodis's novel – impulsively throws from the window a carton of milk that explodes on the windshield of the gangsters' car. Repeated viewings of the film lead one to the conclusion that this scene, which expresses both the plenitude of desire as well as the transgressive exuberance of childhood, is profoundly ambivalent. Through a network of associations, it effectually combines images of pleasure and childhood with those of death. This first network then generates a second one that is manifest in the three following shots: of the milk being swept aside by movement of the windshield-wipers; of the light of the snow-covered mountains on the windshield of the car that takes Charlie toward the house of his childhood; of the traces of snow that Charlie's hand wipes off of Léna's face after her death. From milk to snow, the play leads straight to tragedy. The first instance of the milk blinds the gangster, just as the reflected snow blinds Charlie, with both constituting a whiteness that merges motherhood and death as the target of a visual impulse in which the force of desire is expressed. This desire is extinguished when Charlie, with Fido at his side, closes Léna's eyes.

These symbols are themselves inscribed within the film's larger framework, which presents a journey from black to white, from the darkness of the first night-scenes to the house in the snow; like an ascent from the depths of the cellar, in which Charlie hides after his fight with Plyne, toward the blinding light of the mountains. Above all, *The Piano Player* is a voyage into the past, a return to the point of origin, toward Charlie's childhood; but this return is also a return of the repressed, a return of the violence of childhood that the hero believed he had been able to escape when he left his brothers. Right from the very first images, the irruption of Chico into Plyne's bar marks the reentry of delinquency into the stifled and deadened world of the piano player. The fragile structures behind which Charlie believed he was able to hide show themselves to be incapable of containing the resurgence of this primitive past. A woman has to be the designated victim, since as a being, for Truffaut, she remains inexorably identified with his mother. The trajectory of erotic experience depicted in *The Piano Player* is consistent with the vision presented in *The 400 Blows.* The secret that the piano player harbors is designed – like Antoine Doinel's delinquency – to provide him with a means of awaiting, in a state of agitation and suspense, a resolution of the fusional relationship that binds him to this composite feminine figure. Here the woman dies; in *The Soft Skin,* it will be she who kills.

THE SOFT SKIN (1964)

On the eve of shooting *The Soft Skin,* Truffaut seems to have been particularly concerned to downplay the autobiographical dimension of this work. As he wrote to Helen Scott when he sent her the screenplay: "I urge you . . . not to speak of an 'autobiographical' film, of the order of *The 400 Blows,* but of a *fiction* that was inspired by various events involving passion."[9] Notwithstanding, the autobiographical dimension appears difficult to avoid if one takes into consideration the following remark: "Given that I'm not scared by the thought of committing a breach of good taste, the scenes showing Lachenay's household will be shot in my apartment in the Rue du Conseiller-Collignon,"[10] and also this confidential admission of January 1, 1964: "Madeleine[11] and I are going to separate . . . *The Soft Skin* has been painful to shoot and, because of the contents of the screenplay, I am filled with horror at the thought of marital deceit; in that regard, I am pretty revolted at this time."[12] The shooting of *The Soft Skin* was wound up on December 30, 1963.

Nevertheless, various incidents involving passion certainly did exert an influential role in determining the narrative shape of the film, and chief among them was the "Jaccoud affair" that aroused strong opinions during the early 1960s. Pierre Jaccoud, an elegant lawyer, married and in his 40s, had been conducting a long-term affair with a young woman,

Linda Baud. The clandestine encounters of the pair always took place in secret, to avoid shame and humiliation:

> When they went to a restaurant, Jaccoud would leave Linda Baud in the car, enter into the restaurant, and scan the place to see whether there was anyone in it they knew. If there was, he would get back into the car, go to a second restaurant, choose a table at the back, and make her sit facing the door. Each time the door opened, he would ask her, "Who is it?"[13]

Discarded, Linda Baud eventually took a new lover. Jaccoud, seeking revenge, sent him nude photos of his mistress that he himself had taken. He was accused of having killed the lover's father in order to retrieve the photos. One of the pieces of evidence used in this shady affair was the bloodstained raincoat that Jaccoud sent his wife, asking her to have it cleaned. One can detect important elements of the screenplay in this story: the photos, the garment to be cleaned in which Madame Lachenay discovers the receipt for the giveaway photos, and the raincoat that, in the film, is the one she puts on in order to go and shoot her husband.[14] In particular, we encounter the character of an upper-middle-class man caught in a mass of lies, furtiveness, and guilt that he is unable to confront. Truffaut's interest in Pierre Jaccoud's troubles seems to have been grounded in a feeling of compassion that was tinged with a certain degree of identification:[15]

> My idea was to make a film about adultery, based on the character of Pierre Jaccoud, as one could infer it from the accounts of his trial . . . It affected me deeply, and I thought that through him I could depict a man who is highly effective in his social life, but weak as far as love is concerned, and who, at the age of 40, finds himself confronted by a dilemma that leaves him more and more trapped in a vicious spiral. *The Soft Skin* is the portrait of such a man.[16]

"Vicious spiral" was the term Truffaut had already used to describe the story of *The 400 Blows*. He depicts an internal psychic destiny against which his heroes struggle, but most of them in vain. As far as the denouement of *The Soft Skin* is concerned, it was something entirely different that fueled the filmmaker's inspiration. He found it in *Détective,* which he called "the anthology of human weaknesses,"[17] and which he read every week. In July 1963, a young woman, Nicole Gérard, had shot her husband, who had just left her, in a crowded restaurant, around dinnertime. The weapon used to commit the crime was the same as in the movie: a shotgun. To the critics who found this detail unrealistic, Truffaut was able to retort in good faith that he had not invented it.

Most critics, in fact, panned the film when it came out. In what respects did they find Truffaut wanting? Firstly, for the banality of his subject matter, but especially on account of the disconcerting style, the effects of which seemed gratuitous. *The Soft Skin* is indeed a work that is frenetically cut up. Apparently, Truffaut directed his cinematographer, Raoul Coutard, not to film anything using panoramic shots.[18] The basic unit in the film, he said to a journalist, was no longer the scene, as in his previous works, but the shot.[19] A standard film comprises around 500 shots, whereas this one contains nearly 900. The most disconcerting aspect of the style of *The Soft Skin,* however, relates to the fact that objects, not characters, occupy the foreground of the scene. From the outset, we are plunged into a world that is mechanical, automated, and inhuman. When, at the beginning of the film, Lachenay (Jean Desailly) races by car toward the Orly airport to catch, literally about to take off, the airliner that is to fly him to Lisbon in order to present at a conference, the whole journey, from his apartment in Paris to his hotel room in Portugal, is filmed in eight minutes and 86 shots. Of these 86 shots, 33 are close-ups of objects: the car, starter, clutch, steering wheel, headlight, rearview mirror, clock, loudspeaker, briefcase, microphone, tickets, numbers, aircraft, gangway, illuminated arrivals-and-departures board, the hotel. In contrast to what happens in Hitchcock's films, these objects do not appear to have any particular role within the plot. In *Suspicion,* the fatal glass of milk is a crucial piece of evidence, priming the spectator for the revelation of the truth concerning the characters. In *The Soft Skin,* it is possible, if need be, to imagine that the objects in the first scene are meant to intensify the suspense of this race against the clock, but how can one explain why Lachenay and his wife, who are getting ready to go to bed, go through the rooms of their apartment turning on and off, one by one, all the light switches they encounter? The spectator wonders about the function of this detail. Some find it exasperating, like the critic writing for *L'Express* at that time:

> One has never seen, in close-up, so many shots of ignition keys, of starters being pressed, of payphone buttons. One has never seen so many doors opening and closing. Why make such a fuss over such minute details? To accelerate the pace?

> To give the impression of a breathless "modern life"? To make us think that the hero is oppressed by the practical difficulties that his double life causes him? If that is the reason, it is infantile and, above all, ineffective.[20]

Any critic who wants to reduce everything to the level of the plot is wrong to do so. More than ever, with Truffaut, the plot in *The Soft Skin* is merely a pretext. In speaking about his films, Truffaut said: "I present stories with a beginning, middle, and end, even though I know well that, ultimately, the main interest lies elsewhere, rather than in the plot itself."[21] In this case, the interest resides precisely in this mode of atomized representation. It is the latter that conveys the essence of what the film wants to communicate, as André Téchiné astutely perceived:

> Pursuing a path of making and unmaking, *The Soft Skin* speaks to us of distance . . . Fingers exploring to the limits of propriety, hesitant touchings, tentative caresses, hands held and released then grasped at the gangway, fingers being applied to the buttons of the elevator, making circular movements on a telephone dial, exchanging keys . . . there is no lively impression here of a body, no vital impulse. Only the outer cover, the surface, are still seen as the manifestation of a number of latent symptoms.[22]

The absence of the body, the outer cover, the surface, the skin – one can see in these lines the terminology that is characteristic of the false self, which, in the case of the hero of *The Soft Skin,* takes the form of an empty shell. Charlie hides himself; Lachenay, for his part, remains inaccessible. We are given no flashback that uncovers the origins of his malaise, no interior monologue that reveals his secret thoughts to us. There is only one fleeting trace that is quickly suppressed – the telegram that he writes to Nicole (Françoise Dorléac) in an unguarded moment at Orly: "Since I have known you, I am another man, and this man cannot imagine living without you. I love you." When he accidentally meets the girl in the hall of the airport, he furtively throws it away. The "other man" disappears, and all that remains is this succession of fragmented, disconnected images, in which mechanisms and machines take the place of an absent body. It is in this suite of disjointed close-ups of indifferent objects that Lachenay's interior monologue is to be found. The succession of close-up shots reflects the projection and dissemination of Lachenay's inner being in relation to a reality with which he has lost contact, and which assumes the same hallucinatory quality as occurs in schizoid personality disorders. Adultery, in this instance, is not the cause, but the manifestation of a deeper disturbance. From a psychological point of view, everything about the hero's behavior is crazy. Franca, his wife, is beautiful, loving, and prepared to show tolerance. Nicole, his mistress, accepts the situation without showing any jealousy beyond that which springs from genuine love. Nevertheless, Lachenay allows himself to become enmeshed in a pack of lies, and seems merely to look on, appalled, at the catastrophic developments of a situation over which he has no control.

Lachenay's life is entirely governed by the tyranny of a false self that presents him to the world with all the external markers of success: fame, money, the respectability of a middle-class marriage. Behind this façade, however, the representational system of the film as a whole suggests the presence of a self in retreat, isolated, fragmented, unreal, inaccessible. In a normal situation, a false self serves an important function. By submitting itself to environmental demands, it protects the kernel of personality that is the true self:

> At the centre of each person is an incommunicado element, and this is sacred and most worthy of preservation . . . Rape, and being eaten by cannibals, these are mere bagatelles as compared with the violation of the self's core, the alteration of the self's central elements by communication seeping through the defenses.[23]

The clinical description that applies to *The Soft Skin* suggests a situation in which the danger that threatens the self is so serious that individuality develops as "a sense of depersonalization," involving a "the feeling that the centre of gravity of consciousness transfers from the kernel to the shell, from the individual to the care, the technique."[24] The absence of a true self then creates a condition of chaos and instability that is all the more painful because society regards the false self as the true one.

Lachenay is "invaded" in the true sense of the word; he is constantly having to flee from encroachments and intrusions that are enacted spatially: near the beginning, when he slips away during a party in order to phone Nicole, his wife comes to look for him. In his office, he has to steal away to ward off the curiosity of his secretary. This invasion reaches its height when the presence of an unpretentious young girl who has come to ask him to autograph her book plunges him into a state of near panic, because he dreads the thought that Nicole might barge in. There is nothing inherent in the nature of these experiences that could justify the existential crisis they precipitate in him. His perturbation is the reflection and repetition of an archaic state of emotional deprivation, the sources of which the film leaves completely obscured. *The Soft Skin* describes without analyzing. In doing so, the film faithfully replicates one of the major symptoms observable in the hero. Lachenay lives out his malaise without any hindsight, without insight, without symbolization; he is a man without memory. It is unknown whether he has had other affairs during his 14 years of marriage; he is a man who lacks any means of intimate expression – Nicole reproaches him for not being able to bring himself to say he loves her. Drifting in a perpetual present, cut off equally from the past and the future, he shows himself to be incapable of evoking through memories or associations the threatening primitive environment that is constantly implied but never fully brought into conscious awareness.[25] The elaboration of such a seriously dissociated false self constitutes, in fact, a defense mechanism erected by the individual against the threat of a psychic breakdown, the possibility of which he dreads. In certain scenes of the film, one sees Lachenay on the verge of such a breakdown, which the conclusion of the story will actualize in a form that is both physical and moral.

As in *Shoot the Piano Player,* in this instance dissociation takes the form of a split between mind and body. On several occasions, the film shows the physical unease of the hero – unable to dance; jealous of the athletic looks of Franck, the co-pilot, Nicole's former lover. In a brief scene in which Lachenay is accompanying his mistress to her fitness class, we see him next to a poster displaying the muscled body of an athlete. This creates an ironic contrast with his own body, which is wrapped up in a dark overcoat, with a black hat pulled on his head. He will die in a restaurant in which the walls are covered by photos of skiers . . .

With Lachenay, this physical alienation is matched, as is typical in such cases, with an excess of intellectual activity. This gives the individual an impression of having resolved his problems, whereas in actuality it only serves to aggravate them by producing an impression of emptiness, futility, and pointlessness. As with Charlie, Lachenay seems to derive no pleasure from his activities as a celebrity. His real creative work is, significantly, never shown in the film. We do not see him at work writing on a single occasion, and the story pays no attention to the conferences he attends, showing merely the circus-act aspect, which the hero finds tiresome. In Rheims, Lachenay confesses his stage fright to the audience, after a symphony of malfunctioning microphones, and the constant assaults of the curious, eager, prying faces of the organizers, filmed in close-up, during the dinner that precedes his lecture. As far as he is concerned, the title of the journal that he edits is a confession tinged with mockery: *Ratures* (Crossings-out). Lachenay, in studying the great masters of past literature, has cut himself off from contemporary reality in order to inhabit a dead world. In creating this aspect of the character, Truffaut revealed that he was thinking of the great critic Henri Guillemin: "I was inspired by a man who was more at ease with the dead, with former glories, than with the world of today."[26] Being an anachronistic character who is displaced, and split internally, Lachenay seems to be crushed even by the past that he is trying to bring alive. In Rheims, a long shot shows the shadowy outlines of Lachenay and his friend Clément (Daniel Ceccaldi), after the conference, engaged in conversation behind a cinema screen on which a gigantic picture of Gide is projected. Cultural fathers, taking on a saturnine appearance, seem as if they are about to devour their children.

The encounter with Nicole, at the beginning of the film, momentarily dispels this double malaise of body and mind. After having finished with his conference in Lisbon, Lachenay, returning to his hotel late at night, meets the flight attendant he had noticed on the plane again, in the elevator. She drops her keys, which allows the hero to observe the number of her room: 813, a tribute to Maurice Leblanc, the creator of *Arsène Lupin*. Once she has left the elevator, Lachenay descends again to his room. Truffaut was very proud of his manipulation of time in this sequence:

> The actual duration time it takes this lift to ascend in real life is 15 seconds, and yet the scene in the film, which involves about 25 shots, lasts five times as long, 71 seconds, to be precise. We now arrive on the eighth floor, Françoise Dorléac gets out of the elevator, and we stay with Jean Desailly, who presses the button to go down. This time, the same trajectory lasts only 15 seconds, because it is filmed in a single shot in real time.[27]

What particularly arrests one's attention is the comparison between this scene and the one that immediately follows it. Once he has gone into his room, Lachenay phones Nicole to ask her to have a drink with him. At first she refuses, then, changing her mind, calls him back to accept. The whole scene is filmed in Lachenay's room. The entire sequence – if Lachenay's progress down the corridor that leads to his room is added to the scene in the elevator – comprises 39 shots in two minutes; the second scene involves two shots over three minutes. Extreme visual fragmentation, with numerous close-ups of objects, is succeeded by one of the few passages that are filmed in continuity. In the two shots of the second scene, we see Lachenay first of all cross his room to the telephone, and then, after the call from Nicole, wander through all the rooms in his suite, opening the doors and switching on the lights, one by one, before going to stretch out on his bed. No object is interposed to disturb the visual fluidity of this scene. Filmed in long shot, Lachenay's body seems momentarily to have found a space in which it can evolve without fear, in which it can relax, expand, and project the euphoria that inhabits it. The next day, in the restaurant, shedding his habitual indifference, Lachenay talks about Balzac with such passion and happiness that he forgets the time, meaning that he does not take the girl back to their hotel until dawn. It is then that they become lovers, but we do not see this scene. Once the door to their room shuts, the film switches abruptly to the aircraft on its return trip to Paris, which a string of close-up shots (of levers, instrument panel, runway, and cabin) announce as difficult.

As with the interior monologues in *The Piano Player,* scenes containing a multiplicity of objects never occur in the story by chance, but each time attest to severe emotional suffering in the hero. In this regard, the departure for the tryst in Rheims (Lachenay travels there to give a conference presentation, taking his mistress with him) is attended from the outset by the shadow of dark omens. The couple's car trip to Rheims, seemingly peaceful, is densely packed with close-ups of machines; out of a total of 48 shots, 18 shots are taken up with such things as the car's starter, a gas pump, the car's gas tank, trucks, and numbers. This episode marks, in effect, a moment in which the interior dissociation of the hero reaches an intolerable intensity. The presence of Clément, Lachenay's provincial friend – a loser who is unbearable but disarming – nevertheless places this episode under the sign of the most corrosive black humor. If one wanted to present comically a physical representation of Winnicott's notion of an invasive environment, one would be hard pressed to think of anyone better than this unfortunate man who pursues Lachenay insistently throughout the evening, while Nicole is waiting, finally asking him to give him a lift to Paris. In the café scene in which the two men have a drink after the conference, the pressure Lachenay experiences from the need to cope with the impossible situation in which he has landed himself becomes so violent that it brings him to the verge of physical illness. On the other side of the plate-glass window, he can see Nicole, wandering through the dark streets, being accosted by a passerby who propositions her. Commenting on this passage, Truffaut declared:

> At one moment, I thought of making him faint in Rheims, once he had seen the girl on the other side of the window; after Ceccaldi had drunk his half-pint, he was to have gotten up and then fallen over backward. Then I said to myself: that will mean making a film about a mad man, people are going to think that it is the story of an ill person, and so I abandoned the idea, which I used later in *Fahrenheit*.[28]

Lachenay is indeed stupid for not having confessed the truth to his friend. Commenting on this fact, which earned him criticism, Truffaut remarked: "People condemned the film for something I purposely intended; he doesn't say to Ceccaldi: 'I've come with a girl.' That's because, like Jaccoud, Desailly is a man who can't do that."[29] Lachenay is especially ill-advised, because his actions put pressure on the shell of the false self that makes it ready to crack. When the hero comes to the verge of a breakdown, the sight of him reflects the disposition of the audience in the theater itself. Seated, silent, deprived of mobility and the means to take action, Lachenay, filmed in close-up, has to watch, helplessly, the spectacle of his mistress acting out a little scenario in front of him – by repelling the advances of the creep who is pursuing her – as if he is viewing her from the perspective of a long shot. Other scenes replicate elements of this crucial scene: the plate of glass that separates Franca from her husband at the airport, or Lachenay from Nicole when he notices her in the same episode through the windshield of the car that his wife is driving; the distance between the woman as spectacle and the lover as spectator when Nicole dances alone in front of him in the cabaret where they are spending the evening. This relative disposition reproduces in spatial terms Lachenay's internal flaw. In cinema, the law that governs representation is that of the heterogeneity of spaces: the spectator is never located in the same space as the image on the screen. The split that prevails between Lachenay and the truth of his emotional life takes on the same insurmountable, definitive aspect. That is why this truth, as Truffaut says, cannot ever be revealed to anyone.

In *The Soft Skin,* the solid reality of the women contrasts with the uncertain, fragmented being of the hero. In a way that is quite surprising for a film by Truffaut, the women are only slightly fantasmatic in the way their characters are portrayed. For the most part, they do not participate in the unconscious of the story. These women are real: they eat, dance, gossip, have friends, go shopping. Nevertheless, in the rare moments when they enter into the field of the hero's consciousness, they suddenly change and, losing their solidity, seem to fly to pieces. In the love scene at la Colinière,[30] we see Nicole's erotic body become fetishized under the gaze of her lover. With her eyes closed, the girl lies motionless on the bed. Lachenay caresses her and begins to take off her stockings. The scene is filmed in a series of close-ups that alternately show the man's face and fragments of the woman's body. Fetishism, by isolating a part of the woman's body in order to eroticize it, removes the threat that it represents. Truffaut would later devote a whole clear-eyed and fascinating film to this theme, *The Man Who Loved Women,* but one already finds it, presented fleetingly, in several scenes of *The Soft Skin:* in the airplane that takes him to Lisbon, Lachenay particularly notices the beautiful hostess at the moment when she is changing her shoes behind a curtain that allows only her feet to be seen; during the trip to Rheims, he expresses his regret at seeing Nicole in trousers, and makes her go and change into a skirt, to please him; like Léna in *The Piano Player,* Nicole asks her lover to buy her some stockings, and when they are at la Colinière draws his attention to the women who are wearing leopard-skin blouses – these are women, she says, who like making love.

This dividing up of the female body into pieces reflects the fragility of the hero, who is incapable of apprehending the physical reality of a woman in its totality. But, in splitting up the object of his desire between wife and mistress, Lachenay is also showing his reluctance to unite the

2.3. Pierre Lachenay (Jean Desailly) with Nicole (Françoise Dorléac), his mistress, in *The Soft Skin,* dir. François Truffaut, 1964.

emotional and the sexual in one feminine figure. The script foreshadowed this by inserting a brief excerpt on high-class prostitution on the sidewalk of the Avenue Foch, at the moment when Nicole and Pierre try to rent a room in a hotel used by prostitutes near the Etoile. Shocked by the vulgarity of the place, the girl refuses to remain there. And what does Lachenay do, other than treat his wife like a prostitute, when he seizes the opportunity during a brief visit to his house, after their separation, to make love to her without necessarily wanting to renew their relationship? Furious, she throws him out. The reaction of the women in these scenes displays the same refusal to be treated merely as objects of pleasure. This is confirmed in two other scenes in which we see them, one after the other, fending off the crude desire of an unknown man: Nicole, in Rheims, when she is pursued by an anonymous passerby; Franca (Nelly Benedetti), in Paris, when, with exasperated violence, she repels the advances of a professional Lothario, who retreats, flabbergasted. In contrast to *The Piano Player,* there is no intimacy in *The Soft Skin,* no shared experience that could potentially restructure the hero. At the end of the film, Lachenay remains alone.

Nevertheless, the whole story is carried along in its forward course by a powerful hope of a happy resolution. The aerial metaphor that governs the film's imaginary bears witness to it. Airports, aircraft, and journeys are associated with the adultery. Nicole, given the role of flight attendant, is the woman associated with this flight. With Truffaut, images follow one another from film to film without ever being identical. In this one, the images of flight constitute the same defense mechanism that pertains to the elaboration of the false self. The latter serves to mask depression:

> The false self . . . though a successful defense, is not an aspect of health. It merges into the Kleinian concept of a manic defense – where there is a depression but this depression is denied, by unconscious process of course, so that the symptoms of depression appear as their opposites (up for down, light for heavy, white or luminous for dark, liveliness for deadness, excitement for indifference, and so on).[31]

The image of flight needs to be understood in this clinical context. Flight does not suggest a playful, creative, sexual euphoria so much as a defensive representation of its opposite – a fall, or breakdown, the threat of which weighs down on Lachenay right from the beginning of the film. Two pieces of evidence, cut from the film during the editing, confirm this hypothesis. The first scene of the film was to have followed in great detail the movements of an unknown man on the platform of the metro up until the moment when he threw himself under the train that was transporting Lachenay. There remains only a fleeting vestige of this episode when it is referred to in the dialogue. When he arrives back home in a rush, the hero tells his wife he has been delayed by a suicide. In another scene, Lachenay and Nicole are going together to the airport's theater, in which is playing a film assembled from old clips, *Paris 1900:*

> We see a man, a pioneer of parachuting, who is in the process of leaping off the first level of the Eiffel Tower, with a parachute on his back of his own invention. He hesitates for a long time before jumping, looks toward the camera, looks into the void. We think that he is going to chicken out, and then suddenly he throws himself into the void and smashes into the ground, his device having failed to function.[32]

In these two sequences, falling is linked to a man's death. Even though Truffaut, as he typically did, suppressed these two scenes because they were too explicit, too direct, we still find the image of the fall in the crucial scenes of the film that record the end of the hero's relationships with his mistress and his wife: that involving his breakup with Nicole, and that involving his murder by Franca. Nicole breaks off from her lover while he is making her visit an apartment under construction into which he wants them both to move. After her departure, Lachenay, shattered, remains alone and looks at the girl going into the distance as she moves down the street. One shot, filmed from a high angle from the top of the building, shows her disappearing into a taxi. At the moment when Franca, armed with a shotgun, leaves her apartment to go and kill him, Lachenay is in the process of phoning in order to reconcile with her. The nanny who is looking after their daughter answers him. He asks her to call back his wife, first from the stairway, and then from the window. Two high-angle shots punctuate these vain attempts: one shows the empty stairwell, and the other shows Franca's car moving away in the street.

The entry of Nicole into Lachenay's life brought with it a hope of recovering some contact with his secret self in order to ward off the threat of a breakdown. The images of flight connote this hope. When that disappears, there is no longer any way out, because the hero's wish to reconcile with his wife is, properly speaking, a solution that arises from despair. Moreover, the idea of it does not come to him spontaneously; it is suggested by one of Franca's friends, whom he telephones in his distress. He acquiesces without any real conviction, like a man who is shut down, a puppet who lets himself be pushed around by circumstances. As with delinquency in *The 400 Blows,* or the secret in *The Piano Player,* the defensive construction of a false self indicates a hope that the true self will be able to regain its well-being, lest doubt intervene with suicide as the clinical result: "Suicide in this context is the destruction of the total self in avoidance of the annihilation of the True Self."[33] The images of falling suggest that Lachenay's death, at a psychic level, corresponds to a suicide. It is obviously not inconsequential that the instrument of his death should be Franca, who, in the film's imaginary, is the character who comes nearest to being a maternal figure. It is no less significant that in the final scenes three women come between Lachenay and his wife in a way that precipitates the tragedy: the friend he calls, the girl who is chatting on the public telephone, and his daughter's nanny. Between Lachenay and Franca, there are always too many women. In the last minutes of the film, Franca's character changes rather dramatically, and it was no doubt that, more than the shotgun attacked by the critics, that audiences found shocking. She turns into a dark figure, violent and enigmatic, in whom there suddenly appears the shadow of the maternal mystery. Unable, like Mathilde in *The Woman Next Door,* to set her son free, she prefers to eliminate him. It is the repressed past that kills Lachenay by preventing him from forging a free, autonomous identity. Truffaut said, furthermore, that his hero was "an upper-middle-class man with something juvenile about him that gives the impression of innocence, and of extreme clumsiness in his efforts to act clandestinely."[34] Lachenay carries Antoine Doinel within himself. It is the deprivation of his early emotional environment that the adult hero of *The Soft Skin* is reliving without understanding it or being able to analyze it. And if the murder of a son by the mother is the equivalent of a suicide, that is because the two of them have never separated. Eighteen years later, *The Woman Next Door* would pick up the same syndrome, pushing the logic that informed it up a notch further.

Having been shot by Franca, Lachenay slumps down on the table of the restaurant he regularly uses, *Le Val d'Isère.* The whiteness of the tablecloth picks up that of the snow on the mountains in the photos that line the walls. More indirectly, it relates to the images of Léna's death in *Shoot the Piano Player.* Franca, before she pulls the trigger, throws the photos of Nicole in her husband's face. The atomized body of the young woman, the fragments of which Lachenay has not been able to reunite, symbolize for one last time the interior disintegration of the hero, which, after this, becomes tragically definitive. But it is with a close-up shot of Franca that the story ends. A faint smile, ambiguous, vaguely terrifying, floats on her lips. In the world of *The Soft Skin,* forgiveness has no place and, contrary to what one might expect, it is not the mother but the son who shows himself to be pitiless. He reproaches her, with every image in the film, with having destroyed him.

Shoot the Piano Player and *The Soft Skin* are two films stamped with the seal of guilt in the face of success, of woman, of the past. But it would be a distortion not to acknowledge the considerable humor that ani-

2.4. Franca (Nelly Benedetti) in the final scene of *The Soft Skin,* dir. François Truffaut, 1964.

mates them. Apparent from the first images of *The Piano Player,* it is no less present in *The Soft Skin* – a film that is, however, more discreet and classical. In this respect, the episode that takes place in Rheims is a veritable piece of anthropology, considerably lightening the story in order to rescue it from the tragic. Furthermore, Truffaut saw Lachenay as "a blunderer" (*un gaffeur*) who

> every time he is faced with a difficulty chooses the worst possible solution . . . Rather than being cruel, I wanted to be fairly critical, with the result that the film is full of comments and mockery. There's an Italian left-wing filmmaker, De Bosi, who has said that it's a film characterized by black humor. I think that that's fairly accurate.[35]

What is humor? As we know, it involves a distancing, a liberating detachment, which explains the pleasure Truffaut took in projecting the main elements of his life into his work. "Humor," said Freud, "does not give up, it defies, it reflects not only the triumph of the ego, but also of the pleasure principle that finds in it a means of asserting itself despite unfavorable external circumstances." With humor, he added, it is the superego that "directs itself, full of goodness and consolation, toward the intimidated, fearful ego,"[36] assuming the role of a consoling and protective parental authority. In *The Piano Player,* the presence of Fido, Charlie's little brother, reduces the plot on several occasions to the level of children's games, lacking seriousness. In *The Soft Skin,* Lachenay's daughter, Sabine (Sabine Haudepin), is not enough to defuse the tragedy, but her presence alleviates it by letting us glimpse a desirable dimension that it is not able to attain. For Truffaut, humor and the spirit of childhood are always linked together and, while the adults often carry a suffering child within themselves, the children in his films allow one to imagine a zone of light that is always intact, which brightens and warms large stretches of his work.

3

Queen-Women

Jules and Jim (1962)
The Last Metro (1980)

JULES AND JIM AND *THE LAST METRO* WOULD SEEM TO HAVE little in common apart from an adulterous schema involving one woman and two men. While it is central in the first film, this situation remains marginal in the second one, which depicts the activities of a theater under the Nazi Occupation. Moreover, there is a contrast between black-and-white and color, between the adaptation of a novel and an original screenplay, between the outdoors and an enclosed space, and between the study of a trio as against a polyphonic construction that brings together 15 characters. Nevertheless, both films were made to celebrate Jeanne Moreau and Catherine Deneuve, both of whom played an important role in Truffaut's personal life. *Jules and Jim* and *The Last Metro* are works inspired by the idealization of a female figure. Their autobiographical dimension, however, extends beyond the recent past; each film, like a palimpsest, reveals several different layers of memories in Truffaut that are joined together through a play of analogies. Speaking about *Jules and Jim* in 1975, he made the following admission:

> Much later, I came to realize that the reason I had wanted to make *Jules and Jim* so badly was that the subject matter had deeply hidden roots in my own childhood, and that it would allow me to highlight all the things around me that I had felt were abnormal during the period of the Occupation when I was living at Pigalle, in the midst of trafficking, the black market, the settling of scores involving women, adultery, and everything that was linked to the Collaboration, the Resistance, and the Purification.[1]

This remark turns *Jules and Jim* into a work whose private content coincides exactly with the historical content of *The Last Metro*. Considering the two films together also allows one to compare and contrast two kinds of representation that correspond to the beginning and the end of the filmmaker's career: that is to say, a natural setting as against a studio, an indirect style as against the art of the secret, and the theme of love as against that of creative work.

JULES AND JIM (1962)

In the white house by the seaside in which they live together for the first time, Catherine (Jeanne Moreau) leads Jules (Oskar Werner) and Jim (Henri Serre) on a walk through the woods, "looking," she says, "for the last signs of civilization." The camera, following the movement of their gaze, scans the ground to reveal, among the plants and shrubs, a shoe, a box, matches, a piece of porcelain, a metal cup, a cigarette butt. Later, after the war, Jim goes to rejoin Jules, Catherine, and their daughter Sabine (Sabine Haudepin) in their chalet near the Rhine. One evening, Catherine invites Jim to tell her about himself while they are walking together. He runs through his memories in the course of a long walk through the forest that lasts until dawn. The story, in an attempt to give an impression of what has happened to these characters across a span of nearly thirty years, attempts to absorb into its flow the signs, the traces, the vestiges of a vanished past. As the intertwined journeys through time and space indicate, the action of *Jules and Jim* takes place under the sign of a nostalgic movement. This movement, as the narrator's commentary, which is couched in the imperfect and simple past tenses, constantly reminds us, is never toward the future, but is always directed toward a time that has already taken place. What Truffaut loved about the source novel, written by an old man (Henri-Pierre Roché was 76 years old when he wrote *Jules and Jim* based on his memories), was its ability to take a calm, reconciled look at a time that had been lost: "It was probably ambitious to make a film about an old man's story, but this return to the past, which enabled me to achieve a certain degree of detachment, fascinated me."[2] He would later profess that he had wanted to film the past in *Jules and Jim,* just as he would film the future in *Fahrenheit 451,* with a light touch, without requiring the audience to believe too much in its verisimilitude.[3] Every image in the film is designed to give spatial form to what is represented as a ludic, or playful, time.

From the opening, when a 360-degree panoramic shot follows the movement of Thérèse (Marie Dubois), a young anarchist Jules has picked up, around his room, the film repeatedly presents the image of a circle: the circles involved in the games with Sabine, the whirlwind in Catherine's song. Time in *Jules and Jim* has the circularity and lack of finality of play itself. During this scene, with a cigarette in her mouth, Thérèse puffs out smoke in imitation of a train. Later, Jim encounters her again, in a café, where she stuns him with the incredible story of her life, which takes the form of a journey around the world. From beginning to end, it is the woman who initiates the movement that animates the film. A driving force of immense vitality, she draws men along in her trail: she is the prime mover for their journeys as a threesome, and of the cycling excursions that she leads from the front; she is also the only one who drives the car. Jim's friendship with Jules starts up in Paris, but when they see the image of the statue that fascinates them projected on a screen, they race off to the island in the Adriatic Sea where it is located. The story leaves out the voyage itself in order to transport us abruptly from the dark room of Albert, in which the projection is taking place, to the open-air museum, bathed in sunlight, that contains the statue. The advent of the ideal woman is thus accompanied by an opening up of space, of a magic mobility for the two men, whereas previously their lives had been circumscribed by narrow routines. When they meet Catherine, who resembles the face of the statue, she immediately leads them to the seaside. Then Jim follows the pair to the countryside near the Rhine and, after a number of subsequent reunions, to a mill in the area around Paris. When, by chance, they meet each other again in a cinema at the end of the film, Catherine takes them to a riverside restaurant. This turns out to be their last outing. Any movement generated by Catherine always leads away from towns. The space and time she occupies is inseparable from nature.

Those who are familiar with Truffaut's films may find the high degree of importance that nature assumes in *Jules and Jim* surprising. He himself made the following confession:

> Nature leaves me entirely unmoved. If someone were to ask me to name the places that I have loved most during my life, I might say that it is the countryside in Murnau's *Sunrise*, or the town in the same film, but I would not mention any

> actual place that I had really visited, because I never visit any. I'm aware that it is a bit abnormal, but that's the way it is. I don't like landscapes or things; I like people, I'm interested in ideas and feelings.[4]

Notwithstanding this protestation, the film presents an extensive country landscape full of murmuring streams, the rustling of trees, and the tall grasses of meadows. This is not the countryside of Murnau, but of Renoir. In the fifth shot of *Jules and Jim,* during the stretch of unoccupied time that precedes the arrival of Catherine, we see the two friends drifting idly in a rowboat that glides along the river under the leafy shade of overhanging trees. This shot comes straight out of *A Day in the Country.* Woman belongs to a nature that brings back cinematic memories. Already in *Les Mistons,* Bernadette had appeared to the boys who were spying on her gliding through the woods on her bicycle. A long traveling shot followed her to the stream in which she took a swim. Bernadette was the sister of the ingénue in *A Day in the Country* who, swinging under the boughs next to the water, entranced the boaters. Just like the women in Renoir's films, Catherine in *Jules and Jim* incorporates and amalgamates the landscapes she traverses.

While *The Soft Skin* gives the impression of a surgical film in which the hero is visually dissected, piece-by-piece, in *Jules and Jim* everything is held together. Each fragment is linked to the next through the use of panoramic and traveling shots that become airborne for the sake of enclosing the bodies of the characters in their environment: "It was constantly necessary to take in nature, the environment, which explains why there are so many 360-degree panoramic shots. There was no question of showing the chalet without showing the meadow, nor the meadow without the forest."[5] Neither Jules without Jim, nor Jules and Jim without Catherine. The substance out of which the members of the trio are cast is fluid, aquatic. The epitome of this moist space, protective and uterine, is the lake shrouded in mist where they go during Jim's stay at the chalet near the Rhine, the setting for their most perfect happiness: "All four of them took a walk around a lake hidden in the mist in the depths of a humid, verdant valley." In this leafy enclave, enclosed and secret, in which everything is suspended, with no trace of civilization remaining, they play, as in fairy stories, with white pebbles, learning how to make

3.1. The mist-shrouded lake in *Jules and Jim*, dir. François Truffaut, 1962.

them skip. "The harmony between them was complete . . . Heaven was very near." Catherine's substance eludes the constructions of culture.

Every return to Paris is marked by archival images showing the city during the 1900s. The timeless country landscapes associated with the woman are placed in contrast with historical markers of the period, with their iron and stone structures: the elevated railway on their return from the Adriatic, the Gare de Lyon on their return from the sea, the Eiffel Tower on Jim's return from the Rhine. Catherine's only promenade in Paris takes place along the banks of the Seine, without any trace of an urban landscape. In addition, she jumps into the river, and her hat, followed by the camera, drifts away on the current of the water. The images that depict Catherine are filmed in fluid, continuous shots, whereas static shots punctuate her absences: during the lives of Jules and Jim before she arrives in the story; during Jim's sojourns with his Parisian mistress, Gilberte. When Catherine jumps into the Seine, it is to protest against Jules's comment on women, whom he sees as "natural, therefore abominable." The original screenplay states even more bluntly that women are "primitive, like animals." Similarly misogynistic remarks occur within the larger framework of the film, in which they are expressed in a poetic manner, sometimes attended by fascination, and sometimes by horror. Speaking of Catherine, Jules declares: "She is a force of nature who expresses herself through cataclysms."

Faced with this landscape that is an extension of the female body, Jules does not hesitate: he sets himself up in it to study the flora and fauna. Whereas his father had had him photographed in his youth dressed up as Mozart, one of the most representative figures of art and civilization, Jules becomes a specialist in the most uncivilized forms of life: plants, insects, and other types of animals. When, in the chalet by the Rhine, Catherine shows this earlier photograph of Jules to Jim, the montage of the film juxtaposes it against a shot of salamanders wriggling in a bowl in Jules's room. This cruel shot explains the reason for his survival: Jules does not end up dying because he has the ability to adapt and accommodate. On the rare occasions on which he displays any degree of independence, he is immediately punished: by the slap when he refuses to scratch Catherine's back, by her leap into the Seine when he contradicts her, by her aggressive enumeration of all the famous French wineries when he praises German beer. For his part, Jim often moves away; he is a traveler who is always ready to leave Catherine's countryside: "There is a need in me to have adventures and take risks," he says to her. Although he leaves, he always returns, responding without hesitation to the young woman's tyrannical summons. She regularly intervenes in his story – on six occasions: the first time, she asks him to help her with her luggage and sets fire to her dress in the course of burning some letters; the second time, she sets up a meeting with him in a café but arrives too late; in the chalet, she has Jules call him on the telephone to get him to bring a book back so that she can seduce him; she summons him again by telephone one night in Paris: Jim, who is lying in bed next to Gilberte, whom he is going to marry, hastens to obey, and Catherine tries to kill him with a revolver; the final time, she says to him in the restaurant: "Mr. Jim, I've something to say to you. Would you come with me?" and then leads him to his death.

Just as Jules and Jim seem to complete each other like two sides of a single whole, Catherine also presents a double face that is illustrated by the scenes in which she meets Jim. In the first, she becomes Thomas, and, in her disguise as a boy, proposes a race to her friends. Being a woman who has been placed off-limits to Jim by Jules ("Not that one, Jim"), she erases all signs of sexual difference. As this scene suggests, Catherine's relationship to Jules will be that of a friend rather than a spouse. "You are mad," she says to him when she jumps into the Seine, picking up the theme of the androgynous, undifferentiated woman. Furthermore, on several occasions Catherine is compared to Napoleon: dominating and imperious, she thus classically evokes the phallic mother of children's fantasies. In the original screenplay, one of Jules's remarks confirms this representation of her as an infantile projection: "Until I was 11, I believed that the reason why the statues of women in Paris did not have male genitals was simply because of the tact of the sculptors. Much later, in various studios, I saw naked models, and I almost missed my imaginary women." In contrast, alone with Jim in the scene that follows, Catherine is adorned with all the seductive qualities of femininity: a diaphanous negligee, hair fastened in curls, vulnerability when her garment catches fire. However, she also displays vindictive impulses directed against the masculine: the love letters that she wants to burn, vitriol to throw in "the eyes of lying men." Associated with flaming fire, boiling liquid that steams in the sink where Jim has persuaded her to throw it, Catherine is scarcely more reassuring when she becomes fully feminine than when she was androgynous. The future relationships of the trio are already registered in several paradigmatic scenes in the film: the breathless race that she wins through trickery; the final end of Jim and Catherine in the crematorium.

Just as the instability of the representations of Catherine's sexuality reflects a child's vision of womankind, the intense idealization found in the metaphors in which she is described evokes a maternal figure. When the relationship between the three of them begins to disintegrate, Jim finds Jules alone when he returns to Germany. Catherine has disappeared. During one disillusioned exchange, Jim says to Jules: "You speak of her like a queen." Jules replies:

> But she is a queen, Jim. I'm speaking to you frankly. Catherine is neither especially beautiful, nor intelligent, nor sincere, but she is a real woman, and it is this woman we love. It is she whom all men desire. Why has Catherine, who is in such demand, given the gift of her presence to us two, in spite of everything? It's because we pay complete attention to her, as if she were a queen.

The ingenuous admiration that a young child might experience as part of the vision he forms of his mother shows through this description. Moreover, this dimension of the character is obvious from the beginning of the film. In the villa beside the sea, Catherine calls Jules and Jim "children" on several occasions, and, on the beach, the male characters are constantly infantilized by the way the shots are framed: long shots of the two men frolicking in the waves like boys; close-ups of Catherine stretched out on the sand watching them, with a sulky expression.

This maternal symbolism is reflected in the way Catherine's origins are portrayed. An excavated statue, an archaeological figure, she seems to rise up from a distant past. In contrast to the other statues, which have been damaged by the elements – referring to the one before it, Albert remarks that the latter is "very pathetic," giving "the impression of a decaying face" – the statue whose image they "recognize" in Catherine, with emotion, when they meet her has escaped from all the ravages of time. Intact, like the image of the mother buried in memory, the statue seduces them with its smile: "Had they ever encountered this smile? Never. What would they do if they met it one day? They would follow it." This reminds one of what Freud said in *Leonardo da Vinci: A Memory of His Childhood* regarding the smile of the women in his paintings and, in particular, that of the *Mona Lisa*. This smile, calm but enigmatic because it is tinged retrospectively with conflicts experienced during adolescence, is that of a mother as perceived by a child during the earliest years. The presence of this maternal component in Catherine's character is not surprising. It remains to be seen, however, how it is worked out in the story and what aspect of the mother is involved, given that each film presents us with a different facet.

In 1978, Truffaut told a journalist that he had become aware of the personal dimension of the film some years after it had been made, and described the part his mother had played in the genesis of *Jules and Jim* as follows:

> I am never conscious of the whole meaning of a subject when I choose it and when I tackle it. Usually, I only come to understand it long after I have made the film. I had a very difficult relationship with my family, particularly with my mother, and I only understood several years after making *Jules and Jim* that I had made it to please her and gain her approval. Love affairs played a big role in her life, and given that *The 400 Blows* had been like a knife stabbed in her back, I made *Jules and Jim* in the hope of showing her that I understood her.[6]

Indeed, despite the fact that Truffaut seems troubled by his discovery that he had unconsciously evoked the Collaboration, the Resistance, and the Purification in *Jules and Jim,* as suggested in the quotation above, it is nevertheless clear that the "hidden roots" of the film extend directly into the circumstances of his family during the war years – the same situation that he had described in *The 400 Blows,* involving the infidelity of his mother and the tolerance of his father. In this case, however, instead of blaming the maternal character, he turns her into a radiant, glamorous presence. Catherine is presented as a "pioneer" who wants to "reinvent love," and fails. As Truffaut said, *Jules and Jim* is a "hymn to life and death, a demonstration through joy and sadness that there is no possibility of any combination of love relationships outside of a couple."[7] The film that ensued unequivocally confirms an element of personal identification in the "understanding" he accorded his female character: the feminine adultery depicted in *Jules and Jim* in a lyrical, glorious way was matched in *The Soft Skin* by a masculine adultery that involved humiliation and shame. The shattered hero in the latter film is, however, the son of this dissatisfied, tormented, royal mother depicted in the former. From a clinical point of view, the symptoms from which Lachenay suffers could be directly attributed to a primary maternal environment similar to the one that the heroine of *Jules and Jim* projects around her – because, in spite of Truffaut's attempt to idealize her, Catherine is far from being a mother who has any concern for the development of her children. Relating back to the archaic maternal figure of early childhood, she is presented as a narcissistic and tyrannical woman who dominates, without any trace of paternal mediation – apart, perhaps, from that supplied by an impassive, neutral narrator – her dyadic relationship with her son.

Catherine's relationships with the two men are characterized by a mutual lack of understanding concerning the needs of the other.[8] The young woman keeps Jules and Jim in a state of complete subservience. She pesters them with her requirements, constantly keeps them in suspense over her demands, her changes of mind, her sudden mood swings. She is incapable of providing any sense of security or reliability. Life with her is a permanent "happening," governed by the unforeseen: she arrives, leaves, comes back, sings, reads out loud, seduces, slaps, deceives, delights. Because she is a being who is set apart as someone "special," everything about her is impulsive, ardent, and ephemeral. The two men spend their time trying to read her face, as if it were a stormy and changeable sky, in an attempt to guess her secrets: "She only reveals her goals in the act of attaining them," says Jim to himself when she starts to seduce him in the chalet; "Catherine was smiling, but she had the same look as the evenings when she was up to something," he observes when he meets her at the mill.

Neither he nor Jules can understand why, one day, she decides that she does not want to have anything more to do with them. With regard to Jules, she simply declares that when he returned from the war he was "finished for [her] as a husband," and, when she sends Jim back to Paris, all she says is: "I have no heart, and that's why I don't love you, and why I am never going to love anyone." The docility displayed by men in the face of her caprices, moreover, is astonishing. This is especially true of Albert (Boris Bassiak), her interim lover, who appears and disappears according to the whim of her desires like a puppet whose strings she is pulling. The final instance occurs in a restaurant the couple has just discovered, to which she takes her husband and Jim. Without them knowing why, she has brought along her white pajamas, tied up in a small parcel. At the end of their meal, she slips away to spend the night with Albert. Jim then says to Jules: "Again well-played, a dramatic turn of events, and a parcel of white pajamas. I wasn't expecting that. I'm astounded that she didn't choose someone new to play this role. She has already made great use of Albert." This behavior, and the commentary on it, are typical of the relationships between the members of the trio.

The relations between them reproduce the dependency bond that unites an idealized maternal object with an infant self that is attached to it. The effect of this relationship is to exclude the possibility of a genuine separation that could allow the individuation of the son. The absence of any boundaries between the mother and her child creates the illusion that there is no need for communication, because the two of them are interchangeable. It is this absence of communication that gives the relationship its "special" character. From the moment they become more absorbed, stimulated, and tortured by Catherine, the two men sink into a state of apathy and non-being. In order for the status quo to be maintained, it is essential that the relationship never be allowed to arrive at maturity by becoming mutual; this is what is confirmed by the sequence of amorous desynchronizations presented in voice-off that precedes the opening credits: "You told me: 'I love you.' I told you: 'wait.' I said to you: 'take me.' You said: 'go away.'" Departures, separations, and missed meetings attest to the constant discrepancy that marks their exchanges. At the end, the letters between Jim and Catherine are constantly crossing each other in a way that works to frustrate the fulfillment of the desires and impulses of the two lovers. No matter how much tyranny she exercises, however, Catherine is never satisfied. As with Lachenay, there exists in her a longing and hope for a vital communication of the true self that remains forever unassuaged. That is what explains the "happenings" and the multiplication of love affairs that end in disillusionment. During the time when he is both in love and loved in return, Jules often turns out to be tactless; Jim is constantly brandishing the specter of the faithful Gilberte. When she is "Jim's fiancée, entrusted to Jules," Catherine often asks her husband in a pathetic voice: "Do you think Jim loves me?"

The space that produces Catherine, as the walk in search of "the last signs of civilization" suggests, is located on the borders of culture, in an archaic psychic past that is still under the sway of the reign of nature. This regressive maternal space is the opposite of a transitional space. The idea of play, which has a leading role in this film, reflects this phenomenon. Play is the most important activity through which a child projects his subjective sense of things onto the world. In *Jules and Jim,* one finds traces of this activity in its pure state: disguises, tomfoolery in the chalet, games with Sabine. The lives of the trio, however, are mostly governed by games of chance, like the game of dominos in which the two friends are constantly absorbed.

This structured game is the opposite of a creative experience inscribed in a spatio-temporal continuum that opens out into the external world. Significantly, it is this trivial, sterile game that becomes a symbol for the kind of lifestyle that is depicted in the film. Referring to the happiest moment during their ménage à trois in the chalet, the narrator says: "Jules and Jim had never played with such big dominos." The greatest player in the story, however, remains Catherine. Superstitious (she will not allow hats on the beds) and a cheat, she is constantly conducting her life as if it were a series of gambles: "Pay in cash and start all over again,

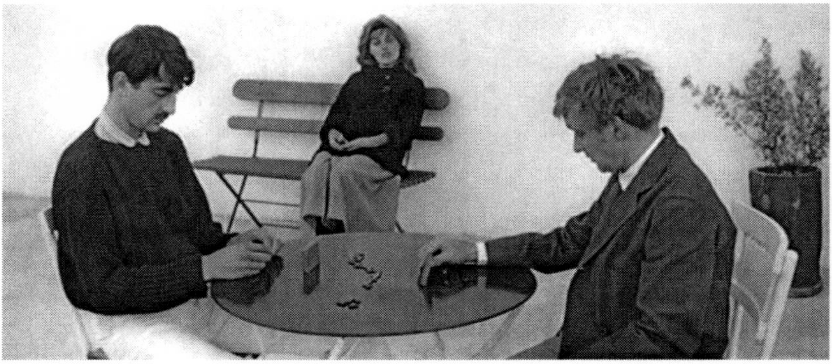

3.2. Catherine (Jeanne Moreau) watches Jim (Henri Serre) and Jules (Oskar Werner) play dominos in *Jules and Jim*, dir. François Truffaut, 1962.

was the basis of her credo." On the day of her marriage to Jules, she punishes him for a *faux pas* by taking a lover, so as to be able to "start from scratch." She does the same thing to Jim, because he delayed coming back to rejoin her in the chalet, and imposes an enforced chastity on him so as to be certain that the child she is expecting is indeed his: "They start all over again." The time involved when someone is playing is a time that does not build, does not lead to the acquisition of any knowledge, and does not transform anyone, since it is subject to endless repetitions of the same thing and consists of a succession of new beginnings. Truffaut included numerous visual markers in the film to suggest the passing of time: women's fashions, Jules's hourglass,[9] and especially the paintings of Picasso:

> I wanted to avoid physical aging, hair that turns gray. Gruault found a way to mark the passing of time that I thought was excellent – this was to place Picasso's masterpieces around the set. They created a real sense of progression: one can see the advent of impressionism, of his cubist period, and of his collages.[10]

But this passage of time as reflected in art, like evolution, progress, and discovery, occurs in the film without leaving any imprint on the characters. That is undoubtedly why they do not age. Their time is not that of experience. Being a story about three young people launched abruptly into life, *Jules and Jim* is the opposite kind of story to that which depicts a process of learning. At the end of the film, Jim rejects the sterile time of the player, together with Catherine. When he announces to her his intention to marry Gilberte, he says: "The promise I made to Gilberte that we would grow old together is worthless, since I can postpone it indefinitely. It is a forged ticket." Jim no longer wants to cheat with life, and others, like Catherine does. He wants to reenter the movement of a time that is adult, civilized, fertile – a kind of time that is alien to the young woman. He wishes, finally, to have a relationship of mutual reciprocity with Gilberte. In the maternal environment, as Jules's example shows, the only thing possible is adaptation – the opposite of communication. That is what Jim reproaches her for in the same scene: "You wanted to change me, to make me adapt myself to you." In response, Catherine brings out her revolver, like Mathilde in *The Woman Next Door.*

By only allowing a relationship that is symbiotic and magical in its nature, Catherine prevents the concrete from being elaborated on in symbolic experience. This is confirmed by the failure of writing that occurs in the film. Announced by the scene involving the meeting with Thérèse – the young anarchist who did not have enough paint to complete her slogan "Death to others" on the wall, and who got slapped by her companion – this failure is reinforced by the epistolary exchanges of the trio. Jules loses Catherine during the war when he writes her letters that she describes as "very beautiful," and Jim when he leaves the chalet to go to Paris. Their correspondence concerns their hope to have a baby together. Like Jules in his letters, Catherine tries to invest words with the immediate reality of the body: "This paper is your skin, this ink is my blood, I am pressing down strongly so that it can enter." This transgressive ritual fails, and their letters attest to the rupture of their relationship.

Mastery of writing implies acknowledgement of the law of the father that the whole film is trying, in vain, to deny. The last words of the story assert the power of this law against the rebellious will of the young woman: she wants their ashes to be scattered – that is, to be given back to nature against the symbolic order of cultural rites – but "this was not permitted." Moreover, the opposition between water and fire that marks her death designates the opposition in the film between the imaginary and the symbolic. The fire of writing at the beginning sets Catherine's garment alight; it will consume her body at the end. From the time of

The 400 Blows, the association of fire with writing expresses paternal anger. In contrast, water – into which Catherine jumps out of a spirit of rebellion, and into which she leads Jim to his death – marks a retreat into a psychic domain in which the law of the father is tragically suspended. *The Story of Adèle H.* depicts a similar phenomenon. In this film, a retreat of this sort becomes synonymous with the madness into which the young woman sinks, signaled by a writing that becomes uncontrollable, disordered, and terrifying.

"Catherine always comes back," says Jules to Jim during one of the young woman's disappearances, underlining his certainty that she is no more able to separate from them than they are capable of leaving her. *The Green Room* will later explore a situation that directly extends the one in *Jules and Jim,* given that the refusal of separation is pursued even beyond death in the later film. It results in a denial of bereavement and a retreat into the self that leads to a fetishistic cult of the idealized maternal object. Like Jules, the hero of *The Green Room* is interested in insects, and collects slides of them, thus marking the distance he interposes between himself on one hand, and humanity and civilization on the other. As in *Jules and Jim,* the First World War has an important symbolic function in *The Green Room.* Whereas Roché's novel simply notes in a few matter-of-fact phrases the interruption it caused in the relationship of the trio, Truffaut subjects it to a lengthy visual elaboration by inserting a series of sequences of archival footage that are specially stretched into cinemascope for the film. These images of destruction, which are also images of a past preserved by cinema, contrast with the idyllic, atemporal landscapes that they frame in the film. War is the indicator of time and the fragility of civilizations. When Jim goes to rejoin his friends in Germany after the Armistice, he spends a lengthy time passing through military cemeteries in which his companions lie buried. This presence of death at the heart of the story foreshadows the end of the film, in which Jules will follow after the two miniature coffins containing the ashes of the incinerated couple. It already evokes the secret cult of the departed dead that *The Green Room* will celebrate in a grandiose fashion.

This analysis underlines the importance of autobiography in the genesis of *Jules and Jim,* a film that extends *The 400 Blows* by projecting a lyrical vision of a fusional bond with the mother. Roché's novel is, nevertheless, far from being merely a pretext for this vision. *Jules and Jim* is not the visual equivalent of a text, but a "filmed reading" (*lecture filmée*) of a novel.[11] The placing of the story within a frame transforms it. As in *Les Mistons,* the narrator's voice-over encloses what we see on the screen in a past that has disappeared, thus marking a distance that is also an exorcism. The time of the story is that of a narrative. Roché's style, which is reproduced in the commentary, brings into being a mediation that intervenes to order and structure the experience evoked by the images. As Philippe Carcassonne observes, with Truffaut, the Oedipal relationship is located not so much between two types of condition as between two types of story: that which says, and that which is said, the present and the imperfect."[12] The film's ceremonial consists of using the voice-over as a support, screen, and shield against the images – a support because it generates them, a screen because it disguises the autobiographical dimension, and a shield because it holds at a distance the violence of the fantasy that they express. This strategy occurs again in the three other films in which a voice-over predominates: *Two English Girls, The Wild Child,* and *The Man Who Loved Women.* In all of these works, its relationship to the image tends to constitute the very subject of the film.

THE LAST METRO[13] (1980)

The imaginary dimension of *Jules and Jim* is constructed in accordance with the logic of the story of adultery taken from the novel. The relationship that exists between the realistic script and the fantasmatic script involves a slightly greater discrepancy than in *The 400 Blows,* but hardly more so. In this case, the primary and the secondary proceed hand-in-hand in each image; the one generates unconscious material that governs the symbolic motifs of water, falling, writing, and maternal and filial representations, while the other presents a *ménage à trois* in a range of aspects that are varied in each scene. Spectators may be disconcerted because of their social, moral, or religious convictions (in both Belgium and South America, the film provoked outrage), but their need for realism, rational coherence, clarity, and continuity in the narrative is always satisfied. The power of the primary operates indirectly, without altering the flow of the secondary.

The situation is very different in *The Last Metro.* Certainly, no one has ever complained about not being able to understand the film, given that its central theme of "The show must go on" does not provide too great a challenge to one's intellect. The situation concerning the lovers is also devoid of complexity: Marion Steiner (Catherine Deneuve) has taken over the management of the theater owned by her husband, Lucas (Heinz Bennent), whom, without anyone knowing, she has hidden in the cellar because it is during the Occupation, and he is a Jew. In the course of events, she has fallen in love with a young actor she has hired, Bernard Granger (Gérard Depardieu). An analysis of two sequences, however, allows us to see that while it is easy to "understand" the film (although there is a question as to what, exactly, it is that one understands), it is difficult to explain "how it is understood." The first sequence occurs near the middle of the story and consists of four scenes:

1. In the course of a rehearsal, Marion forbids Bernard to caress her face, even though the script requires it.
2. One hears the radio, in a voice-over, reporting an assassination attempt on a German officer that involves a booby-trapped record player, while an image is shown of Merlin, the director, leaving the theater.
3. Shots of the corridors of the Metro in black and white. Travelers, all of them unknown, are moving about.
4. Marion is engaged in discussion in her office with a man to whom she wants to sell her jewels. Merlin enters to try to talk her out of it.

There is not the slightest connection between these four scenes in terms of cause and effect, and not the least degree of spatio-temporal continuity. The only information imparted to us concerns the record player that Bernard tinkers with in the wings of the theater and that he carries under his arm, even though it belongs to Marion. The incidents depicted in this sequence are never mentioned again in the rest of the film – which seems particularly striking, given the fearsome consequences the assassination attempt would have had at the level of reality.

The second segment involves one of the most mysterious moments in the film, and also one of the most powerful, given that many spectators remember it vividly after the screening: Marion, forced to go to the Propaganda Staffel to make a plea on behalf of the theater, finds herself alone in a room with a German officer who insistently and vigorously shakes her hand after having told her simply that he greatly admires her. Marion, frantic, does not know how to break free, and it is only the arrival of a young soldier that allows her to get away. This scene, like the other ones, is never mentioned again in the rest of the film.

This style is typical of Truffaut at the height of his maturity as a filmmaker, when his imagination could move from one representation to another with a mastery and surety of touch that were so impeccable as to allow him to engage in all kinds of liberties without incurring any rational censure. The narrative structure of *The Last Metro* is based, like that of all his other films, on a system involving two levels of interpretation; but in this instance, the realistic story is subject to ellipses, short circuits, and lacunae that the spectator hardly notices, so powerful is the welding system that is put in place by the fantasmatic script.

This welding works through a play of repetitions that are no longer linked organically to the story as in *Jules and Jim,* through metaphors (woman-water, woman-as-driving-force, or landscape), but rather enjoy an autonomous function that is independent of the logical meaning of the story. The primary no longer works on the story indirectly, but secretly.

Four series of repetitions can be identified in the film. The first consists of the refusal of the characters to engage in certain kinds of contact (shaking hands, or being touched); the second is apparent in a series of surprised or curious expressions; the third comprises spatial transgressions: doors opened or passed through at inopportune moments. Finally, the haunting presence of a theme of secrecy can be observed. All the characters have something to hide, from Lucas, who has to conceal his presence, to the child who is illegally growing tobacco.

As Peter Brook remarks in his study of the novel genre,[14] the narrative transaction between text and reader can be compared to the psychoanalytic process of transference. The analyst, like the reader, has to work on the problematic relation between the incomplete and distorted story that the patient is presenting to him and the past history that the story is trying to reconstitute. In this work, repetition, as a return of the past in the present, plays a determining role. Within the analytic space, a patient tends obsessively to *repeat* material from the past, as if it were actually taking place in the present, whereas the analyst would like him to *recall* the past as such. Repetition, therefore, as Freud observed, is a form of remembering that "intervenes when conscious memory is blocked as a result of repression or resistance."[15] The violence of repressed desire, as well as the irruption of powerful fantasmatic impulses within logical discourse, is affirmed through the network of repetitions. The four series of repetitions in *The Last Metro* suggest, according to the transference model, that a powerful repression is at work in the shaping of the story. Certain forms of contact, glances, spaces, and revelations are forbidden. It is not too difficult to detect in this constellation the basic taboo underlying all culture, which is that forbidding incest. The repressed material in *The Last Metro* is the maternal body that must neither be touched, nor looked at, nor explored, nor known. These prohibitions arouse feelings of curiosity and fear in the child that are depicted in the film. *The Last Metro* simultaneously tells the story of a theater under the Occupation and the geographical exploration of the maternal body in the imagination of the child.

It is obvious that Bernard embodies this child. In the presence of Madame Steiner, "still strangely beautiful for her age," he adopts the expression of a cowed child. As soon as he arrives at the theater, the story associates him with Jacquot, the son of the concierge. They pass each other in the street to meet at the window of the lodge at the theater. The concierge is scrubbing Jacquot's head vigorously because he had allowed his hair to be fondled by a German soldier. This display of maternal authority is extended into the scene in the theater that follows. Bernard, passing through the corridors, interrupts a conversation between Jean-Loup, the set designer, and Marion: she has refused to hire a Jewish actor, and she charges Jean-Loup with the task of telling him so. Indignant, the young actor futilely invokes the name of Lucas Steiner in an attempt to have him hired. In these two episodes, the authority of a woman prevails over that of a well-meaning masculine figure: the soldier who caresses the head of the child, the Jewish director of the theater. Regarding the young actor who has been sent away, Bernard says to Jean-Loup, defensively: "I am not interested in taking someone else's place," indicating a predisposition that will be reiterated in the hospital scene at the end

3.3. Bernard (Gérard Depardieu) and Marion Steiner (Catherine Deneuve) in *The Last Metro,* dir. François Truffaut, 1980.

of the film. Bernard does not want to replace Lucas as far as Marion is concerned. He fears Marion, in whom he senses an element of mystery from the beginning. At the café, when he sees her passing in the street, he says to his friend: "She is not straightforward, that woman. There is something about her that is not clear."

It is not only Marion who represents a powerful, mysterious maternal manifestation in the story, but also the entire space of the theater itself. Catherine was a substance in which one bathed. Marion is a structure that one explores. With its elaborate organization into enclosed rooms, its staircases, its trapdoors, its concealed exits, the theater suggests the labyrinth that the maternal body assumes for the child. His curiosity in the face of this mystery is inhibited by his fear of transgressing the law of paternal authority. The end of the film eloquently actualizes these fears when Bernard suddenly finds himself in the basement of the theater, face to face with Lucas, the father hidden within the maternal space.

What renders Marion so disturbing is the fact that the identity of the father remains uncertain for such a long time in the story. There is no father, or there are too many of them: Jean-Loup, who directs the theater by proxy, Merlin, who looks after financial matters, and, above all, Daxiat (Jean-Louis Richard), who imposes the dictates of German censorship without any recourse of appeal. Is the law of the father that of the Gestapo? Lucas, as the "Symbolic Dead Father," whose just and generous law is respected, is matched with Daxiat, representing the Idealized Father – like the teacher in *The 400 Blows,* or the captain of the firemen in *Fahrenheit 451* – who exercises an arbitrary, brutal authority with which the son collides during the Oedipal crisis.[16]

The film can be read according to two parameters: one historical, the other fantasmatic. The sequence cited above illustrates this double function. Although the four scenes in no way contradict the historical story (remember that we have seen Bernard carrying the booby-trapped record player), their lack of narrative continuity cannot be explained in terms of any logical scheme; only a fantasmatic reading can make sense of the way they relate to each other. At this level, their apparent complexity is replaced by a scenario that has a childlike simplicity: rejected by the mother, Bernard gives himself over to an Oedipal aggression against the Idealized Father (soundtrack). This aggression threatens the Dead Father (Lucas, hidden in the basement), in place of whom a substitute, Merlin (Marcel Berbert), is expelled from the theater (visual track). The mother, herself exposed to danger, finds herself symbolically dispossessed of her jewels. Merlin, once again replacing the Dead Father, reestablishes order.

This interpretation leaves only one shot unexplained: the third, which depicts the corridors of the Metro. In this case, one of the shots borrowed from a film by Georges Franju, *La Première Nuit,* is involved. Truffaut requested permission from Franju to use scenes from this film, in the following terms:

> I have filmed several shots of the Metro for the sake of justifying the title and linking up several parts of the story, but I can't keep any of them, because they are hopelessly modern: neon lighting, remodeled stations, and always with too much ambient light . . . Your film, *La Première Nuit,* left a big impression on me, and I have just seen it again, with the same admiration. I have noted three or four shots in the first ten minutes – amounting to a total of less than thirty seconds – that would be perfect for the purpose, if you will give me permission to use them.[17]

These few shots, in black-and-white in a color film, thus stand in for archival documents from the historical time depicted in the film. Its temporal setting makes *The Last Metro,* by definition, a film about Truffaut's childhood – he was 10 in 1942. Significantly, it does not appear to contain any direct personal references, in contrast to *The 400 Blows,* the action of which, in contradistinction, had been displaced from 1942 to 1958. In Truffaut's autobiographical works, the filmmaker's childhood seems to consist of carefully repressed material that is not allowed any direct representation. The years of the Occupation, which were crucial for him, were dominated by his love for the cinema and vagrancy. Sometimes he would sleep in the Metro. In *The Last Metro,* the shots of the Metro are purposely emptied of narrative content. These are evocations that have no apparent relevance to the story, serving only to justify the title, but without illustrating its meaning: "the last metro" refers to the last train that spectators must hurry to catch after the show in order to observe the curfew imposed by the Germans. It is possible to see these neutral images, the only document referring to Truffaut's childhood, as representing in filmic space what Freud calls a "screen memory," that is to say, a "childhood memory characterized simultaneously by its singular clarity and the apparent insignificance of its content."[18]

Analysis of such memories reveals how a process of repression has displaced the most significant experiences of childhood into representations that are neutral in appearance. The whole of *The Last Metro* can, in fact, be read as a grandiose screen memory. Truffaut himself has confessed that the film is packed full of childhood memories but presented in an indirect manner, as if a play of sideway glances were involved.[19] One of the characteristics of a screen memory is that the adult subject sees himself as a child in it, while remaining outside the scene as a spectator. Jacquot, the concierge's son, corresponds in the film to this description:

> It is strange that we do not see the child playing a more major role in *The Last Metro,* as he would in reality. Nevertheless, I am persuaded that it is a vision of the Occupation that is my own childhood vision. I was 8 years old at the beginning of the war, and 12 years old at the end. But someone who was an adult during the war would not have created the same scenario. He might, perhaps, write the same story, but he would not have kept the same details. I filled it with the details that impressed themselves on the child that I was.[20]

Moreover, in the earliest synopsis of the screenplay, the character of Jacquot was much closer to the reality of the young Truffaut than in the finished film:

> Jacquot, son of the concierge, 10 years old. He is growing tobacco in the courtyard of the theater. Pinches copper in the theater and exchanges it at the town hall for liters of wine which he then has to sell. Mixed up in the life of the theater and often caught in the act of doing something stupid, he is able to pinch the hollow metal rods that hold down the carpet to make a peashooter out of them.

This summary directly refers to Truffaut's own childhood memories of his activities associated with the Metro:

> I was 11. Lachenay had told me that that one could sleep in the deepest metro stations, which had been turned into shelters. I went there. It was packed with people. They gave us a blanket, but they woke us up at 5 o'clock so that the Metro could swing into operation. At that time, they were giving a liter of wine in exchange for 125 grams of copper, so I would steal doorknobs and sell the wine.[21]

In the film, Truffaut only retained the symbolic role of the child. Associated from the beginning of the story with Bernard, Jacquot finds himself in the room where Marion is changing in the middle of the performance, in a scene that is emblematic of the Oedipal scenario: the dresser tells him to turn toward the wall, thus picking up the prohibition concerning the maternal body that governs the whole fiction.

In an interesting article, Guy Rosolato, playing on the word "screen," has studied screen memories that are memories of cinema.[22] He observes that during the 1940s and 1950s, cinema was the object of a powerful taboo for spectators, not only because intellectuals regarded it with contempt, but also because it represented the site of an initiation for children into the mysteries of passion. This remark tallies with Truffaut's own, in which he confesses that, in order to go to the cinema, he would secretly go out at night without his parents' knowledge, or miss school: "I still have a great anxiety that originates from this time, and films are associated with anxiety, with a notion of secrecy."[23] He also speaks of "extremely adult dialogue" in Henri-Georges Clouzot's *Le Corbeau: The Raven,* which he knew by heart, having seen it twenty times during the Occupation: "I learned probably 150 words of vocabulary that I didn't understand," and "there were things involving love that I thought – I can't say novel, because I hadn't had much experience – somewhat singular."[24]

Cinema, suggests Rosolato, can become "the occasion for an indirect seduction between parents and children and, more precisely, as the majority of cases demonstrate, by the mother."[25] In Truffaut's case, everything suggests that it was at the cinema that he found an answer to the questions that his family situation and, in particular, his mother's attitude were forcing him to ask himself. If one pursues this line of thought, one can see the staging of a fantasy of seduction of the son by the mother in *The Last Metro* through a complex network of filmic memories and allusions. The dynamic of the relationship between Bernard and Marion, with the latter constantly taking the initiative to defend her body against the former, seems to confirm this hypothesis. It is also confirmed by the representation of sexuality in the form of a play of hands, glances, and forbidden spaces – which reflects the prudish shortcuts taken by cinema at that time. A study of *The Last Metro* reveals, in fact, that rather than alluding to memories of the theater, the story is constantly referring to films. Commenting on its origins, Truffaut said: "In writing a preface for the 10/18 collection concerning the earliest articles of André Bazin, compiled under the title of *Le Cinéma de l'Occupation,* I had to draw upon my memory as a young spectator and, immediately, recollections from this period flooded back *en masse,* which made me decide to put substance to my oldest dream."[26] It is also possible that Truffaut's decision to shoot most of the film in the form of night scenes derived not so much from his desire to create a wartime ambience, as he claimed,[27] but quite simply from the fact that he was evoking his own memories of dark theaters and the emotions that he experienced in them.

Freud links the experience of seduction to the emotion of sexual fear. Being passive and ignorant, the child receives the revelation of adult desire as a *surprise* that generates fear. This affect is distinct from the kind of fear that involves preparedness, and it is evoked on many occasions in the film. It is explicitly linked to the female body in the scene in which Nadine and Martine expose their limbs, in order to put on stockings, in front of Marion. At the same moment, the eyes of the latter fall on the title of a newspaper under their feet announcing that the free zone has been invaded. Her face then registers a look of anguish. Another scene occurs when Bernard races out of the cabaret, to which he has invited Marion, after having noticed a large number of

German military caps left in the lobby. In both cases, fear is linked to spatial transgressions that pick up the theme of the hidden father and the dangers of incest.

Repetitions play the same role in *The Last Metro* as rhymes do in poetry. Rhymes have no meaning at the level of secondary discursive logic, but, like the rhythms they generate, they are integrated into the grammatical organization of phrases in such a way as to stimulate the deep layers of the mind in which reside the archives of memory, drives, and, more generally, the emotional potential on which aesthetic compositions play.[28] Symbols represent another means of eluding the vigilance of the conscious mind in order to allow a drift toward a fantasmatic reading. While it is possible to understand them within a framework of logical communication, they are overdetermined, expressing a different meaning according to the level at which they are read. The most effective symbols are those that are the most discreet. They seem slightly displaced in relation to the story, slightly out of context. This slippage prompts one's perceptive mechanism to produce unconscious interpretations and to pass beyond a mode of secondary thinking into associations of a primary type.

The power and effectiveness of the network of repetitions in *The Last Metro* arises from the fact that they never become rigidly fixed within a scheme of symbolic representation. They are floating motifs that, in their constellation, form an unstable collection that is always on the move and open to new configurations. These repetitions present, not only within each film, but also from one film to another, a kaleidoscopic vision that escapes from any system of closure. The scene cited earlier, in which the German officer insistently shakes Marion's hand, resists any logical interpretation when taken in isolation, but the spectator understands it because it is inserted into a whole that is figurative. It reawakens the memory of all the play of hands evoked by the film, which, in turn, through displacement, suggests the erotic impulses of the characters. The aggression to which the German officer subjects Marion's hand marks the extreme manifestation of this: it is the equivalent of a rape. This scene is typical of Truffaut's indirect style, arousing in the spectator an intense unconscious activity and opening up a field of interpretation in which each individual viewer can project his own affective potential. Mobilizing the perceptual apparatus of the spectator, this scene offers interpretations without imposing any particular one and, in spite of its underlying violence, does not threaten the psychic integrity of the spectator.

The embedding and dissemination of the Oedipal script through this system of repetitions suspends the temporal flow of the story in a return of the identical that is a return of the repressed. The displacement involved serves the purposes of censorship and condensation in the representation of desire. With Truffaut, fantasmatic figures relate to the simple, universal constructions that Freud defined as "primal fantasies," those that are inherent in the development of every human being: primal scene, castration, and seduction, this latter fantasy being one of the most universal, as the father of psychoanalysis discovered at his own expense. The signs of an undifferentiated primary organization are manifest in the film through the polyphonic orchestration of the script, which can be summarized as "A mother seduces a son." All the characters enact the affects that this script involves, forming a vast ensemble in which the boundaries between them are obliterated. Truffaut admitted, moreover, that he had been troubled during the shooting: "It was the first time I had presented characters with so little depth, characters that I didn't think were very strong, and who were different, for me, from a character like that of *Adèle H.*."[29] The comparison is justified. In *The Last Metro,* the intensity of a role that Adèle alone plays in the earlier film is shared between fifteen characters.

What transforms the dynamic of the mother/son relationship in *The Last Metro,* however, is obviously the presence of the character of Lucas. It imparts a validity to Marion that Catherine in *Jules and Jim* never enjoyed. The tyranny that Marion exercises is founded on a just and respectable law that the ending will reveal. It is in protecting her husband that Marion finds the positive dimension of her maternal role. The importance of the Jewish theme in the film, which offers a forceful vision of the historical period of the Occupation in a stylized manner, can be surprising. Nevertheless, in presenting this theme, Truffaut is merely giving an account of a crime inflicted as a result of the most intolerable of injustices. Lucas takes his place directly in the succession of humiliated children found in the works of Truffaut.[30] His position as director gives

3.4. Lucas Steiner (Heinz Bennent) listening to rehearsals from the cellar in which he is concealed, in *The Last Metro,* dir. François Truffaut, 1980.

him an exceptional status in the film. Exiled from society by German law, a prisoner, hunted, in danger of death, Lucas at first experiences a moment of intense despair. But as soon as he discovers the system of pipes that allows him to listen to what is happening onstage, he is able to affirm his freedom by secretly directing the play being mounted by members of the company. Nothing escapes him; he controls and directs everything around him, even his wife's love for Bernard, as he calmly reveals to the latter when they meet. One cannot imagine a more perfect representation of transitional space than the stage set onto which he projects the creations of his mind, and through which he affirms the power of the imaginary over the real in the face of the threats coming from the external environment.

On several occasions in the film, this creative space is associated with a liturgical space. When Daxiat comes to find Marion in her hotel to tell her that he knows Lucas is in France, an air raid forces them to descend into the cellar, where he repeats his threats by candlelight. When the Gestapo arrest Bernard's friend, it takes place in a church filled with the singing of a choir of children. These two intrusions into a dark place prefigure the arrival of the Gestapo in Lucas's basement. They also liken this cellar to a crypt, which is reminiscent of the space in *The Green Room* in which the cult is enacted.

Nevertheless, while Truffaut, in this film of his maturity, accords an overwhelming privilege to the dynamic of creative work by proclaiming its primacy in all matters involving emotional conflict, *The Last Metro* is not, like *Day for Night,* a film about creativity. Besides the fact that it strikes one as being not particularly conversant with the practices of the theater, the staging of the play does not produce material that is especially rich visually, as Truffaut himself remarked.[31] It is, above all, the personal problems of the characters that are revealed through the repetitions. Although an aesthetic profession of faith does exist in this film, which is dominated by the sensations, emotions, and memories that are linked for Truffaut to his childhood, such a profession has to be sought in the remarkable epilogue.

In the hospital, it is as if one is assisting in a last attempt by Marion to seduce Bernard. The latter, swathed in bandages, rejecting her advances in a faint voice and invoking the authority of Lucas (believed dead) to protect himself, projects the image of a son castrated by the mother's possessive desire. But then the curtain falls, and we suddenly realize that we have been assisting within a theatrical representation. Those who are watching the play are applauding enthusiastically, when one of them directs his glance toward a darkened box and reveals the secret presence of Lucas in the theater. The acclamation accorded him by the audience forces him to show himself on the stage, where the three of them take their bows. A close-up shows Marion's hands seizing Bernard's hand on one side and Lucas's hand on the other. One can recognize in this the four objects of repetition, but now freed from earlier prohibitions. Thanks to a *glance* that expresses nothing other than admiration, Lucas is able to come out of *secrecy,* in order to penetrate into the *space* of the stage, and the trio join their *hands* in joy. By deceiving the spectator with this ending – and he is deceived, given that at the beginning of the scene the spectator sees real figures in the background of the set, whereas at the end they are replaced by painted figures – Truffaut abruptly shatters the play of investments involved in the unending Oedipal scenario, a play that he himself has created. Refusing, in a moment of derision, to resolve it, he affirms the primacy of creative work. The adulterous trio can live in peace from the moment that he continues to produce plays.

As in *Day for Night,* Truffaut divides himself between two characters. Bernard, the twin of the eternal Doinel, and Lucas, a character who is mature, resigned, a prisoner in his emotional and social reality, but supremely free in the practice of his art. It is the latter that the filmmaker chooses to celebrate at the end of his film.[32]

As Marc Chevrie notes in an excellent article, the main lines of thought of which I am drawing upon here, Truffaut's oeuvre is marked by the continuity of, and fidelity to, the same principles.[33] For him, the big issue was always a need to defend the cinema of fiction against everything that threatened it. If his style changed, it was because, over the course of years, the nature of the enemy had also changed.

In the 1950s, it was a question of fighting against the conventionality of the cinema of quality. As we know, Truffaut placed the issue of the adaptation of literary works at the heart of the polemic he inaugurated with his famous article "A Certain Tendency in French Cinema." He distinguished ideas as articulated by scriptwriters from ideas inherent in mise-en-scène, and criticized the films of his time for privileging the former – the facile words of an author, contempt for the characters, a concern to cater to the public – at the expense of the latter, that is to say, the visual. Adaptation had to respect the literary material and not butcher it or modify it. It is the mise-en-scène that expresses the style of the auteur, with the original text in counterpoint. In that regard, *Jules and Jim* unfailingly applied the critical views Truffaut held in 1954. The film offers not only a magisterial example of the adaptation of a literary work, but also maintains equality between the characters (Jules is not allowed to become a ridiculous cuckold), a rejection of star-worship (the actors playing the characters named in the title were unknown), black and white, natural settings, and an alliance of fiction with the documentary.

Nearly twenty years after the New Wave, the enemy had become television, with its cargo of colorful, informative, "direct" images that were poured into households each day. Television demystifies; it was necessary to perpetuate the myth of past cinema. Truffaut expressed his hatred for documentaries, advocated a return to the studio, used color cautiously, refused to include the merely picturesque or engage in improvisation, and used great actors, to whom he offered carefully written scripts. It was not a question of recovering a lost naturalness but, to the contrary, of fleeing from it – because it had become everyone's compulsory, daily diet to the point of inducing nausea. To control, stylize – these were the order of the day, from that time on. *The Last Metro* is an example of such an attempt. Before anything else, it was necessary to preserve the bewitching power of cinema: to astonish, surprise, captivate, mobilize the imagination of the spectator. For Truffaut, this was the unique law of the cinema.

4

Sentimental Educations
Stolen Kisses (1968)
Two English Girls (1971)

TRUFFAUT WAS NOT EXPECTING THE SUCCESS OF *STOLEN KISSES* any more than he anticipated the failure of *Two English Girls*. He thought that the former movie was too frivolous:

> I nearly abandoned *Stolen Kisses* a fortnight before shooting began, I was so ashamed of it, and felt so uncomfortable. I already had the scripts for *The Wild Child* and *Mississippi Mermaid*. I said to myself: really, I have two good scripts to shoot; there are magnificent novels to tackle, and in two weeks I am going to shoot a film in which nothing at all is said! I was consternated.[1]

In contrast, on the eve of the screening of *Two English Girls,* he seemed optimistic and wrote to Nestor Almendros, the film's cinematographer: "The eight or ten people who have already seen it . . . think that it's the best of my films, owing to the cinematography. I'm of the same opinion . . . The final version, almost complete, is 2 hours 13 minutes long, and it seems that no one is bored by it."[2] After disastrous reviews, he decided to cut 14 minutes from the screening. Truffaut, who ordinarily accepted the judgment of the press and the audience with good grace, displayed an uncharacteristic bitterness in response to the reception of his film. His final act before his death was to restore cut scenes in preparation for a new release of *Two English Girls* in 1985. The film has scarcely enjoyed any greater success than it had in 1971. However, in 1990, twenty years after its creation, a survey of filmmakers worldwide revealed that the two works most often cited as Truffaut's best are *The 400 Blows* and *Two English Girls*.

It seems that the latter of the two can be included in the category that Truffaut called "the great flawed film." He proposed this critical concept in his book on Hitchcock:

> It is simply a masterpiece that has aborted, an ambitious project weakened by some errors in the making . . . In appraising a director's overall achievements, a true cinephile may, on occasion, prefer such "great flawed film" to one of his acknowledged masterpieces – thereby preferring, for example, *A King in New York* to *The Gold Rush,* or *The Rules of the Game* to *Grand Illusion.*[3]

A comparison between *Stolen Kisses* and *Two English Girls* allows the dichotomy that can exist at the heart of a work to be probed further. As with the other titles cited by Truffaut, it is true to say in the case of these two films that an opposition exists between humanist optimism and clinical pessimism, between a classical narrative form and an abstract stylization, between speed and slowness, and between proximity and distance. The presence of Jean-Pierre Léaud, common to both works, compounds this contrast, given that he is able to create an entirely different character in each of these two films.

STOLEN KISSES (1968)

The credits of *Stolen Kisses* are superimposed over an image of the doors of the Cinémathèque with bars across them to prevent access. This shot, from the outset, signals the circumstances in which the film is being made. At this time, that is to say, three months before May 1968, Truffaut found himself completely absorbed by the defense of Henri Langlois, who had just been sacked from the Cinémathèque. He shot the film while leading "a double life as filmmaker and militant"[4] and, for once, the work being made did not take priority. Improvised at the last minute, realized in a climate of play and carefreeness, the sequences of *Stolen Kisses* were shot as if they were a succession of sketches. The extreme segmentation of the film (consisting of nearly 700 shots) was dictated by circumstances. If the marvelous scene in which Monsieur Tabard (Michael Lonsdale) reveals his problems to the director of the detective agency and that of Madame Tabard's monologue in Antoine's room seem very fragmented, the reason is simply that the actors, who had received their words a second or two before shooting, did not know what they were meant to be doing. The film is structured around a flexible schema that Truffaut described in these terms:

> To be truthful, in *Stolen Kisses,* each spectator "imported" his own subject; for some it was *Sentimental Education,* for others a rite of passage; still others

> thought of it as a set of picaresque adventures. Each brought to it whatever he wanted, but it is true that, whatever that was, it was already in it. We had stuffed the film with all sorts of things linked to the theme that Balzac calls "A beginning in life."[5]

In actuality, *Stolen Kisses* follows the classical structure of the apprenticeship story: a young man (Antoine Doinel) leaves the army to enter into adult life, passes through various initiatory phases, and, at the end of the film, is integrated into the social order through marriage. Moreover, it is the only film by Truffaut that ends with the formation of a couple in accordance with the traditional model found in American cinema. There is, however, a series of "snags" in the Truffaldian version of this scenario. At the beginning, the young man does not leave the army, but is expelled out of it and, at the end, just when he has proposed marriage to his girlfriend (Christine Darbon), a madman suddenly appears who accuses him of being an impostor. Meanwhile, a series of episodes intervene that warrant careful attention because, while Truffaut exploits classical motifs found in fiction, he livens them up with the spice of subversion.

While the shot in the credits is showing the barred doors of the Cinémathèque, the song by Charles Trenet that gives the film its title is heard in the soundtrack. The use of this song, which dates from 1942, serves to indicate that, despite the topicality of the image, the film refers to memories of the past. After *The 400 Blows* and the short film *Love at Twenty,* "Antoine and Colette," the continuation of the Doinel cycle, follows the autobiographical story of the auteur:

> I don't have any antennae for picking up what is modern. I only deal with sensations, through things that I have already experienced. It's partly because of this that my films are full of memories of youth. During my preparations for this one, I also noticed that everything had changed, the forage caps of the soldiers, the pawn shop, everything. At that moment, I decided to engage in a deception, to deal with the old, but in the Paris of today. *Stolen Kisses* is a little like a film one would have made in '45, but without saying so.[6]

The prohibition that the shot in the credit sequences shows oppressing the cinema becomes displaced onto the hero: after a panoramic shot of Paris, the camera switches to the sight of him behind bars in a gloomy prison – but for the sake of taking him out of it immediately. Truffaut, the filmmaker, defies all prohibitions, and his film soon sets off, like

Antoine, in search of time past. This nostalgic movement is married to another, more explicitly sexual movement – that of desire. When he is leaving the prison, the other inmates tell Antoine to go and have sex on their behalf at 5 o'clock on the dot. We see him hurriedly crossing the Place Clichy to fulfill his mission. The first girl balks at the job. Antoine moves away and finds another one on the stairs who is more favorably disposed. From the brothel, Antoine makes his way to the apartment of Christine (Claude Jade), a pure young woman who, we learn, did not requite his love in the past – a refusal that prompted him, in despair, to join the army. The momentum of the plot is under way; it does not stop until the end of the film. Moving at top speed, *Stolen Kisses* traces the progress of an irrepressible desire.

Spatially, the film can be described as a vast electric field in which the current circulates from one conductor to another. As the episode with the prostitutes shows, if this electricity meets a resistant terrain, it immediately passes on to a more receptive conductor. Breakdowns occur, as when Antoine meets Colette, "the girl from the *Jeunesses musicales*"[7] whose story was told in *Love at Twenty.* Whereas in the preceding film she was an inaccessible object of desire, in this one she has become a stalwart housewife who introduces her husband and child to the hero. Here, the current does not proceed any further. There are also moments when the circuit overheats and blows its fuses: when the homosexual client at the agency learns that his friend has gotten married, and that the latter's wife has become pregnant, he has a crisis of destructive rage, making it necessary for the dentist on the floor above to be summoned to assist in bringing him back under control, upon which he collapses in sobs. These two examples also suggest that marriage is the most certain means of ensuring that desire will be placed outside of the circuit. Everywhere else, however, it passes from one character to another, without letting itself be arrested by any lesser switch.

Unquestionably, the place most conspicuously associated with the circulation of desire is the detective agency owned by Monsieur Blady (André Falcon), where Antoine (Jean-Pierre Léaud) works. No one ever seems to go there except to consult about problems relating to love relationships. From the minor story of the boss, who has a female employee placed under surveillance – on the pretext that she is thieving, whereas the real reason is that he is in love with her – to Monsieur Tabard (Michael Lonsdale), who comes to complain that he is unloved and learns in the course of the investigation why, and how, given that his wife in the meantime has cheated on him with Antoine, all the clients are driven by blind impulses of passion. The detectives lend them their eyes, and the work of shadowing them involves following the trajectory of strange desires. Antoine, who is incapable of maintaining the slightest detachment, shows himself to be particularly ill-suited to this work. When he commences his job at the agency, clumsily trying to conceal his face behind a newspaper, he starts off by following a woman in black, who ends up complaining about him to a police officer. He ends his time at the agency by finding that he himself is the subject of his own inquiry. Throughout the movie, we encounter a madman in a raincoat who mimics Antoine's movements as he pursues Christine out of lovesickness, but with a greater degree of assurance and effectiveness. Christine herself follows Antoine, the woman detective follows Madame Tabard (Delphine Seyric), and so on. The powerful nature of these impulses was so pressing, so necessary to the imaginary of the film, that Truffaut was so carried away by it while effectuating the mise-en-scène that he was prepared to overlook the need for any realistic motivation:

> I remember having improvised one scene on account of the decor because the facade of the parents' house had two exits . . . This scene completely contradicts the psychology of the characters. We see Jean-Pierre arrive at the home of the girl's parents; the mother on the doorstep tells him that Christine has left, but she insists that Antoine come into the house; on the right of the image, we see the door of the basement open, Claude Jade come out of it, and then pass with her head lowered below the windows. This little dumb-show, which is unexplained, is not linked to anything else; it suggests a degree of complicity between the mother and the girl, that Antoine has not always been well viewed in this house, that Christine has another life beyond him . . . In short, it is a red herring.[8]

Psychology is no more responsible for what happens here than it is for what happens elsewhere in the film. Truffaut improvised this scene because it answers to the film's dreamlike vision, to the unruly and irresistible impulse resulting from a desire that nothing can arrest, not even the complete absence of any narrative justification. One visual motif illustrates the free and unhindered circulation that takes place in the film: half-opened doors, through the gap of which many scenes are filmed. To mark the initiation of Antoine into the work of a sleuth under the aegis of the old detective, Monsieur Henri, we see the two men on a series of landings, ringing doorbells and causing doors to be opened in order to ask questions. But it is especially at the agency that this phenomenon becomes an obsessive preoccupation. Consisting of a suite of rooms that open onto one another, Monsieur Blady's office presents to the gaze a circular space that remains constantly open, like a circuit. Characters enter, leave, and pace up and down in the rooms of the agency like a perpetual whirlwind. Owing to the nature of this unenclosed space, the spectator is able to witness several scenes simultaneously. We will come back to this arrangement, which, in its use of depth of field, makes the style of *Stolen Kisses* resemble that of Renoir. Significantly, however, the story comes up against closed doors on two occasions: in Christine's house, near the beginning, Antoine literally shuts the door of the dining room in which he eats with Christine and her father in the face of the camera. The second occasion involves the door of Antoine's room, which Fabienne Tabard closes in order to be alone with him, with the result that Christine knocks on it in vain. These doors mark the two poles between which the hero oscillates: familial intimacy, outside the exhausting circuit of desire, and the assuaging of that desire through more transgressive activity.

The film illustrates a very simple law concerning desire: to sustain it with the other, one has to flee it. In *Antoine and Colette,*[9] we saw poor Doinel pursuing the girl he loves hopelessly, writing to her, telephoning her, even going as far as to install himself in a hotel opposite the place where she lived, and then intruding himself desperately into her parents' house to the extent that, by the end of the film, he finishes up planted in front of the television with them while Colette goes on a date with another boy. In *Stolen Kisses,* by way of contrast, all he has to do is tell Christine sharply that he does not admire her to make her throw herself into pursuing him. Similarly, with Fabienne Tabard, all he has to do is write a farewell letter, and she appears on his doorstep.

Without desire, life is nothing more than a vacuum, a sleep, an inertia, as can be seen when the two women irrupt into his life. Employed as a night watchman, Antoine is reading *La Sirène du Mississipi,* curled up in an armchair and wrapped in a blanket, when Christine appears

4.1. Antoine Doinel (Jean-Pierre Léaud) in *Stolen Kisses,* dir. François Truffaut, 1968.

behind the glass door of the hotel. She is not able to open it, and the pair exchange several silent gestures through the glass. The obstacle between them is invisible, but present nevertheless, limiting them to indirect attempts at communication that are difficult and full of misunderstandings and breakdowns. Right to the end of the film, the young pair experience difficulty in forming a couple. Paradoxically, however, it is owing to Fabienne Tabard that they are finally able to achieve it. By generously giving them herself as a gift, Fabienne makes it possible for them to get past a symbolic initiation that breaks the deadlock with the girl. Antoine meets Madame Tabard on account of Blady's agency, which sends him to spy in her husband's shoe shop. One evening, after the shop has closed, Doinel, who has been asked to locate a pair of mislaid shoes, is daydreaming among the shelves, perched on a high ladder. We see here the same inertia that was evident before Christine arrived, but this elevated aerial position foreshadows, as does everything associated with flying in Truffaut's films, the possibility of hope, of an opening out of the everyday into another dimension. Indeed, he suddenly hears an enchanting voice and goes in search of it out of curiosity. It leads him into the shop, where he finds a dreamlike creature in the act of trying on shoes. If there is any

4.2. The first appearance of Fabienne Tabard (Delphine Seyrig) in *Stolen Kisses,* dir. François Truffaut, 1968.

woman who is magical in Truffaut's cinema, it is surely Fabienne Tabard. Wrapped in a stole of Arctic fox, she fascinates Antoine from the moment he sees her. One hardly needs to stress the role of legs in the structuring of desire in Truffaut's works . . . Fabienne, when she appears before Antoine, exactly replicates the posture of Madame Doinel taking off her stockings after she arrives home. But in this instance, the seductiveness, instead of being experienced as distressingly aggressive, is enchanting.

In this film, moreover, Fabienne Tabard is associated with a spellbinding form of spoken language. She expresses herself with a dazzling naturalness when speaking to Antoine, who remains constantly stunned and silent in her presence. Having heard her speak English on the telephone, he immediately wants to learn that unknown "maternal" language. We see him at home trying to learn it from records, and the camera ironically follows along the electrical cord of the record player to show us Antoine practicing phrases while shaving in front of the mirror of his bathroom. Monsieur Tabard, like all unsuspecting cuckolds, tells him that the real way to learn English is in bed, with a girl from that country. But, before Antoine can follow this suggestion literally, we find him, in a rather startling scene, hypnotically repeating, in front of his mirror, the names of Fabienne Tabard, Christine Darbon, and Antoine Doinel. Truffaut said of this episode: "When Jean-Pierre Léaud repeats his name in front of the mirror over and over, it is very immodest, but he has to do it."[10] Antoine engages in a kind of magic ritual in which language is the instrument. Like the repetition of the names, the mirror suggests not only a search for identity, but also for a maternal face in which Antoine might find his own identity reflected. In this regard, this episode relates to the one in the parents' bedroom in *The 400 Blows,* during which the child contemplates his reflection in his mother's mirror. But by dislocating the proper names into incantatory repetitions, Antoine is equally searching to penetrate a secret, to break through a prohibition. In a film in which spoken language shows an exceptional capacity for expressing the impulses of desire, Antoine tries to take over the bodies of women by pronouncing their names along with his own.

Fabienne learns about Antoine's love for her from the drift of a conversation that she overhears between two saleswomen. This indirect communication very economically indicates yet again the speed of the circuits of desire in the film, and the way that speech is integral to them; speech takes off at full speed, insinuates itself, infiltrates itself, flows in unexpected places, and even sometimes overflows them. This is what happens, in a justly famous scene, when Fabienne invites Antoine to have coffee in her apartment, and asks him, while she is putting a record on the gramophone, whether he likes music. Antoine, in a state of uncontrollable panic, replies: "Yes, sir." He then takes flight, tipping over his coffee, and scampers off like a rabbit down the stairs. This slip of the tongue, which betrays the young man's consternation, reflects the power of desire as it collides with the forbidden.

After this disconcerting episode, Antoine sets about writing to Fabienne and scribbles at length on a sheet of paper, attempting to compose a farewell letter. Quoting from Balzac's *The Lily of the Valley,* which he was reading in the prison scene, he declares that their love is impossible. These words are dispatched through the pneumatic post, and the camera follows the lightning speed with which it passes through the subterranean tubes that cross the city with apparent pleasure. This memorable scene reveals yet again the speed of the language of desire, but also depicts an exploration of the underground of the city and its internal labyrinth, in other words, of the female body. However, instead of killing desire, writing instantaneously actualizes it. The following day, by 8:15 AM, Fabienne is in Antoine's room, offering herself to him. She does this in the course of a long, gracious speech, a monologue, which replaces the distance imposed by the written word with the proximity and warmth of living verbal interchange.

In the scene in which Christine encounters him at the beginning of the film, she reminds Antoine that he used to write close to nineteen letters to her each day. That was evidently during a time when she did not want him. Antoine no longer loses himself in the meanderings of writing and deferred desire, and, to the extent that he does so, immediately makes up for his mistake. Written models are rejected in *Stolen Kisses*. Madame Tabard tells him that she refuses to be a new Madame de Mortsauf who dies in abstinence. The body courses with desire, and desire courses with the word. In this film, a constant use of the telephone confirms this symbolic effectiveness of language. Another episode in the story gives a further illustration of the simplicity of speech: the old detective writes a report and asks a female colleague to give him alternatives for the word "say" in order to avoid repetition. After she has offered him a list of synonyms, he replies to her that he is going to stick with "say" after all. The film itself imitates this healthy economy. There is no mass, no liturgy, no cult, no candles in *Stolen Kisses*. People speak, and then they act. Direct contact is maintained with reality. Nevertheless, it is also through a monologue that the madman at the end of the movie denies that there is any validity in Antoine's marital pretensions. What is actually happening at that moment?

In a scene placed near the beginning of the film, Antoine, having been summoned by Monsieur Blady, is heading toward his office. As he is passing by, the old detective, Monsieur Henri, comments to him: "I'm only going to say one thing to you. It's what my father told me when he allowed me to make my way to Paris: always be deferential toward your bosses." One can hardly say that the young man follows this wise counsel. This is confirmed by a quick examination of the film's structure. The story, which seems random and disconnected, is actually constructed according to a strict model. It is composed of a series of confrontations between Antoine and older men, each accompanied by what one might describe as a feminine illustration. For example, we encounter the first of these authority figures – the adjutant-major who releases Antoine from military duties – in the process of giving a lecture to young recruits, in which he is explaining how to handle mines, using images: "Defusing a mine is like handling a woman. One has to proceed gently. With a girl, do you put your hand on her sex straight away? No, you play around a bit." He then speaks privately to Antoine and gives a detailed account as to why he holds a low opinion of him. The latter listens to him in a silence laden with sarcasm. Following this sequence, there is an episode involving two prostitutes who illustrate a cursory, unsentimental sexuality that is as pragmatic as that described in the gallant advice of the adjutant.

Having become a night watchman at the Hotel Alsinor, Antoine then meets Monsieur Henri, who performs the role of a kindly mentor for him throughout the film. This old man, full of experience, at first deceives the younger man in order to obtain evidence of adultery. Antoine lets him enter a room, in which they find an illicit couple. The betrayed husband, who is accompanying the detective, tears up his wife's lingerie (we encounter this motif again in *Mississippi Mermaid*) before breaking a vase. Continuing Antoine's sexual initiation, the second older masculine figure introduces him to a primitive scene that is incipiently perverse, since it involves three people. He also offers the young man a new job, and it is because of him that Antoine returns to Blady's agency. It is there that he meets Tabard, who becomes his second patron during his investigation at Tabard's shop.

We now come to the heart of the story. Antoine has just slept with Fabienne and has resolved to tell Blady that he himself is the mysterious lover. He remains alone in his office, getting ready to make his confession. Through the set of half-open doors, three scenes then take place simultaneously on the screen. One of the female detectives in the agency repels the advances of another detective whom she does not want to marry. The old mentor makes an inquiry over the telephone. Antoine and Blady, unseen, are talking together, and we suddenly hear the infuriated voice of the boss: "What am I going to say to Monsieur Tabard? That he has paid 100,000 francs to be a cuckold?" At the same moment, we hear a heavy thud – Monsieur Henri has collapsed, having suffered a heart attack. He is dead. In this brilliant scene, Antoine, a budding Oedipus, has simultaneously slept with his mother and killed his father. He has even symbolically killed three of his father figures, since, with the same blow, he also makes a fool of Blady and Tabard. From this we can see that Antoine is certainly not deferential in his attitude toward his bosses. He is ceaselessly deceiving them and appropriating their women for himself. Death has also irrupted directly into the story. The following scene shows the funeral of Monsieur Henri. After it, Antoine goes to visit a prostitute, displaying an assurance that contrasts with his clumsy ignorance at the beginning. An initiation has indeed taken place. But, as the third of the Oedipal scenes forewarns – in which the woman rejects the advances of the man – a question mark hangs over the formation of the couple.

Furthermore, we find that Antoine is immediately confronted by a new paternal stand-in. He has just crashed into Christine's father's car in the street. Her father takes care of everything. To thank him, Antoine sleeps with his daughter. Antoine, in effect, has become an emergency troubleshooter, and Christine, taking advantage of her parents' absence, calls him under a false pretext to repair a television set that she herself has disabled. The representation shifts from the sight of Antoine, who is starting to become exasperated with the television set, to that of the empty apartment. The camera tracks over the scattered pieces of the television on the floor to lead us to the parents' bedroom, where Antoine and Christine are sleeping together.

Stolen Kisses, in a fragmented and parodic way, thus reproduces the classic schema of the Oedipal myth. It perverts the terms of it somewhat, as the transgression seems to be accomplished in a mood of happiness. Fabienne Tabard offers Antoine incest as a contract, "a real contract, fair for both of us," and then disappears from the story, as if by magic, once the act has been consummated. Her intervention marks the Oedipal passage in the film that allows the couple to be constituted at the end. Who is Fabienne Tabard? First of all, like Catherine in *Jules and Jim,* or Marion in *The Last Metro,* she is an image of the parents combined. Her femininity is beyond doubt, but the message she transmits to Antoine when she visits him is one that the son ordinarily receives from the father in the normal course of things, namely the confirmation of his identity: "Your fingerprints," she says to him, "are unique in the world. You know that? You are unique." Fabienne also passes on a humanist message, for which she draws upon the memory of her own father. She describes how her father, just before his death, had said: "People are amazing." Through these fine sentiments, Fabienne tries to turn Antoine into a man, to convince him of his worth, and to give him confidence in himself and others in order to confront life effectively. The problem is that she appropriates the word of the father and sleeps with the young man. An entry into the symbolic order does not allow for such transgressions. But the sexual act is not actually seen. Fabienne speaks and, like many characters in the film (the adjutant at the beginning, the homosexual, Colette, the madman at the end), her speech takes the form of a monologue. Fabienne also says to Antoine, oddly, that she does not mind that he does not talk to her, but that she wants him to look at her. In her relationship with him, Madame Tabard exactly reproduces the relationship that the spectator can have with the cinematic image. Despite the assurances she gives the young man that she is not an apparition, but a real woman, in the film she occupies the role of a goddess who has momentarily come down from the screen. She can be looked at, she can be listened to, but she cannot be communicated with. Can she really be touched?

In *The 400 Blows,* Antoine also entered into a contract with his mother, but one that involved writing. In *Stolen Kisses,* it concerns the body. But this body is remarkably absent from the story. There are only two kisses, both of them furtive: the one Antoine steals from Christine in the cellar, and the one stolen by the detective at the agency from his reluctant female colleague. In *Two English Girls,* we will see a profusion of wet bodies exuding tears, vomit, and blood. The body in *Stolen Kisses* is dry, light, and mobile. It evades gravity. In the film, the model for its functioning is that of machines that transmit words or images: telephones, record players, the pneumatic post, the television at the end that Antoine does not know how to fix, and of which the scattered components symbolically figure a very technical kind of undressing of Christine's body, offered up in response to the desire of the young man.

Stolen Kisses represents the fantasy of an Oedipal passage experienced as fusion with a dreamlike feminine image whose voice is the only indication of a physical presence. Silent in his bed, Antoine allows himself to be taken over by this disembodied presence that enchants his ears. The spoken word overshadows the body and writing to become the immediate expression of desire. It comes up against death, however. Death is exactly what is signified by the cutting off of speech over the telephone. Monsieur Henri's heart attack cuts off communication, interrupts the flow of words, and silences the voice of the father. Oedipal transgression permits the circulation of desire in the film, but not its articulation in the reality of finite human existence. Cinema is not life. Truffaut evokes this dichotomy in his remarks on the ending of films:

> There is a great contradiction between life and spectacle. Life heads toward deterioration, old age, and death. Spectacle goes toward what I would call exaltation. With circus spectacles, don't we number the acts in ascending order? If one structures a film around an ascending curve, one is respecting the law of spectacle but cheating with regard to the law of life, and vice-versa.[11]

In Blady's agency, a detective tells Antoine that he made love after a burial. The young man imitates this example after the death of Monsieur Henri, but incest, which informs the representation of desire in the film, taking the pleasure of spectacle as its model, is a way of refusing separation from parental figures and of denying the inevitability of their death, which is inscribed in the difference between the generations. Antoine, by fusing with an image who speaks, bypasses paternal authority instead of submitting to it. He thus condemns himself to struggle against it through his whole life in the form of multiple stand-ins.

The ending of the film confirms this. At first, we see Antoine and Christine eating breakfast after the night they have spent together. Writing reappears in this scene, despite the closeness of the couple. The two young people silently exchange notes, and we learn that Antoine is asking Christine to marry him. Along with writing there intervenes the threat of a symbolic castration that the film has constantly avoided. It is therefore highly logical that the madman, the final representative of the father, should intervene at the end of the story to denounce the deceitfulness of young Doinel. But in this undifferentiated world of transgression, this character also becomes a grotesque double of Antoine himself. Declaring to Christine that he will never leave her and will live only for her, the madman is the very image of this wild and unconstrained desire that characterizes a dyadic relationship that excludes the passage toward a world governed by the difference between the sexes, between generations, and by the law of the father – that is to say, toward the socialized world of adults. Truffaut said insightfully about this scene: "With the passing of years, I believe that this final scene from *Stolen Kisses,* which was made with a great deal of innocence, without me knowing myself what it was trying to say, has become a key to almost all the stories that I tell."[12]

TWO ENGLISH GIRLS (1971)

An examination of *Two English Girls* illuminates the following remark by Truffaut: "I profoundly believe that observation involves suffering."[13] In *Two English Girls,* the characters watch each other live – they do not live themselves. The film sets in motion a mechanism that ensures from the outset their exclusion from the life cycle. Sidelined, they endlessly contemplate their reflection. This reflection, from the opening credits, is provided by writing: the text of Roché's novel annotated in Truffaut's hand with a view to its adaptation to the screen. Before the voice of the filmmaker begins to provide the voice-over commentary of the film, we hear a phrase uttered as a prelude by the voice of Claude Roc, the hero, that is to say, Jean-Pierre Léaud: "Tonight I relived our story in detail. One day, I will turn it into a book. Muriel thinks that the story of our trials could be useful to others." Here, yet again, is an affirmation of the primacy of a book designed to channel experience into the mold of language, for the sake of providing a voice capable of communicating it. As Marc Chevrie notes, in *Two English Girls:* "we do not see a love story, but we assist in its *telling.*"[14] From the beginning, life is subjected to a mise en abyme, or self-reflexive mirroring. The characters, caught like insects in the honey of words, show themselves incapable of getting free of them. Moreover, the sky is absent in this film. Apart from one shot of the seaside, Truffaut resolutely points his camera downward throughout the story. Even in the beautiful landscape shots filmed outdoors, one's experience is internal: "In novelistic and cinematic works, most love stories are stories about love that is impeded, but here the impediments are almost never external ones: they are interior, and even mental."[15]

Works that convey a strongly realized vision tend to have prologues and epilogues that are distinguished by their symbolic density. *Two English Girls* confirms this rule. In the first shot of the film, a mother fills the screen: she is reading in a garden. Children's cries draw the camera toward her son, Claude, who is performing acrobatics on a high-pitched swing, encouraged by the voices of two little girls and two small boys (played by the children of Truffaut and those of Suzanne Schiffman, respectively). A close-up captures the process of the rope breaking. The children's cries become tinged with fright. Claude falls. He breaks his leg. The final image, filmed in a high-angled long shot, shows the mother running toward the scene of the accident. Just as flight, accompanied by a panoramic shot of the sky, invests the beginning of *Stolen Kisses* with a sense of hope and defiance, the fall, shot from a high angle, imprints the opening of *Two English Girls* with the mark of failure. This fall is placed under the sign of the mother and the book. The thread that ought to guide Claude through the labyrinth of life is broken: he will not ever become a father, an example for future generations; he returns in the direction of past generations and remains forever under the aegis of his mother: "You have never been, and you never will be, a husband," says Muriel (Stacey Tendeter) to him when she takes her leave of him at the end of the film.

In this film, the heaviness of writing contrasts with the lightness of the word in *Stolen Kisses:* instead of a daydream from an elevated perch, we have the earth, which Anne (Kika Markham), the other English sister, says is filling her mouth, as she is dying; instead of a mother who offers herself generously, we have a jealous virgin mother who passes on to her son the prohibition she has embodied; instead of carefree incest, there is castration. The film's system is designed to immobilize desire, to paralyze its circulation. This blocking occurs in the most economical manner possible: all it takes is for two women, two sisters, to assume responsibility for the maternal prohibition, turn and turn about. Muriel separates Claude from Anne, then, immediately afterward, Anne serves as a barrier between Claude and Muriel. Truffaut said that in this film he wanted to "squeeze love like a lemon" (*presser l'amour comme un citron*).[16] Implicitly, this is the same as saying "love is bitter."

But the great difference between *Stolen Kisses* and *Two English Girls* does not concern the content as much as the container. While in the first film we can consistently trace a realistic script and a fantasy script running in parallel, in the second film, the fantasy proceeds without the encumbrance of a rational justification. The vision presented in *Two English Girls* is purely oneiric. The coexistence of these two scripts in *Stolen Kisses* can be illustrated by a particular sequence. One scene, accompanied by background music, presents a series of shots of staircases, landings, and half-opened doors, through which Antoine and the old detective peer. At a literal level these shots obviously reflect the pair's professional activities, but they are also imbued with powerful symbolic connotations (the circulation of desire, ascent, sexuality). A further scene follows in which Antoine and Monsieur Henri are talking in a taxi. The aged mentor points out a restaurant to his apprentice that serves salted pork with lentils every Thursday. There is no salted pork with lentils in *Two English Girls,* nor a shoe shop with customers and salespeople who seem to have their feet firmly on the ground. Motifs follow on from one another in an impressionistic orchestration, without being supported by realistic references to anchor the journey in an ordinary, reassuring, daily life. Rational thought and fantasy thought have contradictory functions: whereas the first supports the faculty of judgment, the second sustains sexual mobility. In *Two English Girls,* the story is completely informed by the latter. I shall now briefly follow the main markers of its existence.

After his fall, we see Claude coming down the stairway of the house on crutches. A female servant rushes past him to climb the stairs at a run. The castrated masculine is thus matched by a feminine that is mobile and quick; descent is matched by ascent, in accordance with the sexual motif. Claude's mother appears and scolds him because he has been waiting for her: "You are big enough to present yourself, by yourself" – a remark that is unintentionally ironic, since in her eyes he will never be big enough for anything. Claude enters the sitting room alone, where he meets Anne Brown, the daughter of one of Madame Roc's childhood friends, for the first time. His mother joins them and suggests to Anne that she teach Claude English. For Truffaut, perhaps because he never succeeded in speaking it himself, English is always the language of desire – and desire appears suddenly with the arrival of Anne Brown. When she raises the veil on her hat, she reveals her fearless gaze. This gesture, which foreshadows, by way of contrast, the severe blindfold over Muriel's eyes, seems like an amorous invitation. A desire to "see" guided the work of the investigator in *Stolen Kisses,* in which the gaze symbolically figures the projection of desire.[17] In *Two English Girls,* it is exactly at the moment when Anne reveals her gaze that Truffaut's voice-over commentary intervenes for the first time: "When the young English woman lifted her veil, Claude got the impression of a coy and charming nudity." The distance imposed by the text (articulated in the voice-over) cancels out the proximity promised by the image. The following scene confirms this pattern of an impulse, which is then countered by a repression generated by the voice of the narrator. Claude and Anne visit a museum. With the two of them surrounded by the nude feminine statues of Maillol,[18] Anne encourages the young man to abandon his walking stick: "Claude, I am sure that you have no need of that." He gives it to her and advances several steps without support. The nakedness of the feminine bodies, the ascending steps, the erasure of the signs of the fall, all suggest a liberation at this moment from maternal oversight. But the moment is fleeting, because in this scene Anne also presents Claude with a photo of Muriel as a little girl, to the accompaniment of a commentary in voice-over.

In the midst of a movement toward the adult world, therefore, a sign of childhood presents itself; to the immediate warmth of Anne's body is opposed the vision of a woman whom she dedicates to Claude's desire. As in *Jules and Jim, Mississippi Mermaid,* or *Day for Night,* the ideal woman is one whose reflection is seen before she is encountered in her fleshly reality. The mechanism condemning the hero to search for a missing object is primed. The site of desire is always going to be that of a lack. This photo of Muriel will reappear during the final moments of the film to consecrate the failure of this quest.

Having found his wings, Claude flies toward freedom in the shots that follow. A train carries him to England, to the home of the Brown sisters. The narrator's voice says: "Claude's mother had no objection to this trip." But at this very moment, the somber face of Madame Roc (Marie Mansart) appears, superimposed over the image of the train, as if it had arrived to restrain the impulse of this flight. We see Claude pedaling, his cape floating in the wind, along a road that twists next to the seacoast. When he arrives, he sees Anne in the middle of a group who are animated by a heated discussion: someone has just stolen a rowboat owned by Mrs. Brown's aged neighbor, Mr. Flint (Mark Peterson). Anne notices her friend, and explains to him that Mr. Flint does not want to track down the guilty person. He thinks that "the thief has greater need of the boat than he does." In the context of Truffaut's oeuvre, this detail immediately signals that the Browns' house is associated with a benevolent and generous form of justice, with a freedom that allows childhood to bloom without the threat of reprisals. The shadow of the forbidden and delinquency is put to the side. In this little Welsh cottage, Claude is able to experience the promise of a life that is open to the realization of all his aspirations.

Muriel's second incursion into the story is again marked by absence. She does not appear at the family's evening meal, and her empty chair is the only thing that signals her existence. When she does finally appear, she conceals her eyes from Claude's curiosity: a large medical bandage blocks her gaze. As Anne later explains to him: "Muriel has damaged her eyesight by working on a book for her professor at night." Muriel's eyes are going to haunt the film. Speaking to Anne about her, Claude says: "When I have seen her eyes . . . " "When you have seen her eyes," she interrupts, "everything will have changed." When Claude and Muriel break up, she confesses to having lost "the normal use of her eyes," and thanks heaven for not having landed him with "a blind woman." In the fine scene, in which Claude, in Anne's studio, declares his love for her, the young woman places a damp cloth on the face of a statue, thus veiling its gaze from him. Later, Muriel sends her private diary to Claude, in which she reveals, in the course of a lengthy confession illustrated with images, "the harmful use" she has made of one of her "organs": a little girl initiated her into self-pleasuring at a very early stage, and after their separation she has continued these solitary practices.

The metaphor in the film that unites blindness with sexuality arises from associations that have always been acknowledged in popular, mythological, and literary culture: masturbation makes you blind; Oedipus blinds himself when his incest is revealed; in Charlotte Brontë's *Jane Eyre* – engravings of the Brontë sisters can be seen hanging on the walls of the Browns' house – Rochester is only able to surrender himself to the happiness that the heroine promises him after he has undergone a symbolic mutilation: a fire makes him blind. In the heritage of Western culture, masturbation, incest, and castration are associated with blindness. Desire's gaze is merged with its organ: the eye is the sex. In the film, a third term is added to this transparent metaphor: writing, and, in particular, writing at night. To write at night is to abandon oneself to the forbidden language of desire.

In a scene with powerful oneiric overtones, we see Muriel sitting in front of a mirror as she writes her resolutions for behaving better in an exercise book. The final phrase, which she articulates in a voice-over, is as follows: "I must look after my eyes." A close-up then focuses on her enigmatic expression in the mirror. Here, we have a twofold reflection of Muriel's tormented being, first in the mirror, and then in the words on the paper. This double reference to the imaginary and the symbolic is maintained throughout the film. The main structuring image of the reflection of her body in the mirror is split when Claude breaks up with her, and then when Anne admits she is having an affair with him. Her body comes apart at this point, expressing an irrepressible, visceral collapse in the form of tears, fainting fits, and vomiting. Hysterical, it speaks louder than words. The imaginary, under the sign of the dual relation with the mother, cannot escape from the proliferation of binary oppositions. Muriel perpetually remains a prisoner of the mirror image offered by feminine doubles: the little girl who initiates her into sexuality, and her sister who takes Claude to her. This split also resides within her own being. Her body, which her blind gaze cannot encompass, remains fragmented. Her sex becomes "the thing" against which she has to struggle as if it were an unknown and brutal enemy. Desire always remains alienated. This disordered imaginary has no chance of permitting any access to the symbolic, governed by paternal mediation, which could restore Muriel to a subject position.

The powerlessness of writing to inaugurate a relationship of genuine exchange and communications bears witness to this. When Claude declares to Muriel his intention of marrying her, she writes a letter back to him declining his offer. The shot that follows shows her striding rapidly through the countryside, crying: "Claude, I adore you. Everything I have is yours except what you're asking of me." During her nervous breakdown, she composes endless letters expressing her passion, but she never sends them. The one that Claude finally does receive informs him, with a terrifying calm, that her decision is a good one, and that the garden is superb. Her writing conveys lies and, when it tells the truth, it remains ineffectual. Muriel's diary, which contains a confession that is violent and immodest for such a puritan as she is, does not have the least impact on Claude, who regards it as a mere curiosity, a kind of ethnographic document that he hastens to have typed up with publication in mind. Claude's own book, which his mother dreams about him having published, does not seem to contribute anything to his life. We see a saleswoman placing it in a shop window, and an iris-out then effaces it from the screen. Earlier, the same form of visual punctuation erased the face of the dying Anne.

Writing is a form of death. The characters are caught up in the substance of the words pronounced by the narrator, but they have no control over their language, which seems to evolve in a dimension that is separate from that in which they live. In *Two English Girls,* the failure of the fathers traps the three young people within the alienation of an imaginary that can never be constituted in the symbolic. Mrs. Brown (Sylvia Marriott) is a widow. Claude, the voice-over tells us, like David Copperfield, has never known his father. In the absence of being able to refer to the law of the father, their place in the world of human relations remains empty. This disorder is the same that leads to psychosis. Adele H. is not only Muriel's sister, but also Claude's – given that the suffering body of the young English woman is merely the projection of the mutilated being of the hero.

One father figure does exist in the film, however – Mr. Flint, who is frail and timid. We see him officiate in the fine scene of the "Nun's Kiss." Claude, who has lost at a game, owes a forfeit to Anne. Mr. Flint asks him to kiss her through the rungs of a chair. Kneeling, the young people approach their faces toward one other, while a fire is burning in a fireplace in the background. Flames, rungs: desire is forbidden. Before kissing Anne, Claude turns toward Muriel. A close-up focuses on her severe face, on which black glasses are hiding her eyes. This savage feminine gaze, inscribing castration, casts a threatening shadow over this intimate scene, and Mr. Flint's feeble attempt to reestablish some masculine mediation is incapable of dispelling it. We encounter the image of fire again in the two parallel promenades that Claude takes with each of the two sisters, at night, along the seashore. Bars or barriers punctuate the whole story: the fences around the Browns' garden near the mailbox where the messages of hope and despair exchanged between Claude and Muriel arrive; the fence beside which Muriel as a child exchanges secrets with her little friend, Clarisse; the bars of the bed through which Anne and Claude are filmed entwined after the young woman has confessed her affair with Diurka, the publisher.

Another memorable scene establishes the primacy of the feminine that surrounds Claude: that of the "squeezed lemon." Having taken refuge in a cave, following a story that has interrupted their walk in the countryside, Mrs. Brown, the two sisters, and Claude playfully try to warm themselves by sitting and balancing the body of a third partner between the backs of Muriel and Anne. First, this position is occupied by the mother, and then by Claude. In this scene, the masculine subject finds himself at the center of a microcosm in which everything expresses femininity: the cave, the smell of moist earth mixed with that of the young women, the grip that his body experiences when it is caught between those of the young women, the rhythmic movement that evokes lovemaking, but also the oscillations that push him constantly from Muriel to Anne, and from Anne to Muriel.

Alerted to the prospect of marriage between her son and Muriel, Madame Roc rushes in with the very speed of words, since we are given an image of her train arriving while the soundtrack is still in the process of reproducing the contents of Claude's letter to her. Madame Roc will never tolerate any woman possessing her son exclusively, thereby replacing her. The verdict is pronounced by the voice of poor Mr. Flint: the two young people will be separated for one year, without seeing or writing to one another. Apart from this restriction, they are free. It is thus a contract with the mother that again determines the course of events, as in *The 400 Blows* or in *Stolen Kisses*. Maternal authority dictates the terms of the law. It triumphs over Mr. Flint's modest attempt to arrange for the desire of the young pair to find a way of expressing itself. After six months, Claude renounces Muriel, and writes to her to break off their relationship. Thereafter, his Don Juanism frees him to remain entirely in his mother's possession.

4.3. Claude Roc (Jean-Pierre Léaud) and his mother (Marie Mansart) in *Two English Girls,* dir. François Truffaut, 1971.

From this point of rupture, the film unrolls as a hallucinatory play of repetitions. Caught up in a game of mirrors, Claude lives out his story in a series of parallel scenes in which the sisters move around like shadows, acting out the maternal scenario that is forbidden. Two scenes take place in a garden: the first is with his mother, who is talking to him about painting; the second is with Anne, who is talking to him about sculpture. His mother chastises him for having written to Muriel; Anne tells Muriel that she is surprised she has sent Claude a parcel. Mrs. Brown hides Anne's presence in Paris from Claude; Anne hides Muriel's presence. There are two seductions in Anne's study (her own, and that of her sister); two deflorations (Anne and Muriel); two nervous breakdowns (Muriel and Claude); two separations (Claude and Anne leave one another on the island; Muriel and Claude in Calais); two deaths (Madame Roc and Anne). Even Diurka's trip to the Browns' house replicates that of Claude at the beginning of the film.

In this film, in which characters ceaselessly displace one another, nothing moves forward; everything stagnates. Only the mortality of human beings assigns a limit to these exhausting duplications. One could say that the trajectory of the film is inscribed between the photograph of Muriel as a child and the bloodstain on the hotel sheet that marks her loss of innocence. From the most frenzied idealization at the beginning, one moves by the end of the film to the most material sign of bodily reality, to its most crudely organic manifestation. Between these two signs, love is evacuated, together with exchange, giving, communion, acknowledgment of the other. The imaginary asserts its stranglehold on Claude. He is condemned to be alone, confined within an alienated body. This blood, which is his own, through a classic form of fictive displacement, shows us masculine mutilation inscribed on the body of the woman.

To say that the fantasmatic governs the film is not to disregard the clarity of the narrative. To the contrary, nothing appears easier to understand than the course of events in *Two English Girls.* Nevertheless, none of them can be justified in accordance with the order of reason. The conduct of the characters transcends all logic. After their idyllic sojourn on the island where they become lovers, Claude and Anne become separated for no reason. The beautiful image of them rowing different boats in opposite directions reinforces the oneiric nature of this decision. And even though the mother's authority seems to forbid the formation of the couple – so that Claude, after the death of Madame Roc, says to Muriel, who has just kissed him in Anne's studio: "I have to leave immediately," or when Muriel, after Anne's death, has spent the night with Claude and tells him in the morning: "I'm going to leave, Claude," to which he replies, "Leave? Why?" – there is no rational cause for these separations. The prohibition that weighs on the film does not pertain to any ordinary reality; it is inscribed solely in accordance with the logic of an unconscious representation. The world of *Two English Girls* is constituted solely by the presence of the forbidden – so that incest can be accomplished at the expense of narrative reality. The sole objective of the narrative is to delay this moment: when Claude has possessed her sister, Muriel, there is no reason for anything else to happen apart from the epilogue.

When they came out of the theater after *Two English Girls,* some critics concluded that the characters were cold and incapable of eliciting a sympathetic response;[19] others attacked the film for its preoccupation with the description of outmoded feelings "that are no longer relevant" (*qui ne sont plus de saison*)[20] or which are "far removed from real life" (*si loin de notre monde actuel*).[21] The most savage was Jean-Louis Bory, who denounced as excruciating this "festival of subtle psychology with its furtive meanders and precious sentiments."[22] But the majority of them complained of the slowness and length of the film. In short, almost nothing about it pleased anyone – neither the substance of the story, nor the form. Within its own fiction, *Two English Girls* constitutes a work of art that, having received unanimous disapproval at the time of its creation, later, with time, has become recognized as a masterpiece: just like the statue of Balzac by Rodin. At the beginning of the film, in describing the second meeting between Anne and Claude in Paris, the narrator observes: "For a whole week they went to look at the magnificent statue of Balzac that the Société des Gens de Lettres had commissioned from Auguste Rodin but then indignantly refused to accept." In the epilogue, the same voice tells us: "Claude is visiting the Rodin museum today: Balzac's statue has at last been recognized and is admired by everyone." Critical displeasure that the passage of time transforms into acclaim is a phenomenon that seems to be pertinent to Truffaut's film.

Far from being outmoded, the subject of *Two English Girls* is relevant to a development that is necessary in all human beings: the symbolization of desire, the negative side of which is depicted in the film. Clearly, as the prologue explicitly alerts us, this subject is the major preoccupation of the whole film. Georges Delerue's beautiful music underlines the repetition of the elements that reveal this preoccupation. It is not only the threatening nature of this unconscious material, but also its very organization that explains the failure of the film at the time of its release, and the reasons for the harsh critical condemnation it elicited. Unconscious thought requires analysis, focalization, and differentiation of the material; fantasmatic thought, by way of contrast, is syncretic, dispersed, and undifferentiated. In other films by Truffaut, equilibrium is established between these two modes of perception. A realistic story does not only satisfy the rational requirements of the spectator, but also diverts his or her attention away from unconscious representations, thus preventing any censoring reactions. This system can be seen functioning with unusual effectiveness in *Stolen Kisses, The Last Metro,* and *The Woman Next Door.* In *Two English Girls,* the protective screen of a realistic framework does not exist. The only possible reading of the film is an oneiric one. If such a reading is rejected, the film loses all its meaning. In that case, all one can do is conclude that the film is a farrago of convoluted sentiments from another age. Criticism of its repetitions and slow pace arise in response to the undifferentiated nature of the unconscious material, which overturns the spectator's established frameworks of perception, as well as those of the reader – in the same way that criticism leveled at the first volumes of Proust's great work[23] reflects similar arguments.

This kind of work, in fact, displays an extraordinary richness of form. Its success depends upon the link that it is able to establish with the power of primitive drives comparable to those found in dreams. Only a form that is very rigorously structured can mobilize and channel this unconscious flow. *The Rules of the Game* is a film constructed in accordance with this model,[24] attracting the same kind of negative criticism when it appeared as *Two English Girls* did, owing to its repetitions and the absence of a determinate subject. Rodin's statue was rejected because the sculptor, instead of presenting the novelist in a frock coat, dared to show him emerging from a barely formed block of stone. Unconscious perception that is disconcerted, affronted, or paralyzed responds, in the first instance, by rejecting such bold representations altogether. With time, this new style is gradually assimilated, and people learn how to decipher it, with the result that its originality and effectiveness begin to be recognized. It also loses its ability to shock.

In his description of "great sick films," Truffaut attributes their failure to an "excess of sincerity."[25] These are films that do not conform to the norm, given that the latter "privileges a ruse rather than direct confession."[26] The ruse consists in not attacking head-on the perceptual habits and conscious expectations of the viewer. If this ruse is absent in *Two English Girls,* it is owing to the fact that the film is stamped with two "direct confessions": that of Roché and that of Truffaut. The latter was not only inspired by the novel of the former, but also by his reading of the intimate diaries of the novelist:[27] "In his novel, Roché idealizes and softens the suffering of the women. In the diary, in contrast, he does not shy away from truth of any kind, and it is filled with intimate details, often reflecting great cruelty."[28] Moreover, as the filmmaker confesses: "I began the film in a bad moral state that ameliorated in response to the shooting of the film as it proceeded. What impressed itself on me was this phrase of Claude (he has just finished his first novel): 'I feel better now, I have the impression that the characters in the book are going to suffer in my place.'"[29]

The whole film reflects a sad truth that is exposed through the sensibility laid bare by both the novelist and the filmmaker. Its epilogue is marked by a sense of tragedy that was totally absent from the novel. In Roché's book, Madame Roc does not die; Anne and Muriel get married, and raise many children. The death of the former in the film gives rise to a scene imbued with a profound sadness. Truffaut confessed that the scene showing the death of the mother in *The Magnificent Ambersons* was his inspiration for this scene.[30] As for Anne, when she is dying, he makes her utter the phrase spoken by Emily Brontë at her death: "My mouth is full of dirt." With regard to this allusion, Jean Gruault, the scriptwriter for the film, explains: "He was fascinated by the Brontës. There was also the idea of sisters. And this film has always cut close to the bone, as far as I am concerned, even though I have never had any comparable experiences, because I knew two sisters who were just like that. Just as François did."[31] The two sisters were Françoise Dorléac and Catherine Deneuve. Anne's death in the film was inspired not only by the death of Emily Brontë, but also by the premature passing of the actress who played the heroine in *The Soft Skin*. The fine, but melancholic, scene showing the arrival of Muriel in Calais at the end of the film seems to come straight out of *Mississippi Mermaid*. Like Louis Mahé, Claude watches out for the young woman on the gangway of the ship, the black bow of which is depicted in many shots. *Two English Girls* was shot the day after the breakup of Truffaut's relationship with Catherine Deneuve. This crisis in his personal life explains the bitterness in the story.

The epilogue of the film delivers one of the strongest passages in Truffaut's oeuvre. It orchestrates all the motifs of the film in an elegiac mode. "Fifteen years passed in a trice": Mrs. Brown has died, and Muriel, who has married in Wales, has had a daughter. Claude is walking in the garden of the Musée Rodin and looks at the statues made by the great sculptor. A group of young English high-school girls runs past him, laughing. What if one of them is Muriel's daughter? A circular traveling shot moves around Rodin's statue, *The Kiss*. Claude goes to catch a taxi. It is not free; the driver is waiting for someone. Claude draws away but

4.4. Claude Roc (Jean-Pierre Léaud) in the epilogue from *Two English Girls,* dir. François Truffaut, 1971.

perceives his reflection in the window of the car. He murmurs: "But, what do I have? . . . I am looking old today." He heads toward the exit and disappears beyond the partially opened doors of the park, surrounded by the young English girls.

Several scenes at the end of the film are punctuated by the presence of children. When Diurka arrives in Wales, Muriel is giving a lesson of religious instruction to a group of pupils, who then run to admire the visitor's automobile. At Calais, the quay where Muriel embarks, the scene is enlivened by young children who are joyfully running around. This motif, highlighted in the foreground by the epilogue, is reinforced by the insertion of the photo of Muriel as a little girl. What is shown is the passage of time, the movement of future generations from which Claude is excluded. The statues evoke the memory of Anne. The statue of *The Kiss* nostalgically designates the impossible ideal implicit in the film: the hero has never been able to form an adult couple. The image of Claude in the window of the taxi pathetically attests to this failure. An aged child, he contemplates his alienated reflection, which is that of a stranger whom time has disfigured without his knowing it. The taxi will not take him anywhere. In a film in which means of travel – bicycles, locomotives, cars – intervene repeatedly, in order to suggest figuratively the impatient movements of desire, this taxi, which he is unable to use, marks the end of the journey. Someone else will take it in his place. Chased out of this great garden, the image of which, in various forms, has punctuated the story, on each occasion signifying the promise of a renewal, Claude disappears behind the heavy doors that symbolize the final portal of life. So many signs of exclusion, mortality, and death have rarely been united in so few images. The film is not simply brought to a close by the epilogue; it is barricaded like a prison. Experience is a blind lantern, which does not illuminate those who live it. It might be useful for those who look at it, as Claude as was hoping would be the case for him at the beginning of his story.

Only the massive statue of Balzac has benefited from the passage of time in this tragic story. It is hope that its epilogue conceals.

Stolen Kisses and *Two English Girls* contrast with one another insofar as one is a film about cinema, and the other is a film about the book. Speech dominates in the first, and writing in the second, but both show the fundamental importance of language in Truffaut's works. In *Stolen Kisses,* words draw the image along in their train, often replacing it, as in the great Oedipal scene in the detective agency when the voice of the owner, alone, admonishes Antoine. In *Two English Girls,* Roché's text invades the image, passing, as Marc Chevrie notes, through "the body and the mouth" of the characters.[32] Truffaut's cinema attests to a double vocation: to express its content in a purely visual way; and to create a story entirely through a voice-over, in the manner of Sacha Guitry in *The Story of a Cheat.* His entire narrative register is inscribed between these two poles. *Two English Girls,* which Gruault says was inspired on a visual level by the atmosphere of "Swedish silent films" (*films muets suédois*),[33] comes close to realizing the ideal union of these two modes of expression. But, in contrast to Guitry's films, or images that simply illustrate the text, with Truffaut there is a constant confrontation and tension between the visual track and the soundtrack. In *Two English Girls,* the violence and disorder of physical love are expressed in the former; the cold and ironic distance of observation in the latter. *The Man Who Loved Women* will unveil the origins of this narrative tendency that governs the art of storytelling in Truffaut's work.

5

Criminal Women
The Bride Wore Black (1967)
A Gorgeous Girl Like Me (1972)

THE BRIDE WORE BLACK ENDS AT THE POINT WHERE *A GORGEOUS Girl Like Me* begins: namely, in a prison. Julie Kohler and Camille Bliss have both burned their bridges with society and have taken the plunge that tips them from marginality into criminality. Their respective fates are as different as the tone of the films they inhabit, but whether virgin or prostitute, silent or loquacious, they both pursue the impulse of an obsession that imparts a strength to them no one can resist. They move like a hurricane across the lives of five men who are transformed into marionettes in their hands. *The Bride Wore Black* and *A Gorgeous Girl Like Me* share, in fact, a narrative pattern that picks up the schema of Truffaut's first short film, *Les Mistons* (1957). In *The Bride Wore Black,* the woman in mourning who has lost the man she loves is a counterpart to Bernadette in the earlier film: as Truffaut said, "The men whom Jeanne Moreau meets are the *mistons* [mischief makers] who have grown up."[1] Moreover, in *A Gorgeous Girl Like Me,* it is Bernadette Lafont who plays the female character, just as she did in *Les Mistons.* Both of these films display a similar tension that constantly operates between images and words, as well as an extensive use of flashbacks as a device for the truth. These bitter women hide a secret, and the links that tie them to their creator are worth exploring.

THE BRIDE WORE BLACK (1967)

The Bride Wore Black can be viewed as a synthetic work that in various ways picks up all of Truffaut's preceding films. The theme of a murdered childhood is central to its plot, just as in *The 400 Blows*. Julie (Jeanne Moreau) has the same name as Charlie in *The Piano Player*, Kohler. The anger that propels her manifests itself more directly than in the case of her masculine namesake, but it has its origins in a past from which she cannot free herself, just as in his case. As in *The Soft Skin*, the woman kills; as in *Jules and Jim*, she dominates men and takes the initiative; as in *Fahrenheit 451*, Truffaut opts for a fairy story: "*The Bride Wore Black* can seem simplistic and mechanical to anyone who refuses to accept that an adult's film can start with 'Once upon a time.'"[2] Those who know Truffaut's work will recognize that the fantasmatic content of this little story displays an unusual degree of clarity. Its effectiveness resides in "its constant effort to achieve simplification and stylization."[3] In this respect, *The Bride* is a great success. From its very first images, the film affirms and exploits the effectiveness of a language that is precise and economical.

A woman in black is leafing through a photo album in her bedroom. She suddenly rushes toward the window to throw herself into the void. Her mother restrains her. Julie's suicidal impulse becomes transformed into a murderous obsession. This recovered internal self-control is displayed in the second scene, through a close-up shot of a suitcase in which she is carefully packing clothes, all of which are black or white. The number five also makes its appearance in the form of five sets of tickets laid out side by side. Julie leaves the house and has her young niece, dressed in white, accompany her to the station. The woman in black and the little girl pass through the streets together, hand-in-hand. The motif of childhood, innocence, virginity, is thus introduced into the story from the outset. Julie, we are going to learn, has passed without any transition from white into black. Life and its colors have been stolen away from her by her tragic destiny. Child or nemesis, she will never be a woman. The little girl that she holds by the hand is her double, whom she is going to avenge.

On the platform of the station, Julie climbs into the train for Paris only to get off again surreptitiously on the other side, on the tracks. A close-up follows her feet along the rails. This opening, which, apart from a few phrases, is entirely silent, recalls the first shots of Hitchcock's film, *Marnie*, in which we see a woman packing her suitcase and catching a train in a context that loads all her actions with mystery. Like Marnie, another woman who has become a criminal because death intruded into her childhood, Julie is going to claim back a symbolic re-appropriation through her transgressive actions. Instead of stealing, she will kill.

Julie's aborted suicide and the prospect of a fall into the void, which drew her like a magnet, are repeated with a magnificent visual orchestration in the death of the first man, Bliss (Claude Rich). On the day of his marriage, Julie appears at the reception, leads him out onto the balcony, throws her white scarf onto the bars of the signage that overlooks the store, asks him to reach out and retrieve it for her, and then pushes him without hesitation into the void. This fall is successively filmed from four different angles to accentuate its dramatic character: subjectively (we see all the other balconies passing by at top speed as the body falls), objectively from the bottom (at first from a distance, and then from nearby), and from the top of the balcony. The film seems to describe this long descent toward death with disconcerting pleasure. The following scene explains why, through an immediate inversion of signs. The camera undertakes to follow the graceful flight of Julie's scarf as it floats in the sky for almost two minutes, above a splendid panorama of the Cap d'Antibes. It continues on its airborne trajectory by becoming caught in the slipstream of an airplane that is taking off into the distance. The image of the fall is then picked up, with an aerial view looking down on the Alps, filmed from the inside of the cabin in which Julie is sitting, crossing out in a notebook the name of her first victim. Coral, the second of her victims, appears soon after, at the window of a hotel. The camera, roaming over the façade, again frames him when he comes out into the street. The following day he collapses, poisoned, at the feet of Julie who, in a succession of cross-fades in which she seems to float away, dances around him. This play on verticality was not created merely for the sake of making an effect. Just as black avenges white, the fall replaces the aborted takeoff of the heroine into the happiness of marriage. The pleasure of killing becomes a substitute for that of sexuality. The nature of this displacement explains the dissociation we observe between the soundtrack and the visual track: "If you look at the images of *The Bride,* you see a woman who goes from one place to another, who meets men, and then kills them. If one listens to the soundtrack, one hears conversa-

5.1. An uninvited guest: Julie (Jeanne Moreau) appears at Bliss's wedding in *The Bride Wore Black,* dir. François Truffaut, 1967.

tions about love, about the way that men regard women. Killing is never an issue."[4]

The spectator learns why Julie is determined to commit murder from a series of flashbacks: those concerning the assassins, and those concerning the bride. At the moment she pushes Bliss into the void, she is content to say to him: "I am Julie Kohler." The first image of the past occurs during the encounter with Coral. As he is writhing in agony, a shot of the bell-tower of a church appears. The camera moves slowly down it toward the bottom until it reaches a bridal party coming out onto the forecourt: a shot rings out; the groom falls down, dead. In the course of the third murder, the whole story is revealed. While Morane is suffocating in the storeroom in which Julie has managed to imprison him, her explanation for why she has done it takes the form of a long flashback that is almost entirely silent: five idle bachelors are playing a game of cards in a room situated at the top of an apartment building overlooking the forecourt. They amuse themselves by aiming a rifle at the cock on the steeple. One of them, believing that the rifle is unloaded, directs it slowly toward the base of the bell tower – once again, the image follows a descending movement – takes aim at the wedding party, and pulls the trigger before any of his friends can stop him. After this tragic action, we see the five men frantically leave the apartment in haste, hurtling down a spiral staircase, at the foot of which they separate from each other for good. The collapse of Julie's world, connoted by the images of falling, also threatens their world, as this flight downward suggests. By way of contrast, Julie's flashback involves images of a happy childhood. A young boy and a little girl love one another and play at being married in a big country house: David has been Julie's only love; she has always wanted to marry him. Filmed in slow motion, the children, who are skipping about in a field, seem to float above the ground. The grievous act of the idle bachelors has shattered this dream. A visual convergence of the two series of flashbacks occurs when the final image from the childhood sequence shows the church's tower, with its rooster on top, dominating the countryside in the distance. When Morane pleads with Julie to let him out, she replies pitilessly: "You took something from me that you cannot give back."

None of the five men depicted in the film has succeeded in establishing an adult relationship with a woman. Bliss, the Don Juan of the area, regards marriage as a retreat for those who are scared by aging, and indulges in puerile games: he has recorded the noise that his fiancée's stockings make when she crosses her legs; Coral is a pathetic old boy, terrorized by women, who lives in miserable solitude; Morane, the smug politician, is married but believes that his wife does not understand him; the gangster, who fired the gun, does not seem to have realized that women exist; Fergus experiences love too late. Immaturity is responsible for their downfall. They are vulnerable to the knowing and efficacious charms that Julie uses to seduce them by satisfying their fantasies. With each of them, she replaces the woman in their life and identifies herself with their ideal vision. The murder of her husband, then, takes on a symbolic value. It is indeed the act of "mischief-makers," jealous of a couple who represent the flowering of an adult desire that is integrated with the law. Prior to this, their only passion has been women and hunting, as Morane tells us. They have blended the two things together in killing the husband. Trespassing into territory that is out of bounds, they have tried to appropriate for themselves a forbidden woman.

The transgressive nature of the relationship uniting the five men with Julie is signaled by the return of a stylistic motif common to almost all of Truffaut's films: the fragmentation of the female body. During each of the murders – apart from the last one, which takes place off-screen and is only indicated by the cry of the victim – a close-up shot isolates the legs of the bride: after Bliss's fall, we see the bottom of her long white dress caress the black shoes of one of the guests; when she dances around Coral, the camera cuts off her body at the waist; just before his final conversation with Julie, Morane slyly looks at his visitor's legs through the balustrade of the staircase; finally, Fergus, the painter, sketches with pleasure the naked feet of his "model," in charcoal. The murders are also rigorously stylized. In the case of the first three, a record of Vivaldi's music serves to signal Julie's murderous intentions; then, once the pattern has been established, it disappears. Although the film is organized, like a fairy tale, in accordance with a principle of enumeration,[5] its originality derives not only from the way each murder varies the basic pattern, but also from the manner in which the victims are described. With each of them, Julie functions as a means of revealing their nature. The attention that is devoted to describing them also explains the form of the film:

> Having only 400 shots, it is the film of mine that has the least number of cuts. I felt it like that. The form of a film generally presents itself to your mind at the same time as the idea for it. There are many sequence shots, because each of the male characters in the film has only a quarter of an hour of projection time to exist in front of us.[6]

The portrayal of these men is remarkable for its precision, and each time Truffaut found the quickest formula for sketching it: brief dialogue between childish seducers and pranksters in the case of Bliss and his friend Corey (Jean-Claude Brialy); a concert scene with Coral (Michel Bouquet), in which the duet on the stage between the pianist and the cellist figuratively suggests the ideal amorous exchange between male and female to which he aspires (in real life, the only thing he shares with a woman is a bottle of gin when his dreadful lodger comes to drink in secrecy); a hollow monologue by Morane the politician on his pathetic ambitions.

By the time the third murder has taken place, the spectator knows the full story. Interest is sustained because of the vulnerability shown by the heroine in the best episode in the film. In this scene, Charles Denner

5.2. An avenging nemesis: Julie (Jeanne Moreau) as Diana with Fergus (Charles Denner) in *The Bride Wore Black,* dir. François Truffaut, 1967.

acts the role that he would later reprise in *The Man Who Loved Women,* that of the unrepentant but clear-eyed womanizer. The floor of his bathroom is covered with plastic breasts; he nevertheless ends up confessing to Julie that he loves her. To find the courage to continue with her plan, the latter had gone to take confession. To the priest who urges her to renounce her quest for vengeance so that she can reenter life, she replies: "I am already dead." The episode with Fergus (Charles Denner) proves that she was deceiving herself. In contrast to the other men, the painter touches her body to help her assume her poses. She feels somewhat mortified at failing in her first attempt with the bow of Diana, the huntress. The second attempt, however, is successful. There is no flashback during this sequence. The painter's canvases take their place. Fergus had painted portraits of a woman resembling Julie many times before meeting her. This detail suggests that the image of the bride, briefly glimpsed on the day of the murder, has been unconsciously haunting him. Fergus has a memory, a conscience, and a heart. It is the only time Julie is tempted to give over her quest for revenge. Under his paintbrush, she becomes that which she will never become in life: a beautiful naked woman open to masculine desire.

In spite of the clarity of the fantasmatic script, the character of Julie remains a complex creation. Impelled into delinquency by grief, like Antoine, she has an innocence that is apparent in her relationship with children. With Cookie, Morane's son, who enters into this dark film like a ray of sunshine, she becomes transformed into a cheerful woman who is capable of tenderness. Her potential capacity to be a benevolent maternal figure who displays love for children is further inscribed in the film through a very beautiful image: when, because of Julie's intervention, the teacher who has been falsely accused is released, a long shot with a zoom-out shows a group of children running toward her to greet her in the school courtyard. But Julie kills adult men with a terrifying cruelty. When speaking of the murders she has committed, she says to the priest: "This is not a mission; it is a job." Significantly, Truffaut asked Jeanne Moreau to play the role as if she were "a semi-skilled worker":

> Nothing is more satisfying for the audience than the spectacle of a character who keeps on going right to the end. And as far as this trajectory in a straight line is concerned, I got her to agree that it should be pursued without artifice, without any signs of vanity, both seriously and lightly at the same time. It was my hope that Jeanne Moreau, in *The Bride,* rather than conceiving of her character as the goddess of revenge, would think of her as a person who was obstinate and competent.[7]

Such an apparent absence of emotion recalls Franca when she shoots her husband in the final shots of *The Soft Skin.* Julie's desperate determination also resembles that of Mathilde in *The Woman Next Door.* The significant woman in Truffaut's past rises up in the present; Julie takes on certain of his mother's characteristics. She is a hybrid character who evokes the strange fusion of the suffering son and the death-dealing mother. The fact that she is always dressed in black or white and stages a brilliant spectacle for each man also inevitably evokes cinema itself: Julie is a silent film that each man watches. A revealer of truth, it unrolls in a place that is no longer located in real life. Being a work lacking in any other complexities, *The Bride Who Wore Black* is a film whose power resides in its simplicity. In it, Truffaut affirms his mastery of a symbolic system and means of expression that he exploits with consummate mastery. Significantly, it was when he emerged from the making of this film that he articulated, for the first time, his understanding of the elements that constituted the secret of his art – that is, the art of the secret:

> My dream is to achieve a form of secret persuasion. I want people to go away feeling as if they have seen shots that are not there, so that they are prompted to think back to their own background and delve into their own past. I would like to provoke associations of ideas, cause memories of coincidences to resurface, put the focus on encounters that were more or less predetermined.[8]

Here, the filmmaker is pointing to the collective unconscious that was the special terrain of all of his work.

A GORGEOUS GIRL LIKE ME (1972)

With Camille Bliss (Bernadette Lafont), the heroine of *A Gorgeous Girl Like Me,* Truffaut created a wonderful character – anarchic, crude, and insufferable – that no one can resist. However, the film was not well-received at the time of its release: "It is indisputably a failure and even, it could be said, a mistake," wrote Marcel Martin in *Les Lettres françaises,* who criticized the film for its despairing cynicism and the absence of any social context that could justify Camille's revolt. Even the film's supporters agreed that the character was a little bitch – capable of eliciting laughter, but as vulgar as she is superficial.[9] At best, the film was labeled a trivial entertainment of no importance in which Truffaut had distanced himself uncharacteristically from his characters.[10] The filmmaker emphatically corrected this misapprehension:

> I don't regard any of my films as aberrations, even *A Gorgeous Girl Like Me,* which is perhaps the most controlled and coherent of them all, complementing the others. I think that there is a compelling logic to it, a real reason for its being. It does have some weaknesses, but I don't at all see this film as a parenthesis or a cop-out in any kind of way.[11]

We should accept that he was correct to defend this surprising film that, along with *The Green Room,* marks one of the two extreme poles of his oeuvre. *A Gorgeous Girl Like Me* might not be a great film, but it is a certainly a successful film, revealing a tendency that is deeply embedded in Truffaut's personality. From the outset, it should be regarded as a continuation of, and a response to, *Two English Girls;* it complements this earlier film on account of its theme:

> In *Two English Girls*...I tried to destroy romanticism by being very physical, which explains why there is an insistence on illness, fever, vomiting, etc. *A Gorgeous Girl Like Me* was the continuation of this attempted destruction: it mocks romantic love, it affirms the brutality of reality, of the struggle for life . . ."[12]

It is the final phrase of this quotation, in particular, that one ought to keep in mind. Camille Bliss illustrates a vitally important notion in Truffaut's work – the need to know "how to survive": "She is fighting for her life throughout this film, and I'm not at all concerned with the issue of sympathy or antipathy. When people came to me and said that she's a real bitch, I was very surprised. It seemed to me that they hadn't paid much attention to the film."[13] Indeed, the world into which Truffaut throws his heroine is entirely devoid of any moral criteria. It is a jungle governed by indifference to the plight of others, and by drives that are as primitive as they are self-regarding: "It is a cruel film without a single ounce of feeling, a mocking comedy in which everything is scorned, but I hope that it is too light-hearted to be regarded as bitter."[14]

A Gorgeous Girl Like Me is also a response to *Two English Girls* in that Camille, instead of submissively and sadly surrendering herself to the inevitability of death as her fate, reacts to each new turn in the story with a staggering energy: "The real theme of the film," said Truffaut, "is vitality."[15] After *Two English Girls,* with its depiction of what the filmmaker described as "a nervous breakdown typical of that period," *A Gorgeous Girl* marks a striking return to health, one that involves a foray into the very sources of Truffaut's work, namely, the antisocial tendency: "*the nuisance value of the antisocial child is an essential feature,* and is also, at its best, *a favorable feature* indicating again a potentiality for recovery of lost fusion of the libidinal and motility drives."[16] Camille illustrates this pattern in a highly comic way. Like a jack-in-the-box, she affirms the power of an amazing vital force that overturns and devastates everything around her. Jumping up at every turn in the story, she is the insufferable child who refuses to allow herself to be suffocated by her environment at the same time as she destroys it. As the sociologist's secretary primly observes, the environment is the victim of Camille Bliss, not the other way around. Her strength, her verve, and her self-confidence irresistibly suggest a return to the state of infantile omnipotence. Moreover, by describing her criminal maneuvers as "a gamble with fate," she is affirming

5.3. A harlot, wild, colorful. Camille Bliss (Bernadette Lafont) in *A Gorgeous Girl Like Me,* dir. François Truffaut, 1972.

her belief in a magical control of the reality that she confronts. One of her lovers, Sam Golden, attests to the effectiveness of the fusion of her ability to act with her libidinal drives when he characterizes her as a "somersault artist." In this caricatured rendering of the scenario that produces delinquency, the antisocial tendency is presented as an alternative to depressive withdrawal. Instead of being the victim of internal obstacles, like the paralyzed young bourgeois characters of *Two English Girls,* Camille projects her aggressiveness outward – onto a world populated with persecutors – in a way that reflects a newfound faith in life: "*The antisocial tendency implies hope.*"[17] Furthermore, far from imprisoning her in the past, the flashbacks in the story open the doors of the prison, and those that lead into the future. The signs of a predestined fate are inverted here, as is proven by the way the themes of writing and the fall are handled.

The beginning of the film emphasizes the failure of a book. A young woman goes into a bookshop to look for a work, the publication of which has been announced. The book derives from a thesis by Stanislas Prévin (André Dusollier) on criminal women, but it has not yet been released. What has happened to it? The film begins with a flashback that shows the young sociologist entering a prison, one year earlier, to meet the subject of his study. He arrives armed with a tape recorder, on which he is going to get Madame Bliss to record the story of her life – progressively illustrated in a second series of flashbacks. The tape recorder is at the center of the story: "In *A Gorgeous Girl,* the construction of the film is organized from the beginning around the tape recorder. Everything departs from there and returns to the same place."[18] The structuring of the film around the recording of an experience creates a parallel between *A Gorgeous Girl* and *The Wild Child:* "Bernadette is the savage, and this time, we are do not sympathize with the educator, who understands nothing about life."[19] The sociologist's powerlessness when confronted by Camille is translated into a linguistic relationship. *A Gorgeous Girl* does not merely contrast the feminine with the masculine, and spoken language with writing, but also an extraordinarily dynamic slang with the empty verbiage of Stanislas. As Truffaut observed, this language is no less elaborate that that in *The Two English Girls:*

> It was merely a different literary form that attracted me: after the beautiful language of Roché, constructed out of short phrases, with an incredibly refined sensitivity, I committed myself to a completely invented language, a very coarse kind of slang, for sure, but also less vulgar than that used by Queneau in *The Adventures of Sally Mara.*[20]

Stanislas decides to transcribe Camille's words faithfully into his book: "Language, he explains to his secretary, is an important vehicle for conveying one's personality." In this instance, his own personality is singularly lacking in any distinctive features. We see him duped, taken over, and finally annihilated as a result of his linguistic competition with Camille. At the film's conclusion, the young woman's testimony causes him to be thrown in prison for a crime that she herself committed. Stanslas immediately writes a long plea that has no effect: Camille escapes from the nets of writing, which land on the empty-handed fisherman.

In the original screenplay, after one of the countless new developments that take place in her story, the heroine remarks: "In my story, there is no ending, but there are many instances of falling." Indeed, two memorable falls frame the film. The first is that of her father: Camille, a child, surreptitiously takes away the ladder he was using to climb into the barn of the family's farm; he does not notice that this has happened, and falls. This is one example of a "gamble with fate." This indirect murder earns the little girl a spell in a reformatory. The second fall is that of her lover, Arthur (Charles Denner), the puritanical rat exterminator who sets himself against the "evil beasts" with as much passion as he represses his sexuality. Having realized the perverse situation into which he has led Camille, his "poor little bird," he decides that there is no other way but for them to kill themselves together. Camille tricks him into jumping from the top of a church by himself. She again finds herself in prison for this crime, which is about the only one that she has actually not committed. These falls display her vigor. She brings them about without ever being subjected to them. She does not fall; she refuses to jump. She does not display the least sign of a suicidal tendency. Camille clings tightly to life, because she has a single goal that guides and orientates her efforts.

In *A Gorgeous Girl,* two forces govern human relationships: money and sex. Wads of banknotes, stolen or extorted, circulate freely; all the characters are mobilized by their sexual drives. Even the very dignified young bourgeois woman who types up Stanislas's thesis reveals through her words and actions the attraction she feels for the sociologist. Camille's lovers display the same pattern of desire in a less rarified form: Clovis (Philippe Léotard), her husband; Master Murène, the corrupt lawyer; Sam Golden (Guy Marchand), the singer; and Arthur, the rat exterminator have only one thought in mind – to throw themselves on the heroine. Furthermore, the last two display strong fetishist tendencies: before being able to perform, Sam needs to listen to a record that reproduces the sounds of race-car engines on the track at Indianapolis, while Arthur, by means of a very contrived setup, tricks himself into believing that his "fall" onto Camille's body is an unavoidable accident arising from the pet-control process! As she explains to Stanislas, Camille heroically accepts the insatiable sexual demands of all four men as a given, but it is clear that she herself, unlike them, is never at any moment a slave to her instincts:

> *Stanislas:* Are you telling me, Camille, that you had ulterior motives when you got involved with each of them?
>
> *Camille:* Of course! Come on, I wouldn't have slept with them unless I had a good reason. I'm not that kind of girl!

Camille is the only character in the film with an ideal. She is an artist who wants to become famous. The sincerity of her belief that this is her vocation is not in doubt. After all, as a young girl, she kills her father because he smashed her banjo with a stomp of his foot. She asks Stanislas to bring her another one in prison, and reacts with childlike joy when she sees it. In one of the most sincere moments in the film, she confesses her admiration for Sam Golden, having been deeply impressed by seeing his name displayed on the shabby nightclub where he sings: "I've always had heaps of respect for people who can get their names written on walls: I say to myself that they must really know what life is about . . . to have a knack like that, eh?" While she is uttering these words, the camera moves close to her face in one of the rare close-ups in the film. Camille is fascinated by the media. At the beginning, we see her entranced by the advertisements on television; by the end, she succeeds in becoming a rich and famous singer. Furthermore, the media seem to give back to her the love that she bears toward them. She is freed from prison because of an amateur film proving that she did not push Arthur off of the church. This sequence results in a delectable pastiche by a cinephile who is crazy about technique. The film has been shot by a little boy, Michou, and at the moment when Arthur's body smashes onto the ground, Michou invites Stanislas and his secretary to admire the effects of a beautiful zoom; the epidemic of mockery in this film spares neither children nor cinema itself! At the end, newspapers announce Camille's release and the imprisonment of the sociologist. When the latter wants to read aloud a letter in which he recounts the truth, he cannot find anyone to listen to him apart from his fellow prisoner, and he is not able convince even his cellmate of his innocence. Camille with her lies successfully persuades everyone to believe the contrary; the final image shows her in the process of giving a television interview while a bulldozer destroys the last remaining evidence of her guilt. Stanislas remains in prison.

5.4. Camille (Bernadette Lafont) visits the imprisoned Stanislas (André Dussollier) in *A Gorgeous Girl Like Me,* dir. François Truffaut, 1972.

When Camille goes to visit Stanislas in his gloomy prison, she says: "Prison is a weird thing. There are those who know, and those who don't know. Ah, well, as for you, now you are the same as me." Indeed, in this scene, filmed in close-up shots, in which each character in turn seems to be positioned behind the bars that separate them, a single identity appears to have been established between Stanislas and Camille. To the critics who accused him of ridiculing intellectuals, Truffaut replied:

> The film has been seen as scornful – that's wrong, because one does not disdain oneself. The film was made *against myself:* this is what people don't seem to have understood. The film is ambiguous, for the reason that it is secretly no less autobiographical than my other films. In *A Gorgeous Girl Like Me,* both of the characters are me: Camille Bliss and Stanislas, the sociologist. I am making fun of someone who persists in viewing life through a romantic lens: the rational one is the girl, who is kind of a guttersnipe – someone who has learned to mistrust everyone and fight for survival. I oppose one to the other, but I am fond of both.[21]

Truffaut could certainly be both of these characters simultaneously. Like Antoine Doinel, Camille is detained in an observation center for delinquent minors; like Antoine Doinel, Stanislas spits out the coffee that he discovers is contaminated. These are details, for sure, but the kind of details that always proclaim the truth in Truffaut's films. Where the filmmaker does indeed seem to display bad faith is when he insists that he is fond of both of them. While it is clear that he takes endless pleasure in playing along with his female protagonist, it is blatantly obvious that he disapproves of Stanislas. *A Gorgeous Girl* is a superb example of autobiographical splitting, with a killing-off of the disowned part. Truffaut divides himself in two in order to release the feminine component in his personality and celebrate its triumph. *The Bride Who Wore Black* tentatively initiated this movement whereby he projects himself onto a female character. In this film, the filmmaker pushes this process to the extreme by identifying completely with this "gorgeous girl," who frees herself by telling the story of her life. "Had I been a woman, I would have been like her,"[22] Truffaut said, adding further: "I am more interested in the femininity of artists than in their virility."[23] From *The 400 Blows* onward, he placed creativity, like delinquency, under a female sign.

The originality of *A Gorgeous Girl* resides in the fact that Camille does not possess any trait that could associate her with a maternal figure. She is Antoine Doinel's double. In an attempt to console Stanislas for the fact he is in prison, she says: "Look at me, it's thanks to prison that I've become a star," which is very close to what Truffaut himself might have said. The splitting-off of the feminine allows him to put aside everything that impedes the vital impulse that drives toward success. In *The Green Room,* Julien Davenne represents the other side of Camille, in a form that is not devoid of a degree of satiric mockery. Truffaut associates the feminine with vitality, creativity, and delinquency; the masculine with withdrawal, melancholy, an absence of ambition, the cult of the past and the dead, and a temptation to commit suicide. Camille Bliss and Julien Davenne constitute the two faces of their creator that all of his other films try to unite. As we will see, *Mississippi Mermaid* presents the most elaborate version of the process involved in this attempt to reunite the split-off elements in his psyche.

One can understand why Truffaut remained fond of this film, one that revealed an essential component in the autobiographical mosaic that makes up his oeuvre. The energies that the film sets free are also reflected in its form: "By giving Bernadette Lafont a multiplicity of opportunities for displaying her vitality, I attempted to create an experience of cinematographic vitality in *A Gorgeous Girl*."[24] Indeed, like Camille, the representation is animated by a striking dynamism, with its dialogues that take dazzling shortcuts and its images that link the present to the past. Above all, Truffaut made a profession of aesthetic faith in *A Gorgeous Girl* by affirming a tendency that would prevail during the second half of his career: a hatred of the documentary.

When Stanislas shows Camille his manuscript at the end of the film, Camille, when reading the transcript of what she has said to him, exclaims: "Wow! Holy shit! Come on . . . it's so badly written! . . . I thought you were a professor!" Stanislas replies that her words function like "fingerprints." By throwing him into prison immediately after this, Truffaut is denouncing the narrative impotence of the sociologist's method. A book should not content itself with merely recording reality without any kind of mediation. It needs to have an author who controls its order, and who invests it with meaning. A work of art necessarily involves a manipulation of reality; Camille knows that. In the film, the visual track often denounces the lies of the soundtrack, in which it tells its story in its own way. But it is Truffaut, in particular, who keeps his distance from "real-life documents." In contrast to Stanislas's book, the film surrounds Camille with a system of critical devices that expose the fragility of recorded "reality." The sociologist, armed with a tape recorder, goes crazy because he is in love; his secretary, armed with a typewriter, corrects his interpretations with a lucidity that is inspired by jealousy. In short, objectivity is an illusion and, in any case, the audience only enjoys lies that are shaped according to some kind of implicit order. At the end of the film, under the pretext of "transforming the environment," Camille, on live television, obliterates the proof of her crime through the use of a bulldozer. The nature of her art is reflected in the image of this machine: primitive, brutal, lying, but ruthlessly efficient. Truffaut's next film, *Day for Night,* picks up the problem of creativity in a way that is both serious and lyrical, by making an inventory of the obstacles that a director has to surmount in order to create a work of fiction. *A Gorgeous Girl,* as Truffaut insisted, is indeed a film that is "coherent, controlled, and complementary to the others."

Both *The Bride Wore Black* and *A Gorgeous Girl Like Me* are adapted from American novels, the first by William Irish, whose *Waltz into Darkness* Truffaut later turned into *Mississippi Mermaid,* and the second by Henry Farrell. While the issue of Truffaut's relationship with literature is essential, the question of how he adapts novels seems less important. The director displays an extreme freedom in his treatment of the source texts, which he usually chose because an idea or a theme directly bore upon his personal preoccupations. As Jean Gruault observes, based on his work as Truffaut's scriptwriter: "Basically, the only material he used from the scripts you brought to him was what he already had in his head."[25] Truffaut's treatment of crime novels is imaginative and lively, but a comparison between the film and the book yields nothing of any great interest. Roché's case is an exception, given that Truffaut had an especial fondness for his style. The film versions of *Jules and Jim* and *Two English Girls* reproduce texts that he loved – but he takes the same liberty in adapting these novels as he does in his adaptations of crime novels. His most faithful adaptation is undoubtedly that of *Fahrenheit 451;* Bradbury furnished him with a fairy story that might have come directly out of his own imagination. Adaptations often allowed Truffaut to stage situations that he would not have dared to invent. In the second part of his career, having gained in self-assurance, he increasingly preferred to use his own original scripts.

6

In Search of the Father

Fahrenheit 451 (1966)
Day for Night (1973)

FAHRENHEIT 451 AND *DAY FOR NIGHT* BOTH PRESENT AN IMAGE of a small human community, the function and organization of which are clearly delimited. The team of firemen and the film crew both have their head (captain/director), their base (fire station/hotel), their equipment (cranes and trucks), their work-instruments (flame-thrower/camera), and their goal (to achieve their respective missions). The first burns books; the second is shooting a film. In these two works, lyrical shots – "magical," as Truffaut called them – rather than depicting human exchanges, dwell on moments of speechless ecstasy when fire is consuming pages or when film is coiling at the foot of the editing table. In these microcosms, in which human activity more than ever takes on the appearance of play, destruction and construction confirm the status of two cultural objects: the book and the film. "Confirm" is a term that is too weak to describe the veritable cult devoted to these two objects. Both reign supreme in human affairs; in *Fahrenheit 451,* as in *Day for Night,* we find that the economy of desire is entirely subordinate to their power. These films are peculiarly complementary because they raise the question of cultural experience, and of its roots in an affective experience that is dominated by parental figures. But these works – and their power resides in this – lead one into a larger reflection on the transmission of knowledge, on communication, and on death. In studying them, we come to appreciate the filmmaker's gift in being able to invest autobiographical specificities with a universal relevance, in which everyone can find elements of his or her own experience.

FAHRENHEIT 451 (1966)

Despite the crackling of the flame-throwers that endlessly occupy the screen, *Fahrenheit 451* – the title indicates the temperature at which papers ignites – seems at first sight to be a cold film. Feelings remain hidden, and speech is rare. Filmed in England, which left Truffaut feeling hugely isolated because he could not speak English, and shot, significantly, at the time when his "Hitchbook" was being published, *Fahrenheit 451* seems to exemplify the law of the master: "Whatever is *said* instead of being *shown* is lost on the viewer."[1] In this, the first of the films he made in color, Truffaut accords great prominence to the image: "The scenes with dialogue are to be kept short, and I am making a rule for myself not to shorten the 'privileged moments,' that is, scenes that are purely visual: the comings and goings of the firemen, emergency departures, fires, and various odd happenings."[2] The silent interventions of the pyromaniac firemen, for which Bernard Hermann's martial music supplies a revealing commentary, constitute particularly successful moments of visual art.

In *Fahrenheit 451,* two great forces confront one another: fire and the book. A force that is natural, primary, and elemental is opposed to a force that is cultural, secondary, and sublimated. The members of the human population comply with this double polarity, aligning themselves with the power of one or the other of these forces. In the course of the narrative, the journey of Montag (Oskar Werner), the hero of the film, consists of fleeing from one camp to the other. A fireman blasts out flames in the first images of the film; by the end of the story he becomes a living book who utters the words of a dead author in the depths of a snow-covered forest. In the science-fiction world of *Fahrenheit 451,* the options are indeed limited to these two types of engagement, and the forest camp at the end is, in many respects, as constrained and austere as the fire station at the beginning. The firemen are robots, and the book-men resemble automatons. In this disturbing film, the only freedom consists of choosing one's respective mode of alienation. Real life is absent; all that exists is its reflection in words.

The empire of fire is depicted as being as resolutely masculine as it is childish. Strapped into their black uniforms (inspired by the tunics of

6.1. The captain (Cyril Cusack) in *Fahrenheit 451*, dir. François Truffaut, 1966.

the Russian army),[3] stationed rigidly on their gleaming truck, the firemen in *Fahrenheit 451* embody the dream of every young boy: to see the things he is playing with suddenly enlarged to a human scale. From the opening images of the film, the spectator plunges directly into the world of childhood: "If I were to do the film all over again, I would instruct the set designer, the costumier, and the cameraman to make a film about life the way children see it: the firemen would be lead soldiers, the fire station a superb toy, etc."[4] Such a conception of the world as a model makes the film seem like a fable, like a malicious fairy story. Moreover, the ferociously policed society of *Fahrenheit 451*, through its ironic mode, suggests not so much a right-wing or left-wing totalitarian regime as the projection of unconscious representations. Surrounded by his docile, brutal cohort of young men, the captain of the firemen (Cyril Cusack) bears no small resemblance to the father of the "primitive horde" that Freud describes in *Totem and Taboo*. Comparing the development of the child to that of humanity in general, Freud traces the social order and its prohibitions back to the originary murder of the father by the son, jealous of his power. In the Freudian myth, the father-king keeps his sons in a state of dependency and immaturity in order to maintain his reign.

From the opening of *Fahrenheit 451,* the firemen's relationship with their chief reflects this kind of schema: a close-up of the captain sitting enthroned on his truck, while his men are busy destroying books, signifies the absolute nature of his authority. Using the third person whenever he addresses Montag, he treats him like a child whose submission is beyond question, throughout the entire length of the film.

This paternal figure is full of ambiguity, and the arbitrary law that he exerts remains mysterious. Although he is benevolent and seductive in his dealings with Montag, we see the captain display a brutal violence toward less submissive recruits. In an enigmatic scene that provides a good illustration of a son's anxiety in the face of the unpredictable behavior of the father, Montag, who has been summoned to his office, sees the captain, through a window of frosted glass, in the act of beating up two young firemen because of his displeasure at their friendship. This primitive scene, which connotes a latent homosexuality pertaining to masculine communities, suggests the tonality of this pre-Oedipal world. The law of the father is founded on fear and violence; it does not reflect any higher order. Kept in a state of regressive dependency by fear, the sons are trapped in a state of rivalry with each other, with the chief as object. Throughout the film, Fabien, Montag's colleague, displays his resentment at the favors that the captain accords the latter, and keeps him under surveillance with a jealous eye. The captain deliberately fosters this atmosphere of adulation by handing out a medallion with a "very lifelike" effigy of himself to his men, with a puerile air of self-importance.

Even if the firemen are married, like Montag, they are not independent adults with a well-defined identity. During the sacking of the old lady's library, the captain, in his diatribe against books that "have nothing to say," particularly targets autobiographical works whose authors claim the privilege of a unique identity: "We all need to be the same. Only equality can guarantee happiness for everyone." It is not equality that power is advocating, however, so much as uniformity: among the firemen, any difference between men is not tolerated.[5] Moreover, Truffaut borrowed the salute exchanged by two firemen in one scene from the Ku Klux Klan. In *Fahrenheit 451,* the greatest differentiating factor arises not from racial, religious, or political distinctions, but from the affective register: emotion is the enemy. This is what the firemen are seeking to banish from their world by burning books. In the second part of the film, Montag literally pumps emotion into the heart of Linda's female friends by reading Dickens to them. One of them starts to cry. Montag the fireman throws flames onto books; Montag the reader projects from the text onto humans. In both cases, he sets his targets ablaze.

With Freud, the castrating father demonstrates his power over his sons by reserving for himself the exclusive use of the women of the horde. In *Fahrenheit 451,* the father bars access not to women, but to culture. It is against this prohibition that Montag revolts, first by engaging in reading, and then by killing the captain. In this instance, all the sexual metaphors are replaced by cultural metaphors. A case in point is the famous pole in the fire station that the firemen use to ascend to, or descend from, one floor to the next. Montag can no longer use it once he has read books – this pole evokes a pre-Oedipal autoeroticism that access to sexual maturity renders obsolete. For Montag, it is access to culture that marks such a transformation. In this desexualized world, books constitute the erotic force that makes possible the assertion of the individual. To read is to become an adult, in defiance of the law of the primitive father.

At the beginning of the film, the appearance of one of these universal symbols, which Truffaut handles very effectively, sums up the messages that are dispersed throughout the rest of the film. In the first scene, a man, alerted by gunshot to the imminence of a raid by the firemen, rushes out of his apartment. Before leaving, however, he seizes an apple that he bites into while fleeing. We encounter him again in the camp of the people-books. He is holding an apple in his hand, an apple that Clarisse eventually bites into. This apple, of course, is the fruit of knowledge, forbidden in the domain of the firemen, but prized in the camp in the forest. It is also, nevertheless, a symbol of seduction. Simultaneously, then, this image associates culture with sexuality, and the book with the woman.

In *Fahrenheit 451,* the book is as resolutely feminine as fire is masculine. The anonymous voice on the telephone at the beginning was that of a woman. In Montag's case, the person who initiates him into reading is Clarisse, the friend of an old lady who is a book-lover and a staunch member of the Resistance – a commitment that is confirmed by the fact that she would rather be burned with her books than be separated from them. Linda (Julie Christie), on the other hand, who regards books with horror, is not accorded any autonomous existence in the imaginary of the film. She is inseparable from Clarisse, of whom she is the negative double. It is for this reason that the same actress, Julie Christie, plays both roles. In *Fahrenheit 451,* Truffaut splits the feminine in the same way one separates the white from the yolk of an egg: on one side, there is Clarisse, eccentric, talkative, eager for exchanges and conversation; on the other side, there is Linda, conventional, taciturn, absorbed in the television programs she constantly watches. The two women are not only contrasted like word and image, but they also have contrasting sexual identities: the former is childish, the latter adult. As far as Truffaut was concerned, it was a question, above all, of "rendering of Clarisse asexual so as not to involve her or Montag in an adulterous situation . . . Neither mistress, nor Girl Scout, nor girlfriend, Clarisse is merely a little girl who is full of questions, and someone who reasons."[6] In contrast, Linda is a kind of mechanical female with neither thoughts nor emotions. Permanently filled with pills, one day she suffers an overdose, and then becomes an inert chemical body whose blood has to be changed just as one drains a machine. Her sexual advances toward her husband are modeled on the judo holds that are taught on television. There is no eroticism, but instead a sportive, aggressive kind of sex. Representing a cultural woman and a sexual woman, Clarisse and Linda have one thing in common: they both emasculate Montag with as much determination as the captain infantilizes him. Commenting on Clarisse, Truffaut said that she picks Montag up, on the monorail that takes her to work, just like a boy would.[7] For her part, Linda offers a sharpened razor to her husband as a prelude to their lovemaking; it is difficult to see that as an innocent gesture . . .

As is indicated by each woman's relationship with children, the maternal is associated with the feminine. Consistent with her icy image, Linda detests them. In the course of a conversation with her friends in front of the inevitable television set, she expresses her horror at the idea of motherhood. She admits, however, that it might be "entertaining" to have children, because they resemble oneself – an observation that picks up the leitmotif of narcissism in a minor key. In contrast, Clarisse, being a teacher, takes her mission as an educator to heart, and breaks down in tears when her young pupils run away from her after her return to the school. Moreover, like Clarisse, children are linked to books from the beginning of *Fahrenheit 451*. In the first scene, we see a young boy leafing through the pages of one of the books that the firemen are getting ready to burn. His father forces him to throw it back into the brazier. A flash-shot shows a very young child in another part watching the maneuvers of the firemen from behind the window of an apartment building. In the following image, Montag, protected by a perspex visor, sets fire to the heap of books that his colleagues have seized from the apartment. These two shots establish an analogy between the child and the man, both being separated from the books by a transparent screen. The analogy is reinforced in the fine surrealistic scene that follows Montag's first act of reading. The text, *David Copperfield,* invades the screen in close-up, while Montag, in a loud voice, deciphers the syllables with difficulty. It involves an evocation of David's childhood. Here is how Truffaut describes the sequence that follows:

> I try to depict a square in which children are playing. The firemen "comb" the square and search people: old men, nurses, etc. While frisking an old man, Montag detects the presence of a book under his overcoat, but nevertheless lets him go. When leaving the square, the captain, to amuse himself, frisks a 1-year-old baby, finds within a small pocket in its baby clothes a tiny book of "Chinese sayings," and confiscates it.[8]

This rebellious baby, whom the captain reprimands with an amused indulgence, is not without resemblance to Montag, who has just been born, metaphorically, because of his discovery of what books can offer. In the camp of the people-books, we encounter a small boy who is reciting a text as the film closes. The child-book at the end thus embodies a reply to the child at the beginning who was forbidden to read.

In the corridor of the school, Clarisse meets two little boys one after another, each of whom runs off when they sees her. Two male nurses come to change Linda's blood. On the television, during the families' game in which she is participating, two presenters share the screen. Two recruits are reprimanded for having sat side by side in the firemen's school, and are then beaten up by the captain. In the camp of the people-books, Truffaut even has fun inventing two twin books: "I chose two twins to be 'Jane Austen's *Pride and Prejudice.*' Then Montag asks them: 'You are both the same book?' and they reply: '*My brother is volume one. – My brother is volume two.*'"[9] This proliferation of minor doubles only reinforces the major duality of the principal characters: Linda doubles Clarisse, whom the old lady redoubles; the captain is both benevolent and brutal; Montag will see his double die on television during the final chase, and divides himself into the black Montag, who burns books by day, and the white Montag, who, wrapped up in a large robe with a monastic look, reads them by night.

This constant division of identities is a sign of their precariousness and instability. The characters seem to be engaged in a search for themselves, and, in the absence of any stable model, appear to be condemned to gaze endlessly at their reflection without ever attaining an identity that is separate and permanent. The theme of narcissism, absent in Ray Bradbury's novel, is very prominent in the film:

> For several days, I felt that something was lacking in the screenplay for *Fahrenheit 451,* an idea that could be expressed visually through different details that one would place here and there. I decided upon narcissism . . . In the sequences involving the aerial railway, I would show a traveler rubbing himself on the cheek with his wrist like a little girl who is falling asleep, another person kissing their reflection in the glass of the window. Linda, in her kitchen, would caress her chest – in short, there was an embarrassment of possible choices inherent in this idea that could really work across the whole film.[10]

This presence of narcissism confirms the pre-Oedipal nature of the world of *Fahrenheit 451*. The characters, like young children, seem to be arrested at the mirror stage, which, according to Lacan's theory, occurs in the developmental process at about the age of 2 years old, that is, before the acquisition of language. They play with an egotistical delight in their own image and their own body. By the end of the film, the only stable identity is that of the people-books, who find peace by taking refuge in the words of the great masterpieces of literature.

But books themselves are doubles: book-objects and book-contents; the firemen burn the former, the material objects, while the people-books learn the latter, the texts. Truffaut was highly aware of this polarity:

> As far as *Fahrenheit 451* was concerned, I had been influenced by certain articles written by Roger Caillois in the NRF about books and reading. He said that books are valued differently according to the individual concerned. He was

> speaking of people – especially university academics – who are interested in the content, and others – especially autodidacts – who treat the book like an object with all that that entails in terms of memories and sentimentality. In this context, which is that of my film, the book becomes an object that one cherishes more and more. Even the binding, the cover, and the smell of the pages acquire great sentimental value.[11]

Nevertheless, in *Fahrenheit 451*, as in *The Man Who Loved Women*, which also posed the same problem for him, the book oscillates ceaselessly between these two poles. For Montag, it is both a fetishistic object, the material qualities of which are cherished as such, and a textual object that opens a way into the cultural and artistic heritage. This double function has complex origins that are gradually uncovered. One thing is certain: reading is an act of love, of possession, of extreme violence. One absorbs a book, one merges with it, one becomes fused with it. Underneath its cold exterior, *Fahrenheit 451* is a film that is burning with passion. The people-books shown at the end of the film fill themselves with text, drain themselves, and efface themselves to the limits of nonbeing in order to make themselves into book-contents. They incarnate these living books, which Montag declares to be his family, and which Truffaut filmed as human beings: "I only noticed today that to let books fall outside the frame is impossible in this film. I have to follow their fall right to the ground. Books here are characters, and to cut off their trajectory is equivalent to leaving the head of an actor outside the frame."[12] This allusion to books falling refers to several scenes in the film. During the first intervention of the firemen, books, placed in a sack, are thrown out of a window of the apartment block; a dreamlike, slow-motion shot follows their movement toward the ground. At the old woman's house, the firemen throw books down from the upstairs balustrade. As they are being consumed by fire, the books display the opposite tendency by rising up, twisting and raising their pages in an aerial movement. The direction of this movement is captured in Montag's nightmare, which materializes the fantasy of a book-bird:

> Another "magic" shot: an attempt to film in slow motion a pile of books that are falling without any obvious reason. It took two days before I achieved the shot of my dreams. To finish off the magical effect, we are trying to make a book fly, like a seagull, in an empty setting, so that we can insert this image into the nightmare being experienced by Montag, who is ill.[13]

With Truffaut, vertical space is always a space that is heavily sexualized, and this double movement involving falling and flight is linked with the feminine. In *Fahrenheit 451,* this space is also that of Clarisse. While Linda always moves on the flat surface of the marital home, Clarisse floats in the air on the monorail, confides to Montag in an elevator, climbs and descends staircases several times. Her escape, before the arrival of the firemen, is achieved, curiously, in an ascending manner that is greatly emphasized in the film: "Clarisse takes her clothes, throws them on a wardrobe, places a stool on her bed, climbs up, opens a skylight, picks up her clothes, throws them on the roof, and hoists herself outside. We continue to see her in pajamas on top of the roof, passing between two chimneys against the night sky, lit with stars."[14] The old lady is also associated with vertical space. She defies the firemen from the top of her stairs, before descending them majestically, slightly in advance of the flight of the books toward the floor. Both book and woman obey the same imaginary laws and, through a process of symbolic analogy, occupy the sexual space of desire.

Ideological interpretations have been proposed to explain the fable of *Fahrenheit 451,* but Truffaut himself had very definite views about the subject of his film:

> You know, people are going to see all kinds of grand ideas in *Fahrenheit.* They are going to say that it is a film about culture and liberty, a social critique, or perhaps even a diatribe against countries in which books are burned. But I don't give a damn; that doesn't interest me in the slightest. It may be in the book, but, personally, I am not interested in grand ideas, at least not of a formal sort . . . As far as I am concerned, I can only make a film that springs from ideas that relate to me personally.[15]

Truffaut declared that, above all, he had made the film "while thinking constantly of the Resistance and the Occupation,"[16] that is to say, the period of his childhood. He intended that Montag would be "a kind of Gestapo-type who was interested in the Resistance."[17] Truffaut also often compared his hero to Antoine in *The 400 Blows,* even going as far as to say that *Fahrenheit 451* was one of the possible continuations of his first film.[18] Furthermore, in directing the actors, he ordered both Jean-Pierre Léaud and Oskar Werner never to smile, which provoked a violent conflict with the latter, who felt he was being stifled in this taciturn role.

Like Antoine, Montag lives in a state of disobedience and then of delinquency, absenting himself from the fire station – just as Antoine plays truant from school – and going to steal files from the captain's office. The difference is that Montag gets around authority more adroitly than Antoine does, thus avoiding imprisonment. Truffaut made the following remarks on this aspect of the film:

> I am not against violence because of idealism, or because of any commitment to the idea of nonviolence. I am against it because violence means confrontation . . . that arises from my childhood, in fact. For me, escape is what replaces violence; not escape from what is essential, but escape in order to obtain what is essential. That, I believe, is what I have illustrated in *Fahrenheit*. It's an aspect of the film that has escaped everybody, but that, for me, is the most important: it's an apology for craftiness. "You don't say! Books are forbidden? Very well, then, we're going to learn them by heart!" That's a supreme ruse. No one could ever persuade me to join with filmmaker friends in signing a petition against censorship, because I believe that there are fifty ways of getting around censorship, and of triumphing over it.[19]

Truffaut also indicated that the books that appear in the film do not constitute a catalogue of favorites. Only the album by Dali, the pages of which turn slowly in a current of air, is there as the result of deliberate choice – because Dali is "the only great artist who declared himself in favor of all forms of censorship."[20] Prohibition does not muzzle desire, but increases it tenfold, as a fantasmatic reading of the film confirms.

It is particularly with respect to its fantasmatic dimension that *Fahrenheit 451* resembles *The 400 Blows*. Like Antoine, Montag is a loner caught between the arbitrary orders of a father whose authority he is going to be led to contest – the captain is a sympathetic version of the instructor in *The 400 Blows* – and of a mother who is divided into two complementary characters, the one coldly sexual and the other warmly cultural. Madame Doinel united, in a less sharply contrasted way, these two attributes. It is she who encourages her son to write, and who leads him to read Balzac, causing Antoine, already, at this early stage, to become a pyromaniac. In Truffaut's own life, books were tied to the feminine. He said he had learned to love them as a result of his maternal grandmother, who had herself written a novel. His mother also read to him a lot, which, in an admittedly indirect way, led him to reading for himself: "My mother couldn't bear noise, and required me to remain motionless,

6.2. The old woman (Bee Duffell) surrounded by her burning books in *Fahrenheit 451,* dir. François Truffaut, 1966.

without budging or talking, for hours on end. So, I read; it was the only activity in which I could engage without getting on her nerves. I read an enormous amount during the period of the Occupation."[21]

The Man Who Loved Women depicts this scene, investing it with a fantasmatic content that the mechanisms of fiction render more precise and dramatic. We see a son immersed in reading while a feminine, seductive mother remains at a distance while arousing him. In this film, the erotic impulse is divided almost equally between women's legs and books. The book-object, which, for Truffaut's heroes, elicits a sentimental attachment that sometimes borders on fetishism, derives its power from its associations with the maternal presence. The materiality of the book is that of her body. To read is to obey the mother, to identify oneself with her, to stay in her presence, to fuse indirectly with her. In *Fahrenheit 451,* a striking cross-fade merges Montag's face with that of Clarisse, the mother-book, while they are both in bed in their respective houses. The fire that devours pages with passion and violence is not only an image of the sublimated pleasure of reading, but also an image of the desire that ties the son to the mother. To read is to transfer this desire from the body to the text.

That is why, in the film's imaginary, vertical space is associated with both Clarisse and books. But it is equally for this reason that fire represents the instrument of paternal prohibition. The huge, devastating infernos of *Fahrenheit 451*, which combine prohibition and transgression, become transformed in Truffaut's more melancholy films into the trembling flames of candles, by the light of which the characters celebrate the mournful cult of doomed love.

Fahrenheit 451 is presented as a work of repair aimed at salvaging the maternal character, from which Truffaut carefully separates the good from the bad: the mother-book from the mother-sex. There are father figures that correspond to these two maternal images. The first of these is the captain, who forbids fusion with the mother-book and enjoys a close relationship with the mother-sex, who in turn respects his law and denounces Montag so that the captain can punish him. Montag is then forced to liquidate this tyrannical father. During this putting to death, achieved with flame-throwers, Montag performs a revealing action. When his house is invaded by firemen, he first burns the marital bed, associated with Linda, before turning the murderous fire against the captain. After this double symbolic execution of an archaic parental couple who were forbidding the child access to a passage toward maturity, Montag runs away to join Clarisse's people-books. It is there that the figure of the good father appears, the Oedipal father who opens up the cultural order for the son and transmits his knowledge to him. The final images of the film show an old man who, before enjoying a peaceful, natural death, has a young boy learn by heart the book that he incarnates. It is, however, disturbing that this image of reconciliation should be associated with words that seem to contradict it. Here, in fact, is the text that the child comes to learn from the lips of the old man: "How to love my father, a man who never thought of me, never had a word for me, nor ever a gesture, nor a smile. He was scared of dying too young, was concerned about his own health, and he died nevertheless, as he feared, when the snow came." The parental representations in *Fahrenheit 451* are extremely complex, but they are what inform the organization of the film, together with its mode of representation, at a deep level.

Finally, what is to be said about the people-books who stem from this conflict-ridden lineage? They are free men, according to the play of words that we find at the end of the film. They have a stable identity, but they have also become removed from life. That is exactly what Truffaut said about himself: "I have always preferred the reflection of life to life itself. If I chose books and cinema, from the age of 11 or 12, it was because I preferred to look at life through books or cinema."[22] The people-books live in the reflection of life. In the snow-covered forest at the end of the film, men and women affirm that the transmission of truth and the safeguard of cultural heritage assure the triumph of the human spirit over oppression and death – that they are sufficient in themselves to justify the brief passage of an individual through the world of the living. *Fahrenheit 451* is one of the most autobiographical and personal of films that François Truffaut ever made.

DAY FOR NIGHT (1973)

When he undertook *Day for Night,* Truffaut had behind him the difficult years when he racked up his two "absolute flops,"[23] *Mississippi Mermaid* and *Two English Girls,* as well as two films that had received a very lukewarm critical reception, *Bed and Board* and *A Gorgeous Girl Like Me.* In fact, between *Stolen Kisses* in 1968 and *Day for Night* in 1973, he had achieved only one big success, *The Wild Child* in 1971. This was also the period in which he was most seriously attacked for the bourgeois themes and conventional aesthetic of his films. In 1974, Truffaut summed up the situation in a long letter addressed to the critic in the *Nouvel Observateur,* Jean-Louis Bory. This self-criticism, which is also a passionate plea for the kind of cinema he was making, was triggered by one small phrase written by the journalist that had touched him to the quick: "Truffaut, Chabrol, Demy, Rohmer have sold out to the system,"[24] a phrase which summed up fairly accurately the prevailing attitude at that time toward the elders of the New Wave. In this letter, Truffaut defends his "purity" (*pureté*)[25] as a director and reviews all the films he had made in his career up until that point: "Good or bad, my films are those that I wanted to make, and *only* those ones."[26]

In this overview, he sums up the origins of *Day for Night* in these terms: "I pulled myself together and became reconciled to myself thanks to *Day for Night,* which simply deals with my reason for living. (You adore your mother, I hate mine, even though she is dead – how likely is it that we could have even two ideas in common?)."[27] This declaration surprises us because of the hiatus between the declaration about his films and the personal parenthesis. Moreover, the reference to his mother is almost the only one in the 600 pages of his correspondence. Truffaut's mother had died just after *Stolen Kisses*. In a letter written on August 25, 1968, he proclaimed to a friend: "Well, apart from that, my mother is dead; you don't give a damn? Me neither, but all the same, I have to take part in the final unctuousness."[28] His biographer, commenting on these remarks, observes that "he [Truffaut] does not seem to have been greatly moved by his mother's death."[29] One wonders whether that was actually the case. Whatever the truth was, a complex maternal figure plays a leading role in the films that followed *Day for Night* (a happy turning point in Truffaut's career). *Day for Night* did indeed have a liberating effect, as Truffaut admitted to Jean-Louis Bory, as far as his creativity and unconscious representations were concerned.

From the beginning, as Jean Aurel (who worked with the director during the editing of the film) explains, *Day for Night* struck those involved in its making as a jigsaw puzzle that lacked any continuity:

> The screenplay for *Day for Night* was unreadable: it was a succession of sketches . . . One got the impression that Truffaut's understanding of his own film grew better and better as our sessions proceeded. It became clear to him that it was not a film about love affairs between cinema folk, behind the scenes during a shooting, but a film about cinema, which glorified the work of cinema. I have the impression that the metamorphosis took place during the final editing of the film.[30]

The work itself, which the filmmaker originally conceived as a report on the shooting of a film, displays a powerful imaginary component that rigorously shapes its structure, even though it remains masked by the polyphonic construction of the story. For the first time, Truffaut was working with a dozen actors of equal importance and, as in *Small Change* or *The Last Metro*, the meaning is dispersed across a constellation of characters and situations. Truffaut was not merely content to show what goes on behind the scenes in cinema, as we are encouraged to think by the title of the film – which makes reference to a technical procedure allowing a night scene to be shot during the day – and by the credit sequence, which presents an image of the soundtrack alongside the visual track. The real problem he tackles is that of creativity itself. Far from being charming entertainment about the shooting of the films of yesteryear, *Day for Night* can be read as the imaginary projection of a director wrestling with all the internal conflicts, excessive emotional expenditure, and renunciations that his work imposed on him, or rather his "reason for living."

Winnicott describes creativity as a mode of perception "that makes the individual feel that life is worth living."[31] Without creativity, "there is no psychic life, but only survival, no existence, but a habit that is maintained by automatic behaviors that are equally indifferent to life or death."[32] Winnicott does not treat it as the manifestation of an exceptional gift, but, in an original way, as a feeling of being. To be creative is to feel alive. For him, it is not the use or the content of creativity that is most important, but the description of the psychic place in which it is exercised:

> What, for instance, are we doing when we listen to a Beethoven symphony or make a pilgrimage to an art gallery or reading *Troilus and Cressida* in bed, or playing tennis? What is a child doing when sitting on the floor playing with toys under the aegis of the mother? What is a group of teenagers doing participating in a pop session?
>
> It is not only *what are we doing?* The question also needs to be posed: *where are we?*[33]

In Winnicott's topography, creativity corresponds to that intermediate area that is developed at the beginning in the space of separation between the mother and her child, and in which come to be united me and not-me, personal psychic reality and the control of real objects: "The creativity that we are studying belongs to the approach of an individual to external reality."[34] In *Day for Night,* a simple detail like the hearing aid that Truffaut wears when he plays Ferrand, the director of the film, already suggests that the passage from the outside to the inside is not accomplished without difficulty.

Nevertheless, at the beginning of the film, the first images plunge us into the euphoric sense of a perfect control over reality. A busy square, a metro exit, a red car, a woman and her dog: everything is moving with a perfect naturalness, observed from the perspective of a long shot. Suddenly the screen is filled with an enormous close-up of a face, that of Ferrand, who cries out "Cut!" The scene freezes, and the spectator becomes aware that he has just witnessed the shooting of a film. The contrast between the scale of these two types of shot shows the power of man over reality. We are in the play area of infantile omnipotence in which the world is made to submit to the desire of the stage director.

Adult creativity represents a direct extension of the games of childhood. We see instances of playing with a simulated fire in the fireplace, with a false candle, with artificial rain, with dry ice, with a cat that does not know its role. We see playing with feelings, as in Ferrand's decision to incorporate into the screenplay the words that a star utters in a moment of despair. Time is played with, and even death, as when Ferrand, in the editing suite, reverses the scene in which the stuntman drives his car over the edge of a high cliff road. The euphoria that is generated by this harmony between the internal world and reality is suggested at the end of the first sequence by a long, ascending, panoramic shot that follows the crane on which the camera is resting. Happy music accompanies this imaginary flight in its hold over reality.

But the camera soon slows down. The transitional space becomes full of persecutors, and we quickly become aware that the threat emanates from the feminine. The first big problem arrives with Séverine (Valentina Cortese). Drunk, she is unable to act her part. We then discover that Stacey (Alexandra Stewart) is pregnant and will not be able to continue acting her role to the end. We next learn that the insurance companies are refusing to cover Julie Baker (Jacqueline Bisset) on account of her emotional fragility: she is recovering from a nervous breakdown. As if that were not enough, Liliane (Dani), the continuity girl, is beginning to flirt outrageously with the photographer, despite being engaged to Alphonse (Jean-Pierre Léaud), the star. She will end up leaving with a third scoundrel, the stuntman, which precipitates a major crisis that culminates in a fit of hysteria by Julie. The latter spends a night with Alphonse to console him and prevent him from quitting the film. Alphonse hurries off to alert Julie's husband and declare his intention of marrying the latter's wife. Even though Alphonse is culpable, he is less so than Liliane, who triggered this series of catastrophes. Women thus sow disorder on all sides. Even in the film that is being shot by the crew, *Meet Pamela,* we see the heroine leaving her young husband to take up with her father-in-law. At the beginning of the story, women are conspicuous by their absence (Julie has not yet arrived, Séverine never goes to see the rushes), while the ending of the film is marked by their successive departures: the departure of Stacey, of Liliane, of Séverine, and of Julie. Finally, the wife of the assistant director, who persistently plants herself on the set with her knitting so that she can keep an eye on her partner to ensure his (staunch) fidelity, also ends up throwing a hysterical fit, howling: "Your cinema, I find it so oppressive. I despise cinema . . . Yes, I despise it."

In the playful space of the filming, women pose a constant threat. They deceive, lie, desert, or quite simply encroach on the transitional space of play. Ferrand keeps himself carefully shielded from their interferences. He virtuously sends away an unknown young woman who comes to hook up with him one evening so that he can devote himself to a working session with Joëlle (Nathalie Baye), his faithful assistant. The latter escapes from the curse of the feminine by masculinizing herself. For her, sex is something that is perfunctorily performed, as is shown by her brutally aggressive sexual overture to the props man who helps her to change a tire. When she surprises him the following morning in the bed of the wardrobe assistant, all she displays is a smile that is amused and indifferent. After Liliane's departure, she declares, indignantly: "As far as I'm concerned, I would leave a guy for a film, but I would never leave a film for a guy."

Liliane's betrayal marks a decisive turning point in the film's structure, dividing it into two sections: "I think that one laughs more in the first part, which is descriptive, and less so in the second, which is more narrative. The dividing line occurs, roughly, with the first departure, that of Dani."[35] The first half culminates in the grand lyrical passage: "Cinema reigns," in which, to the accompaniment of Georges Delerue's lighthearted, urgent music, a series of shots of the film-shoot follow, involving both day and night scenes, that illustrate the cohesion of the team as a result of the passion and happiness they experience while they are working. An aperitif offered by Alexandre at the bar of the studio brings this section to a close in a festive atmosphere marked by good humor. Here, Ferrand meets the English stuntman who has to double for Julie in the scene involving the car accident.

It is after this last scene that Liliane leaves the team. This desertion takes place in the context of a group of complex figurations. The stuntman doubles for Julie in the role of Pamela at the moment when she is killed at the steering wheel of her car on a winding road atop a cliff. This death takes the spectacular form of a fall into the bottom of a deep ravine, which the camera follows at length. As soon as this scene has finished, Liliane decides to leave for England with her new lover. She meets Julie and explains why she is leaving Alphonse: "He needs a woman, a mistress, a nanny, a nurse, a little sister; I'm not capable of playing all those roles at once." Both the death of Pamela, Alphonse's wife in the film, and the departure of Liliane, his mistress in real life, are tied to the image of a fall. The stuntman who plays Pamela in Julie's place and takes Liliane away joins these two female characters together. In this collection of displacements, we find the theme – familiar from the rest of Truffaut's films – of the disappearance of a hybrid feminine figure (both woman and mother) who provokes chaos within the metaphorical family (composed of the cinema team). As in other films by Truffaut, the fall suggests a failure of the environment and the disintegration of internal supportive structures that maternal love should generate in the early stages of life. Despite the fact that it is Alphonse who manifests the symptoms of this drama in the light and humorous mode that prevails in *Day for Night,* it is Ferrand – the adult double of Alphonse, according to the Truffaut/Léaud formula established by the Doinel series – who remains the true subject.

We find a reference to this image of a denigrated femininity in Ferrand's dream. On three occasions the film presents a digression in the form of an obsessive dream, with each occasion unveiling a little more of the scenario. The sleeping director sees himself in the guise of a young boy, at night, who is going to steal some photos of *Citizen Kane* from behind the iron grating of a theater. The third dream is presided over by a replica of Julie whose voice resounds in Ferrand's head: "Like thieves, like thieves."

This episode relates, of course, to the practices of the young Truffaut, who would go with his friend Lachenay to pilfer from cinema displays in order to enlarge his collection of film photos. One of the dream segments is immediately followed by a shot of the barrier that bars access to the Studios de la Victorine. This collocation of symbols places cinema, for Ferrand, under the sign of the forbidden and the transgressive. The dream sequences, which seem to have no relation to the action, are perfectly integrated within the fantasmatic dimension of the film. If transitional space is threatened by persecutory elements, it is because the harmony between the internal world and external reality is always put in question because of a failure of the feminine: in this instance, maternal love defaults, causing regression and anxiety. To struggle against this failure of the environment-mother, delinquency appears again. The game becomes transgressive, and the theme of theft relates to the defense mechanisms that *The 400 Blows* describes in detail. For Truffaut, "the director is a thief."[36] The choice of *Citizen Kane,* a great film about maternal abandonment,[37] also suggests this schema. When he is dying, Kane utters the word "Rosebud," which is the name of the sled with which he was playing on the day when his mother left him.

Nevertheless, *Day for Night* is a film about repair, and everything is restored to order: Séverine organizes a party for his departure, Stacey is able to complete her role before her pregnancy becomes too visible, Julie reconciles with her husband, and there is even a suggestion that Liliane may come back. The announcement of a marriage between two members of the team in the last moments of the film marks a reconciliation of the masculine and the feminine. Beautiful and charming, the women are forgiven, and disappear.

In contrast to the book, which Truffaut places completely under the sign of the mother and the feminine, the practice of cinema has its foundation in masculine figures who are stable and strong. Significantly, we find in Truffaut's biography that the primary influences that shaped him as a filmmaker were those of André Bazin, and great masters such as Renoir and Hitchcock. *Day for Night,* in fact, insistently addresses problems involved in the relation between the generations, paternity, and filiation, as Truffaut himself observed:

> From the continuity girl who is pregnant by an unknown father, to Julie Baker who (in real life) has married a doctor who could be her father, and who (in the film) goes away with her father-in-law, through Léaud who kills his father, and Valentina Cortese who drinks because her son has leukemia . . . All of that stunned me afterward, when I became aware of it during the course of the editing.[38]

One could also add to this list the mystery surrounding the comings and goings of Alexandre at the airport. We discover that it is not a woman, but rather a handsome young man whom he has come to collect. He tells Séverine of his intention to adopt the young man – Truffaut derived his inspiration for this episode from the couple formed by Jean Cocteau and his adopted son, Édouard Dermithe.[39]

Out of this new figurative gathering, one dominant feature emerges. In the world of *Day for Night,* in contrast to Truffaut's other films (with the exception of *The Wild Child*), powerful fathers reign supreme: Alexandre (Jean-Pierre Aumont), Doctor Nelson (David Markham), the assistant director, and Ferrand himself, who adopts a paternal and benevolent attitude toward all the actors. Alphonse, who always finds himself in the position of a son – in the film of *Meet Pamela,* as well as in his life as an actor – is obliged to bow before their power: Alexandre takes Pamela for himself, and Doctor Nelson takes Julie. If one recalls that the stuntman, described by Liliane as "the only real man," has stolen her away, we see that the fathers win on all fronts. Furthermore, in the course of a conversation with Joëlle, Ferrand evokes Hollywood, which he believes is "full of famous people who are trying hard to achieve the stature of their parents: the Fairbanks, the Barrymores." In the car that is taking them to the airport, Doctor Nelson and Alexandre talk at length about the vulnerability of actors and their need for love. Julie's husband immediately rushes to her aid after the crisis precipitated by Alphonse. His pardon comes so naturally that the film does not bother to register the way in which it happens: Nelson arrives smiling, and the door of Julie's dressing room is closed on the couple's intimacy. Above all, however, it is the fathers of cinema that the story of *Day for Night* celebrates. In another grand lyrical moment in the film, Ferrand opens a parcel of books that contains monographs on all the great directors: Dreyer, Lubitsch, Hawks, Bresson, Rossellini, Hitchcock . . . The telephone rings at the same moment: it is the musician from the film who wants him to listen to the playback of the scene involving disguises. The names of the filmmakers fill the screen to the accompaniment of nostalgic music, that which underscored the tranquil love of Anne and Claude on the island in *Two English Girls.* The love that unites Ferrand to his cultural fathers and his craft is the only kind over which no question mark hangs.

6.3. Cultural fathers: the cinema. Ferrand (François Truffaut), Alphonse (Jean-Pierre Léaud), and Léon Gaumont in *Day for Night,* dir. François Truffaut, 1973.

The shooting of the scene involving disguises takes place to the strains of the same music. Shot in period costumes and by the light of candles, it separates off the rest of the film, marking the successful conclusion of the second part. The glorious moment "Cinema reigns" that punctuates the end of the first half of the film is matched by a melancholy passage in which Julie-Pamela utters the words that Ferrand has stolen from her: "I know that life is disgusting." The shooting is interrupted by a new catastrophe: Alexandre has been killed in a car crash on the road to the airport where he was going one more time to look for his companion. This passage gathers together a constellation of figures. The scene is played out first between Alphonse and Julie, marking the return to work of the team after the personal storms have been resolved. Doctor Nelson has reclaimed his rights over his spouse. The long black dress that the heroine is wearing and the liturgical appearance of the decor evoke a religious ritual, in the course of which Alphonse seems to accept the loss of the forbidden woman. But this symbolic castration is experienced as bereavement. It is accompanied by trappings that are usually associated with a fetishistic cult of nature in Truffaut's works, of which *The Green Room* is the apotheosis. The fetish masks a lack and generates an illusion that allows the reality of separation to be denied. In this context, the renunciation of the object of desire takes a transgressive turn. Alexandre's death confirms this hypothesis. As Jean Collet has very pertinently observed, Alexandre dies "in Nelson's place" (*à la place de Nelson*).[40] Twinned from the beginning, Nelson and Alexandre both occupy, with respect to Julie, the role of the husband-father who steals her from the son. From the first sequence in the film, the murder of the father is enacted in the course of the fiction: Alphonse takes aim at Alexandre in the street. In addition, the same scene, filmed with a double standing in for the dead actor, closes the shooting of the film. This murder arises from a pre-Oedipal impulse to rebel against paternal authority, and not from a passage toward maturity.

At a symbolic level, however, the real-life death of Alexandre refers to the death of classical cinema. Alexandre is an experienced actor who has a long career behind him, just like Jean-Pierre Aumont, who is playing him. In this second scenario, it is no longer Alphonse who is confronted by a paternal image, but Ferrand, who is living through his mourning for the fathers of cinema and the art that they have handed down to him. The scene that follows is very moving in this respect. As Jean-François Stévenin explains,[41] it was improvised during a shoot that took place on a rainy day. In it, we see Ferrand, in a long shot, making a round of the studio's square in a small vehicle, while he utters the following words in a voice-over:

> Ever since I have been making cinema, I have been dreading what has just happened: the stalling of filming because of the death of an actor. A whole period of cinema is going to disappear at the same time as Alexandre. Studios are being abandoned; films are being made in the streets without a star and without a screenplay. There will be no more films like *Meet Pamela*.

The immense statue of Lincoln that technicians take onto the set in the sequence "Cinema reigns" announces this melancholy reflection and the irruption of death in the form of a grandiose paternal figure frozen in a glory that is past. We should not see this tragically tinted vision as delivering a judgment on classical narrative cinema, which Truffaut would defend to the end, but rather as the image of an internal landscape in which the conditions of creativity are inscribed for Ferrand. Cinema, the space of creativity, assumes the value of a fetish in Ferrand's imaginary. The practice of it prolongs the cinephilia of childhood; it also masks a lack and a deprivation. Death marks the limits of this system of defense; this is the reality that the edifice carefully erected by Ferrand turns out to be incapable of erasing. The shadow side of *Day for Night* manifests itself in this gloomy realization. In the final moments of the film, Ferrand refuses to speak to the reporter about Alexandre's death. He tells him to go and talk to Alphonse. The reporter: "He doesn't want to either . . . He doesn't want to talk about death." Ferrand: "I am sorry, it is too special."

The passage of time, and death, are the true enemies of the creative activity that the film depicts. The photographs that punctuate the story underline this fact. Each time a photo is taken of the team, someone is missing: Liliane, Alphonse, or someone else. Séverine, before leaving, with tears in her eyes, looks at the photos of the film-shoot, the end of which marks the dispersal of the family of the film: "Life's funny, isn't it. We meet, we work together, we love one another . . . And then afterward, we don't have the time to take anything that . . . pffftt . . . it's no longer there. You see, it's no longer there!"

But on the level of the imaginary, the airport and the car are also associated with death, with that of Alexandre combining the two. There is no need to stress the importance of cars in this movie. We can see in this motif, which extends throughout the film, the impact left on Truffaut's sensibility by the tragic death of Françoise Dorléac, who died at the wheel of her car on the road to Nice in 1967. The last words uttered by the assistant director to the members of the team who are dispersing in different automobiles at the end of the film is to wish them a safe journey, and to urge them to take care. The airport is a more ambiguous symbol. It represents the opening of the studio onto life, its mysteries, and its dangers. Julie arrives at it in a fine scene that is full of excitement and bristling with the curiosity of journalists. Alexandre waits patiently for love in it. Doctor Nelson departs from it without any inkling of the drama that will bring him back to it. The noise of jets that interrupts the shooting symbolically suggests the threat residing in the outside, in private life, of the unforeseen. Given that the film contains several references to Cocteau, one can imagine that Truffaut derived his inspiration for the association of the airport with death from an episode in the *Testament of Orpheus.* Analyzing the scene of the death of the poet transfixed by Minerva's javelin, Truffaut, in *The Films of My Life,* wrote: "The stroke of genius that makes this scene work was, in the end, the addition of sound. The enormous roar of a jet taking off accompanies the spear-throwing. The poet dies in the inhuman noise that everybody is familiar with at airports."[42] The jets that cross the sky above the Studios de la Victorine allow a shadow to float over the protected world of the film-shoot: the possibility that life is a force whose swift movement propels one toward death. In *The Soft Skin,* Pierre Lachenay yields to the temptation to embrace this flight, which is placed under the sign of the feminine, and meets a brutal and premature demise at the end of its trajectory.

Truffaut summarized the real question posed by *Day for Night* thus:

> Through the young actor played by Jean-Pierre Léaud, I always deal with the question that has tormented me for more than thirty years: is cinema more important than life? To ask that question is about as intelligent as asking: "Do you prefer your father or your mother?" But I think of the cinema for so many hours each day, and have done so for so many years, that I am not able to prevent myself from making life compete with films, and from reproaching life for not having been as well-constructed, as interesting, as dense, as intense as the images that we organize. "There are no traffic jams in films, says Ferrand to Jean-Pierre Léaud, no troughs, no downtimes. Films move forward like trains in the night."[43]

Despite the emotive words Truffaut uses to evoke it, the dichotomy between life and cinema is not straightforward. Although creativity corresponds to the feeling of being alive, it must be able to manifest itself in a continuous way and encompass all aspects of the relationship to reality and to others. In Ferrand's internal world, the intermittency of this experience, which translates into a contrast between the euphoria of filming and the emptiness of reality once the work has finished, reveals an internal deficiency that the other films describe. Sustained by strong paternal representations, the creative moment allows the persecutory elements that, in real life, prevent a free expansion of one's personality, to be put aside. It is clear that the other great question in *Day for Night* – "Are women magical?" – directly relates to the first one. If woman can become real and not magical, cinema would be inscribed within the continuity of life and not against it, and death would cease to be "special" by becoming the natural fruition of things. The success of

Day for Night is in having been able to describe, in spite of this deficiency, the "other scene," in which day transforms itself into a fertile night of the imagination in order to make possible the creation of a magical object. This magic reflects back onto the women who participate in its creation, that is to say, the actresses, as can be seen with Lillian and Dorothy Gish, to whom *Day for Night* is dedicated.

The book and the film inscribe being within the continuity of a communication with the world and a transmission of experience, which, for Truffaut, represent the two royal avenues of approach to external reality. The achievement of *Fahrenheit 451* and of *Day for Night* is to have been able to evoke simultaneously the intensity of this phenomenon and the violence of the conflicts that provide an obstacle to its free manifestation. In this regard, the two films represent inverse trajectories. *Fahrenheit 451* describes a progressive coming together of the internal world and external reality, while *Day for Night* follows the slow crumbling of the harmony that the first images celebrate with such passion. The conflicts evoked by the two films are particularly profound, given that they involve murderous confrontations with parental figures, transgression, delinquency, and fetishism. Nevertheless, every human being can recognize in this itinerary exaggerated and stylized aspects of his or her own existence. This oscillation between living and not living, whatever the specific forms of it might take for particular individuals, is, in fact, universal. It is through cultural experiences that an individual comes to know a continuity that transcends personal experience. Creativity as a feeling of being is a fundamental, permanent gift that is inherent in the human condition because, as Winnicott observes, acceptance of reality is a task that remains forever unachieved.

7

Marriages
Mississippi Mermaid (1969)
Bed and Board (1970)

AT THE TIME WHEN *BED AND BOARD* WAS RELEASED, TRUFFAUT made the following observation:

> I class myself among the group of directors for whom cinema is an extension of youth, who, just like children who have been sent to play in a corner and remake the world with toys, continue to play as adults by making films. This is what I call "cinema from the room at the back," involving a refusal to accept life as it is, or the world in its real state and, in reaction, an acceptance of the need to re-create something that has a bit of the quality of fairy stories about it, rather like the American cinema that made us dream when we were young.[1]

This declaration, while it applies to all his works, reflects more than anything else the degree to which Truffaut remained distanced from his own times during the years following May 1968. *Mississippi Mermaid* and *Bed and Board* are both characterized by unreality. Removed from ideological commitments, Truffaut cultivated the style of the masters. In the first of these movies, he adopts the formula of a melodrama that combines the influences of Renoir and Hitchcock, and in the second one, those of Lubitsch's comedies seasoned with a dash of Guitry. Being the works of a cinephile that were aimed at a mass audience, these films were not very successful when they were released. Nevertheless, their experimental nature does not mean that they are devoid of emotion. The sincerity of the representation of love in *Mississippi Mermaid,* and a degree of awkwardness in the handling of certain aspects of its structure, turn it into what one could describe as "a little sick film" that appeals to those who love Truffaut's works. The power of the film derives from its melodic line, from the continuity of its interior vision, which follows the course of a metaphorical journey that is not spatially interrupted. In contrast, *Bed and Board,* a static film that centers on an apartment building, exploits discontinuity. Gags, improvisation, and wordplay are uppermost in a story in which the scene forms the narrative unit. Although one is a film-river and the other is a film-mosaic, these two works both have as their subject the early stages of the life of a married couple, describing the pitfalls that threaten its precarious harmony. Both end on a note that is full of ambiguity. But their deep subject remains the eternal dialectic between solitude and intimacy, which is at the very heart of the experience of the spectator who is watching cinema.

MISSISSIPPI MERMAID (1969)

The original screenplay of *Mississippi Mermaid* includes a scene in which the hero, Louis Mahé (Jean-Paul Belmondo), goes to buy stockings for Marion (Catherine Deneuve), the woman he loves. Truffaut had already shot this scene in two other films, *Shoot the Piano Player* and *The Soft Skin,* in which Léna and Nicole ask their lover to get them a pair of stockings. The scene takes place in a shop: "There are saleswomen, and seeing this man buy stockings makes them smile, and there it is. It was a scene about nothing at all, but it was difficult to do."[2] Truffaut had cut this scene from the two earlier films because on each occasion he considered that it had been muffed. The reason he invested these images with such importance that no representation of them could ever satisfy him is because they sum up, in condensed form, the dilemma of the characters: that is to say, the impossibility of socializing desire. To buy stockings, in the imaginary of Truffaut's oeuvre, is to lay claim publicly – but the audience here is composed exclusively of women – to ownership of the female body. Charlie Kohler, like Pierre Lachenay, is incapable of it. Louis Mahé is their brother. His story is going to illuminate the other side of these tormented personalities. At first sight, he does not appear to show the slightest signs of dissociation. He consistently follows the impulses arising from his inner being, and his words and actions reflect these throughout the story. Nevertheless, as Winnicott notes, "the healthy person's inner world is related to the outer or actual world and reality and yet is personal and capable of an aliveness of its own."[3] This harmony between the inner and outer worlds is missing in Louis, just as it is lacking in the pianist, or Lachenay. The link bridging the two spheres of experience is broken. Louis is content with eliminating one side of the equation. External reality troubles him; he abolishes it. In the face of the constraints of the external environment, he chooses to steal away and strip himself, little by little, of everything that constitutes the social being of an individual. The rich owner of a cigarette factory on the island of La Réunion, having fallen in love, he abandons his house, his position, and his goods, only to find himself a penniless vagabond, a murderer, and a fugitive. And even if there is no trace of the shadow of a false self attaching itself to him, there is equally nothing to suggest that he has found a true self. Prisoner of a passion that is deaf and blind, he exposes himself, vulnerable, to wounds inflicted by the other. This irrational inclination constitutes the beauty of the film, conferring on it a lyrical power that likens it to Godard's *Pierrot le Fou*.

Louis's madness is not entirely lacking in lucidity, as a powerful scene in the second half of the film shows. Being hunted by the police, and with no money, Louis returns to La Réunion to suggest to his authorized representative, Jardine (Marcel Berbert), that he buy back his cigarette factory. One shot shows him, looking from the outside at the Jardine family at dinner through a window: the mother is serving the meal; we hear the laughter of two children. This is the impossible image of conjugal life that he was pursuing when, at the beginning of the story, he was waiting for the young unknown woman from Noumea who had replied to his advertisement in the personal columns offering marriage. As Truffaut remarked, "when all is said and done, *Mississippi Mermaid* is the story of a guy who marries a woman who is exactly the opposite of what he wanted. But love entered into the scene, and he accepts her just as she is."[4] This is what Louis tries to explain to Jardine, the realist who, throughout the film, converts life into statistics. Louis rejects these normalizing criteria. For him, it is a matter not even of happiness, but of survival. "I don't know if I am happy," he says to Jardine, "but I can't live without her." So deeply true is this that, during the only time in the film when he is separated from Marion, he suffers a nervous breakdown. The conflicts that torment Charlie and Lachenay are absent from this film, but Louis is, nevertheless, like them, a man who is damaged and fragmented. His loneliness is as profound as theirs.

Vincent Canby, one of the few critics to have recognized the unusual beauty of this film,[5] noted that the credit sequence of *Mississippi Mermaid* contains a tragic expression of this loneliness in the background music. Men and women's voices, among which we recognize that of Truffaut, are reading wedding announcements. In the course of the film, Louis says to Marion: "I think that people who place ads in the personal columns are idealists. In five lines they try to transform their life and, in five lines that they spend hours trying to compose, they try to capture everything in a few words . . . their hopes, their dreams, their ideas about life as it ought to be." Hope, in this story, is translated into a breathless spatial movement. In contrast to Charlie and Lachenay, Louis has no fear of the outside; he rushes into it from the first image of the film, which follows the course of a car on a road atop a cliff. Not only does he leave La Réunion, but also the Heurtebise clinic,[6] as well as the house in Aix-en-Provence, and the apartment in Lyon. Each departure marks a point of no return. The external world no longer exists in *Mississippi Mermaid;* the hero's field of vision is restricted solely to the object of desire. When he leaves the little house in the snow with Marion – the same one used by Charlie at the end of *Shoot the Piano Player,* the house of childhood – it is not so much the Swiss frontier that they are looking to attain together, as the mythical frontier of adult love.

From the beginning of the film, Louis knows, along with the spectator, that he has been tricked: Julie Roussel, the fiancée from Noumea, will never descend the gangway of *The Mississippi Mermaid.* Disappointed, Louis goes back to his car and finds there a beautiful, unknown young woman who pretends to be the one he was expecting. She does not resemble the photo he had been sent: a lie, she admits. Louis accepts that. Signs that her arrival marks a deception multiply. In the end, the false Julie absconds with the fortune of her new husband. When the sister of the real Julie announces the imposture, he hires a detective, Comolli (Michel Bouquet), to find her, and then pursues her into France, where he catches up with her. She is called Marion, and it turns out that she assumed Julie's identity on the ship when Julie's lover threw the latter overboard. Caught up in his passion, Louis kills the detective who is on their traces, for her sake. The lovers flee ever further to escape the police.

As she is descending from the ship, Marion is holding a cage that contains a singing canary. It will soon die. The image of the imprisoned bird suggests Louis's dream as much as the young woman. Immediately after her marriage, we see her suffocating during the night in the marital bedroom. She cannot bear being shut in the darkness, any more than she can bear the chains of marriage, and constantly seeks a means of getting away. In the house on La Réunion, one shot shows her with her head on her husband's lap, one morning, filmed through the balustrade of the stairway. The bars seem to enclose her in a cage like a bird. Throughout the film, Louis hinders her ability to take off, and at the end she decides to poison him in order to free herself.

In *Mississippi Mermaid,* the feminine is presented as a series of attributes that are impossible to grasp and unable to be deciphered. When he discovers the simultaneous disappearance of his wife and his fortune, Louis, in a fit of rage, tears up Marion's white lingerie and throws it in the fire. But his is a rage that burns with passion. We later encounter the image of flames again, in one of the most beautiful scenes in the film – the fireside scene in which Louis describes Marion's face in the words of someone madly in love. Dazzled by her splendor, he has to shut his eyes: "No, it's too much . . . It makes my eyes hurt to look at you . . . I have my eyes shut, and yet I can see you perfectly . . . I swear . . . If I were blind, I would spend my time caressing your face."

Marion is a vision that it burns Louis to touch. Photographs and mirrors abound in the story: the photo of Marion which, as an expression of his possessive love, Louis has had reproduced on the cigarette packets made by his factory; the mirror in which she is reflected during her confession at the Hotel Monorail.[7] It is because of an image that Louis is able to find her again: he sees her dancing on television, dressed in red and black. She has become a hostess at a nightclub, the Phoenix. An evanescent reflection that one can neither embrace nor detain, Marion is a being from the imaginary. But Comolli, who finds the hero by chance at Aix, points out that no one who has seen her ever forgets her – just like an image from a beautiful film. It is appropriate that, on the same afternoon, Louis goes to the cinema.

The originality of *Mississippi Mermaid* derives from the isolation of the lovers. It is the only film by Truffaut in which love escapes from a

7.1. An idealized vision. Louis Mahé (Jean-Paul Belmondo) and Marion (Catherine Deneuve) in *Mississippi Mermaid,* dir. François Truffaut, 1969.

ternary structure: "There is no second man and no second woman, and I was able to concentrate exclusively on the intimacy of a single couple."[8] The happiness the two of them have together is expressed in many scenes, especially those depicting a series of breakfasts taken in a tender tête-à-tête. The film also reflects, through a constant oscillation between the use of "vous" and "tu," the indecisiveness of the couple concerning distance and closeness. A third term exists, however, that is revealed just beneath the surface of the film: first of all, Comolli, with a very paternal authority, begins by separating Louis from Marion, by cutting the photo of their marriage in two; then, after Comolli's death, the police naturally take over his role as the representative of a symbolic law that forbids the fusion of the couple. These symbolic figures of the father, however, play only a secondary role in a story that unfolds entirely under the sign of a two-way relation with a female figure. In a way that is very complex, the prohibition that weighs on love emanates from her.

Who is Marion? A whore or a fairy? This film raises the question that was posed in *The 400 Blows.*While the scene by the fireplace presents an idealized image of her, two other monologues by Louis define her in a way that is singularly more brutal. When he finds her at the Hotel Monorail, Louis compares her with the first girls who came to settle in La Réunion – not orphans, as he had said earlier, but prostitutes. In the course of a second confrontation, in Lyons, he speaks of a certain type of modern women: "Not really tarts, nor adventuresses, nor whores, but a kind of parasite who lives outside of normal society." Although Marion escapes definition, she expresses herself in the film through two particular modalities: sexuality and money, neither of which answers to the emotional needs of Louis. Whether Marion abruptly refuses to make love, or wants to make love fully clothed, as occurs immediately after Comolli's murder, the film presents her sexual impulses as an unknown continent that her husband docilely explores. Her attitude toward money is more direct. As soon as it is in short supply, she displays an icy indifference toward Louis that pushes him as far as murder. During the latter's voyage to La Réunion, however, she records a disk that she sends him containing a declaration of love that is full of emotion: "For some time, as you well know, I have not been able to live without you." The record falls on to the ground and shatters into a thousand pieces, carrying with it the secret of this avowal.

Truffaut said that he had wanted to attempt a traditional subject of the kind found in pre-war cinema: "We see it in *The Woman and the Puppet, The Blue Angel, La Chienne* . . . This theme of the femme fatale, of a vamp subjugating an honest man to the extent that he becomes a puppet; all the filmmakers I admire have tackled this theme. I say to myself: it has to be done . . . And then I realize that I can't do it."[9] Marion is, in fact, a complex being in whom calculation never seems entirely to exclude sincerity. She explains to Louis: "One day you got angry at me because I didn't want to read a book that you had chosen for me. You have accused me of wasting my time reading trashy romances like *A tout coeur, Confidences, Nous deux.* What you don't know is that what is contained in those books resembles the life of girls like me." As far as the mode of representation is concerned, the film conforms to this model rather than that of the classics cited above. Speaking of *Mississippi Mermaid,* Truffaut said that he had wanted to make "a sincere film, which nevertheless would try to look like a photo-romance . . . I tried to find ways of introducing in the same sequence both a 'cliché' and an emotion; viewers predominantly registered the 'clichés,' they were less receptive to the sincerity."[10] The film also contains an overt reference to this kind of work. When the couple are coming out of a cinema in which they have seen *Johnny Guitar,* Marion says to Louis: "It is not only a film

7.2. Rat poison signals Marion's intention to kill her husband. Louis Mahé (Jean-Paul Belmondo) and Marion (Catherine Deneuve) in *Mississippi Mermaid,* dir. François Truffaut, 1969.

with horses." "No," Louis replies to her, "it's a love story with emotions." In the same way, *Mississippi Mermaid* is a "false adventure film" (*faux film d'aventures*).[11] There are numerous examples of its double nature. One might cite, in particular, the scene in which Louis arrives at the Hotel Monorail to kill Marion. He abandons his project when he sees her, remarking: "A revolver is not a magical object." But the most powerful example occurs at the end of the film. While reading, by chance, a cartoon describing the poisoning of Snow White by the witch, Louis suddenly realizes that Marion has done the same thing to him. He says so to her, adding that he accepts it. The "tart," instead of fleeing or denying it, bursts into sobs, crying out: "I'm ashamed. No woman is worthy of being loved like that. I am despicable." This rupture of tone creates a mysterious aura around *Mississippi Mermaid.* But what is the nature of the emotion in the film? What does it really say about love? Who are Marion *and* Louis?

The most intriguing aspect of *Mississippi Mermaid* concerns the sexual identity of the characters. Truffaut drew attention to the complexity of this question when he explained: "A secret preconception drove me on in my work when I was making this film: for me, Catherine [Deneuve] was a boy, a hoodlum who had had all kinds of fun and games, and Jean-Paul [Belmondo] a young girl who was expecting everything from her marriage."[12] He added that, in spirit, Belmondo was "a virgin." When she recounts the story of her life, Marion describes a past that resembles, blow for blow, that of Camille in *A Gorgeous Girl Like Me:* precocious sexuality, thieving, and delinquency. We know the kinship that unites Camille with her creator. As in *A Gorgeous Girl,* Truffaut projects himself doubly in *Mississippi Mermaid,*[13] but the two characters in it are equals. Louis and Marion represent two sides of the same human being, a strange couple that can be explained by drawing on Winnicott's profound insights regarding bisexuality. In Winnicott's view, the feeling of being that constitutes the basis of all identity is linked, for both men and women, to the transmission of a maternal, feminine element that finds its fulfilment in the exercise of creativity: "The male element *does,*while the female element (in males and females) *is.*"[14] Being depends on a primary identification between a child and its mother in the phase of non-separation; it contrasts with doing, which only arrives on the scene at a later stage of development: "After being – doing and being done to. But first, being."[15] A deficiency in the environment-mother paralyzes the capacity of the child to be, and provokes a split between the feminine element and the masculine element that hinders the maturation of personality. Truffaut's films show the source of this inner dissociation at work in a variety of forms. "The mother who "is" to a lesser extent than she "does" imparts an identity to the child that is that of someone who *does as if,*"[16] that is to say, someone who operates through a false self. In *Day for Night,* creativity is defined as a feeling of being, the intermittent nature of which is tied to a failure of the environment-mother. In *A Gorgeous Girl,* and to a lesser extent in *The Bride Wore Black,* Truffaut liberates this dissociated female element, depicting both its shortcomings, which are apparent in antisocial behavior, and also its irresistible vital force. To mark this split between being and doing in *Mississippi Mermaid,* Truffaut projects the feminine element onto the man and the masculine onto the woman. This schema is recurrent in his films, as he himself remarked: "Usually, it is the heroine who takes the initiatives; usually, it is the hero who is affected by the story."[17] It is the damaged feminine element, however, that is of interest in this instance. This is what leads to lack of satisfaction, theft, and delinquency. Louis seems to contemplate this dissociated part of himself – without which he will never be able to become a man – helplessly.[18] Dedicated to Renoir, *Mississippi Mermaid* alludes to a passage from *La Marseillaise* in which the revolutionary and royalist troops fraternize instead of fighting with one another. The name of the island of La Réunion commemorates this event. This film buff's metaphor strikingly illustrates the subject of a film that follows an attempt to achieve a "reunion" of the split-off feminine with the masculine. Such a return to unity is difficult, full of conflict, and painful: "I am starting to experience love, Louis, that hurts . . . Does love hurt?" says Marion at the end of the film. The couple then depart in the snow toward the unknown, just as at the end of *The Grand Illusion*.

Mississippi Mermaid is also a love story about a real-life man and a woman. During its shooting, Truffaut and Catherine Deneuve began a relationship that was very important in the life of the filmmaker. When *The Last Metro* reunited them in 1980, Truffaut included in the passage that Marion Steiner recites the final lines from *Mississippi Mermaid* spoken by Marion.

BED AND BOARD (1970)

The Doinel cycle owes its unity to the strength of the character created by Jean-Pierre Léaud because, stylistically, nothing is more disparate that the series of films that comprise it. Compared with the realism of *The 400 Blows,* which reflects the influence of Rossellini, *Stolen Kisses* displays a kind of genial improvisation, constituting the most natural language that Truffaut spoke in any of his films. In the first film, the subject matter is of supreme importance; in the second, a rare balance is established between the content and the containing form. *Bed and Board* presents a third formula. The subject of the film is no longer the story but the act of narration. Saying takes primacy over the said. The discrepancy between them reflects the influence of Lubitsch and his American comedies on Truffaut's work. In this film, which is rather anachronistic, Truffaut tries to recover the cinematic language of a bygone era:

> For some years now, I have been influenced by Lubitsch, whose films I have looked at very closely, being enthusiastic about this very singular kind of wit that disappeared after having had an enormous importance in its own time, especially for McCarey and Hitchcock. It consists of arriving at things via a

> circuitous route, of asking oneself: given that one has to make such-and-such a situation understood by the audience, what is the most indirect, roundabout way of presenting it?[19]

An indirect style implies a distancing and a certain degree of abstraction in the way the mise-en-scène is contrived: "Lubitsch wasn't looking to make the spectator believe the story. He takes us by the hand and systematically demonstrates the mechanisms that he sets in motion. He tells us a story and pulls a prank every two minutes to show us that he is telling a story."[20] *Bed and Board* is certainly not Truffaut's most successful film, but it contains many scenes in which the ingenuity of formal devices and strategies wins over the viewer. For Truffaut, the subject of "Doinel married" provided an ideal terrain for this kind of exercise. Doinel's character presented him with particular problems, and the filmmaker noted that he tended to express himself more spontaneously in his other films:

> I have a great propensity for talking about myself, and a great reluctance to do so directly. For this reason, I get the feeling that I've been more intimate and more sincere in films based on borrowed subjects – *Mississippi Mermaid, The Wild Child, Two English Girls* – than in the Doinel films, in which I was constantly dreading an identification of Jean-Pierre Léaud with me.[21]

Bed and Board was all the more problematic given that Antoine's age was close to that of his creator. Moreover, Truffaut had not anticipated making a sequel to *Stolen Kisses,* and it was Henri Langlois who advised him to show "the little couple" married. He then thought that *Bed and Board* would be the last of the series because the continuation of the film existed already: "It is in *Shoot the Piano Player, The Soft Skin,* and, if one wants to include it in dream form, in *Fahrenheit.* I think that I have always filmed the same leading character, and that I have asked everyone to act like Léaud does. I even think that he is the character in *Mississippi Mermaid.*"[22]

The second problem more directly concerns the subject of the film, that is to say, adultery. After *Jules and Jim,* Truffaut was criticized for having presented an ideal, complacent vision of this phenomenon: "Because people loved *Jules and Jim,* I felt a kind of irritation, and said to myself that it was my fault because I hadn't made the film sufficiently pessimistic, not hard enough; for that reason, I then wanted to make *The Soft*

Skin to show that love is something far less euphoric, less exalted."[23] The failure of this film, however, again caused Truffaut to feel "dissatisfied, and *Bed and Board* was a response to *The Soft Skin*."[24] As he explained, it was a light-hearted "remake" of the earlier film: "And in the end, when *Bed and Board* had been finished, I realized that it, too, was sad . . . When one is dealing with adultery, it is not funny and, in order to make it light-hearted, it is necessary to tell lies, as in certain American comedies."[25] This takes us back to Lubitsch and confirms, yet again, that Truffaut never used style gratuitously. The devices furnished by the "American comedy" genre allowed both the character and the subject of the film to be placed at a distance. Moreover, Truffaut, by adopting an indirect style as the main focus of his work, was able to explore the attributes of the kind of dissociation that we have seen operating in different forms in all of his adult masculine heroes. The piano player, Lachenay, and Louis Mahé are Doinel's doubles; the latter is by no means exempt from their symptoms. The stylistic devices exploited by Truffaut in *Bed and Board* serve, in fact, to reveal his illness. As Annette Insdorf has demonstrated, the subject of the film is communication, in all its various forms, and, in the end, its failure.[26] The problem of languages dominates this work, in which the hero, like Victor in *The Wild Child,* tries endlessly to unite the two terms of a signifying system that eludes his control.

Bed and Board depicts Antoine Doinel (Jean-Pierre Léaud) as being lost in a forest of signs that he is trying hard to decipher. There is a lot of talking in this film, in which we almost never see a character alone on the screen, with conversational exchanges taking place in each scene. Moreover, the central space in the story is a courtyard, which evokes that in Renoir's *The Crime of Monsieur Lange,* where many characters encounter one another, eager to express themselves. Nevertheless, the sense of a profound solitude emerges out of this bustling crowd. As Antoine's colleague at work says: "When I am home alone at night, I am scared. I would marry a gas lamp provided it gave me some conversation." Above all, the multiplication of signs seems destined to fill in a void; for most of the time, it does not relate to any reality. Everyone pursues his or her obsession, from the waitress who wants to sleep with Antoine, to the pensioner who will only leave his house when Pétain is buried at Verdun, through the opera singer who, tired of waiting for his wife, throws

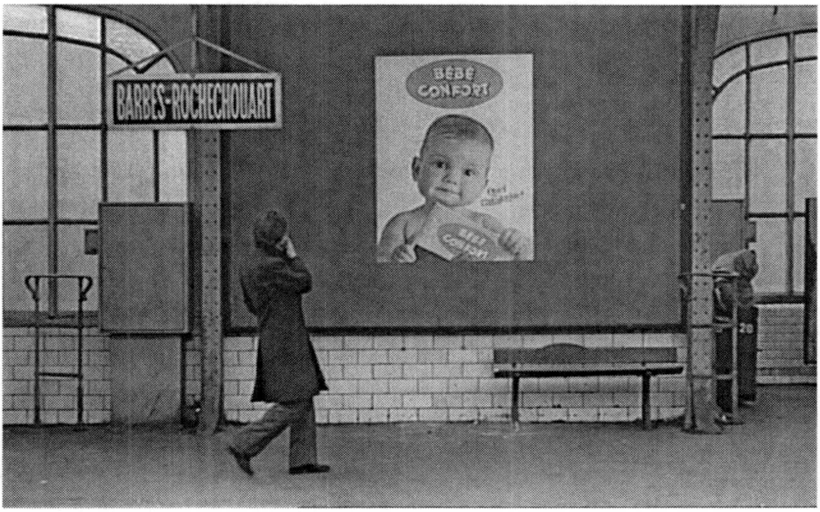

7.3. Antoine Doinel (Jean-Pierre Léaud) lost in a forest of signs, in *Bed and Board,* dir. François Truffaut, 1970.

her coat and bag down the stairs. These messages have no effect. Space is encumbered with useless objects, such as the library ladder Antoine buys when he has no library. This piece of equipment is ingenious and available, but the reality that it is designed to address is absent. There are also messages that go astray en route and arrive at the wrong destination. Antoine has no reason to be anything other than happy when a letter of recommendation designed to pull strings for a young man of means is taken as referring to him, which allows him to obtain a job. But when the tender words that his Japanese mistress has concealed in the tulips literally fall under Christine's nose, the affair turns sour.

The first scene poses the problem from the outset. Christine's legs traverse the screen, and in a voiceover we twice hear a shopkeeper who has addressed her as "mademoiselle" being corrected: "No, not mademoiselle, madam." Here is the first message that has been imperfectly received: Madame Doinel does not give the impression of being a married woman. There is another disconcerting message: the legs of desire have become those of the law. This transferral is perhaps the original cause of the malfunction that operates throughout the film. Marriage blurs the codes, alters the language of desire, of the couple, of social exchanges, and distorts the relationship between words and things. An example of this can be found in the "remake" of the kiss in the cellar: as in *Stolen Kisses,* when the pair descend to look for a bottle of wine, Christine (Claude Jade) asks Antoine to kiss her. Ritual replaces desire; the sign has become empty.

In a moment of anger, Christine accuses her husband of taking pleasure in "what is blurred, vague, equivocal, ambiguous," while she only likes "what is clear-cut." These adjectives could be applied to the different kinds of communication that the story depicts. Examples of different types of language abound in the film. The language of flowers: Antoine, who, at the beginning of the film, colors carnations for his living, is looking for a uniform red; the flowers become black, denoting the failure of his marriage. The language of images: Christine refuses to tell him where she is going when she goes to visit a gynecologist; Antoine guesses her destination when he sees a baby on a poster on the walls of the metro. Foreign languages: Antoine has an Ionesco-like conversation with his American boss in which he replies to questions that he does not understand with phrases from a learner's textbook; with his Japanese mistress, he sinks into a linguistic no-man's land that transforms their intimacy into a nightmare. Silent language: after she discovers Antoine's adultery, Christine welcomes him back into the house, dressed as a geisha, with tears in her eyes. Even when he finds himself alone in a brothel with a prostitute, Antoine delivers a brief monologue that she does not understand: "I hate everything that ends. It's the end of the film." For a system of communication that is well constructed and functional (for example, Christine playing *La Marseillaise* on a violin so that Antoine can intercept a client who has forgotten to pay, in the courtyard), what a lot of messages there are that are lost, ineffectual, or wrongly interpreted! The mysterious man whom the inhabitants of the courtyard fear and call the strangler turns out to be merely a simple variety-show performer. One day he appears on television, demonstrating how faulty the collective attempt to decipher him has been. The most powerful example of the complexities of communication, however, is that of the telephone. The Doinels do not have one. At the beginning of the film, Christine is alerted to the fact that her mother is calling her to the café in the court-

7.4. Silent language: Christine (Claude Jade) dressed as a geisha in *Bed and Board,* dir. François Truffaut, 1970.

yard through a byzantine system of human relays. When they do get a telephone, thanks to the intervention of a senator, Antoine tries to call the speaking clock, but gets the Cochin Hospital instead. Then, when Christine criticizes his letter of thanks, he falls into a black rage, declaring that he has no need of any telephone because "he never gets bored." However, at the end of the film, alone in a téte-à-téte with his mistress at the restaurant, he sinks into such a depression that he spends the evening telephoning his wife. The final time he returns to the table, he finds that the Japanese woman has left him a sarcastic note: "Go and fuck yourself." That is the end of the adultery. The message in these scenes is twofold: the telephone does not work well; no one can pretend to do without it. It is the telephone that reconciles the couple.

The epilogue of the film also presents an ambivalent message:

> I originally had a happy ending, but we see Jean-Pierre Léaud behaving like the opera singer behaved, that is to say, he takes the coat and purse of his wife and throws them down the stairs; he has become a husband like him. But I had wanted to counterbalance that, to show that it is not very serious, by making the singer's wife say to the neighbor: "You see, dear, they are like us – now they truly

> love one another." But I don't want to finish it like that any longer: I show the singer grimacing, which lets us know that he doesn't agree with what his wife is saying – in other words, each shot contradicts the preceding one in this film, in which two happy manifestations are followed by two unhappy ones.[27]

In *Bed and Board,* Antoine is writing a book. During one of the most successful scenes in the film, Christine accuses him of "smearing the family" by recounting his childhood, and says to him that "a work of art is not a settling of scores." With this film, Truffaut seems to uncouple himself from his double, subjecting him to a particularly harsh critical scrutiny. But while Doinel is sometimes revealed in it as pitiful, the film as a whole celebrates the art of storytelling and the pleasure of toying with the spectator. Even though messages do not always arrive at their destination, and they are too confused to coincide with any kind of reality, as Truffaut says in the words with which he dedicates the film to Sachy Guitry, "[his] genius flourished in dialogue" that gives the impression of "definitive improvisation." The exchanges between the Doinel couple often attain this elevated state in which language reigns supreme. One only has to recall the scene in which Antoine undertakes to describe his wife's breasts, which he views as dissimilar, naming them "Laurel and Hardy" and "Don Quichotte and Sancho Panza." Christine tells him he is completely mad, but the charm of the sign prevails over any realities.

In the chronological order of Truffaut's works, only *The Wild Child* separates *Mississippi Mermaid* from *Bed and Board.* One can scarcely imagine three more different films as far as their mode of expression is concerned. Nevertheless, each of them represents, in various ways, an attempt to find a common language for an ill-assorted couple. Like Itard and his wild child, Louis and Marion, and Antoine and Christine are searching through a forest of opaque and recalcitrant signs to read themselves, understand themselves, and possess themselves. The endings of these three films, as ambiguous as they might be, consolidate a union, the fragility of which has been repeatedly underlined in the story. Instead of endorsing the inevitable return of a repressed past that is destructive, these films attempt to exorcize it. Itard, Louis, and Christine grant to the other – the wild child, the antisocial person, or Doinel the "madman" – a gift that is rewarded by the beginnings of trust. But it is cinema, above all, that triumphs in these films, by providing Truffaut with all the registers of its language, thus giving him a means of orchestrating his improbable dialogues. *The Wild Child* would be the only real success of this series. Giving up working in classical styles, Truffaut invented an entirely original form of expression for this film that would reveal itself in the process of depicting its subject.

8

Words and Things

The Wild Child (1970)
The Story of Adèle H. (1975)

AT THE BEGINNING OF *THE WILD CHILD,* THE YOUNG BOY, who still does not have a name, is placed in an institution for deaf-mutes. That night, in the dormitory, being unable to bear the sheets and mattress, he hides under the bed to sleep. At the end of *The Story of Adèle H.,* Victor Hugo's daughter, who no longer knows who she is, takes refuge in an asylum for the night and, terrified that someone might steal from her, goes to sleep under her bed to protect her suitcase. These paired images mark the link between these two characters, one of whom is condemned to live on this side, and the other on the other side, of the world of exchanges and communication. Even the way in which they sleep is marked with the sign of exclusion. Their narrative destinies reflect one another like an image in a mirror. Referring to the life of Adèle Hugo, Truffaut said: "This biography moved me greatly. Perhaps because it displays the other side of the coin as far as *The Wild Child* is concerned. Like the child of l'Aveyron, Adèle has a problem of identity, but here it is of the opposite kind, given that she is the daughter of the most famous man in the world."[1]

Victor undergoes a difficult process aimed at rooting him in society, while each scene shows Adèle drawing a little further away from her fellow human beings to retreat into madness. For each of them, language manifests the malfunction of their relationship with the world. Victor will never be able to master the principle that unites words with objects; Adèle ends up drowning herself in an ocean of writing, the proliferation of which does not relate to any reality. Things without words, words without things, the dislocation of the system of signification upon which the very notion of culture is based gives rise to an austere reflection in these two films that is extended into the nature of their respective systems of representation. Inspired by "authentic" histories, as stated in their respective credit sequences, both of them illustrate the articulation of the real and the imaginary, of the written record and of fiction.

THE WILD CHILD (1970)

The Wild Child, the second film in the trilogy Truffaut devoted to the theme of childhood, addresses the question of origins – of language, of communication, and of culture. It is a film about "first times": "This child has grown up removed from civilization, so much so that everything he does in the film is being done for the first time."[2] It was also the first time that Truffaut had acted in one of his own films, marking a reversal in the play of identifications: "Up until *The Wild Child,* whenever I had children in my films, I would identify myself with them; then in it, for the first time, I identified myself with the adult, with the father."[3] His decision to play Doctor Itard, who undertakes to educate the wild child, and whose two reports are faithfully reproduced in the film,[4] was, said Truffaut, the "trigger" (*déclic*)[5] that persuaded him to film this story: "From the day I decided to play Itard, the film assumed an all-engrossing purpose for me."[6] As was typically the case, every time he was preoccupied with an idea so deeply that he could not bear to discuss it, Truffaut did not mention this to anyone. When the shooting of the film was already in progress, he wrote to his faithful friend and collaborator since *Jules and Jim,* Jean Gruault, who was the co-author of the screenplay with him: "Forgive me for having been secretive about my intention to act the role of Itard; I was trying to keep it secret until the last moment."[7]

This film also marks the beginning of a remarkable collaboration between Truffaut and Nestor Almendros, "one of the greatest directors of photography in the world,"[8] who would work on eight other films by the director. In his book *Un homme à la caméra,* Almendros provides the following information:

> *The Wild Child* is a homage to the photography of silent films . . . Their style, without any touching-up, had the precision of a fine drawing that has

> disappeared today . . . The techniques of silent cinema achieved an exceptional degree of refinement, but its secrets would disappear with the death of its creators. It is necessary to rediscover these techniques.[9]

Each image in *The Wild Child* reflects the beauty of this early cinematic gaze on the world, which, in film, came to be associated with the regular use of the iris for punctuation. Coming to the conclusion that the iris-effects able to be obtained by contemporary techniques were too mechanical, Truffaut succeeding in finding some actual equipment from the silent era, "an antediluvian vestige" (*vestige antédiluvien*), that was used for the shooting.[10] A film about the secret of origins, *The Wild Child* also celebrates the origins of cinema itself.

From the first shot, an iris aperture on a black screen isolates a peasant woman in a forest. It is through a female glimpse that the existence of the wild child is revealed. The peasant woman is gathering mushrooms when a noise attracts her attention. An indistinct creature races along the ground through the undergrowth and leaves that surround her. The woman looks at this sight for a moment, and then runs away, scared. In the deserted forest, a naked child then appears, moving on four legs, and comes to sniff the abandoned mushrooms. Grabbing them by the handful, he crushes them against his mouth to eat them. We follow him through the forest for a while: he drinks from a stream, lapping the surface like an animal; runs under the leafy branches; and then climbs nimbly to the top of a tree. He settles himself among the branches and rocks himself with a slow movement, to and fro. The camera draws back in a zoom, and an iris-out closes this first sight of the wild child.

A nurturing mother without knowing it, the peasant woman who abandons him in the introduction will be replaced in this metaphoric role by Dr. Itard (François Truffaut). The self-cradling of the wild boy at the end of this sequence is characteristic of young autistic children. The child who has never been cradled in the arms of his mother becomes himself the mother who cradles. Because of this, he loses his identity.[11] In the absence of any object with which he is able to unite himself, he isolates himself from the external world. The development of a relationship between Itard and the child is enacted in the course of the film. We have to wait until the final image in the movie before the child returns the gaze of which he is made the object at its opening. During the story, the camera does not adopt his point of view; he remains sightless, an object, a spectacle. He does not reflect the world, but confuses himself with it.

The first scenes all enforce a visual effacement of the wild child (Jean-Pierre Cargol). He is erased by his environment, into which he blends to the point that on several occasions we do not immediately see his presence in the image. In the first sequence, the forest seems to absorb the child. Later, we again find him buried in the hay of a barn after his capture, so well-disguised that he has to move before we notice him. At the institute of the deaf and dumb, the nurse who is looking for him outside literally has to pull him out of a heap of dead leaves that are covering him. Filmed in long shots, these early scenes also show the child masked by the crowds of people who surround him – at first peasants, then curious Parisians, and finally the young deaf-mutes of the institute, who harass him. It is while he is in the midst of the latter that Dr. Itard, outraged, eventually seizes him bodily in order to protect him. Because of Itard, the wild boy is separated from the environment in which he is merged. Thereafter, he acquires a visual identity and become an autonomous body on the screen. The story has foreshadowed this symbolic birth a little earlier.

Itard's first appearance in the film occurs well before his meeting with the wild child. Straight after the capture of the boy in Aveyron, we observe Itard in his office, the neatness of which contrasts with the confusion that reigns in the scenes set in the country. His voice utters the first intelligible speech in a story that, until then, has been dominated by either silence, or the cries of peasants. In the first image, his face crosses in front of a large anatomical poster of a human face, indicating his scientific vocation. He reads a journal article that describes the events we have just seen, dissects it,[12] and affirms his interest in the child in his commentary (which is delivered in a voice-over, as if it were the text of a newspaper). A flute solo accompanies these images. We find the same musical punctuation repeated, which contrasts with the absence of music in all the other scenes, when an old peasant succeeds in cleaning the face of the wild boy with a sponge moistened in water. For the first time, the boy's features appear on the screen. Washed like a newborn infant, he emerges into the world. The repetition of the flute melody associates Itard with this event.

Vertical space comes to signify the symbolic itinerary of the wild child. From being perched in his tree during his last moments of freedom, he then tries to seek refuge in a burrow when he is being pursued by peasants, who fumigate the hole in order to make him come out. His entry into civilization corresponds to a fall from which only Itard can raise him. When Itard snatches him away from the crowd of young deaf-mutes, he leads him toward a staircase on which he meets the old scholar, Pinel. It is there that he utters the word "education" with respect to the child for the first time. On his arrival back home, Itard makes the child go up to the first floor of the house; the ascending movement is invested with importance by a close-up shot of Victor's bare, muddy feet on the stairs. At the end of the film, it is from the top of the same staircase that the child, having come back by himself after running away, finally returns Itard's glance. During his escape, we saw that he had lost his ability to climb up a tree quickly in the way he used to do. His socialization takes place between these two ascending moments, between the tree and the staircase.

In the prologue, the scene that most clearly marks Victor's emergence into a separate identity simultaneously outlines Itard's pedagogical project. It is one of the great moments in the film; a study of the different drafts of the screenplay confirms that Truffaut rewrote it several times before attaining its semiotic perfection. This silent scene owes nothing to the real-life Itard's original texts. In it, we see Pinel (Jean Dasté), Itard, and the wild boy in a library. On the wall there is a giant diagram showing the anatomical dissection of an ear, the organ through which sound passes, and hence knowledge. A remarkable shot shows the image of the three males in a mirror. Itard, placed behind the boy, offers him an apple, the reflection of which the boy sees in the mirror. Books on the shelves frame the glass of the mirror. Here, as in *Fahrenheit 451,* the apple of knowledge is set in direct relation to cultural objects. The wild child grabs it, with the intention of eating it. This action, reflected in the mirror, marks his potential access to the status of a subject, whereas the preceding scene had reduced him to the condition of an object, naked on an examining table. But this is not the most important aspect of the scene. This image, in which three generations of men are present, for the sake of depicting a patrilineal transmission of the cultural heritage, also symbolically figures the autobiographical elements in the film. Dedicated to Jean-Pierre Léaud, *The Wild Child* is a homage by Truffaut to his favorite actor, whose teacher he had been, just as Itard is for Victor: "While I was shooting the film, I was partially reliving the shooting of *The 400 Blows,* during which I initiated Jean-Pierre Léaud into cinema."[13] *The 400 Blows* was dedicated to Bazin, for whom Truffaut had been the wild child. This image therefore refers to this triple relationship of filiation. Whereas in *The 400 Blows,* Antoine, alone in his home, looks at himself in the three mirrors of the parental bedroom, here Victor is supported by the strong masculine presences who frame him in the image. Nothing could better evoke an environment conducive to the development of a child than Dr. Itard's house, a representation of the transitional space between inside and outside, child and mother, nature and culture. The window – which, along with the mirror, constitutes one of the visual structuring principles of the film – is the very place of this passage. It is there that Victor receives his name, a mark of his social integration; it is there that, on numerous occasions, he comes to dream during exercises; it is through there that he will escape. Itard also goes there often to observe his pupil silently, with his face behind the windowpane.

These examples indicate how the system of representation in the film involves a stylization that excludes any tendency toward documentary: "I succeeded in making an anti-documentary out of very real subject matter," said Truffaut about the film.[14] In a report he wrote on the subject of the screenplay for *The Wild Child,* Rivette insisted on the necessity for this approach:

> *Everything,* in this film, is necessarily "composed" (we are not living in 1798, and "Victor" doesn't exist): both staged and acted. Any attempt to simulate a "documentary," any shooting strategy based on the idea of being a fly-on-the-wall (or wanting to give the illusion of that) would be a lie, and therefore a fault . . . What is needed, it seems to me, is a very obvious, explicit mise-en-scène . . . a precise reconstitution of social conditions and attitudes: a well thought-out "fabrication," and *therefore* poetic.[15]

In this respect, *The Wild Child* is a film that owes a great deal to Hitchcock. In the book that he devoted to him, commenting on *The Wrong Man,* a film that was also based on real events, Truffaut said to Hitchcock: "The main trouble, I think, is that your style, which has found

8.1. Dr Itard (François Truffaut), Professor Philippe Pinel (Jean Dasté), and Victor (Jean-Pierre Cargol) in *The Wild Child*, dir. François Truffaut, 1970.

its perfection in the fiction area, happens to be in total conflict with the esthetics of the documentary . . . Faces, looks, and gestures have been stylized, whereas reality can never be stylized."[16] This formula describes his work in *The Wild Child*. Truffaut has translated the story of Victor into a vast symphonic collection of signs that reflect universal realities. As in *Adèle H.*, the system of representation displays an exceptional economy and legibility: "It is a work characterized by an exhilarating exactness . . . like an electrician, I lay bare the wires, I reduce the number of elements."[17] Several examples will suffice to illustrate the ways in which he stylized reality.

Water is so strongly associated with Victor that Itard on one occasion calls him "our drinker": the water of the streams that the child goes to drink when a coach is taking him to Paris; the water of his first bath that makes him happy, and the rain that drenches his face in the garden; the water that, in accordance with Itard's educational method, founded on the withholding of needs, rewards his exercises. Water, without which life does not exist, is also the vital element that enables the blind-and-deaf girl in Arthur Penn's film *The Miracle Worker* to discover the use of words.[18] It is his sensitivity to the sound "o" that gives Victor his name, without his needing to master a linguistic usage of the phoneme.

From the beginning, fire is associated with civilization. The peasants smoke out Victor's burrow to force him to come out to them. At Itard's house, this fire becomes the less threatening flame of a candle. Two beautiful silent nocturnal scenes frame the story; in them, we see Itard, alone at night, sitting on the edge of his bed, musing by the light of a candle. The first of these scenes precedes his decision to take Victor into his house; the second alternates twice with shots of the child asleep in the forest during the time of his flight, evoking not only the contrast between nature and culture, and sleep and reflection, but also the link that unites the two orders of experience at the end of the film. Another scene suggests the union between the master and his disciple. When an official letter arrives announcing that the government has judged that Victor is incapable of learning, and will not renew Madame Guérin's pension, Itard leaves for Paris to plead her cause. The following shot shows the child alone, playing with the flame of a candle. This silent, peaceful image refutes the clinical aridity of the voice-over in which the text of the letter is being read. In the calm of the night, Victor displays the happiness that he is feeling at handling the instrument of knowledge – not the alphabet, but fire. In the scene that follows, Itard comes into the child's bedroom at night with a candle in his hand. He sits down on his bed, and Victor takes his hand to place it on his face. This gesture of mute tenderness also contradicts the letter, which declares him "incapable of sociability."

In this filmic orchestration, water and fire are joined by milk, which the story associates with the gracious image of young Madame Lemeri with her beautiful blond baby under her arm. During Victor's visits, on several occasions she opens a cupboard to take out her jug of milk so that she can pour a bowl for the child. As in *The 400 Blows,* milk, a maternal element, here serves to emphasize the most fundamental need of children. The insertion of such passages, which involve purely visual lyrical fragments, seizes and captures the imagination of the spectator. They speak across all the languages of the world, and Truffaut's use of them in *The Wild Child* is masterful.

At the heart of the problem addressed by the film is the constant tension we observe between the words of Itard's voice-over reports and

8.2. Victor (Jean-Pierre Cargol) in *The Wild Child,* dir. François Truffaut, 1970.

the image. The first constitutes the dry, realistic observation of a failure: Victor, one is told, will never speak; the second, in contrast, follows the lyrical movement of a successful adaptation to society that Truffaut invests with the power and beauty of a myth of origins. In addition, one is surprised to see the filmmaker talk not only of the child's "spectacular progress," but also of "his acquisition of a certain written vocabulary."[19] As Octave Mannoni explains in his essay on Itard's reports, published before the shooting of the film,[20] words always remain objects for Victor. He never mastered the symbolic function. It is pointless to dwell at length on Itard's pedagogy here,[21] the instructional methods of which, being inspired by Condillac,[22] could only end in an impasse, given that they depended on a faulty theory of language. Furthermore, Victor is not the "natural man" envisaged by the doctor. Truffaut, a greater realist, says that the original "wound" suffered by the child is "beyond healing."[23] But, using Itard's reports as a pretext for projecting elements of his own experience, he transforms the story from an account of failure into one of victory.

Truffaut himself also confirmed the autobiographical element in the film. After declaring that what he loved most about Itard's works was his distinctive style and manner of writing, he noted: "There is, however, an episode in which I found myself represented when I was reading the *Rapports,* and it is that which made me decide to make the film. It is also the only dramatic scene: the unjust punishment Itard inflicts on his pupil in order to make him rebel."[24] This rebellion picks up the theme of delinquency dealt with in *The 400 Blows,* but here it is given its true interpretation, provided by an intelligent, sensitive teacher. Read as a positive message, it is deeply validated. The natural bite that Victor inflicts on the doctor in the institution of the deaf-mutes at the beginning of the film is replaced by the imprint of culture at the end that raises him to the dignity of a moral being. Delinquency has become what it has always been: an indication of the child's psychic integrity, of his will to survive, and of his hope for a just world that will recognize his rights.

An autobiographical reading, here as elsewhere, is indispensable for an understanding of the film's system of representation, if not its appreciation. The basic structuring device in the story is presented as a system of shot/reverse shot that alternates a close-up of Itard, who is watching, and a long shot of Victor in action, whether he is learning to eat with a spoon, light a candle, play with a wheelbarrow, or simply swaying in the rain. As Rivette remarks in his report on the film, Itard is Victor's "first spectator," occupying a position relative to the latter that is analogous to that of James Stewart in *Rear Window.* Once again, we encounter the metaphor of cinema. The film adopts the dynamic of an exchange between the man-as-camera and the child-as-spectacle. In the course of a play involving relationships of filiation and identification, Truffaut engages in a dialogue with himself in *The Wild Child.* The adult-become-filmmaker ponders the meaning of this double, branded by childhood, that constitutes the subject matter of his film. Significantly, Victor's mobility contrasts with Itard's rigid impassiveness. The boy participates without any mediation in the mystery of a natural world, the reality of which is imparted through the constant use of sequence shots, in accordance with Bazin's theories; in contrast, the only space in which Itard can act is the white page in his journal, in which reality becomes translated into signs. In this regard, one of the most moving episodes in the story shows Itard at night, at his window, with a candle in his hand, looking from upstairs at Victor in the garden, whose face is lifted toward the moon. The candle, a symbol of civilization and the illumination of the mind, is contrasted with the moon, which a close-up isolates when Itard raises his meditative glance toward it. Bathing the wild child's body with its natural light, it seems to communicate to him a happiness of which Itard has lost the secret. The doctor tries to break this union, but the image betrays the nostalgia that it inspires in him. The symbiotic relationship between the child and the elements is contrasted against the symbolic mastery achieved by Itard through writing. Whereas the one lacks language, the other lacks immediate contact with the world. The process of dissociation observed in Truffaut's other films can also be seen operating in this one. As indicated by the windowpane that separates them, the two orders of experience are irreconcilable.

In the image, Itard's journal comes to play the literal role of a link between them. Its composition stages the very act of writing; this is what is validated by a story that repeatedly stresses the material representation of writing: a hand tracing words, letters being written down on paper. Certain juxtapositions of shots allow us to measure the gap that separates the two characters at the fundamental level of expression: a close-up of Victor's dirty hands, the nails of which Madame Guérin is cutting, followed by one of Itard's hands while he is writing; a shot of the text of Itard's manuscript, preceding one of Victor's alphabet book. The paradox of the film is that the symbol of the separation between them becomes the instrument of their reunion, thanks to Itard's creative act. The doctor's words give a voice to the wild child, and they come to confer an order, coherence, and meaning to his experience. It is through them that he comes out of silence in order to enter into the world of human exchanges. Truffaut's decision to act the role of Itard himself is hugely significant in this context. Owing to his presence, the composition of the journal emerges as an act of exorcism that abolishes the distance between the adult man and the child. An actor would never have been able to evoke so strongly the mystery inherent in this act of creation. Itard's journal is as much his son as Victor is, and the role that Truffaut performs is close to that of Ferrand in *Day for Night.* Truffaut-Itard gives birth to a text that consecrates his reunion with Victor; Truffaut-the-filmmaker creates films that reconcile himself with himself, by representing the mothering of the split and asocial child that he carries within himself.

The Wild Child, moreover, confirms the feminine nature of creative work: "All these happy changes," Itard notes toward the end of his journal, "occurred within the short space of nine months." In *The Man Who Loved Women,* an old doctor – played, like Pinel, by Jean Dasté – says to the writer-hero: "There is nothing finer than to write a book, except, perhaps, to give birth to a baby." In *The Wild Child,* Itard achieves this double act of creation.

Nevertheless – and this is the second paradox in the film – Victor's "language of action"[25] finally prevails over writing by candlelight, the castrating function of which is amply illustrated in *Two English Girls.*[26] The elision of the presence of mothers – Victor renounces the forest, and Madame Guérin plays a secondary role – suspends the petrifying action of writing. Itard's solitude and his withdrawal from the world are obvious in the film, but it is Victor's vitality that imposes its dynamic on the story. Unable to speak, he communicates his needs with a growing facility, frolics around in the countryside to the joyous sounds of Vivaldi's *Concerto for Mandolin,* even invents a chalk-holder, and wins over the audience when he gets rid of the doctor who has come to treat Itard. The use of the journal in the story confirms the primacy of the image over the word. As one interesting article on *The Wild Child* notes, we observe in this film a progressively widening gap between Itard's journal and the "reality" that it reflects.[27] At the beginning, it serves to convert scenes that have already been represented in the film into the order of language. In the episode of Victor's punishment, this natural order is reversed: Itard's text lays out in advance what the image is going to represent. The project to punish Victor, announced in writing, thus assumes the same arbitrary character as a linguistic sign. Dissociated from reality, it does not reproduce it. In fact, it manipulates it. The child's mouth, unable to speak, ends up biting the hand that writes in order to express his revolt against the unjust tyranny of words. The final scene of the film (the spontaneous return of the child after his escapade) confirms the widening discrepancy between the journal and reality. Itard at his desk has just expressed his certainty that the child will not come back. An extreme close-up of his writing allows us to read the words that are being pronounced in a voice-over: "Unfortunately, young Victor has escaped." At this very moment, the child's face appears at the window. What then happens is remarkable:

Itard stops writing to go and join Victor and welcome him back, thus reversing the schema of the film in which we see him constantly leaving the scene of an action in order to record it in writing. The voice-over, in this final episode, no longer imposes a distance on the expression of joy at the reunion; it leaves that to the emotive words of the doctor: "You are no longer a savage, even if you are not yet a man." Victor's action has not only contradicted the somber message of the writing, but it has also interrupted its flow. By coming back to "his house," the wild child has unquestionably demonstrated his need of others; he has also allowed Itard to emerge out of the reflection of life in order to gain entry to a reality in which the exchange of a glance marks the triumph of direct communication and a reciprocal gift.

At the end of the story, the language of action triumphs over writing, the image over the word, reality over its representation – a triple homage to childhood, to cinema, and to Bazin.

THE STORY OF ADÈLE H. (1975)

In contrast to *The Wild Child*, in *The Story of Adèle H.*, water is not the primary element that is indispensable for life, but a natural force ready to swallow up things human. Adèle's fate is symbolically inscribed in the credit sequence itself. The drawings against which the actors' names are superimposed – all of which relate to Victor Hugo's works – are dominated by massive silhouettes of impregnable castles and citadels, providing an image of crushing paternal power; the name of Isabelle Adjani, however, is nested in the trough of a high foam-crested wave that is about to close over on itself. The father, a bastion of culture, is thus opposed to the daughter, whom nature is in the process of claiming for the purpose of erasing her. In this film, the sea signifies the madness that threatens Adèle (Isabelle Adjani). Her vow will be to travel over the waves, cross the oceans, to go and join the imaginary man she has created – the only gangplank that protects her from the abyss of the oceans.

Victor emerged from a forest; Adèle will come out of the waters. The nocturnal shot with which the film opens shows a boat pulling away from a ship that has arrived from Europe and heading toward the shore of Nova Scotia. When Adèle ascends onto the wharf in the midst of a somber crowd of passengers, the red color of English uniforms is the only thing that introduces a bright element into the surrounding gloom of twilight – the red of passion, of obsession that dominates Adèle's clouded mind, the only thing that still attaches her to reality. Almendros's camera work in this film is perhaps even more remarkable than that in *Two English Girls*. The sepia and brown colors of the image, from which Adèle's pale face detaches itself, stylize reality, investing it with an abstract quality in order to suggest the tonalities of an internal world. We only see as much of the world as Adèle sees, that is to say, signs that are scattered, unconnected, and alarmingly parsimonious, which her logic cements irrevocably into delirious constructions. When she gives up the struggle after her arrival in Barbados, her withdrawal from reality is underlined by a return to the image of a world bristling with voices and sparkling with colors.

When Adèle approaches the customs officers, a passenger in the foreground is challenging one of them: he lacks his identity papers. The young woman slips through in the crowd, evading all control, while this encounter is taking place. In these early scenes, she presents herself under different names, each of which begins with an H. Who is Adèle, to whom even the title of the film refuses to give a surname? What law is she trying to bypass? An exemplary exposition provides us with this information. It is framed by two episodes in which we are shown Adèle, who has moved into the house of her landlady, Mrs. Saunders, asleep.

The first shows her in bed, in a state of agitation, with her eyes alternately shut and then open in the darkness. We see her at a solicitor's office, where she presents herself as a married woman looking for her niece, who is infatuated with a British officer, Lieutenant Pinson (Bruce Robinson). The latter's departure for Halifax has put their marriage plans on hold. She would like the solicitor to make inquiries as to his whereabouts. One slip betrays Adèle: speaking of her niece's family, she says "my parents" before recovering herself; but especially at the moment when she declares in an assured voice: "I am completely indifferent to Lieutenant Pinson," Lenoir brandishes his ear trumpet and forces her to repeat this apparently pointless phrase in a louder voice. The repetition is already an avowal. The second scene clarifies these particulars. Adèle, filmed from its interior, approaches a bookstore, in which a young man and woman are in the act of making a purchase. When she sees them, she quickly hides herself. Once they have left, she in turn enters to request a ream of paper and, at the same time, ask for news about the lieutenant, given that it was he who was in the store in the company of a woman. To explain the reason for her inquiry, she describes him this time as her "sister's brother-in-law" (*le beau-frère de sa soeur*), which, as Jean Collet astutely observes, could make him *her* husband.[28] Pinson and an obsession with writing thus make their appearance together in the story, as well as a visual disposition – Adèle spying on her lover from behind a window – that recurs in several important scenes. This introduction to the subject of the film tells us everything we need to learn about Adèle's quest; all that remains is for us to know the depth of her suffering. This is revealed in a third episode at Mrs. Saunders's boarding-house. Learning that Mr. Saunders (Sylvia Marriott) is going to serve food at a banquet at the Officers' Club, Adèle hastily composes an impassioned letter that she asks him to give to her "cousin," the son of a minister who has become an officer and is in love with her. That evening, she leafs through her photo album with her landlady, who mistakes a portrait of Léopoldine for that of Adèle. Adèle tells the story of this elder sister, dead from drowning, who was so greatly loved by her husband that he preferred to die with her. Her father collapsed, she says, becoming mad with grief when he heard the news. This introduces the twinning motif that pursues Adèle until the end. She is always the double of a woman who is stronger and more prestigious than her: "You don't know how lucky you are to be an only daughter," she says to Mrs. Saunders. When Mr. Saunders comes back, he has to admit that there is no reply to her letter. Adèle rushes out, in tears, while the old man lists in detail the items on the menu of the banquet. The juxtaposition of Mr. Saunders's voice-over and the image of Adèle's distress suggests, with a remarkable economy, the distance that separates her from the world of bodily pleasures. Her psychic condition means that her body is shut off from the nourishments and pleasures of the outside world; it is eaten away and deformed from within by the sufferings of the mind. The prologue ends with the first of the scenes involving nightmares, which recur like a leitmotif. In this scene, we see Adèle's body distorted with grief, struggling against the threatening waters that are starting to cover her face. Instead of sleep observed from the

8.3. Adèle's dream of drowning. Adèle (Isabelle Adjani) in *The Story of Adèle H.*, dir. François Truffaut, 1975.

outside, as in the earlier scene, we now see Adèle's sleep as experienced from the inside.

Adèle's conversation with Mrs. Saunders sheds light on the meaning of this obsessive fear of drowning. She is claiming as her own the place of her dead sister, "adored by the whole family," but especially by their father who, as Adèle's nightmare suggests, would have preferred her to die instead of Léopoldine. Psychosis is born from the parental figures' desire for the death of the child. The only common trait linking the insipid puppet who is Pinson and the great Victor Hugo is that neither of them wants her. Adèle chases after the phantom of a father from whom she has emptied any kind of reality, with the result that she merely preserves the aspect that has destroyed her: the absence of love. In the course of her first meeting with the lieutenant, we see her run through a whole gamut of passionate emotions: love, rage, hate, despair, supplications that are made to a man who remains passive and cold. Pinson, a fetishized object, has no function other than to reveal a lack by masking it. It is impossible for a relationship based on a reciprocal exchange to be established between them: "From the beginning, I show that it is messed up: the

8.4. Adèle pleads with Lieutenant Pinson. Adèle (Isabelle Adjani) in *The Story of Adèle H.*, dir. François Truffaut, 1975.

lieutenant is never going to love Adèle."[29] While the prologue shuts the door on hope once and for all, it also convinces us of the vigor and fertility of the heroine's imagination. The ensuing film plays this as its trump card. Its only purpose is to show how Adèle is going to be able to survive in this untenable situation. When madness overtakes her, it stops.

Shortly after her disastrous exchange with Pinson, a silent nocturnal scene occurs that confirms the symbolic position of the two characters. Descending from a carriage that has been following that of Pinson, she sees the latter enter the house of the young woman who was with him in the bookstore. She draws closer, concealing herself, and sees, through the illuminated windows of the house, the couple in the process of ascending the staircase to go to a room on the upper story. Hoisting herself into a tree, she observes the lovers embracing on the bed. Pinson is pulling up the petticoat of his mistress . . . The camera then fixes on Adèle's fascinated face in a close-up, focusing on a strange smile of triumph that spreads across it. In this superbly primitive scene, Adèle is not a jealous or wounded woman, but a child who is fascinated by having been able to witness the secret activities of the parental couple. The branches that partially hide her face reinforce the sense of a transgression of the forbidden. Pinson occupies the place of her father who, by preferring her sister to her, has alienated her desire, her identity, and her language.

The Story of Adèle H. presents such an astonishingly precise clinical demonstration of what, since Lacan, has been called "the foreclosure of the paternal metaphor" that one wonders whether Truffaut spent more time reading psychoanalytic texts than has been commonly supposed.[30] The paternal metaphor points to the foundational role of the father in facilitating the entry of all subjects into culture: it is a metaphor because there is a substitution of one word for another, paternal because it is the name of the father that invests the signifier with power for the child. Should the father fail to fulfill his symbolic role, the filiation of the subject, and hence his or her inscription in the world of human exchanges, remains void. Such a failure of the paternal function is what Lacan means by the term "foreclosure." Preventing the formation of a chain of signifiers, it renders impossible the stabilization of identity, the socialization of desire, and the mastery of language; abolishing all stable referentiality, it leads to madness. *Two English Girls* began the exploration that *Adèle H.* completes. In the former film, the law of the mother is substituted for that of the father; in the second film, paternal failure is even more tragic, insofar as the father, far from being absent, occupies a prominent cultural position. Many of the scenes in the film suggest the power of the father. When his name appears for the first time on the letter that Adèle, who is ill, asks Mrs. Saunders to post, the doctor explains to the latter that Victor Hugo is "the greatest living poet, like Homer, Dante, and Shakespeare." At the end, old Madame Baa, who takes Adèle in, begins the letter that Adèle asks her to send with the words: "I am only a poor woman from Barbados. I don't know how to read, but I know the name of Victor Hugo." Victor Hugo is a powerful signifier, but for Adèle this signifier does not answer to anything. If the title of the film hides her surname, it is not so much for the sake of leaving the mystery of her identity floating in the air as for reflecting this fundamental lack. What Adèle requires from Pinson, above all, is not love but marriage – that is to say, a name, an identity, an inscription in society. He can keep his mistresses, she tells him, but she wants to become Mrs. Pinson and to free herself from the crushing weight of a name that annuls her.

The struggle that drives Adèle takes the form, moreover, of an endlessly redefined relationship with the facts surrounding her marital status. Three major events sum it up. When she receives a letter containing the consent of both her parents to her marriage, Adèle is at the bank where she regularly goes to collect her mail and the money sent by her father. When she arrives, a little boy asks her what her name is, to which she replies: "Léopoldine." After she has read her letter, she comes back to him and says: "I lied. I am called Adèle." By acknowledging Adèle's right to merge her desire with the law, her father is permitting her for the only time in the film to assume her identity in peace. The second event is that of her greatest revolt: alone at night in her bed, she writes feverishly some words that she repeats out loud: "I denounce the fraudulence of the married status and the scam of identity. Born of an unknown father. I am born of an unknown father." At this very moment, she suffers the same symptom as Muriel: her eyes burn – an image of the prohibition of incestuous fusion against which she struggles in vain. The third event takes place when she leaves Mrs. Saunders's boarding house under the pretext of returning home, when in actuality she is going to follow Pinson's regiment. As her landlady is congratulating her on having given up the lieutenant, Adèle tells her that she never wanted to marry him in the first place: "Think of the name I bear, Mrs. Saunders, think of my father. I wouldn't give up calling myself Mademoiselle Hugo for anything in the world." By identifying herself with her father, she is signaling the end of her struggle. She surrenders herself, accepts being erased, annihilated. Henceforth, she enters into madness.

When the film was released, certain critics accused Truffaut of having distorted the actual facts of Adèle's story. Indeed, we can see the temporal distortion the filmmaker imposed on the representation of the facts, given that the film furnishes all the necessary dates. Born in 1830, Adèle arrives in Halifax in 1863 and returns to France in 1875. The story thus covers twelve years. Adèle is 33 years old at the beginning and 45 at the end; Isabelle Adjani, whom Truffaut cast in the role of Adèle, was only 19 years old at the time of the shooting. We can see from this discrepancy in age that, in making this film, Truffaut was even less interested in the real facts than ever before. Adèle had left reality behind, and the film reproduces the hallucinatory quality of this inner world that human time has ceased to irrigate. Very few scenes are linked together with a chain of cause and effect, or by any kind of temporal continuity. To the contrary, the sequences are separated from each other by numerous fades-to-black. Time does not pass; it repeats itself. It is virtually impossible, even after having seen the film a number of times, to recall the chronological order of the scenes. They all repeat the same places, the same conflicts, and the same struggle. The successive drafts of the screenplay – which was one of the ones that Gruault had to rework the most often during the six years of its genesis[31] – show that Truffaut progressively suppressed everything outside Adèle: "I didn't want to hear any more talk of sun in a period film, nor of the sky. The film of *Adèle* became tighter and tighter, claustrophobic, the story of a face."[32] Out of the seventy-three segments in the film, twenty-eight occur at night, nineteen are silent, and eleven are accompanied in the soundtrack solely by the text of Adèle's diary, or that of her letters. This threefold absence of temporal links, of light, and of dialogue has the effect of suspending the operation of ordinary logic in order to submit the unfolding of the story to the shortcuts of the imaginary. Such a telescoping of the rational is what gives the film is remarkable power to fascinate. All that remains of reality is a network of signs, a deciphering grid similar to that which dreams impose on lived experience, which they filter and organize according to the laws of the unconscious. This translation of ordinary facts into a signifying structure corresponds to the work of fiction itself, involving the transformation of life into a "story."

Two elements guided Truffaut in his achievement of this stylization: Maurice Jaubert's music,[33] and the films of Charlie Chaplin. The idea of using Jaubert's music was, he said, "decisive,"[34] persuading him, indeed, to move forward with this project, which had been suspended for a long time: "Because I had the feeling in shooting *The Story of Adèle H.* that I was making a film that didn't require me to take into account the preoccupations of the present day, I was happy to use music from 1930–1940."[35] Jean Gruault explains further that in *Adèle H.*, at the beginning, each scene had to correspond to a film by Chaplin.[36] This intertextual allusiveness, which almost entirely vanished in the final draft of the screenplay, reflects, like the choice of music, a desire to anchor the story in the cinematic past. This inclination links up with the autobiographical project that informs Truffaut's entire oeuvre. In all the films he made, he tried endlessly to reproduce his experience as a young spectator. His aim was to recover the emotions of this hidden personal film that had formerly been evoked by the works of the masters. Their secret becomes merged with his own. With Jaubert, Truffaut went back to the origins of the masterpieces of his youth.[37] For him, the choice of Chaplin was justified in many ways – as a homage to the genius of cinema, to silent cinema – but it was also determined at a deep level by the very subject matter of the film.

In his preface to the book by André Bazin and Eric Rohmer on Chaplin, Truffaut, after having commented that the latter, whose mother died in a state of madness, had narrowly escaped insanity on account of cinema, continued thus:

> For several years, the cases of children who have grown up in moral, physical, or material distress have been studied more seriously, and specialists now describe autism as a defense mechanism. Thus, as we can see clearly from the examples Bazin draws from the films of Chaplin, all of Charlie's antics and actions are a defense mechanism.[38]

The nature of these mechanisms fascinated Truffaut all the more in *Adèle H.* because they were expressed in writing, that is to say, a creative activity. As was already apparent from *The Wild Child,* Truffaut was very interested in autism, which had been drawn to his attention by his reading of Bruno Bettelheim's *The Empty Fortress: Infantile Autism and the Birth of the Self.* Like Winnicott, Bettelheim accorded considerable importance to the earliest relationship between the mother and the child. It is not a matter of seeing Victor Hugo as a Madame Doinel with a white beard (his paternal function is well established in the film), but Truffaut certainly projected an important part of himself into the character of Adèle – an unloved child, humiliated, outside the law.[39] Winnicott explored the Lacanian notion of foreclosure using a very different terminology. It was a matter of what he called "the fear of breakdown."[40] The patient who fears breaking down does not know that this breakdown has already taken place. This experience has not been able to be integrated by the self because it occurred at a time in early childhood when the self was not sufficiently organized for living. Here, it is the past, in which this psychic death took place, that is foreclosed. Psychosis is a highly sophisticated defense mechanism against the return of this catastrophic event, to which Winnicott gave the name "unthinkable anxiety," or "primitive agony," which has been experienced without being processed: "It is a mistake to view psychotic disorder as a breakdown. It is a defensive organization linked to primitive agony."[41] Many of Truffaut's films reflect fear and breakdowns, from *The Soft Skin* to *The Woman Next Door,* which, like *Adèle H.,* engages in the study of a dual relationship that has no outcome. A false self, dissociation, anxiety at the thought of disintegration, and a fear of falling are all phenomena that relate to primitive agony.[42] In Truffaut's oeuvre, it is the exercise of a creativity that is fully experienced as a feeling of being that forestalls this threat, in a manner that is temporary but effective. The struggle conducted by Adèle bears only a tragic resemblance to this activity.

The fear of a breakdown reflects a failure of what Winnicott calls the primitive "holding" of the infant, that is to say, the structure of support that procures an environment favorable to his or her development. This term takes its literal origin from the action of the mother who carries, or "holds" the infant; there is always the possibility that she will drop him or her, and it is the thought of this fall without end, the feeling of falling forever, that is linked to the unthinkable anxiety. In contrast to Victor in *The Wild Child,* who is reborn into the world owing to the putting in place of a protective mechanism, nothing supports Adèle. Her dread of drowning and the two fainting fits that punctuate the story – one on a snowy day when she comes out of the bookstore, and the other in Barbados – give a visual form to the void that is threatening her. Fear of breakdown creates an inner hole, an absence, a nothingness. Adèle's response is to fill it with a bulimia of writing. Writing and the fantasmatic life she maintains are reflections of both the desire to fill in an "irreparable breach"[43] and the need to dissociate herself from reality in order to reconstruct it. By opting for this defense mechanism, Adèle once again expresses her dependence on a father who owes his prestige, his fame, and his money to writing. She is seeking to appropriate this power for herself.

In this regard, the two most important sequences that structure the story are the one in which we follow the journey of the letter in which Adèle announces her marriage to her parents, and the one showing her meeting with the magician. Both scenes visually disrupt the obsessive

8.5. A bulimia of writing. Adèle (Isabelle Adjani) in *The Story of Adèle H.*, dir. François Truffaut, 1975.

rhythm of the film – bank, bookstore, bedroom, street – and correspond to a bold plunge into the unknown. To understand the first, it is necessary to examine the two scenes that precede it. After having received the consent of her parents, Adèle, disguised as a man, goes to find Pinson at a dance being held at the Officers' Club. The scene takes place at night, as does the voyeurism episode; Adèle moves along the outside of an illuminated picture window that separates her from her lover. Someone goes to find him upstairs, where he is with a woman. Once again, it is at the top of the stairs, in the company of a woman, that we later find him in an episode that takes place in Barbados. Adèle's fear of a breakdown is matched by the involvement in vertical space of the man in whom she hopes to find salvation. Pinson and Adèle then withdraw into a cemetery, where they hold a conversation in which he asserts that he will never marry her. A scene then follows that shows the young woman in tears before a small altar, on which a photo of Pinson is sitting surrounded by black and candles. Love has become the religious cult of a dead object, picking up the theme of the cemetery in which Adèle's male disguise also announces, as a premonition, the death of her femininity. Davenne, the hero of *The Green Room,* is not far away. This ceremony of despair, however, is associated with a sumptuous mise-en-scène: we see a close-up of Adèle's face as she announces her marriage to her parents, while superimposed over it are drawn the ocean coasts between which her letter is going to pass. We are able to follow the passage of this letter owing to a series of cross-fades showing the maps of the Americas, views of the Atlantic, a map of Europe in which the name of Guernsey is picked out, and finally a grand house, which is that of Victor Hugo. An old woman in black exits from it with a letter in her hand, continuing the motif of mourning, and goes to the headquarters of the newspaper in Guernsey to arrange for a marriage announcement to be published. Maurice Jaubert's music accompanies both the scene of the funereal ritual, and also that of the letter's journey, indicating the link that unites the idea of death to this lyrical passage. The two are equated because this marvelous episode, although it marks Adèle's triumph – in sliding over the surface of the waters, imposing her word on the world, and giving the power of truth to her fantasy – also attests to her final rupture with the real. Like the words of her father, hers will be published and disseminated throughout the world, but, dissociated from reality, their power will be ephemeral. At first, we see Lieutenant Pinson being harshly scolded by his superior for this fanciful marriage, which the latter imagines took place in Paris while he was in Halifax.[44] Soon after, however, it is Adèle whom the paternal voice condemns, accusing her of lying. As if to confirm its failure, the Name of the Father finally appears on the copy of *Les Misérables* that the lovesick bookseller inappropriately offers her. This book attests to the distance between the writings of the father and those of the daughter, between the language of an imaginative creator and that of a delusional fantasist. Moreover, the young bookseller occupies the role of Adèle's double in the story: while he is passionate about her, she brutally rejects him; the written word that should draw them together separates them; his slight limp picks up the motif of Adèle's psychic infirmity. When he goes to visit her during her illness, we notice him throwing a glance at the young woman's white underwear, which is drying on a line on the other side of the window, a fragment of the body that is inaccessible to desire. This detail shows how everything in the film relates to the main character and her conflicts.

Adèle's meeting with the magician marks the second attempt at exorcism through the word. Having seen him place a spectator under his power through hypnosis, the excited Adèle goes to find him in his lodgings. The scene that follows unites language, the Name of the Father, magic, and money, which is to say, Adèle's whole defensive panoply. She asks the magician if he can force a man to marry against his will, that is, to alter reality through the power of words. The magician, sensing a good thing, does not say "no" and asks for an enormous sum, "payable in advance." Adèle promises to give it to him. Her father's money, upon which Adèle cruelly depends for her survival, has served on several occasions as a means of trying to buy Pinson. In this instance, it is not only his money but, for the first time, his name that Adèle is going to brandish, thus doubly exploiting the weapons of paternal power. The magician demands a guarantee to ensure that he will be paid; Adèle silently writes the name of Victor Hugo in the dust on a mirror in which her image is reflected. The Name of the Father has never seemed more formidable than in this scene. In the absence of any power to attribute its symbolic function to it, Adèle tries to put it to use through magic. This scene continues the occult séance in which, like Victor Hugo, she invokes the name of Léopoldine in front of a pedestal table. The image of Adèle, obscured by the dust of the past, is blocked by the imposing name that overwrites her. The whole drama of Adèle's identity is summed up here in the mirror and the name. The "anonymous spectator" brings back his costume: he was an accomplice, and the magician is a swindler. Adèle runs away. Having once again wanted to control things through words, she has failed. This scene is followed by the hysterical outburst in which she declares herself to have been born of an unknown father. Her two final acts of exorcism consist of breaking off Pinson's engagement by producing the announcement of his marriage to her, and then by going to accost the lieutenant on the parade ground to throw money at him in silence. She also pulls out in front of him the cushion hidden under her dress that gave her the silhouette of a pregnant woman. Usurped words, money, and the body – in other words, her last rounds of ammunition.

Having left Mrs. Saunders's house, Adèle departs from reality at the same time. The ending marks her descent into madness, her absence from the world, her withdrawal into a psychic retreat. She leaves for Barbados and, dressed in rags, with a hallucinated expression, encounters Pinson in a street, without recognizing him. This scene, in which the camera follows her lengthily through a maze of streets, evokes the labyrinth in which she is lost from now on. She has called herself Mrs. Pinson, but there is now a real one, given that the lieutenant has married. There is no longer a name for her; she is also dispossessed of her language. The final letter in the film is dictated to a scribe by Madame Baa. A voice-over describes Adèle's return to Paris and her confinement for forty years in an asylum, while the visual track, using period photographs, presents the grandiose funeral of her father, followed by the twin tombs of Adèle and her mother, who has the same first name. Even in death, Adèle does not have the right to a separate identity; she will never be anything other than the double of another woman, and will end up merged with her parents. The film concludes, however, with the triumphant image of the young woman perched on a rock in Guernsey, overlooking the sea and the waves, repeating the profession of faith that she had made during her final moments of lucidity in the house of Mrs. Saunders: "This incredible thing – for a woman to cross the sea, travel from the old world to the new world to rejoin her lover – such a thing, is what I will do."

One recalls a statement made by Truffaut in 1979: "I deliberately created *The Wild Child, The Story of Adèle H.,* and *The Green Room* to be like objects and even, in my heart of hearts, like ivory eggs that one can see and touch, but never bite into."[45]

The extreme concision of these films reveals Truffaut's art with particular clarity. The economy of representational signifiers is such that even the least informed eye cannot fail to notice the ingenuity of the constructions which, like variations on a musical theme, construct a complete and hermetically sealed system from a few notes. One can apply almost any system of interpretation to these films, knowing that it will work. The perfection of the packaging ensures its adaptation to all of the contents. Ultimately, one could say that these films present a set of logical relationships to the spectator emptied of signification. Truffaut constantly constructed his films around autobiographical elements because he sensed that the very truth of this unconscious material would guarantee the rigor of the thought that organized it. It is this organization that interested him; it is also what ensures the transcultural accessibility of his films. In his work, Truffaut rediscovered the laws that govern the formation of myths. Comparing them to dreams, Lévi-Strauss wrote in *The Jealous Potter:* "the universal need motivating dream-work is, contrary to what Freud sometimes appeared to think . . . a need to impose a grammatical order on a mass of random elements."[46] This discipline is what Truffaut embodies in the process of stylization he adopts.

9

The Child King

Small Change (1976)
Love on the Run (1979)

SMALL CHANGE AND *LOVE ON THE RUN,* IN VERY DIFFERENT ways, both deal with the past, reassembling fragments of a childhood, a time of life, an experience. Of the sketches that make up *Small Change,* only the final one (the summer camp) is directly autobiographical. The others are snippets of stories found in newspapers, invented, or borrowed from others. Nevertheless, this film seems in many respects to be like a rereading of *The 400 Blows,* with all the young heroes being a composite of Antoine Doinel. *Love on the Run* picks up the story of Antoine through flashbacks of the series that bears his name, and also of *Day for Night, The Man Who Loved Women,* and even *A Gorgeous Girl Like Me. Small Change* disperses memory across the space of a town that owes more to one of Trenet's songs than to the actual reality of France in 1976; *Love on the Run* looks for images of a lost time in the memory of cinema, in this way definitively consummating the divorce between myth and life. Both films reflect a wish to exorcize the past by subjecting it to the gaze of an appeased maturity. The way they are edited transforms the story into a puzzle in which the key piece is that of inscribing a new vision of the relationship between the son and his mother.

SMALL CHANGE (1976)

Whenever Truffaut speaks of his two passions, cinema and childhood, aerial metaphors come into his mind. To those who asked him whether he was worried about demythologizing the craft that he loved so much by making *Day for Night,* he replied: "An aviator can fully explain everything that he knows about flying a plane, but he never succeeds in demythologizing the intoxication of flight."[1] Describing his work with children in *Small Change,* he compares it to shooting a scene from a helicopter: "You think a lot of time is going to be wasted by doing that. But as soon as the camera is in the helicopter, one gains an immense amount of time. Thirty kilometers can be filmed in ten minutes."[2] *Small Change,* like *Day for Night,* adopts a narrative organization that reflects a bird's-eye view of reality. Polyphonic and collective, the story simultaneously encompasses a multiplicity of settings, actions, and characters. Childhood and cinema reassemble and accelerate life. *Small Change* is a film that also displays a slightly exhilarated perspective on things. It is delirious, but in such a deliberate way that when the teacher claims the right to vote for children in his speech, the message is delivered like a letter through the mail. We are entirely in the realm of fairy stories; children have seized power. In this fantastical town in which "Monsieur Sequin's aftershave" is sold, people immediately construct a pulley to send food to a little girl who says from her window that she is hungry, a baby survives a fall from the tenth story without hurting himself, a son supplies provisions for his paralyzed father who lives surrounded by extraordinary machines for turning pages and making telephone calls, and cruel mothers with long hair live in strange huts built in the middle of trees.

In the opening, Martine, a little girl, sends a postcard to her cousin Raoul from Bruère-Allichamps, in the center of France. The approval of her father – played by Truffaut – ensures from the outset that childhood is going to enjoy the protection of narrative authority. In contrast to the beginning of *The 400 Blows,* no prohibition is going to intercept and stifle freedom of expression and the relationship between the feminine and the masculine. The teacher confiscates the postcard that little Raoul is looking at in class, but instead of chastising him, he seizes the opportunity to turn the event into a geography lesson. Antoine's fateful pin-up is replaced by the instructive message of a girl who is the same age as the pupils. The lesson is interrupted by the arrival of the teacher's wife, who is pregnant. She calls her husband out into the corridor, and they embrace one another behind a glass door, which allows the children to observe this comforting vision of marital happiness. This model implanted in the beginning of the story licenses the formation of a young "couple" exchanging their first kiss at the end of the film. In between, however, the film takes a somber detour in order to flush out and free a child martyr, the victim of not one, but two women.

In *Small Change,* childhood is not experienced as a curse, but taken on as a state of grace. Truffaut said that he had made the film while thinking of a phrase from Bernanos: "I know that youth is blessed, that it is a risk to run, but that even this risk is a blessed one."[3] While the film picks up the schema of *The 400 Blows* – the negligence of mothers, the resignation of fathers, a complete rupture between the world of adults and that of children – it reverses the signs of power. The effectiveness of children is emphasized by the relative absence of big people. Truffaut enhances this distortion of reality by not having any professional actors in the adult roles. This allows the sparkling naturalness of children to assert itself effortlessly in the film, with everything that parents and teachers do being characterized to a greater or lesser degree by clumsiness. Truffaut openly admitted as much: "The adults are depicted as rather weak, sometimes out of commission or handicapped in some way, like Patrick's father, who is disabled, but this is not shown in a negative or malicious way. Far from it."[4] An investigation of the film, however, quickly reveals, as in the case of *Day for Night,* signs of maternal shortcomings. Such shortcomings can be found not only in the wicked stepmothers, but also in the mother who allows her baby to fall out of a window, blissfully ignorant of the fact, and in the woman who, with staggering hypocrisy, coldly admits that she detests the children she looks after. At the end, the female teacher, feeling guilty at having failed to realize the plight of the child martyr, bursts into sobs when it falls to the male teacher to deliver a paternalistic speech. With the exception of this warm-hearted pedagogue, the image of a benevolent mentor who is a spokesman for Truffaut, paternal weakness is treated even more satirically in *Small Change* than it is in *The 400 Blows:* Patrick's disabled father literally cannot lift his little finger.

Truffaut asserted: "The film is not autobiographical, because that there is no precise match between me and any of the characters."[5] Notwithstanding this assertion, it is more autobiographical than ever, given that the author is apparent everywhere, dispersed through his horde of charming imps and skipping a generation to become the teacher. Truffaut even imagined the character of a grandfather with whom he could identify himself:

> When I made *The 400 Blows,* I was the elder brother of the main character; in making *The Wild Child,* I was Victor's father; in making *Small Change,* I felt as if I were a grandfather, and, furthermore, I shot a scene that I had to cut because it was poorly acted, which was the staging of the poem "Jeanne était au pain sec," drawn from *The Art of Being a Grandfather.*[6]

This dispersed representation of the narrator gives the film its unity despite its extreme fragmentation. All the stories spring from the same center and tend toward a demonstration of the same thing. Two among them structure the narrative: that of Patrick (Geory Desmouceaux), the little blond boy who looks after his sick and lonely father, and that of Julien (Philippe Goldmann), the taciturn dark boy who is mistreated by the mothers. The former extends the dream of *Stolen Kisses,* while the latter protracts the nightmare of *The 400 Blows.* The framing of the second by the first gives *Small Change* its optimistic flavor. While Julien disappears from the story as abruptly as he came into it, Patrick leaves for a summer camp where he will meet Martine.

Like Antoine Doinel, both of them suffer from the twofold absence of maternal love and paternal authority. Patrick makes up for this lack by falling in love with the wife of the hairdresser, the beautiful Madame Riffle (Tania Torrens), whom the original screenplay called Madame Tabard. Like Antoine with Fabienne, Patrick experiences in her presence the failure of words to realize the impulses of desire. Concerned to use a learned term to express the pleasure he has taken in eating the sumptuous meal she has served him, he describes it as "frugal." When he arrives to offer her some red roses he has bought with his pocket money, he finds her in the classical seductive pose assumed by mothers in Truffaut's films: sitting, her half-open dressing gown revealing her naked legs. Madame Riffle intercepts the channel of desire, to Patrick's great disappointment, by asking him to thank his father for the flowers. In the Riffles' house, we once again see the fetishized poster that had already appeared in *The Bride Wore Black* and *Stolen Kisses* – one that enchanted Truffaut during his childhood, according to Suzanne Schiffman.[7] The poster depicts a couple ready to go to bed in the compartment of a sleeping car. He is smoking on a bunk above; she draws near in a nightdress, with a smile on her lips. The happiness of a couple, the momentum of a train on the rails, a journey toward the unknown: an impossible ideal of stability created out of movement and adventure.

While Patrick lives in a world of exchanges and contacts, Julien's existence is marked by solitude, wandering, and a silent relationship with objects that are scattered, dismantled, broken, lost, or stolen. Just like Antoine did with his milk bottle, we see him throw the pieces of a broken plate, which he had hidden in his satchel, into a sewer. The silent scene in which the child roams through the nocturnal setting of a deserted carnival, alone, follows the comparable night scene set in Paris in *The 400 Blows*. In it, Julien picks up forgotten objects that are foregrounded in a series of close-ups: coins, a comb, a nail file. Deprived of the essentials, Julien retrieves everything that falls[8] from the normal world from which he is excluded. Marginalized, he is condemned to a clandestine existence, as is illustrated by the note that a shady man asks him to hand to a squalid woman. During the night at the carnival, prostitutes appear in several shots. Above all, Julien, like Antoine, is a child who commits theft: money in the corridors at school, the hood ornament of a Mercedes, a compass box, a seat at the cinema.

With Truffaut, theft is indelibly associated with abandoned children. At the beginning of the film, the teacher makes the children recite Harpagon's monologue, replacing the grotesque poetry of Petite-Feuille in *The 400 Blows* with Molière. Not only does this choice enhance the status of the teacher, but it also functions as a comment on Julien, who appears in the courtyard of the school, and then in the class, exactly during the middle of this scene. The leitmotif of theft, articulated by the cries of the dispossessed miser, coincides with the arrival of the child martyr. It also relates to the very title of the film – *Argent de poche* in French (literally, "Pocket Money"). As Winnicott explains, "pocket money absorb[s] some of the antisocial tendency that is normally to be expected."[9] In other words, pocket money is the antidote to theft. By choosing to place his film under the sign of this gift granted by adults to children, Truffaut is indicating his desire to dispel the specter of delinquency and exclusion. The film is punctuated by petty thefts, but theft, far from triggering a fatal spiral, as in *The 400 Blows,* is repeatedly played down. It does not lead to tragic consequences, even in Julien's case. For example, the teacher asks the pupils to give back the little plastic revolvers stolen by the Lucas brothers without anyone being punished. *Small Change* is placed wholly under the sign of making amends. Even the treatment of maltreated children is lightened by the insertion of the famous scene of the little girl who is hungry. She replicates the story of Julien in a minor key, but in a liberating fashion, given that everything in this scene happens as a result of the child's agency. At the end, Sylvie states in a satisfied tone: "Everybody looked at me."

In this episode, the window plays a major role. It is the site of an opening onto the outside that permits the circulation of glances, words, and food. It is also through a window that the camera penetrates to reveal Julien's secret in a terrifying zoom. It plunges into the darkness of the room in which the lady doctor discovers his badly injured body. A single traveling long shot then follows the frantic dash of the nurse in the courtyard to find the director. This horizontal movement contrasts with the inevitable control of vertical space by the children. Adults and children live in two radically heterogeneous spaces that only encounter one another in tragic circumstances. When Gregory falls, the passersby remain riveted to the spot as powerless spectators. This scene provides the most flagrant example of the reversal of signs in this film, in which the strength of children displays itself by the absence of any fear of falling. From the opening-credit sequence, we see children hurtling in irresistible, joyful cascades down the narrow streets of the small town. In *Small Change,* children can abandon themselves, without fear, to the natural laws of gravity. Their space reflects an instinctual mobility that has not yet been repressed by the censorship of the cultural order. The same is true of their language.

The spoken speech of adults is repeatedly contrasted with other forms of expression: the nursery rhymes recited in the playground by the children, the language of flowers unsuccessfully practiced by Patrick with Madame Riffle, the names that Sylvie gives her fish, Plick and Plock, which her father admits he is unable to understand. The parents have no greater success in understanding why the girl is so attached to the grubby, old bag in the shape of a cuddly soft-toy from which she cannot imagine being separated – a good example of what Winnicott calls a

9.1. The children at the opening of *Small Change*, dir. François Truffaut, 1976.

transitional object. The relationship that children establish with reality escapes adult logic. The film's subversive power lies in its celebration of this lost secret, together with its affirmation of its superiority over the rational communication maintained by adults.

A fantasmatic reading of the film allows a message to be extracted that is as obvious as it is crazy: children have no need of adults; they are completely self-sufficient on their own. If fear of falling is absent, it is because the children do not need any support structures: Sylvie (Sylvie Grezel), Patrick, and Julien provide for their own needs, alone; the Lucas brothers make themselves a breakfast one Sunday morning that is described as "excellent"; even the son of the beautiful Madame Riffle considers his mother inconvenient when she smothers him with kisses at the school entrance. Better still, while his wife is breastfeeding her baby, the teacher is moved to read her one of Bettelheim's essays evoking the anxiety of the nursling crushed against the maternal breast! It is when the lady teacher has left that the children finally recite the passage from Molière with passion, and Patrick, his eyes fixed on the clock, waits impatiently for seconds to tick by so that he can be liberated from the constraints of adult knowledge. The film is a veritable symphony in

9.2. The absence of a fear of falling: Little Grégory in *Small Change,* dir. François Truffaut, 1976.

which each child plays the tune of "Parent, teachers disappear" on their own instrument. In this regard, the greatest scene in the film is the arrest of the cruel mothers. Instead of describing the internment of an innocent child as in *The 400 Blows, Small Change* depicts, with a degree of brutal satisfaction, the incarceration of the guilty mothers, who, according to Richet in his speech, are going to be stripped of their maternal rights, with Julien henceforth living happily without them. Even in this long monologue, the teacher teaches nothing. He translates adult reality into a language that is accessible to his pupils. He is the children's interpreter and the protector of their rights. Truth belongs to them.

The film goes still further. In the course of a cinema session where the whole town has gathered, there is projected on screen the quirky story of Oscar, whose parents from different nationalities have not been able to find a common language that can be transmitted to the child. No matter; Oscar manages alone, and whistles to express his needs. The son of a Madeleine Doinel and an American, he transforms even his handicap into an advantage, becoming a music-hall star! In this episode, which sums up the lesson of *Small Change,* one can easily read the history of the author of the film himself, transposed into an ironic mode. This little Doinel, who appears on the screen and has been able to create a language that has made him famous, is, like Antoine, Truffaut's double.

The film's ending sanctions the exclusion of adults. The summer camp is a community where children reign. They are literally going to stage the initiation of Patrick and Martine into love: they send them into the corridors by telling each of them that the other is looking for them to give them a kiss. When their ruse has succeeded, and the kiss has been exchanged, they noisily applaud the young couple, marking the end of the story. This conclusion reveals the underlying message of the film. Childhood is a spectacle, and children actors who are lacking an audience. The big moments in the film all involve the visual staging of scenes in which the young heroes attract the attention that Antoine so cruelly lacks: Grégory, Sylvie, and Oscar present themselves as a spectacle before adults who are appalled, tender, or fascinated. In the radio scene, Julien becomes the center of a horrified and particularly compelling gaze since it calls forth tears. In Truffaut's oeuvre, the relationship with reality comes down to two privileged positions: that of the spectator and that of the spectacle. Childhood corresponds to the blessed age in which action dominates. To become an adult is to become a spectator, and to leave the center for the periphery of life. The work of the *metteur en scene* is merely a never-ending return to this time of mobility and innocence in the past. Truffaut remarked: "Like Simenon, I believe that we are working with all that happens to us between birth and the age of 14."[10] Childhood, as the aerial metaphors suggest, merges with cinema, of which it is the inexhaustible subject matter.

The charm of *Small Change* derives from its sheer volume: scenes are not juxtaposed, but jammed together; the story is composed of particles held in suspension that delay the moment at which they will become bound together in history. This restraining of the narrative movement mobilizes the spectator's attention and effectively masks the work of fantasy in the film. *Small Change* is not a charming film about childhood. It reactivates the vow buried in the past of the adult to escape from the effects of filiations and to steal away from the constraints of cultural order. In it, we recognize the violence found in fairy stories, which, as Bruno

Bettelheim has shown,[11] translate the unconscious impulses of the child into images and actions: "Children," said Truffaut, "are the privileged spectators of this film."[12]

LOVE ON THE RUN (1979)

Love on the Run is not one of Truffaut's masterpieces, as he himself freely admitted: "It is a film that greatly depressed me, and I released it only reluctantly."[13] After learning how the manager of a theater in Copenhagen had projected this series sequentially as a cycle, following the chronological order of the films, he had the idea of making a sequel to *Bed and Board* in which passages from the Doinel series would be inserted.[14] The film's honesty consists in the fact that it did not add anything to Antoine's character. The Rastignac[15] of *Stolen Kisses* has not kept his promises. He has published a book without it having made any impact on his life, and remains the focal point of a range of female glances on the part of women who judge him with a frequently exasperated indulgence. Refusing to make Doinel pass into adulthood, the story of *Love on the Run* exaggerates the artifice of situations, of dialogues, and even of the acting – which has the effect of investing images from the past with a truthfulness that is all the more moving because it seems unchanging. Out of a running time of one hour thirty-five minutes, these inserts occupy only eighteen minutes, but they carry the film.

Only two scenes in the new story have the same density as the flashbacks. Instead of serving, like the others, simply as a pretext for returning to the past, these two scenes actually prolong it, acknowledging how the passing of time can alter the meaning of memories and transform the nature of our perception of human beings. Both of these scenes are linked to the irruption of death into this comedic world: the death of Madame Doinel and the death of Colette's child.

It is in the printing house where Antoine (Jean-Pierre Léaud) works as a proofreader that an incarnation of past time resurfaces. Enclosed within his glass cubicle, Antoine notices an aging man on the other side of the window who appears to recognize him. This fine scene in which Antoine and Monsieur Lucien (Julien Bertheau) silently stare at one another with a series of hesitant glances reflects the trial-and-error work-

9.3. A dialogue with the past: Antoine (Jean-Pierre Léaud) and Monsieur Lucien (Julien Bertheau) in *Love on the Run,* dir. François Truffaut, 1979.

ings of memory, the slow deciphering of features that the years have altered, but in which there are still traces of a shared experience. Monsieur Lucien is the former lover of Madame Doinel, fleetingly glimpsed one day during childhood when Antoine was playing truant. He takes the younger man to a café, and then to his mother's tomb in the cemetery at Montmartre. This sequence, like that which follows it, in which Antoine describes this meeting to the woman he loves, is marked by twelve flashbacks drawn from *The 400 Blows.* There is a perfect balance between the images in black and white, which focus on the experience of the lonely adolescent, and the present in color, over which floats the shadow of a woman who is "one of the most hard-hearted characters in the whole of post-war French cinema."[16] Emotion is generated not only by the metamorphosis undergone by Madame Doinel, who has become simply Gilberte, and who, Monsieur Lucien reveals, loved her son, and was "a little bird" in their intimacy; it also derives from the spectator's discovery of the human reality of this character, who had remained anonymous in *The 400 Blows* but now suddenly acquires a Balzac-like dimension. The same thing happens with Colette (Marie-France Pisier), "the girl at the youth music concerts" in *Love at Twenty,* when she recounts the death of her little girl, who she had introduced to Antoine in *Stolen Kisses.* The tragic scene in which she breaks down in grief simply shows a series of shots filmed in a dark corridor through which the frantic young woman is passing with the body of her child in her arms. This flashback, which has no relation to any other film, transforms our perception of this character, determined and full of self-assurance, who, from adolescence to maturity, is Antoine's Colette. In these scenes, life has passed; the reality of time has become palpable. But Antoine himself remains a stranger to this rooting of life in time.

Both of these scenes concern relationships of filiation and the passage of generations. Even a film as slight as *Love on the Run* contains its share of fantasy. Specifically, it affirms the power of forgiveness and effects an imaginative reconciliation between the mother and the son. Colette has not only lost her child, she is getting ready to defend a client who has killed his own. The only flashback from *The 400 Blows* that did not appear in the sequence involving Monsieur Lucien rises up when Colette leafs through Antoine's book. It involves the episode at the Observation Centre in which the supervisor slaps him for having eaten his bread; the young woman's face reveals the emotion she experiences upon reading this. These two details emphasize her maternal position. *Love on the Run* reunites a mother who weeps for her child and a son who goes to visit the tomb of his mother. If we add to this the fact that in the film both of them love one of a pair of siblings, Xavier and Sabine, who are reunited by the story in a theater, we can see that it is flirting with incest. An early draft of the screenplay directly alludes to just such a theme. In it, Truffaut anticipated inserting long extracts from recorded interviews between Robert Mallet and Paul Léautaud, with the latter describing the details of his abortive idyll with his unknown mother, whom he had discovered when he was 20 years old, and with whom he had fallen in love.[17] One trace of this idea remains in the film: Sabine presents Antoine with the nineteen volumes of Léautaud's journal.

The return of the incest theme loads the lesson of *Love on the Run* with ambiguity, as the sequence on the night-train attests. After an argument with Sabine, Antoine, without thinking, jumps on to a fast train on which Colette is traveling. Their renewed encounter in a sleeping car, far from fulfilling the dream of the poster in *Stolen Kisses* and *Small Change,* turns sour. Colette once again rejects Antoine, and ends up telling him that she works as a prostitute during the night in the sleeping cars. Antoine sounds the emergency alarm and leaps off the train to run away. At the very heart of this film about forgiveness, the image of the mother-whore who expels the child in the night resurges. It is, however, Colette who returns to Antoine the photo of Sabine that he had lost in the sleeping car, and the story ends with a double kiss, sealing the formation of two couples: Colette and Xavier, and Antoine and Sabine.

As a kind of finale to the Doinel symphony, the final image of the film picks up the scene of the rotor from *The 400 Blows.* Suspended in air, the child experiences the intoxication of a flight that no return to reality can ever restore to him. A metaphor for cinema itself, the rotor remains forever the place in which the legend of Antoine had its birth, and in which he remains a prisoner. "Films move forward," says Ferrand in *Day for Night,* "like trains in the night." *Love on the Run* marks the end of the journey, and illustrates in a fairly poignant way the divorce of reality and illusion, of life and its reflection, and of childhood and maturity. With regard to the film, Truffaut observed: "I would like to quote a phrase by Scott Fitzgerald: 'The whole of life is a process of demolition.' We know that life does not proceed toward anything exhilarating and uplifting. You will always find more freshness in the face of a child."[18] A refuge from an unloved childhood, cinema, when it ends, leaves Antoine on the platform. To Sabine, whom he embraces, he proposes to "do as if," as if love ought to triumph, and the train be able to leave once more.

Truffaut had at first thought he would have the credit sequence of *Small Change* roll with images that were "strongly colored and bright like those that one can see in the Palais de la Découverte," images of the sky, then the earth, of Europe, of France, and finally of the small town situated in the center of France. A geographical and cosmic vision organizes the system of representation in this film. It isolates an imaginary kingdom at the heart of the universe in which children reign. As Marc Chevrie observes, Truffaut's entire oeuvre reflects a desire to construct, on the margins of reality, a "little planet,"[19] protected, functioning as an autarky. The increasingly frequent recourse of his films to auto-citation – the return of names, characters, and situations from one film to another – amply attests to this. *Love on the Run,* constructed from extracts borrowed from past films, marks the apotheosis of this system. In it, Antoine falls in love with Sabine by reassembling the fragments of her photo that has been torn up by an unknown man. Truffaut, who reunites here the faces of his actors from different moments in their life, is, like his hero, fighting against dispersion. Cinema is the site of a cult that celebrates, in a manner that is simultaneously profane and liturgical, a confrontation with memory and oblivion.

10

Fetishism and Mourning
The Man Who Loved Women (1977)
The Green Room (1978)

BEING IMPRISONED OR DEAD, MOTHERS WERE SIDELINED IN *Small Change* and *Love on the Run*. The two films that frame them, however, *The Man Who Loved Women* and *The Green Room,* are among the films in Truffaut's oeuvre that most powerfully and tragically address the problem of the relationship between the son and the mother, and the oppressive constraints that its failure imposes on the mature adult. They also represent, fairly explicitly, an allegorical projection of the very process of creation. As *The 400 Blows* announced, the maternal figure is inseparable from cultural accomplishments. *The Man Who Loved Women* and *The Green Room* explore the modalities of this interaction, which is underlain by a piercing anxiety about time and death. Whereas abundance and scarcity, anachronism and linear temporality, and the search for pleasure as against privation seem to be opposed to one another, we find a meticulous diptych that identifies a series of formal similarities. The triadic structure of these films includes a lonely man who has been shocked by death (Morane/Davenne), a woman who is destined to survive him (Geneviève, the editor/Cécilia the guardian of the temple), and an obsession[1] (a multitude of living women/a single dead woman). An obsessive fear of the past also appears in the form of flashbacks and photos, narcissistic fusion with a female figure who has disappeared, the benevolent mediation of a male mentor (played in both cases by Jean Dasté), behaviors verging on the psychopathological, and especially in the celebration of an object that is over-valued, a fetish and a relic, that impregnates these works with the aura of what Freud calls "the uncanny." Maurice Jaubert's music accompanies both films, which together complete, in an unconventional mode of black humor, the reflection on creative activity begun in *Day for Night* and *The Last Metro.*

THE MAN WHO LOVED WOMEN (1977)

In *The Man Who Loved Women,* Truffaut weaves the strands of time together like the wickerwork of a basket. He was more preoccupied with the container in this instance than what it contained. Four temporalities intertwine in a story that tries to remove a man's life from the constraints of linear progression. The story begins and ends in 1976, at the cemetery in which Bertrand Morane (Charles Denner) is being buried. It presents itself as a flashback that retraces the composition that the hero wrote in 1975, before his death. Images from the recent past, that is to say, ones that involve his pursuit of women, and well as images of his childhood, ruled over by his mother, come to be inserted in the present of the narration. When Bertrand thinks he has finished his book and reunited all the strands of his past, he meets a woman by chance, Véra, who has escaped from his written inventory despite her major role in the life of the hero. A fragment of forgotten time has resurged to make a hole in the texture of his reconstruction. While Bertrand's novel, at the moment of its publication, is a pierced basket, Truffaut's film does not even allow the joins between the willow canes to be seen. Think, for example, of the superb transition at the beginning whereby Bertrand is restored to life: the women's legs, filmed in a low-angle shot from his grave, are replaced by those that the hero, while still alive, was pursuing in the street. Truffaut deserves the title of "king of the invisible flashback"[2] that he awarded to Lubitsch and Buñuel. All the inventive work of the film inheres in the making of a container of which the ingenuousness, the complexity, and the beauty reflect the skill of a craftsman who has fully mastered his craft. Concerning the content, the filmmaker makes his hero say, when speaking about his mother: "One doesn't invent such things."

By the time he was making the film, Truffaut had come to understand the autobiographical nature of the unconscious projections that his films reveal. *The Man Who Loved Women* plays on this knowledge with a certain irony. Bertrand resembles Antoine Doinel, Charlie Kohler, Pierre Lachenay, Montag, Louis Mahé, and Claude Roc. Furthermore, his story had already been presented in the dialogue of *Shoot the Piano Player* when one of the two gangsters tells how his father died – an inveterate womanizer who was hit by a car while he was looking at a woman's legs. This character is also an extension of Fergus in *The Bride Wore Black,* who was similarly played by Charles Denner. Additionally, Truffaut was partly inspired by the intimate diaries of Henri-Pierre Roché when inventing his own Don Juan. The episode involving the secretary who refuses to type up the rest of the story, because she cannot deal with so many stories of interchangeable women, actually happened in real life when the filmmaker wanted to have a first draft of the private writings of the novelist transcribed. It is appropriate, therefore, that this seducer is turned into a writer in the film, because it enabled Truffaut to realize a cherished dream: "I have wanted for a long time to show in a film everything that occurs in the production of a book: a book is written, then it is typeset, printed, you are given the proofs to correct, you choose the cover, and then the book is there, finished, like an object."[3]

Bertrand, as the narrator of his own life, displays a curiosity concerning it that seems to hold out the promise of truth. He undertakes to write a novel not because of literary ambition or idleness, but because he is undergoing a crisis and wants to understand the mystery of behavior that he cannot control. In this respect, the film is presented as if it were the real-life psychoanalysis of a case that one could label, in accordance with a Freudian model, "Leg Man," given that this is the major obsession of the hero: "Women's legs," he writes, "are compasses that measure the physical world in every sense, giving it its balance and harmony."[4] The fragmentation of the story, with its absence of chronological continuity, reproduces the detours that operate in amnesia when a patient is trying to reconstruct his history out of pieces of incomplete memories, forays into the distant past, and returns to the surface of present time. But it is also the overwhelming importance placed on words that makes the film seem like an analysis. Images are constantly submitted to the control of a discourse that orders them, keeps them at a distance, and exorcises them. Words are used recurrently to control the brutal force of fantasies expressed by the image. Analytical listening is even present in the film, in the form of the character of Geneviève, the editor, whose voice-over commentary at the beginning and end of the film balances that of Bertrand in the central part. The nature of his case, which he recounts to her, is epitomized in the film in three narrative sections.

The first of these extends to the evening spent with Hélène (Geneviève Fonanel), the beautiful lingerie-merchant. It shows how Bertrand's life is rigidly compartmentalized between the masculine world of work and his feminine conquests. His occupation requires him to manipulate model airplanes and boats in a way that is strongly associated with the idea of childhood – a constant paradigm in the film. His erotic compulsion suggests the quest for a lost object that always disappears, the lack of which he is able to mask only by engaging in a clever game of substitutions. It also reveals a fetishistic fixation with legs, which excludes any close emotional relationships. The shadow of an inaccessible mother floats over this first section. Hélène, with her retro lingerie and her preference for young men, reawakens painful memories in the hero by momentarily taking on her traits. It is fitting that she turns down his advances in front of the illuminated window of a shoe shop. Her rejection of him causes Bertrand to have a psychological crisis, the nature of which is suggested by the following clinical description: "The fetish cannot function as such, and the ensuing decompensation takes the form of depression, which is what prompts the patient to seek help."[5] For Bertrand, the consultation takes the form of the autobiographical account that he commences on the very evening of this incident.

The second section, which corresponds to the composition of the book and ends with his meeting with Geneviève, marks the return of the repressed and explains, through an incessant movement of coming and going between the present and the past, the origin of Bertrand's obsessive fixation. It is here that the greatest narrative complexity occurs with flashbacks, stories of dreams, and visual hallucinations.

The third part is devoted to the formulation of a diagnosis by the blond editor/psychiatrist. She is the one who gives the book the title of *The Man Who Loved Women,* whereas Bertrand had wanted to call it "The Skirt Chaser." We can read it as both an attempt to rehabilitate the patient and also a description – owing to the use of the imperfect tense – of an illness that has been mastered. Then follows a declaration of the prescription for his cure: "You have to learn to love yourself." The simplistic concision of this aphorism evokes the heyday of the clear-cut treatments with which the "psychoanalytic" films of Hollywood, including those of Hitchcock, regaled us. Despite the transference to the analyst that has taken place, the end of the film, ignoring its previous optimism, amounts to an acting-out that leads to the death of the patient.

When the readers at the publishing house are discussing Bertrand's novel, which only Geneviève defends, one of them says: "The best thing about this book are the pages in which Bertrand Morane tells the story of his childhood, especially the parts that allow us to catch a glimpse of his mother. Unfortunately, that occupies only one chapter: for me, it skirts around the real subject."[6] This wink at *The 400 Blows* lets us know that *The Man Who Loved Women* is an expansion of the basic story found in Truffaut's oeuvre. It weaves together a meticulous network of correspondences between early experiences and those of adult maturity, thus demonstrating, in a way that is both thematic and structural, the truth of what was affirmed in *Small Change:* childhood is the center of a human being's life. The film is constructed like a series of Russian dolls that are progressively opened – with the burial at the beginning and the end being the outer layer, as the before and after of the book – to reveal the miniscule segment in black and white that governs the whole. The five flashbacks that form the heart of the film's narrative last respectively fifty-eight, sixty-seven, twenty-seven, twenty-six, and twenty-nine seconds, making a total of three minutes twenty-seven seconds. If their impact on the spectator seems disproportionate in relation to their length, it is because each detail in the film picks up their lesson, which it develops and illustrates in the description of Bertrand's adult relationships with women. These brief reflections of childhood cast an aura around the hero's destiny with their somber vividness. The use of black and white invests these images with the impact of a real event, such as those one would find in a documentary, of which the fiction film in color is merely the fantasmatic mise-en-scène. All of that adds to their character as flashbacks, a cinematic device that suggests "the irrepressible emergence of the truth"[7] and invests these moments with great intensity. In accordance with the tendencies of amnesia, the order of their appearance corresponds to the slow erosion of repression, which allows reassuring images to emerge first, in order to authorize, little by little, the return of the most traumatizing memories, which, as a result, are the most heavily censored. Truffaut included the following quotation from Bruno Bettelheim's *The Empty Fortress* in the press kit for his film as an epigraph: "It seemed that Joey could never succeed with his mother." Each of the fragments illustrates the pertinence of this phrase.

The first three, by Bertrand's own admission, consist of good memories. He first remembers the circumstances of his sexual initiation. We see him entering the room of an aging prostitute who, understanding the situation, offers to set him up with a woman who is younger and more beautiful than she is. While she goes to look for her replacement, Ginette, Bertrand notices that there are "shelves without books" on the walls. With the exception of this detail, which is a mystery left hanging by the film, everything in this scene is consistent with the normal enactment of the Oedipal scenario. The difference between the generations in it refers to the taboo against incest, which is respected, given that another woman is substituted for the mother. The second segment visually likens Madame Morane to a prostitute who is walking rapidly along a street. After having framed her head and shoulders, the image splits off to focus on her legs, which are hurriedly pacing down the street. The mother-whore is going to encounter Bertrand in conversation with a young girl, also named Ginette. This passage exactly replicates the big moment when Antoine encounters Madame Doinel and her lover in the Place Clichy, but with a reversal of the gazes. In this instance, it is the mother who is alone, and who is watching the motionless couple – filmed, like Antoine, in a traveling shot. Bertrand abandons the girl to go running after her. This scene undoes the preceding one, and marks the fatal impact that the maternal gaze exerts on the son's ability to sustain a sense of his own independent being. In the third, Bertrand "plays" with Ginette at night while her little brother is crying alone in his cot. This abandoned child transforms the young Ginette into an indifferent mother whose only concern is the satisfaction of her desires. The displacements brought about in a few seconds through these flashbacks – Ginette = prostitute = bad mother = object of desire – mark the striking fusion of the mother with the woman. Instead of taking on separate identities, they blend inexorably together, effectively destroying the momentum of Bertrand's movement toward maturity and adult sexuality.

This sequence is followed by three important episodes from the recent past that illustrate this failure. The first depicts Bertrand's obsession with looking, showing him walking in the streets to devour passing women with his eyes. As in the depiction of Madame Morane, shots of their legs alternate with those of their busts, relentlessly fetishizing the female body. His break-up with Fabienne confirms this impression of his behavior: she refuses to see him again, complaining of his emotional indifference. For him, a woman simply remains a beautiful, impersonal object. His affair with the deaf-mute girl reinforces the sense of a relationship that excludes any spoken communication, allowing the series of flashbacks to be picked up exactly where they had been left, that is to say, with the neglected child. Significantly, the young woman punishes her son in order to be alone with Bertrand: "The misfortune of this sacrificed child took me right back to the unhappiest period in my own childhood, when my mother left me alone for several days on end to be with her lovers."[8] These words are accompanied by shots of Bertrand in the act of searching through a suitcase on top of a wardrobe, from which his mother's love letters drop down. The body of the adolescent, in his turn, is then split by the image, just like that of his mother: head and shoulders in one part, legs in the other, with the letters and photos of lovers slowly falling. This fragmentation, which reproduces that of an absent paternal figure who is unknown and inaccessible,[9] seals the narcissistic fusion of the son with the mother: "As for me, Bertrand, the son of Christine Morane, what was I doing that was any different, with my countless mistresses, my letters, my drawers full of photographs?" This segment is followed by the presentation of Delphine (Nelly Borgeaud), who tyrannizes over Bertrand in a delightful manner and shoots her husband like a rabbit, and then of the waitress who practices judo – two images of phallic women challenging paternal representatives. After Delphine's arrest, a string of conquests illustrates the frenetic hunt of a desire that is ignorant of the limitations imposed by the Oedipal process.

Out of this confused and undifferentiated female hodgepodge, which is the manifestation of an extreme erotic dysfunction, the most important memory arises, one that informs all of the fantasmatic representations to be found in the works of Truffaut. A voice-over articulates the law imposed on the son by the mother: "Once and for all, she had forbid-

10.1. A flashback to the young Bertrand (Michel Marti) with his mother in *The Man Who Loved Women,* dir. François Truffaut, 1977.

den me to play, to budge, or even to sneeze. I couldn't leave the chair to which I had been assigned, but on the other hand, I could read as much as I liked, on the condition that I turned the pages without making a sound."[10] This son who is petrified by the presence of his mother, a son who is silent, motionless, and lacking any other refuge apart from life as reflected in books, secretly inhabits all of the filmmaker's heroes. *Fahrenheit 451* picks up the exact terms of the mother's injunction: become a book; *The Man Who Loved Women* liberates the sexual component of this memory. The images in flashback show the son absorbed in reading while his mother strolls around near him in a state of undress that allows her silk-clad legs to be seen: "My mother was in the habit of walking semi-naked in front of me – not to arouse me, obviously, but rather, I suspect, to confirm to herself that I didn't exist."[11]

This scene exactly describes the source and dynamics of Bertrand's fetishistic fixation. Fetishism has its origins in the child's discovery of the castration of the woman. This revelation is often linked "to a premature and recurrent exposure to sexual reality as a result of the mother's immodesty in failing to preserve the boundaries of privacy."[12] In order to combat his anxiety, which in a normal situation is dispersed by the delegated gaze of the father, the fetishist chooses to deny the reality of his perception. Owing to this disavowal, he maintains a twofold belief summed up by Octave Mannoni in the formula: "I know for sure [that women do not have a penis] . . . but even so."[13] Such a denial of reality provokes a fixation on the last object seen before the revelation of the maternal lack, which explains why the fetish is often a feminine accessory associated with the lower part of the female body: lingerie, a shoe, or a stocking. The fetish corresponds to an arrest of the glance, to a voluntary forgetting of what has been glimpsed. Thereafter, it is indispensable for the arousal of desire. In *The Man Who Loved Women,* the book that Bertrand is holding while his mother walks around him half-naked is titled *La Peur Blanche* (literally, "White Fear"),[14] a title that sums up the situation with a certain degree of humor. Both the son's anxiety and the mother's hysteria are revealed in this scene. Madame Morane, with her collection of lovers, seems to be like a single woman who is waiting for love letters that never arrive, in complicity with a son who has become a support for her neurosis. There is a good reason for why they never arrive: Bertrand, having been entrusted to post the letters that she writes, throws them in a sewer: "The mysteries of the postal service are unfathomable." Like the mysteries of the absent father who governs the desire of the mother, and whose place the son, in this instance, happily usurps:

> The perverse fetishist is defined by the fact that he has never got beyond desiring the mother, who in turn has made him a substitute for what she is lacking. Because he is the living phallus of the mother, the perverse subject's entire effort consists of enacting the role required by this mirage of himself, and through that, of finding the accomplishment of his desire.[15]

In this important scene, *The Man Who Loved Women* sheds light on the significance of reading in proximity to the mother's body, the origins of Truffaut's passion for language. Here, the text literally occupies the role of a protective screen between the son and the mother. It keeps at a distance, and structures, a desire that, without it, would be irremediably subject to the law of the mother. From *Les Mistons* onward, Truffaut was inclined to make adaptations of novels in which the soundtrack reproduces the text in voice-over, while the image follows the movement of desire toward death. This narrative formula appears to have been deeply anchored in the circumstances of his autobiography.

One image from the credit sequence sums up the fantasmatic vision that governs the representation presented in the film. Among the horde of women who are going to Bertrand's burial, we first notice a tall redhead, with a bandaged nose, dressed in a skirt that is slit high up her thigh, revealing her legs at every step: castration and fetish are brought together in a single body – because for Bertrand, the fetish is not simply a leg sheathed in silk, but a leg that is moving. Madame Morane, the phobic mother who forbids all contact and whose silence bars access to the slightest symbolization, stamps her relations with her son with the seal of distance, movement, and the glance. The film does not contain any sexual scene; for Bertrand, the erotic moment occurs when his eyes fix on moving legs, in accordance with an indefatigably repeated staging of the scenario of maternal seduction. His nightmare shows what happens when, instead of being the spectacle, the women become spectators, stopping to direct their gaze at the hero: in this nightmare, Bertrand sees Hélène dressing a mannequin in his likeness with gestures of cold possession, while, on the other side of the shop window, the crowd composed of the women he has conquered are watching the scene, laughing. It is this horrific vision that his exhausting amorous quest is seeking to avert. The only alternative that exists for him is to fetishize, or be fetishized. The very moment of his death involves a repetition of this childhood scene. Confined to a hospital bed, having been ordered not to move, he notices the legs of a young nurse through the half-open door, owing to a play of light: "... Her legs are outlined with the precision of a shadow puppet against the whiteness of the gown ... He, who should not be moving at all, sits up and extends his arms toward these legs, which draw him like a magnet, just as the golden crucifix draws Grandet, the miser, when he is dying."[16] Transgressing the maternal taboo, Bertrand's movement kills him.

The childhood scenario also accounts for the tragic loneliness of the hero, which is shared by all of Truffaut's characters. If Bertrand cannot tolerate the presence of another, it is because it reduces him to the state of an object, of living death. In an admirable article titled "The Capacity to be Alone,"[17] Winnicott explains that the ability to remain alone in a positive way arises from the infant's experience of being alone *in the presence of his mother:* "Being alone in the presence of someone can take place

10.2. Bertrand's nightmare of himself as a mannequin in *The Man Who Loved Women,* dir. François Truffaut, 1977.

at a very early stage, when the *ego immaturity is naturally balanced by ego support* from the mother."[18] The child's well-being is manifest in his playing, and later allows him to associate solitude with the experience of relaxation or creation. Nothing like this happens with Bertrand, who is forbidden to play and who remains in the presence of his mother is a state of sadness and anxious vigilance. All that is left is the book, the only thing Madame Morane allows in this unbearable situation. Its existence opens up the possibility of a liberating form of symbolization. There is no doubt that the book is far from being an innocent object for the hero. As the scene with the prostitute suggests, there is a logical relationship between its absence and the expression of an unimpeded sexuality. In fact, the adult Bertrand shows his dependence on his mother by surrounding himself with objects that are loaded with reminiscences. A competition between love and reading is established even in his relations with women. Delphine, in an act of spite, throws the book Bertrand has been reading out of a window, in his presence. When he goes to retrieve it in the street, he runs the risk of being run over – an incident that prefigures his demise at the end when he is hit by a car while running after the legs of an unknown woman. Symbolically, books, like legs, are a fragment of the maternal body. The book is also a cultural object that reactivates the only positive aspect of the childhood scenario for Bertrand. In contrast to his erotic quest, writing permits him a control over his experience that suspends the petrifying effects of maternal seduction. Everything changes with the advent of this creative activity. For the first time, the mediation of protective, identifiable paternal figures enters into the story: the old doctor that Bertrand goes to consult and who, after having forbidden him to engage in all sexual activity, encourages him to pursue his work; the diarists whom he rereads to give him strength to finish in spite of the criticism of the typist: "I noticed that there are no rules, that each book is different and expresses the personality of its author. Each page, each phrase, regardless of which author wrote it, belongs to him alone; his writing is as personal as his fingerprints."[19]

Released from the control of women, oriented toward the pathways provided by symbolization, Bertrand constitutes himself as an independent subject who is able to affirm his identity for the first time. While respecting the law of the mother – the immobility of writing corresponds to that of reading – he experiences an exhilarating freedom. The fact that, at the last moment, he changes the color of the dress of the little girl in his manuscript attests to the autonomy of the writer who can reconstruct reality as he wishes. The book as a transitional object is substituted for the book as fetish, opening up the way for cultural creations.

This new relationship with reality is matched by a new vision of women. The composition of his novel brings Geneviève into the picture, the editor who supports and protects Bertrand's efforts. As in *Fahrenheit 451,* the maternal figure abruptly splits at the end of the film to produce a confrontation between the good and the bad mother: Geneviève and Véra. Like Hèléne, Delphine, Aurore, and the typist, who are all associated with mothers who reject or abandon the hero, Véra, prior to this, has reopened the narcissistic wound of the child. In the course of their tête-à-tête, we learn that the rupture of relations between them has triggered a deep depression in Bertrand. The return of this dramatic episode, when he thought he had settled his accounts with the past, reflects the ephemeral nature of the euphoria that is generated by creativity. The work of repair is never complete, as the melancholy ending of *Day for Night* suggested. Bertrand would like to revise his book to include this female character who has made an impression on his life. Geneviève formally refuses to allow him to do this, thus separating Bertrand from the endless string of castrating mothers. Véra, who has caused Bertrand's breakdown, is thus replaced by a woman who fulfills the function of maternal "holding" for him. She reflects a positive image of himself back to him, advises him to write another book, and opens up for him a space of play and creativity. With her appearance in the story, the desired woman, instead of fusing with the maternal figure, separates from her. In the hotel room in which they have spent the night, Geneviève is no longer filmed in close-up, but in long shots that, for the first time in the film, show the woman's whole body in its entirety. A new female type emerges: no longer a pair of impersonal and undifferentiated legs, but a woman who is affirmed in her distinctiveness, no longer an object, but a subject, no longer the double, but the other of Bertrand. This movement toward an intimacy that snatches for the first time the Don Juan out of his loneliness is interrupted by the return of his obsession. Bertrand remains a dead child, but from this time forward, one whom the gaze of a benevolent mother protects. His voice joins with hers in celebrating the book that, together, they have caused to be born.

Truffaut cast two actresses in the roles of Véra and Geneviève who, in contrast to the other women in the film, have an important cinematic past: Leslie Caron and Brigitte Fossey. The first recalls the luster of Hollywood comedies; the second is inseparable from her role as a child in *Forbidden Games.*[20] This incursion of cinema is not surprising in a work that describes the relation to the female in terms that apply to the spectator watching a film: immobility, distance, looking. A very arresting shot at the beginning of the film provides a visual transcription of this metaphor: Bertrand, in the interior of a basement laundry, is looking at the legs a woman he cannot identify, who, framed by the window, exactly suggests the movement of images on the screen. *The Man Who Loved Women* is, as Annette Insdorf suggests,[21] the man who loved films, with cinephilia being the archetypal form of fetishism for Truffaut.

The Man Who Loved Women is presented as the circulation and transformation of unconscious representations deriving from a matrix that was formed in childhood. It is not the representations themselves that interest Truffaut, but their organization. In the film, everything highlights the way that the narrative manipulates time. To tell a story is to create a network of relationships that between them join together the partial fragments of memories. A story continually juxtaposes episodes that, in real time, are separated by months and years. Out of this juxtaposition arises a structure, a hidden order, which imparts sense and coherence to life. Meaning is nothing other than the generation of correspondences. *The Man Who Loved Women* does not reveal anything about the psychology of the Don Juan. The film reflects a mode of thought that eludes the laws of the rational, and that intervenes with every human being as soon as he tries to communicate the realities of his experience.

When *The Man Who Loved Women* was released, Truffaut declared that in cinema: "one constantly needs to abandon psychological laws for musical laws."[22] In contrast to a novel, a film unrolls in the irreversible time that comprises the projection. Truffaut's stories play with this duration. Time does not flow in them; it folds in upon itself as is shown by the play of repetitions, parallels, and flashbacks. This system creates a perceptual field that sweeps up the spectator's gaze. The time of the projection is that in which a fragment of duration is attached to temporal flow. According to the apt formulation by Lévi-Strauss concerning the detailed analogy he draws between music and myths, "it is as if music and mythology needed time only in order to deny it. Both, indeed, are instruments for the obliteration of time."[23] With Truffaut, the whole art of the story consists in investing the film with the same power.

THE GREEN ROOM (1978)

To suspend time is not only the aim of the narrative, but also the very subject of the story in *The Green Room*. The film begins in 1928, ten years after World War 1. Already haunted by the disappearance of his comrades, Julien Davenne (François Truffaut)[24] has not been able to accept the death of his wife, Julie, which occurred eleven years earlier, shortly after their marriage. He has devoted one of the rooms of his house to her memory, a house that he inhabits with his housekeeper and a deaf-mute child; this is the "green room" in which are gathered photographs and objects of those who have disappeared. Freezing time, Davenne refuses to forget: "In this cruel and pitiless world, I want to have the right not to forget, even if I have to be the only one." Three events, however, come to overturn this life on the fringe of duration: his meeting with a young woman, Cécilia (Nathalie Baye); the death of a former friend who had become his enemy, Paul Massigny; a fire that destroys the green room, leading to Davenne's decision to construct a chapel devoted to the dead. Deep links are gradually going to unite Cécilia with the hero, who asks her to become "the guardian of the temple" and to maintain a watch over the chapel with him. But when Davenne learns that she has been the mistress of Massigny, he breaks off their relations and sinks into a state of prostration that will lead to his death.

Like *Adèle H., The Green Room* is constructed in accordance with the principle of "emotion through repetition" (*émotion par répétition*):[25] "I believe in restrained emotion, in emotion generated not by a paroxysm, but by accumulation. I would like people to watch *The Green Room* with their jaws dropped, moving from one astonishing event to the next, and that emotion grips us only at the end, only on account of the lyricism of Jaubert's music."[26] Like Adèle, Davenne falls prey to an *idée fixe*[27] that each scene looks at from a different angle: "The film rests on the classical idea of making something out of nothing."[28] If Jaubert's music plays an essential role in structuring the story, it is because the story itself obeys the principle of a musical composition: *The Green Room* performs a suite of variations on a single theme.

Of all of Truffaut's films, this is the one that goes farthest in terms of seeking an economy of means. As in *The Wild Child* and *Adèle H.*, Truffaut reduces the number of elements, "strips bare the wire" so as to create an object that is smooth and closed. Here is one example of this narrative sobriety: Davenne is going to give a series of lectures in Scandinavia; a single flicker-shot of the wheels of a locomotive is all that is used to represent this journey. With the exception of four isolated scenes, the entire action takes place in five places: Davenne's house; the office of *The Globe*, the newspaper where he works; the auction room where he meets Cécilia; the cemetery; and the chapel. Furthermore, the whole film was shot in the same surroundings, as Nestor Almendros explains: "*The Green Room* was practically all filmed in a single house rented in Honfleur. Decorative devices allowed us to use the same place for different settings."[29] A single staircase thus served for that of Davenne, of Cécilia, and of *The Globe;* the newspaper's office was situated in the loft of the house, and the cemetery in its garden. *The Green Room* is just as economical in its use of light as it is in actions and locations. Out of 47 scenes, only 14 are explicitly shot during the day; 17 take place at night, and the other 16 are situated in interiors with lighted lamps to suggest evening. Even more so than in *Adèle H., The Green Room* distances itself from ordinary logic in order to allow the compelling laws of an inner world to prevail. Nevertheless, in contrast to Adèle, who constantly reveals herself to the spectator through the mad entries in her diary, Davenne does not confide his inner thoughts to anyone. The story approaches him from the outside, and it is his actions that reflect his obsession. Several scenes end with the mystified gaze that this behavior elicits from the other characters in the film: Cécilia in the auction rooms; Imbert, his boss, at *The Globe;* an employee at the newspaper who secretly observes him while he is composing Massigny's obituary. These expressions triggered by surprise are precisely those that Truffaut wants to provoke in the spectators. The film prevents the establishment of any complicity with the hero. Davenne is a man who, in terms of the dynamics of the narrative strategy, is kept at arm's length, alone.

The first images indirectly and silently reveal the interior landscape that he inhabits. The credit sequence of *The Green Room* is among the most beautiful in Truffaut's films. Captions file past over shots in blue-shaded monochromes of the First World War showing soldiers launching into an assault, running toward the enemy, or mown down by bullets. Twice, a close-up of Davenne's face, poorly shaved and topped by a helmet, is superimposed on the vision of this slaughter. His fixed stare prefigures his future declaration: "I have become simply a spectator of life." Davenne has cut himself off from a world that has moved on to the "post-war" era; he remains haunted by the images of an unbearable carnage that has marked the end of an epoch, in which, as he says, all his friends have died. By substituting a blue tone for the black and white of the documentary-style shots, Truffaut empties them of their realistic character in order to invest them with a subjective value. Davenne lives in an interior landscape beyond the grave.

In *The Man Who Loved Women,* different temporalities crisscross with a frequency that imposes a frenetic rhythm on the work of composing the narrative that Bertrand Morane undertook to write; in contrast, *The Green Room* somberly develops a confrontation between two times that are juxtaposed immediately after the first scenes. This confrontation takes the form of a stylistic contrast. The story begins with a gloomy wake for the wife of Mazet (Jean-Pierre Moulin), one of Davenne's friends. In despair, the widower wants to commit suicide at the moment when the lid is closed over the coffin of the dead woman. Davenne then chases all the assistants out of the room – and especially the priest, whose words of comfort about the prospect of eternal life strike him as insupportable – in order to convey to his friend his own belief: "Our dead can continue to live." The following scene shows him trying to track down a ring that had belonged to his wife, in the auction room where he meets Cécilia. The first scene comprises 36 shots; the second consists of a single sequence-shot. In this film, in which there are comparatively few shots – 458 in the whole of the film – intricately cut passages, in which fixed-camera shots dominate, alternate with traveling sequence-shots. Among these, the most beautiful is the long shot showing Massigny's burial, in which the camera moves through the cemetery to find the sobbing Cécilia, disguised in a veil, in an isolated corner. In fact, the sequence-shots are associated with the young woman. They are the only manifestation of continuity in a film that is composed of disjointed scenes separated by black dissolves that isolate them. Nothing ties the two first scenes together, for example, and one never knows how much time will ensue between fragments of action that are rarely linked in terms of narrative causality. Scenes follow one another as if they were static moments that could be arranged into a different order. To counter this sense of dispersion that eliminates all sense of duration and logic, the sequence-shots impose their own form of coherence. They manifest Cécilia's desire to accept the passage of time, which is the reverse of Davenne's violent inclination: "I believe firmly that it is necessary to move on," she says to him. In a second scene at the auction rooms, we notice that Davenne's memory is inaccurate, while Cécilia's has retained an accurate recollection of all the details of their first encounter, fourteen years earlier. Davenne lives in a state of near-madness that cuts him off from reality. His memories are distorted by his fight to resist time, which he has already lost in advance: by refusing to undertake the necessary work of grieving, he gives himself over to that of death. The whole film is structured around this contrast, which is reflected in the contrast between the hero and the young woman.

The scene that follows the first two completes the exposition of the subject and foreshadows its denouement. Davenne returns home and retreats into his study with Georges (Patrick Maléon), the deaf-mute child, to show him some magic lantern slides. First, he presents some images of insects, and then images of soldiers who were killed in the war: corpses hanging in trees, or scattered over the ground. In the course of this projection, the child repeats, in his confused, indistinct words, the description of this horrible spectacle supplied by Davenne. The association of these images with disjointed language suggests, poignantly, a failure of humanity in this collective disaster. The scene picks up the motif of the credit sequence, as do many other allusions to the war that occur in the film: invalids being pushed in wheelchairs, disabled men, commemorative plaques. Signs of the war are everywhere, and Davenne, although his body is in one piece, bears the traces of this mutilation in his mind. But in this scene, cinema is also explicitly associated with the memory of those who are dead. When he is speaking to Mazet, Davenne turns down a small lamp so as not to allow it to shine more brightly than the light of the candles. Georges also turns off the electric light in order to look at the plaques. The half-light of a funereal wake is merged in this simple act with that of the dark theaters. The cult of the dead is inseparable from that of cinema.

In the three stories by Henry James that inspired Truffaut's film,[30] there is no child. In *The Green Room,* as Truffaut noted, Georges is "a replica of Julien Davenne" (*une replique de Julien Davenne*).[31] He plays a role that is analogous to that of the concierge's son in *The Last Metro.* The latter sums up the fantasmatic subject of the film, that is to say, the prohibition concerning the mother's body, in the scene in which the dressing lady tells him to turn toward the wall while Marion is changing. In *The Green Room,* Georges, punished by Davenne for having broken a lantern slide, consoles himself by escaping into the night. He surreptitiously slips down the staircase of the house, as the hero will do at the end of the film when he goes to join Cécilia in the chapel. We then see him on a dark street where he breaks the glass window of a shop with a stone in order to grab the mannequin of a woman whose face is surrounded by curls. At the moment he is seizing it, the hand of a policeman claps down on his shoulder. Cécilia comes to get him out of prison. This sequence, the only one in the film in which the scenes are carefully linked together, symbolically replicates Davenne's quest: to break the separation between two orders of experience, life and death, the present and the past, the spectator and the spectacle, in order to grab hold of the dead mother against the law of the father. The dark, deep place in which the child is imprisoned evokes the sites associated with delinquency that we often find in Truffaut's films: Antoine Doinel's cell, Lucas Steiner's cellar. But little Georges's escapade is also reminiscent of the dream in *Day for Night,* in which Ferrand sees himself, as a child, in the act of stealing photographic stills of *Citizen Kane* through the bars of a cinema. *Citizen Kane,* the lost mother. In an early version of the screenplay for *The Green Room* (which was titled *The Woman Who Disappeared*), Truffaut called the protagonist Ferrand, like his director in *Day for Night,* who was also deaf like Georges. With Truffaut, the play of analogies is endless.

The mannequin that the child seizes in the night suggests two other networks of images. The first consists of the images relating to Madame Mazet in her coffin at the beginning of the film, whose radiant face is surrounded by a mass of sumptuous curls. The visual representation of death can indeed be surprising. Her beauty and her freshness make her the most carnal person in a film in which even the charming Cécilia will never be as attractive as she is. The vision of this "exquisite corpse" proclaims Davenne's cult of the dead woman. In the scene of the funereal wake, close-up shots of her face alternated with those of a little anonymous boy, who was blond like her, which in itself already invests a maternal function in the dead woman. The mannequin also relates to the episode in which Davenne loses his temper with the sculptor from whom he had ordered a life-sized replica of the body of his wife. This night scene, in which the artist draws back a curtain, just as in a theater, to reveal the mannequin,[32] resembles that in which Adèle went to find the magician in his lodgings. In both segments, the same Oriental woman plays the role of the artist's assistant, who silently observes the scene. Like Adèle, Davenne tries to constrain reality; like her, he fails.

During the destruction of the mannequin, demanded by Davenne, the camera passes abruptly from the interior to the exterior and films in a long shot, through the plate-glass window of the workshop, taking in this literal enactment of the fragmentation of a feminine body, fetishized beyond what is tolerable. This shot is an extension, pushing it to its limits, of that in which Lachenay caresses the inert body of the sleeping Nicole.

In this scene, Davenne displays terrible anger. His rages punctuate the film. Like Charlie in *The Piano Player* or Julie in *The Bride Wore Black,* Davenne could indeed bear the surname Kohler; like them, he is looking to fill in a rift that can never be filled in, which separates him from his past. Incapable of forgetting or forgiving, he rages against anyone who questions the soundness of his mission. At the beginning of the film, we see him violently attack the priest and the teachings of the church. Cécilia criticizes him for the brutality of his comments, and Imbert, his boss, for his hatred of Massigny. This anger finds its most remarkable expression in the scene in which Mazet, who has remarried, comes to *The Globe* to introduce his new wife. Davenne comes across the couple in the stairway and, to avoid meeting with them, hides behind a door, the top part of which is covered in frosted glass. Distorted by the glass, his face seems overcome by grief and gnawed at by death. The glass, which separates him from the normal course of a time that is oriented toward the future, picks up the theme of the "spectator of life." It also recalls the scene in which Adèle is looking, through a window, at Pinson and the woman with dogs going up the stairs to their room. Adèle manifests the curiosity of a child still capable of hope, Davenne the intransigence of an adult who has renounced human happiness once and for all.

In "Mourning and Melancholy," Freud contrasted the normal work of grieving with the pathological obsession of a lost object. According to his view, melancholy arises from ambivalence toward the dead person that prevents the normal process of disinvestment to take place. Hate and love struggle against one another. Davenne's anger is never directed against death; it is endlessly displaced onto other objects. But the very excess of love that it bears with it suggests the necessity of masking a powerful component of unconscious aggression. Imbert wonders whether it is guilt at having survived his friends in the war that has driven

Davenne to withdraw from the world and to commit himself to "everything that is good in life." Unable to renounce the lost object, the melancholy person identifies with it, and turns his hatred back onto his own self, taking pleasure in punishing himself. Taken to its logical extreme, this inner process leads to suicide.

Davenne's narcissistic identification with death is apparent in the analogy between his name and his wife's: Julien and Julie Davenne. As in Truffaut's other films, passion is grounded in identification and not differentiation: the lovers in *The Woman Next Door* who double one another; the twin coffins of *Jules and Jim*. Davenne would also like to base love for Cécilia on similarity. For him, the ideal of love is in the photograph that he shows Cécilia in the chapel: a man and a woman who were never apart; "not for a day, not for an hour," dying "several days apart, like Siamese twins"; a consuming dual relationship without any differentiation, any separation, any end except death.

Cécilia, however, never stops affirming her difference. When Davenne says to her: "We are the same," she replies: "No, we are not the same." Massigny becomes the symbol of what separates them. In *The Man Who Loved Women,* a film about a book, the mother rules, as in *Two English Girls.* In *The Green Room,* a film about cinema, we see the opposite, as in *Stolen Kisses* or *Day for Night* – namely, several representatives of the father: Imbert, the good father, the bishop, and, above all, Massigny, whose paternal function Truffaut confirms by saying that he plays the same role that Victor Hugo played in *Adèle H.* The green room catches fire immediately after Massigny's death, when Davenne drafted an obituary in a state of anger.[33] This act of defiance separates him in two different ways from the character who is a stand-in for the mother. One shot shows Cécilia who, struck down with grief, lets the telephone ring without answering it, while a storm is rumbling in the distance. In the following shot, we see Davenne, disappointed, replace the telephone in its cradle; several seconds later, the fire, ignited by the storm, breaks out in the green room. Fire from the sky descends on the son who has rebelled against the prohibition forbidding fusion with his mother. In an act of despair that is sublime as it is redemptive, Davenne appropriates these heavenly flames to celebrate his funereal cult in the chapel: "I have invented a ritual for them," he says to the bishop's representative. The fire

10.3. Love displayed as if it were a mass. *The Green Room,* dir. François Truffaut, 1978.

of nature is replaced by that of candles, official religion by a parallel celebration. *The Green Room* marks the climax of what Truffaut described as his "liturgical films" (*films liturgiques*) in which love is displayed as if it were a Mass.[34]

From the green room, in which objects relating to the body of the dead woman are assembled, to the chapel, in which signs of the present of the dead are dominant, we pass to the matter of the mind. The same itinerary was observable in *The Man Who Loved Women,* in which the cult of the book replaced that of women's legs. These two films celebrate, in effect, like *The Last Metro,* the triumph of a creative activity that takes place against a backdrop of transgression. As a creator, Davenne is the equal of Lucas Steiner or Bertrand Morane. "Skilled in the writing of obituaries" at the beginning of the film, in the course of the story he gradually invents a form of expression that gives form and structure to his obsession. Like Itard in *The Wild Child* and Ferrand in *Day for Night,* he invents an original language to fight against incoherence, loneliness, and death. In the great scene in the chapel, we find, orchestrated in a sumptuous manner, the leitmotif of the photograph. From *Jules and Jim* to *Two English Girls*, from *Mississippi Mermaid* to *Love on the Run*, passing through *The 400 Blows* and *Day for Night*, the object of desire is displayed in the form of a photograph, the original of which the hero is waiting impatiently to find. In *The Green Room*, Davenne has given up this impossible wish, given that the photographs are those of men and women who have died. But the flames of the candles that sparkle with all their reflected brightness in the glass that covers the images of the dead animate their faces and give them an eternal life. This chapel, along with the rotor in *The 400 Blows*, is the most beautiful metaphor for cinema in Truffaut's oeuvre. Like the rotor, the chapel is a maternal space placed under the double protection of Julie, whose photograph is enthroned over an altar, and of Cécilia, who will continue Davenne's mission after his death. But, as in *The Man Who Loved Women*, "the face is never gained." Just as Véra did, Massigny reawakens a past grief that renders null and void the work of reparation. The original lack can be provisionally masked by the creative act, but it can never be filled in. The slaughter of the First World War serves as a symbol in the film for this catastrophic failure that separates the past from the present. It is an image of the primitive agony that the creative activity is trying to efface. The tragic force of this image gives an idea of the psychic destruction against which Truffaut's hero is fighting; this destruction, like the war that marked the end of a world, is irreparable, and Davenne's task interminable.

The Man Who Loved Women and *The Green Room* end with a communion between the hero and a benevolent maternal figure who gives him the love of which he has been deprived. While Davenne, alone in the green room, is ready to let himself die in a surge of suicidal fusion with the lost object, Cécilia, shattered, goes to see Imbert at *The Globe*. He advises her to confess her love to Davenne: "Julien Davenne is a man like the others, he has a need to be loved. If he is pretending to make do with solitude, he is lying to himself . . . No one, you understand, no one genuinely likes being alone. Let him know about your feelings for him." This judgment refutes the comment made by Bertrand Morane: "I like solitude" Davenne, dying, chases away the doctor, muttering "I am independent." Nevertheless, as soon as he receives Cécilia's letter, he sets off in the snowy night for the chapel, in which he joins her to die in her arms. The chapel, like the book in *The Man Who Loved Women,* allows the protagonist to escape from the influence of the archaic mother, in order to place himself under the protection of a female figure who will perpetuate the work of creativity. It is no accident that Nathalie Baye, the actress who had the role of Ferrand's assistant in *Day for Night,* acts the part of Cécilia in this film.

In *Fahrenheit 451,* the men-books lived in a reflection of life. *The Green Room* contains a striking allegory of this other dimension in which the imaginary reigns: it is found in the large mirror in which the camera recurrently captures the image of Davenne, while he is going up or down the stairs of the house. The whole action of the film represents the interior drama that this reflection symbolically points toward.

In Truffaut's oeuvre, *The Man Who Loved Women* and *The Green Room* form a remarkable diptych on the subject of creative activity. In particular, they shed light on the complex links that unite the transitional object to the fetish and the relic. Even though these three things relate to different fundamental needs, all three are informed by an analogous principle: they depend upon an illusion. Having a mediating function, they fill in a lack or mask an absence. A transitional object allows an infant to bear the absence of his mother; a fetish suspends the threat of castration, the relic abolishes anxiety at the thought of death. The latter objects are not symbolic substitutes – pre-symbolic forms, the materiality of which guarantees their effectiveness. In contrast to a transitional object, which is progressively abandoned and replaced by cultural activities, the fetish and the relic resist the test of disillusionment, and sustain an infantile belief as a shield against adult knowledge (of sexual difference, of the finality of death). For Truffaut, creative activity corresponds with the moment in which the fetish and the relic are provisionally liberated from their pathological component in order to be commuted into a transitional object allowing access to communication and maturity. These two films describe this process, the limits of which they identify, with great precision.

11

The Role of Play
Confidentially Yours (1983)

A MISTY MARSH IN THE EARLY MORNING, A HUNTER RETURNING from his hide; a rifle shot, the hunter collapses, his face covered in blood. This is how *Confidentially Yours* begins. Massoulier is dead. Those who are familiar with Truffaut's films know him without ever having seen him: his name appears recurrently from the time of *The Bride Wore Black* – Massoulier is Corey's friend, from whose dialogue we learn that Massoulier "did" the hostess on the Montreal-Paris flight. In *Two English Girls,* the female photographer tells Claude Roc that she could meet him as a soirée at Massoulier's place – where he waits in vain for her; in *The Last Metro,* Nadine makes the same remark to Bernard Granger. We also encounter, once again, the detective agency from *Stolen Kisses,* and the perverse fetishist from *The Man Who Loved Women.* As in *The Soft Skin,* the heroine, Barbara (Fanny Ardant), occupies room number 813 in the hotel, as a tribute to Maurice Leblanc;[1] her surname is Becker, in homage to the director.[2] At the beginning of the film, while the wife of Barbara's boss lies murdered, one shot alludes to a phrase by Cocteau by framing a watch on the corpse's wrist that continues ticking away the seconds;[3] at the end, to unmask the murderer, the police inspector gives a recipe for potato salad over the phone that comes straight out of *The Rules of the Game.* The declaration of the lawyer – "Life is not a novel" – plays on the title of Resnais's film.[4] *The Green Room* points to cinema as a celebration of memory; *Confidentially Yours* illustrates this affirmation in a playful mode. The film is packed with internal references to Truffaut's other works and citations of the master filmmakers. There is practically no shot, no phrase that does not involve a cinematic memory of one sort

Figure 11.1. Barbara Becker (Fanny Ardant) and Julien Vercel (Jean-Louis Trintignant) in *Confidentially Yours,* dir. François Truffaut, 1983.

or another. Even the use of black and white is meant to evoke images from the past: "*Confidentially Yours* attempts to restore the mysterious, brilliant, nocturnal atmosphere of the American crime comedies that delighted us in years gone by. I think that the use of black and white will help us to recover that vanished charm."[5]

Truffaut thought of *Confidentially Yours* as "a Saturday-evening film designed to entertain."[6] It is set apart from his other films, however, on account of both its gratuitous nature and its unforeseeable status as the last of them. With this crime comedy, which is, from the beginning, a tribute to fiction and the art of storytelling, Truffaut magisterially illustrates his conviction that a film *has nothing to say.* He happily empties it of all content so as to emphasize narrative devices, with which he plays with an astonishing brio. In contrast to his treatment of other adaptations from American crime novels, Truffaut does not use Charles Williams's *The Long Saturday Night* as a framework for the projection of his own personal preoccupations. The film is presented as a meditation on the laws of cinematic storytelling. It is a veritable art of poetry.

At the time of its release, Truffaut said: "I regard cinema as a classical art. Above all, it is magical. And it hasn't ceased being so because of television. My work is an attempt to recover this magic."[7] With *Confidentially Yours,* Truffaut conjures up this magic in a pure state. An *in vitro* creation cut off from reality, the film works on the perceptual system of the spectator with scientific precision:

> I wanted the members of my audience to be constantly captivated, absorbed. So that they would leave the theater dazed, and astonished to find themselves on the sidewalk. I would like them to forget the time, the place they are in, like Proust, when he was absorbed in reading at Combray. Above all, I wanted to make them experience emotion.[8]

Despite its arsenal of citations, *Confidentially Yours* is not a work merely for cinephiles. The allusions are part of the pleasure, but they are not indispensable to it. In an age in which television trivializes the image, Truffaut seeks first and foremost to rivet the spectator to his or her seat. Above all, *Confidentially Yours* reflects "a hatred of the documentary," which "presents things or people for viewing without the allure of fiction."[9] His aim was to avoid "everything that seems like an interview, everything that resembles improvisation. Everything that looks like an evening news broadcast."[10]

Truffaut suppresses color, light, and the blue sky, and breaks clichés with every image. The film takes place in Provence: it is shot in settings of rain, night, and solitude. To escape from narrative convention, it also observes a principle he said he had found in Henry James, that of an odd number of characters: "The unforeseen, the bizarre always involves an odd number."[11] The film is constructed around a poisonous blonde who is soon murdered (the wife), a falsely accused man hunted by the police (the husband), and a female Sherlock Holmes (the secretary). It is when he saw Fanny Ardant wearing a raincoat to shoot the final scene in *The Woman Next Door* that Truffaut decided he wanted to have her play this role, which was what had seduced him in Williams's novel, and to turn her into the heroine of a Série Noire film: "I have always thought that stories – tales – could only be built around a woman, because women – and this is just as true of literature – convey the story more naturally than men do . . . Action belongs to women."[12]

While her boss, Julien Vercel (Jean-Louis Trintignant), remains shut in a cellar (with the name Julien recalling Julien Davenne; the cellar, recalling Lucas Steiner), Barbara follows the tracks of the real murderer by plane, by car, and on foot. Truffaut observed in the press kit that the word "secretary" embodied the word "secret." Barbara's function is to discover these secrets and reveal them.

In *Confidentially Yours,* Truffaut follows the prescription of his master Lubitsch, in particular: do not tell the story, and never treat the subject directly. Only the beginning and the end of the novel remain: "We had to invent the entire middle of the film in order to have something visual on the screen."[13] This invention always moves in the direction of digression. The plot concerns a suite of murders without head or tail, among which an astonishing procession of episodic characters file past in burlesque scenes. The comedy is no longer played out by three, but by seven, nine, eleven . . . Thus, we see a substitute secretary who can only type with one finger, a client in the real estate office who is looking for "a mountain chateau with its feet in the water," a reveler who lets a bra drop out of his pocket in an elevator, a busy peeping-Tom accompanied by his dog Pyrrhus, an Albanian who turns up at the police station at eleven o'clock at night, seeking political asylum. These scenes, seemingly removable, appear irrelevant to the logic of the story. However, if one were to suppress them, the film would deflate like a failed soufflé. They are what fill in the gaps, stitch the story together, impart to it its texture and lighthearted, subversive tone. As Jean Aurel, who co-wrote the screenplay for the film with Suzanne Schiffman and Truffaut, remarks: "It is a crazy film; there is no logic of place or time in it. It is created to entertain. We had to make sure that viewers could follow the thread of what is important, in a way that effectively reveals the other things; the film's subject is not really the action that takes place – it exists to support the rest."[14]

The "rest" reflects Truffaut's taste for the observation of details that are both ordinary and unusual, between "the true and the extraordinary," the accumulation of which frees the story from the constraints of reality in order to allow a subterranean architecture to emerge. Entertaining in a strong sense, because they amuse and distract our attention, these scenes play with details: glances, fragments of the female body, words that quickly become the only point of reference for the spectator. The glances are furtive, stolen, indiscreet; they are the glances of children who worm their way through half-open doors, fanlights, and basement windows; over gates; in the corner of corridors. Sometimes, the camera is seized by this innocent curiosity in the middle of a scene: it suddenly leaves faces that are speaking to focus on the feet of the interlocutors. As far as women are concerned, one is struck by the fact that all of them are distinguished by one unusual trait: black stockings, a scar, a leopard-skin coat, hysterical sobbing, a little white apron. Barbara starts out on her investigation dressed in the costume of an Elizabethan page, and ends it disguised as a prostitute. In this labyrinth, language occupies the role of Ariadne's thread.[15] The search for the murderer receives renewed impetus from a name, a verbal tic, a scrawled phrase. Punning abounds: "Barbara, I am 'dans l'embarras.'"[16] One also finds linguistic mannerisms: "Je vois le topo" (I get the picture). The dialogue pursues word associations, playing on the proper and figurative sense of clichés that are illustrated in the image: "The bird has flown," say some policemen at the airport as their eyes follow a jet, off-screen, that has just taken off. Truffaut had a field day in this film playing with the motifs he had used during twenty years of filmmaking: voyeurism, the fetishized woman (the photo of a skeletal and unrecognizable Judy Garland that reveals to Barbara the secret passageway in the lawyer's office), the mannequin with a wig in the secret hairdressing salon. In this film, in which men prefer brunettes, the lawyer who turns out to be the lover of the unfaithful blonde says, before committing suicide: "I don't belong to the society of men," picking up the leitmotif of the delinquent heroes, marginalized and transgressive, to be found in all of Truffaut's films.

Confidentially Yours is not a "great sick film," but a little film full of health. Nevertheless, these two formulas are strangely similar in the way that both shrug off the story. In a great sick film, it is the excess of sincerity that is conducive to the emergence of unconscious figures; in *Confidentially Yours,* the distancing and the conscious use of narrative configurations produce schemas that also fly from realism, but in a different way. Facility replaces sincerity: "The idea of sincerity is important at the beginning . . . Afterward, one has to think about a career. Sincerity is no longer enough. One is formed by codes. One obeys them."[17] Abstract motifs emerge, playing out from one scene to another, and function like metaphors. The playing with the spectator carries him away: "The pleasure has to be stronger than the analysis. Lubitsch, for example, took great amusement from making members of the audience believe that they had guessed what was going to happen. And at the end of the scene, there is a big surprise. He moves on to other things. It's a game."[18] The pleasure comes from emotion; analysis involves discursive logic. The entire art of Truffaut consisted of forcing the spectator to move from the second register to the first. To illustrate this phenomenon, one can take the case, cited by Bruno Bettelheim in *The Empty Fortress,*[19] of a young autistic patient who, "when asked to subtract four from ten," answered simply: "'I'll draw you a hexagon.'" Truffaut's indirect, oblique style arises from a principle that is analogous to this metaphoric response. It is a question of never giving a direct answer, but of providing a concrete illustration by playing on the abstract relationship that exists between an object and its metaphoric equivalents. The difference is, of course, that the young autistic person is *unable* to furnish information directly, whereas Truffaut *chooses* not to do so, and goes to great lengths to capture in scene after scene the twists and turns of the mind. As one can see, fiction, and all forms of art in general, reactivate a mode of thought that operates in the same way as dreams, psychiatric disorders, and the representation of the world in the experience of children. In the first shots of *Confidentially Yours,* Nestor Almendros's camera aptly abandons the subject of the scene – Barbara's marriage to her boss – to frame the children in the choir who are amusing themselves by pushing around the lens cap of a still camera with their feet. The discreetly happy music of Georges Delerue accompanies their game. Such is the final image that Truffaut has left us of his work as a storyteller.

Conclusion
The Art of the Secret

TEN MINUS FOUR = A HEXAGON. AS I HAVE SAID, THIS FORMULA can serve as a paradigm for understanding Truffaut's narrative procedure. Instead of explicit and abstract information, we find an indirect response formulated in a metaphoric, figurative language. Puzzling at first sight, it can be exposed through an imaginative and ingenious analysis. It requires the interlocutor to engage in mental gymnastics that disobey conventional channels of communication. I will now study the details of these gymnastics because they produce the emotion and constitute the foundation of the psychic well-being that is procured by fiction.

We know that at the very first screening of moving images, organized by the Lumière brothers, the audience, seeing a train arrive at a station, was seized with panic. This was emotion in its raw state. Silent cinema played on this extraordinary power of the image and harnessed it in order to create very refined forms of expression. Fifty years later, emotion had become dulled. "The golden age is behind us," said Truffaut in 1982 to journalists from *Cahiers du cinéma,* adding: ". . . in the work of directors who began making films in the silent era, there is an authoritative aspect that subsequently has been irremediably lost."[1] What he envied in these pioneers was their direct impact on the imagination of the spectator. Being the inventors of cinematic language, they were able to adopt "the most radical solution,"[2] when faced with a problem, without fearing that they would appear naive. With them, the effect of surprise was assured from the outset. Truffaut knew that he no longer enjoyed the same privilege. The guilty party responsible for this was "French quality" cinema, with its commonplaces and clichés, as he observed in his first critical article published in March 1953, titled "Les Extrêmes me touchent": "Twenty years of contrived grand subjects, twenty years of *Adorable Creatures, Return to Life, Don Camillo,* and others like *Moment of Truth* have created a blasé audience whose sensibility and judgment have been alienated by the ugly and contemptible "fear of being duped" that Radiguet had already denounced."[3] In the post-classical era, in order to achieve the same effect as the great filmmakers of the past, it was necessary to use a new type of coding to give the film power over the imagination. In an age of wariness, Truffaut put in place a narrative system that was meant to elude the perceptual predispositions of the spectator. It depends upon the principle of "clandestine persuasion." Instead of the direct style of early cinema, he used an indirect style, as in "the raw and the cooked."[4]

The emotion generated by a fiction film is the product of a double operation: a suspension of ordinary reason in order to force the mind to produce unconscious associations. The psychic apparatus is set up to resist this process, which has the threatening potential to eventuate in chaos. In the context of ordinary exchanges, all data that is presented to the mind is automatically organized in accordance with schemes and logical structures. Awakened consciousness thus creates "a protective network to prevent any unorganized material from penetrating into the deeper layers of the mind."[5] This blocking process facilitates communication and an ability to adapt to reality. Its weakening during sleep explains the return of fantasmatic thought in the form of dreams. The formal components of works of art also have the effect of inhibiting the organizing functions of the conscious mind, and of opening up a new kind of receptivity in the perceptual system: "the formal elements of art are, in essence, intricate and ingenious techniques aimed to bypass, evade, or penetrate the logical, reality-oriented protective layer, to arouse the deeper levels of the mind."[6] The aspects of experience with which works of art are concerned – emotions, memories, desires – are, in effect, stored in these depths. They arise, then, as multi-layered structures intended to deliver a derivative from the conscious to the unconscious.

Truffaut provoked this derivative, which early cinema had produced through the simple magic of the image, much more deliberately than his elders had done. It is furthered in his films by a dynamic relationship between ellipsis and repetition. Ellipsis is the most powerful strategy whereby the mind is normally able to create logical relationships and interpret the facts that are submitted to it. The main tool for this work, which arises in the mind as the result of a conscious search and represents the goal of all its endeavors, is information. This is what Truffaut calls "the pleasure of organizing the composition" (*le plaisir de l'agencement*): "In life, what does the most harm is a lack of imagination and an inability to classify information according to a good order."[7] The careful construction of his screenplays aims to leave in suspension clearly formulated questions that completely absorb the attention of the spectator. Spatio-temporal fragmentation of scenes that are rarely joined together by relationships of cause and effect, together with the multiplication of micro-stories, atomize the narrative into a mosaic that delays the moment in which it becomes constituted as a story; the accumulation of different pieces of information in the same fragment blocks the perceptual system; techniques such as the voice-over, which create a tension between the image and what is spoken, or superimposition, which mixes iconic referents, interfere with any direct information. All of these procedures impede the flow of the story, paralyzing reflection and suspending rational functioning by preventing the material to be immediately interpreted. They also powerfully mobilize the perceptual apparatus of the spectator, pinned to his or her seat and on the lookout for a solution that the almost-suspect clarity of each detail (one thinks, for example, of the maps that Truffaut often inserts in his films) always authorizes him or her to hope for. Having thus mined the logical function, Truffaut fires up the emotional function through the use of affective stimulants.

It is at this point that repetition intervenes. Its use in stories involves a much less deliberate search than that involved in ellipsis. It arises from "instinct," one of Truffaut's favorite words for designating decisions relating to the mise-en-scène. The absence of narrative links is countered, in effect, by a system of rhymes and parallels, forming a network that one can trace from film to film. The presence of this network creates a subterranean continuity that compensates for the absence of rational links. Truffaut's handling of it is extremely delicate, given that the mind normally rejects as meaningless anything that it does not understand.

In order to get around this natural censorship imposed by the psyche, such stylistic devices need to reconcile realistic perceptions with fantasmatic ones, and lead us to read material that is organized according to the laws of the unconscious as if it obeyed the conscious rules of perception. This phenomenon can be constantly observed in films. Such figurative devices, without contradicting the logic of the story, seem to be slightly displaced in relation to it – in particular, their obsessive repetition exceeds the strict requirements of the narrative. This "excessive" material activates the imagination of the spectator, inviting him or her to enter into another mode of thought involving unconscious associations. When Truffaut's films are studied closely, it is amazing to see how certain scenes, which function entirely at an oneiric level, succeed in evading the vigilance of the rational, like those involving the little girls in a cage in *The 400 Blows,* the raid of the firemen in the children's garden in *Fahrenheit 451,* and the handshake of the German officer in *The Last Metro.* These enigmatic scenes, devoid of any identifiable information, are those through which Truffaut really takes the spectator "on board."

As we have seen, the unconscious flow created by repetitions relates to simple, universal fantasies that are called "originary fantasies"[8] because they concern the problem of origins: in the primitive scene, it is the origin of the subject; in fantasy, it is seduction, the origin of sexuality; in fantasies of castration, the origin of the difference between the sexes. The repressed material of films, as in collective myths, deals with all the mysteries that present themselves to the child in the course of his or her development. In this regard, what Truffaut demonstrates is much better defined than is the case with most directors. We recall his declaration: "I believe, with Simenon, that one is dealing with everything that happens to us between birth and the age of 14 years." His works explore the great staging posts that mark out the route to maturity: the acquisition of language, separation from parental figures, the quest for identity, integration into society, the discovery of the other, emotional relationships, sexuality, initiation into culture, the expression of creativity. In working with this material, Truffaut does not propose any solution but, to the contrary, represents the most difficult situations involved in the process of maturation: the failure of language, of love, of the couple, of socialization. The most accurate metaphor for describing the clinical picture he presents is that of the organs of the body: in health, we completely ignore their functioning; in sickness, we discover their exact place and role in the physical dynamic. Films fulfill the same function, as far as revealing psychic realities is concerned, by accurately depicting the dramatic consequences of affective, social, or cultural dysfunction. Each turning point in adult life is liable to threaten the structures put in place during childhood, test them, and modify them. It is these moments of crisis that form the subject matter of stories. Love and creativity remain Truffaut's great themes, because both of them profoundly question our relationship with the world and plunge us back into the sources of our most personal and secret experiences. Before concluding this general survey of the preoccupations of films, one needs to confront the question of Truffaut's so-called "prudishness." Arising from his preference for an indirect style of representation, it is designed to express the violence of drives. In an era in which cinematic conventions dictated that the least one might show in a love scene would be four naked feet wriggling at the end of a bed, and the most tongues, breasts, body hair, etcetera – things that are relentlessly boring when reproduced on the screen – we find, in *The Woman Next Door,* for example, the subversive power of the sexual instinct revealed in those moments in which the lovers, without removing a thread of clothing, murmur gently: "Wait, wait." Such short-circuiting of amorous rituals, like all instances of litotes, has an effectiveness that owes nothing to prudishness and everything to a wish to depict the forbidden dimension of desire.

Nevertheless, in Truffaut's films, it is not simply the repressed content that is at issue in the story, but also the nature of their organization. Freud remarked that if censorship did not exist in dreams, they would be no more intelligible than they already are, because it would still be necessary to translate their symbolic language into the language of conscious awareness. This language is coded. It reflects a mode of thinking that is opposite to that of logical reflection, the laws of which it had been the first to define. The study of neurotic symptoms and the analysis of dreams provide confirmation that whereas classical psychology saw only chaos and meaninglessness in these phenomena, there does indeed exist a form of mental functioning in them that has exact, rigorous mechanisms. Pursuing Freud's line of thinking, Anton Ehrenzweig and

Pinchas Noy have studied the role of this form of thought in aesthetic phenomena, particularly in the case of music and painting. Whereas conscious thought divides, separates, and distinguishes, unconscious thought is scattered, syncretic, and undifferentiated. For Ehrenzweig, creativity consists of "the capacity for transforming the chaotic aspect of undifferentiation into a hidden order that can be encompassed by a comprehensive vision."[9] Works of art thus reactivate the syncretic mode of perception that one finds in the primitive structure of the vision of the world held by children. Moreover, one can assume that the interest Truffaut always showed in the construction of fairy tales relates to the kind of perception that they elicit, which he was trying to reproduce in his own work. Furthermore, by drawing the subject matter of his stories from the circumstances of his own childhood, he was ensuring the accuracy of the way it was organized, owing to the truthfulness of the raw material.

Truffaut's films are meant to provoke the spectator to entertain a double reading, one that involves an opposition between two different modes of thought: a logical mode that is continually suspended by the detours in the story; and a fantasmatic mode elicited by repetitions that organize the coherence of the overall vision at an unconscious, undifferentiated level. This coherence distinguishes creative work from psychiatric symptoms in which a lack of differentiations leads to catastrophic chaos. The effect of this double reading is to orientate the spectator's mind constantly in the direction of "that region of indeterminacy that lies between the fantasmatic and the secondary,"[10] a region containing the barrier against contact between the conscious and the unconscious, a region of "scanning," as Ehrenzweig calls it, that is to say, a kind of perception that is close to the free association of psychoanalysis. The analyst, while he is listening to a patient, is not so much interested in following the conscious flow of his or her words as in identifying the accidents of language – slips, hesitations, repetitions – that reveal unconscious structures behind the logical sequences of discourse. Truffaut's films are constructed in such a way as to activate this kind of reception in the spectator. Undifferentiated perception, in an instantaneous, comprehensive way, brushes aside any structures having a complexity that poses problems for conscious thought. It involves an immediate seizure of the material at the point where conscious attention comes up against the complex network of a story that is constantly slipping away, mobilizing the investment of a considerable quantity of psychic energy. It is the gap between these two modes of perception that generates emotion – that is to say, the pleasure produced by the narrative:

> formal esthetic pleasure is derived from an economy of perceptual energy. If works of art which are generally acclaimed as being "great" from the point of view of structure are regarded in the light of this assumption, it will be apparent that all show this discrepancy between the effort to be invested by conscious perception and that needed by unconscious perception. It may be assumed even that the degree of "greatness" is proportional to the extent of this discrepancy.[11]

Ehrenzweig and Noy believe that the function of artistic constructions is to channel the energetic forces of the unconscious through their formal constituents. Responding to the demands of both fantasmatic thought and logical thought, they unite them in a single structure. The degree of pleasure that they generate is the function of a harmonious dynamic between the two systems. A work that is too undifferentiated will be particularly rich from a formal point of view, but will initially repel understanding. The short-circuit between the two types of perception is at first too radical. There are plenty of examples of the negative reception this type of original work tends to elicit, from cubism to Rodin's statue of Balzac, and the "great sick film" identified by Truffaut. To return to the modest example at the beginning of this chapter, we see that the model "ten minus four = a hexagon" also juxtaposes two modes of thought and plays on the gap between them. As with Truffaut, the anticipated information is left hanging, to be replaced by a response that directs the mind toward another mode of representation. There is a void between these two moments, a rupture that generates emotion in stories.

We have followed from film to film the expression of a kind of metaphorical and symbolic language that is characteristic of unconscious thought. It is composed of terms that are simple, concrete, and universal: fire, milk, water, mirror, window, sea, falling, and spatial representations. Able to be understood immediately by every member of any audience, it easily bypasses linguistic, cultural, and historical barriers. There are no "true" signifiers in this language: "A film doesn't say anything." The supple and flexible structure that it forms allows every spectator to project the content of his or her personal experience. It plays on the affective potential of each person as on an instrument: "Myth and music," writes Lévi-Strauss, "are like the conductors of an orchestra, whose audience becomes the silent performers."[12] This concept could be applied with equal pertinence to the films of Truffaut, which, as this book has shown, succeed in an empirical but exact way to "recover," as Lévi-Strauss says of music, "the structures of mythological thought."[13] The latter, fallen into disuse in the eighteenth century because of a preference for realistic expression, remained present in the unconscious, where it sought a new use. Lévi-Strauss sees music as the heir of mythological thought in so far as both "appeal to mental structures that the different listeners have in common."[14] Having become weakened in novelistic expression, it seems that it has found in the fiction film a medium capable of nurturing it.

Truffaut has often declared that film is much closer to music than literature: "Because of its uninterrupted projection, a film can be likened to a piece of music played in a concert hall – but to nothing else, and especially not to a visit to a museum, nor to the reading of a book."[15] In an interview published in *Cahiers du cinéma,* Lévi-Strauss made similar remarks: "Cinema is an art that has many more dimensions than painting or literature and which, from this point of view, seems commensurable to music, to me."[16] Furthermore, we find in the conclusion of *The Naked Man*[17] a famous description of musical emotion that can serve as a model for the functioning of what Truffaut calls "the emotion" of cinema. In both cases, we see the putting in place of a system that is meant to short-circuit Cartesian thought for the pleasure of the listener or spectator. Like music, the fiction film seems to operate a perceptual system of a sort that is analogous to that found in myths. This hypothesis explains the passion with which Truffaut, intuitively aware of this phenomenon, always defended it during a time when his reputation had declined; it also explains the obstinacy with which he tried to restore the power of the language of classical cinema in his own films. In addition, it accounts for the transcultural appeal of his films and their hold over the collective imagination.

It remains to define the role of this mode of thought, which consciousness, geared toward action, accomplishment, and productivity, represses, but which film reactivates. If works of fiction are necessary for our psychic equilibrium, it is because they put into play mental structures that allow meaning and coherence to be imparted to experience. In order to define the term "experience" in this context, it is necessary to draw a contrast between it and "knowledge." When a child wants to hear the same story each night without tolerating a single word being changed, what is he or she seeking? It is certainly not any knowledge, or information that one gathers in: one time only would be sufficient for that. The child is testing mental mechanisms, executing a kind of psychic gymnastics that brings him or her a sense of well-being and comfort. Each reading appeases the same fears, reassures him, and organizes reality by putting him in contact with a form of mental functioning that enables a transmission of the experience of the story to take place. Childhood is the time when experience of the world needs to be assimilated in high doses, given that the child faces massive problems of adaptation to reality and to the "other" during this period. This primitive form of adaptation is then repressed in the course of the educational process, which delivers the first stage of the acquisition of knowledge. In adult life, these mechanisms continue to be necessary for our equilibrium. The fiction film provides a terrain on which they can be practiced. It represents a form of psychic regulation that allows us to situate ourselves in the world, to accept time and death by giving meaning to our lives.

Above all, the pleasure of films comes from recognizing in fiction a magnified reflection of the structures of our mind when it attempts to organize experience. Truffaut aptly used the metaphor of enlarged-print as a paradigm for defining his work:

> I learned a while back that there were books printed in large characters for people who were beginning to have problems with their eyesight. I ordered some of these books, only to have them ready at hand, not because I have poor eyesight – mine is good. But I wanted to touch these books because they represent what I want to do.[18]

At the end of *The Jealous Potter,* Lévi-Strauss applies the same metaphor to mythological thought, in somewhat different terms: "With an authority that cannot be denied, it arises from the depths of time, setting before us a magnifying mirror that reflects, in the massive form of concrete images, certain mechanisms by which the exercise of thought is ruled."[19]

The example of the child who asks for the same story each night, invoked above to describe the role of fiction, was not gratuitous. It relates to the young Truffaut, who would go to the cinema each night to seek refuge and comfort. It is there that he learned the functioning of these complex processes, the components of which I have attempted to analyze. For this troubled young boy, who was sparkling with intelligence and bubbling with imagination, there was never any other language apart from the one he learned in the cinema while playing truant; it was this that enabled him to impose an order on his life. In 1957, that is to say, in the year in which he released *Les Mistons,* he wrote this about Charlie Chaplin: "An artist can create works for himself to 'do himself good,' or to 'do good' for others. Perhaps the greatest artists are those who simultaneously resolve their own problems and those of their public."[20] It is possible that the secret of great storytellers is in uniting ingenuity with generosity in their work. Truffaut understood this secret. He put it into practice in his films.

Notes

PREFACE TO THE ENGLISH EDITION / ANNE GILLAIN

1. Antoine de Baecque and Serge Toubiana, *François Truffaut* (Paris: Gallimard, 1996).

2. Carole Le Berre, *Truffaut au Travail* (Paris: Cahiers du cinéma, 2004).

3. "J'ai envie que mon public soit constamment captivé, envoûté. Qu'il sorte de la salle de cinema, hébété, étonné d'être sur le trottoir. Je voudrais qu'il en oublie l'heure, le lieu où il se trouve, comme Proust plongé dans la lecture à Combray. Je souhaite avant tout l'émotion." Anne Gillain, *Le Cinéma selon François Truffaut* (Paris: Flammarion, 1988), 415.

4. Dudley Andrew, Anne Gillain, *A Companion to François Truffaut* (New York and London: Wiley-Blackwell), forthcoming.

5. To be published in *A Companion to François Truffaut.*

6. Anne Gillain, "Reconciling Irreconcilables: An Interview with François Truffaut," *Wide Angle* 4.4 (1981): 26–37.

7. Gillain (ed.), *Le Cinéma selon François Truffaut.*

8. Madame Morgenstern gave all these documents to the BiFi in 1998 and 1999 when she finally closed Les Films du Carrosse.

9. *The Mississippi Mermaid* or *The Last Metro,* to name only two.

10. *Truffaut au Travail,* 228.

11. *François Truffaut,* 539.

12. For a more detailed discussion of these theoretical issues, see Anne Gillain, "Aesthetic Affinities: François Truffaut, Patrick Modiano, Douglas Sirk," in *"A Companion to François Truffaut"* (forthcoming).

13. Raymond Bellour, *Le Corps du cinéma, hypnoses, émotions, animalités* (Paris: P.O.L., 2010); David Stern, *The Interpersonal world of the Infant* (New York: Basic Books, 1985); David Stern, *The Present Moment in Psychotherapy and Everyday Life,* (New York: Norton, 2004).

14. Bellour, *Le Corps du cinema,* "L'émotion . . . équivaut à l'hypnose" (122).

15. "L'*Infant* de Daniel Stern *est* le spectateur de cinema" (Bellour, *Le Corps du cinéma,* 152).

16. See Bellour, *Le Corps du cinema,* 151–177

17. Stern, *The Interpersonal world of the Infant,* 57.

18. "Une équivalence frontale . . . entre les affects de vitalité dans les comportements spontanés et le style dans l'art" (Bellour, *Le Corps du Cinema,* 163).

19. Quoted from an article to be published in *A Companion to François Truffaut.*

20. "Le pianiste, je crois que je l'ai fait pour une image. Dans le livre de Goodis, à la fin, il y a une petite maison dans la neige,

des sapins et une petite route en pente et on dirait que cette voiture glisse sur la route sans qu'on entende le bruit du moteur. J'ai eu envie de réaliser cette image" (*Le Cinema selon François Truffaut,* 109).

21. "*La Peau Douce,* c'est parti d'une image . . . d'un couple dans un taxi. Je voyais cela vers 19 h 30. Ils doivent rentrer diner. Ils ne sont pas mariés ou, s'ils sont mariés, c'est chacun de leur côté avec des enfants, c'est un baiser terriblement charnel dans ce taxi, dans une grande ville" (ibid., 152).

22. Stern, *The Present Moment,* 200.

23. Anne Gillain, "Reconciling Irreconcilables: An Interview with François Truffaut," *Wide Angle* 4.4 (1981), p. 32.

24. Stern, *The Present Moment in Psychotherapy and Everyday Life,* 113.

EMOTION AND THE AUTHORIAL FANTASMATIC / ALISTAIR FOX

1. See Jacques Rivette, "Notes sur une révolution," *Cahiers du cinéma* 54 (Christmas 1955), 18–19. Truffaut used this quotation as an epigraph for his collection of his critical writings, *The Films in My Life* (New York: Da Capo Press, 1994).

2. For Tsai Ming Liang's moving account of the overwhelming impact made on him by his viewing of *L'Histoire d'Adèle H.,* the first of Truffaut's movies he had seen, see Tsai Ming Liang, "On the Uses and Misuses of Cinema," *Senses of Cinema* 58 (March 2011) http://www.sensesofcinema.com/2011/feature-articles/on-the-uses-and-misuses-of-cinema/. Accessed November 9, 2011.

3. Michel Marie, *The French New Wave: An Artistic School,* Richard Neupert (trans.) Malden: Blackwell, 2003), 159.

4. David Kehr, "A Poet of Darkness Who Longs for the Light," *The New York Times,* May 16, 1999.

5. Such a preference can still be found today, as, for example, in Colin McCabe's review of Antoine de Baecque's *Godard: Biographie* in *New Statesmen,* May 27, 2010: "Godard's relationship to his films is much more complex [than that of Truffaut to his]. Plot is of minimal importance for him, and is always made up of fragments of narrative rather than a full-blown story."

6. Kehr, *The New York Times,* May 16, 1999.

7. "un 'Truffaut-Jekyll,' respectable et rangé, qui plaît aux familles, et un 'Truffaut-Hyde,' asocial, solitaire, passionné à froid, fétichiste" (Serge Daney, *Libération,* September 30, 1981).

8. Thomas Jefferson Kline, "Cinema and/as Dream: Truffaut's 'Royal Road' to *Adèle H,*" in the same author's *Unraveling French Cinema: From* L'Atlante *to* Caché (Chichester: Wiley, 2010), 10.

9. See Raymond Bellour, *L'Analyse du film* (Paris: Éditions Albatros, 1980); reprinted in an English edition as *The Analysis of Film* (Bloomington: Indiana University Press, 2000); Laura Mulvey, *Visual and Other Pleasures* (Bloomington: Indiana University Press, 1988); Teresa de Lauretis, *Alice Doesn't: Feminism, Semiotics, Cinema* (Bloomington: Indiana University Press, 1984); and Mary Anne Doane, *The Desire to Desire: The Woman's Film of the 1940s* (Bloomington: Indiana University Press, 1987).

10. Barthes' influential essay "The Death of the Author" (1967) is reprinted in Roland Barthes, *Image/Music/Text* (New York: Hill and Wang, 1977), 142–148.

11. See Michel Foucault, "What Is an Author?" Donald F. Bouchard and Sherry Simon (trans.), in Donald F. Bouchard (ed.), *Language, Counter-Memory, Practice* (Ithaca, N.Y.: Cornell University Press, 1977), 124–127.

12. Diana Holmes and Robert Ingram, *François Truffaut* (Manchester and New York: Manchester University Press, 1998), vii.

13. See Antoine de Baecque and Serge Toubiana, *Truffaut* (Berkeley: University of California Press, 2000).

14. See Annette Insdorf, *François Truffaut,* Revised and Updated Edition (Cambridge: Cambridge University Press, 1994).

15. See Carole Le Berre, *François Truffaut at Work* (London: Phaidon Press, 2005).

16. See Robert Stam, *François Truffaut and Friends: Modernism, Sexuality, and Film Adaptation* (New Brunswick and London: Rutgers University Press, 2006).

17. For an example of such Lacanian criticism, see Eliane DalMolin, "A Voice in the Dark: Feminine Figuration in Truffaut's 'Jules and Jim,'" *Literature Film Quarterly* 22:4 (1994): 238–245. DalMolin draws heavily on Kaja Silverman's *The Acoustic Mirror: The Female Voice in Psychoanalysis and Cinema* (Bloomington: Indiana University Press, 1988), which also draws upon Lacan.

18 Andrea Sabbadini, "Introduction," in Andrea Sabbadini (ed.), *The Couch and the Silver Screen: Psychoanalytic Reflections on European Cinema* (Hove and New York: Brunner-Routledge, 2003), 5–6.

19. Ibid., 6.

20. Andrea Sabbadini, "Cameras, Mirrors, and the Bridge Space: A Winnicottian Lens on Cinema," Projections 5:1 (Summer 2011): 17–30.

21. Bernardo Bertolucci and Andrea Sabbadini, "Psychoanalysis: The 11th Muse (A Conversation), Psychoanalytic Inquiry 27:4 (2007): 381–394.

22. See François Truffaut, "Pourquoi ce film? Pourquoi pas?" L'Avant-Scène Cinéma 165 (January 1976): 4–5.

23. Ibid., 388. This observation recalls Truffaut's confession that he only comes to understand the meaning of his films long after he has made them – for example, the fact that he had unconsciously made *Jules and Jim* to please his mother and gain her approval (see Chapter 3).

24. See Virginia Wright Wexman (ed.), *Film and Authorship* (New Brunswick, NJ: Rutgers University Press, 2003); Barry Keith Grant (ed.), *Auteurs and Authorship: A Film Reader* (Maldon, MA: Blackwell Publishing, 2008); David A. Gerstner and Janet Staiger (eds.), *Authorship and Film* (New York: Routledge, 2003); and Alistair Fox, *Jane Campion: Authorship and Personal Cinema* (Bloomington and Indianapolis: Indiana University Press, 2011).

25. See Francis Vanoye, L'Adaptation littéraire au cinéma (Paris: Armand Colin, 2011), esp. Chapter 2.

26. See Deb Verhoeven, *Jane Campion* (New York: Routledge, 2009), 11, and Timothy Corrigan, *A Cinema Without Walls: Movies and Culture After Vietnam* (New Brunswick, N. J.: Rutgers University Press, 1991), 106.

27. See Patricia Ticineto Clough, *The Affective Turn: Theorizing the Social* (Durham and London: Duke University Press, 2007).

28. Quoted from an interview with Antonio Damasio posted on YouTube: http://www.youtube.com/watch?v=Q25upippE (accessed January 28, 2012). For Damasio's detailed account of his theory, see his book Self Comes to Mind: Constructing the Conscious Brain (New York: Pantheon, 2010). The importance of Damasio's earlier findings regarding the emotions is also extensively discussed by Raymond Bellour in *Le Corps du cinéma: Hypnoses, émotions, animalités* (Paris: P.O.L., 2009).

29. Michael Hardt, "Preface," in *Clough, The Affective Turn,* p. ix.

30. For another magisterial exploration of affective issues as they relate to cinema, see Raymond Bellour, *Le Corps du cinéma.*

31. "je suis bien obligé de me rendre compte que seul le domaine affectif m'occupe et m'intéresse" (Truffaut, "Pourquoi ce film? Pourquoi pas?" L'Avant-Scène Cinéma 165 [January 1976]: 4–5).

32. Jane Campion, "Director's Commentary," *Sweetie,* DVD, directed by Jane Campion (Irvington, NY: Criterion Collection, 2006).

33. Simona Argentieri, "Truffaut and the Failure of Introjection," in Glen Gabbard (ed.), *Psychoanalysis and Film* (London and New York: Karnac, 2001), 107–113, esp. 112–113.

34. Argentieri, who is a Full Member of the International Psychoanalytical Association and a Training and Supervising Analyst of the Italian Psychoanalytical Association based in Rome, appears to have been unaware of Gillain's earlier work, which would have provided copious evidence to substantiate the former's hypotheses.

PREFACE TO THE ORIGINAL FRENCH EDITION / JEAN GRUAULT

1. Jean Gruault is a French screenwriter and actor who worked with Truffaut on the scripts for some of his most important films, including *Jules and Jim, The Wild Child, Two English Girls, The Story of Adèle H.,* and *The Green Room.*

2. Les Films du Carrosse was Truffaut's own production company, created with financial backing from UFIC, an organization that financed movies. It was named after *The Golden Coach* (*Le Carrosse d'or* in French) by Jean Renoir, one of the earlier filmmakers Truffaut greatly admired (see Antoine de Baecque and Serge Toubiana, *Truffaut: A Biography* (Berkeley and Los Angeles: University of California Press, 1999), 109 *et passim.*

INTRODUCTION

1. "J'ai toujours pensé que si on a quelque chose à dire, il faut le dire ou l'écrire mais pas faire un film. Un film ne dit rien, un film véhicule des informations émotionnelles trop bouleversantes, trop sensuelles, trop distrayantes, pour qu'il en résulte un message flegmatique" (Serge Daney, Jean Narboni, and Serge Toubiana, "Entretien avec François Truffaut," *Cahiers du cinéma* 316 [October 1980]: 33).

2. Ibid., 26.

3. "On a du mal aujourd'hui, probablement à cause de la banalisation des personnalités par la télévision, à se représenter ce que fut la célébrité de Chaplin. Une photo de *L'Illustration,* dans les années vingt, le montre de dos, saluant d'un balcon de l'hôtel Crillon la foule massée sur la place de la Concorde pour l'acclamer, oui, mais aussi pour le remercier d'exister" (François Truffaut, *Le Plaisir des yeux* [Paris: Cahiers du cinéma, 1987], 71).

4. "Pendant la décennie de terrorisme idéologique, on a essayé de nous convaincre que les films devaient être 'ouverts' et constituer des 'dialogues' avec le public. Alors, j'ai revu mes films préférés, je les ai fait défiler dans ma tête et je me suis aperçu que presque tous étaient des films 'fermés' et ressemblaient à des monologues. Mon dégout de la mode et mon esprit de contradiction faisant le reste, j'ai délibérément tourné *L'Enfant sauvage, Adèle H., La Chambre verte* pour les faire ressembler à des objets et même, au fond de moi, à des oeufs en ivoire que l'on pourrait voir, toucher, mais pas entamer" ("Entretien avec François Truffaut," *Cinématographe,* 44 [February 1979 60]: 59–63).

5. "Travaillant de façon plus instinctive qu'intellectuelle, je ne comprends mes films que deux ans après leur sortie. Cette lucidité à retardement constitue une aide plutôt qu'un handicap, car il me semble que je manquerais d'élan chaque matin pour aller au tournage d'un film dont la signification serait préétablie" (François Truffaut, "Pourquoi ce film? Pourquoi pas?" *L'Avant-Scène Cinéma,* 165 [January 1976]: 4–5).

6. Claude Lévi-Strauss, *The Raw and the Cooked,* trans. John and Doreen Weightman (Harmondsworth: Penguin, 1986), 11–12.

7. "Hitchcock, dès le début de sa carrière, a compris que si on lit son journal avec ses yeux et sa tête, on lit un roman avec ses yeux et son coeur battant et qu'un

film doit se regarder comme se lit un roman . . . Il ne s'agit pas pour Hitchcock de nous apprendre quelque chose, de nous instruire et de nous réformer, mais de nous intriguer, nous empoigner, nous captiver, nous faire perdre le souffle et surtout nous faire participer émotionnellement au récit qu'il a choisi de conduire . . . Les nouveaux cinéastes américains sont presque tous des enfants de Hitchcock, mais, derrière leur goût pour un usage dramatique de la caméra, nous nous apercevons qu'il leur manque quelque chose qui est essentiel dans le cinéma hitchcockien: la sensibilité, la peur ressentie, l'émotivité, la perception intime et profonde des émotions que l'on filme . . . Tout s'apprend, mais tout ne s'acquiert pas et si les disciples peuvent prétendre, un jour ou l'autre, égaler la virtuosité du maestro, il leur manquera sans doute l'émotivité de l'artiste. Alfred Hitchcock reste, encore aujourd'hui, en 1980, même si son état de santé l'empêche de tourner son cinquante-quatrème film, non seulement l'homme qui en sait le plus, mais aussi le cinéaste qui nous émeut le plus" (*Le Plaisir des yeux,* 81–82).

8. "J'aurai à peine l'impression d'exagérer en disant que le cinéma m'a sauvé la vie. D'où le fait que je ne puisse pas en parler intellectuellement. Il m'est arrivé d'employer l'expression 'drogue' avant que ce mot ne devienne à la mode" (Anne Gillain (ed.), *Le Cinéma selon François Truffaut* [Paris: Flammarion, 1988], 19).

9. "plus un écrivain est enraciné dans son environnement et plus il est compris par tous. Plus il est national et plus il devient international" (Isaac Bashevis Singer, *Contes* [Paris: Stock, 1985], 286).

10. "Je classe mes livres par auteur. Mais je voudrais réserver un rayon de ma bibliothèque aux livres sur les mères. C'est le meilleur livre de chaque écrivain. Regardez Simenon, Roger Peyrefitte, Bataille, Pagnol, Albert Cohen. Si on n'avait qu'un seul sujet, ce serait celui-là. Pour moi, c'est peut-être trop tôt" (*Le Cinéma selon François Truffaut,* 386–387).

1. FAMILY SECRETS

1. This chapter reprints, with some modifications, the article by Anne Gillain, "The Script of Delinquency: François Truffaut's *Les 400 Coups,*" first published in *French Films: Texts and Contexts,* ed. Susan Hayward and Ginette Vincendeau (London: Routledge, 1990), 187–199.

2. "Voilà un type qui est cocu, il ne s'en aperçoit pas. Il ne se rend compte que d'une chose: on lui a pris son guide Michelin" (François Truffaut, "Entretien avec Georges Franju," *Cahiers du cinéma* 101 [November 1959]: 4).

3. "Pour donner plus de force au démarrage, je pense renoncer à la révélation de la bâtardise pour la remplacer par une autre: en faisant l'école buissonnière, Antoine rencontrera sa mère avec un jeune type, son amant" (François Truffaut, *Correspondance* [Paris; Hatier, 1987], 142.

4. D. W. Winnicott, *Playing and Reality* (London and New York: Routledge, 2005), 19.

5. Winnicott, *Playing and Reality,* 69.

6. One scene, cut from the commercial version of the film, shows Antoine and René in the process of shooting paper bullets at passersby with a peashooter. They make the bullets by gleefully tearing out the pages from the Michelin guide of Antoine's father.

7. D. W. Winnicott, *The Child and the Outside World: Studies in Developing Relationships,* ed. Janet Hardenberg (London: Tavistock, 1957), 177.

8. Winnicott, *Playing and Reality,* 149.

9. Rabindranath Tagore, quoted by Winnicott, *Playing and Reality,* 128. The commentary of the latter is worth quoting: "Tagore's image has always intrigued me [. . .] as a student of unconscious symbolism, I *knew* (one always *knows*) that the

sea is the mother, and onto the seashore the child is born." In French, there is a homophone between "mer" (sea) and "mère" (mother) that is lacking in English.

10. Melanie Klein, *Love, Guilt and Reparation: And Other Works 1921–1945* (New York: Free Press, 1975), 236–247.

11. Anne Gillain, "Reconciling Irreconcilables: An Interview with François Truffaut," *Wide Angle* 4:4 (1981): 33.

12. François Truffaut, *Correspondance,* 624.

13. Ibid., 608.

14. This chapter was written in response to an excellent study written in 1986 by Elizabeth Halstead, in the context of a seminar on Truffaut that I was conducting at Wellesley University.

15. On this subject, see the article by Pascal Kané, "Qui y a-til sous les jupes des femmes?"*Cahiers du cinéma* 329 (November 1981): 51–52.

16. He says to his longstanding friend, the gay editor: "You see, I never set out to look for the ideal woman . . . or any woman at all . . . but when I met Mathilde, I knew that she offered some kind of assurance."

17. When Mathilde looks at Bernard's house for the first time; when Bernard hides in the dark to avoid the Coudrays; when Mathilde faints in the parking lot; when the telegraph-operator arrives; when Bernard leaves in his car to find Mathilde in the hotel; when Odile Jouve's lover returns; when the lovers embrace in the car; when Bernard's violence is unleashed at the garden-party; during the conversation between the two men in the toilet about the woman-neighbor on the same floor; during the murder-suicide of the final scene.

2. DECEPTIONS

1. "J'ai traversé davantage de périodes de vide et de tristesse après les succès qu'après les échecs: j'ai eu de violents coups de cafard après *Les 400 Coups* et *Jules et Jim,* par example" (*Le Cinéma selon François Truffaut,* 165).

2. This chapter reprints part of an earlier article by Anne Gillain, "La scène de l'audition," *L'Avant-Scène Cinéma* 362–363 [juillet/août 1987]: 69–75.

3. "David Goodis m'a écrit une lettre et j'ai compris que *Le Pianiste* sous-titré lui plaît moins que lorsqu'il n'y comprenait rien et croyait le film beaucoup plus fidèle à son livre." (*Correspondance,* 217).

4. "les hommes n'y parlent que des femmes et les femmes m'y parlent que des hommes; au plus fort des bagarres, des règlements de comptes, du kidnapping, des poursuites, on ne parle que de l'amour: sexuel, sentimental, physique, moral, social, conjugal, extra, etc." (*Le Cinéma selon François Truffaut,* 112).

5. *Série Noire* is a series of crime thrillers published by Gallimard, which includes many works by American writers.

6. "Un jour que j'étais à l'hôpital militaire, on m'avait envoyé dix ou douze romans de la Série noire que j'avais lus à la suite et je m'étais rendu compte qu'ils étaient très féeriques. Bien plus, certaines choses de ces bouquins de la Série noire me faisaient penser à *L'Aigle à deux têtes* ou aux *Enfants terribles.. Tirez sur le pianiste,* ça a probablement été cette idée là: prendre une Série noire – quand même déjà poétique parce que Goodis n'est pas n'importe qui – et la pousser au bout de son extravagance four en faire apparaître le côté conte de fées pour adultes."(*Le Cinéma selon François Truffaut,* 122).

7. "En revoyant le film, je me suis rappelé qu'il y avait toute une partie dans les rapports avec Nicole Berger qui est influencée par *Le Mépris* de Moravia. Il est passé une partie de cette historire de la femme qui a favorisé le succès de son mari; lui pense qu'elle le méprise," (*Le Cinéma selon François Truffaut,* 121).

8. D. W. Winnicott, *Collected Papers: Through Paediatrics to Psycho-analysis* (London: Tavistock, 1958), 212.

9. "Je vous demande instamment . . . de ne pas parler d'un film 'autobiographique,' genre *400 Coups,* mais d'une fiction inspirée de faits divers passionnels" (*Correspondance,* 245).

10. "Comme je ne recule devant aucune faute de goût, les scènes de ménage Lachenay se passeront dans mon appartement rue du Conseiller-Collignon." (ibid., 252).

11. Madeleine Morgenstern, whom Truffaut had married in 1957.

12. "Madeleine et moi, nous nous séparons . . . *La Peau douce* a été pénible à tourner et, à cause du scénario, j'ai pris en horreur l'hypocrisie conjugale; là-dessus, je suis assez révolté en ce moment" (*Correspondance,* 257).

13. "Jaccoud allant au restaurant avec Linda Baud la laissait dans la voiture, entrait dans le restaurant et commençait par regarder s'il n'y avait personne de connaissance. S'il y avait quelqu'un, il remontait dans la voiture, il allait dans un deuxième restaurant où il choisissait une table au fond et la faisait asseoir face à la porte. Chaque fois que la porte s'ouvrait it lui demandait: "qui est-ce?" (*Le Cinéma selon François Truffaut,* 155.)

14. Details supplied by Truffaut in an interview given on January12, 1982.

15. In addition, the filmmaker signaled his closeness to the hero in *The Soft Skin* in the name he gave Pierre Lachenay: Pierre, after Jacoud, and Lachenay, after Robert Lachenay, his childhood friend, whose name he would use for many critical articles he wrote during the early days of his journalistic period.

16. "Mon idée était surtout de faire un film sur l'adultère en m'inspirant du caractère de Pierre Jaccoud tel qu'on le connaît par les récits du procès . . . Il m'a beaucoup touché et j'ai pensé qu'à travers lui on pouvait montrer un homme fort dans la vie sociale mais faible en amour et qui, à quarante-qhatre ans, se trouve devant un dilemme plus aigu et de plus en plus 'coincé' dans un engrenage. *La Peau douce* est le portrait de cet homme" (*Le Cinéma selon François Truffaut* 154–155).

17. Ibid., 154.

18. Gilles Cahoreau, *François Truffaut* (Paris: Julliard, 1989), 224.

19. Ibid.

20. "On n'a jamais vu, en gros plans, tourner tant de clés de contact, presser tant de démarreurs, de boutons de taxiphone. On n'a jamais vu ouvrir et fermer tant de portes. Pourquoi avoir fait un sort à de si infimes détails? Pour accélérer? Pour donner l'impression d'une 'vie moderne' haletante? Pour faire sentir que le héros est harcelé par les difficultés matérielles que lui cause sa double vie? Si c'est cela, c'est enfantin et c'est surtout sans effet." (*L'Express,* May 28, 1964).

21. "Je raconte des histoires avec un début, un milieu et une fin, même si je sais bien que, finalement, l'intérêt est ailleurs que dans l'intrigue elle-même." (*Correspondance,* 465).

22. "Trajectoire se faisant et se défaisant, *La Peau douce* nous parle de distance . . . Doigts parcourant leur propre limite, tâtonnements entremêlés, frôlements provisoires, mains liées et déliées puis agrippées à la passerelle, doigts appuyant sur les boutons de l'ascenseur, effectuant quelques mouvements circulaires sur le clavier téléphonique, échangeant des trousseaux de clés . . . Du corps ne subsiste ici aucune trace vivante, aucun élan . . . Seuls l'enveloppe, la surface, l'épiderme se manifestent encore par quelques symptômes latents." (André Téchiné, "D'une distance l'autre," *Cahiers du cinéma* 157 [July 1964]: 50).

23. D. W. Winnicott, *The Maturational Processes and the Facilitating Environment* (London: Hogarth Press, 1965), 187.

24. Winnicott, *Collected Papers: Through Paediatrics to Psycho-Analysis,* 90.

25. Claude Geets, *Winnicott,* Editions Universitaires, coll. "Psychothèque" (Paris, 1981), 49.

26. "je me suis inspiré d'un homme plus à son aise avec les morts, les gloires anciennes, qu'avec le monde d'aujourd'hui" (*Le cinéma selon François Truffaut,* 162).

27. Ibid., 160.

28. "j'avais envie un moment à Reims de le faire s'évanouir, quand il a vu la fille de l'autre côté de la vitre, Ceccaldi lui boit son demi, et lui se serait levé et seait tombé en arrière. Puis on s'est dit: ça va faire un film sur un fou, les gens vont penser, c'est l'histoire d'un malade, et on a supprimé l'idée qui est allée atterrir dans Fahrenheit" (*Le Cinéma selon François Truffaut,* 162). In *Fahrenheit 451,* it is at the moment when the captain of the firemen surprises Montag in the act of searching through his desk that the latter faints.

29. "On a condamné le film sur une chose que j'ai profondément voulue; il ne dit pas à Ceccaldi: je suis venu avec une fille. Or, comme Jaccoud, Desailly est un homme qui ne peut pas faire ça" (*Le Cinéma selon François Truffaut,* 155).

30. Truffaut gave this name to the country inn to which the lovers retreat, after the disastrous evening at Rheims, as a tribute to *The Rules of the Game,* by Jean Renoir, in which the action is set at a country house called La Colinière.

31. D. W. Winnicott, "The Concept of a Healthy Individual," in *Home is Where We Start From: Essays by a Psychoanalyst,* ed. Clare Winnicott, Ray Shepherd, and Madeleine Davis (Harmondsworth: Penguin, 1986), 33.

32. First draft of the screenplay for *The Soft Skin,* Archives des Films du Carrosse.

33. Winnicott, *The Maturational Processes,* 143.

34. "un grand bourgeois mais avec quelque chose de juvénile qui donne une impression d'innocence et d'extrême maladresse dans la clandestinité." (*Le Cinéma selon François Truffaut,* 155).

35. "chaque fois qu'il se présente une difficulté choisit la plus mauvaise solution . . . Je ne voulais pas être méchant mais assez critique, si bien que le film est rempli d'annotations, de moqueries. Il y a un cinéaste de gauche, italien, De Bosi, qui a dit que c'était un film d'humour noir. C'est assez vrai." (*Le Cinéma selon François Truffaut,* 154,158–159).

36. Sigmund Freud, *Le Mot d'esprit et Ses Rapports avec l'inconscient* (Paris: Gallimard, 1978), 408. Gillain is quoting here from an essay by Freud on "Humour" that first appeared in *Imago,* 1929, vol. XIV, fasc. 1, and that was printed in the French edition of *Jokes and Their Relation to the Unconscious* as an appendix.

3. QUEEN-WOMEN

1. "J'ai compris beaucoup plus tard que si j'avais tellement voulu tourner *Jules et Jim,* c'est que ce sujet avait des racines très cachées dans ma propre enfance et que cela me permettait de tirer un trait sur toutes les choses que j'avais ressenties comme anormales autour de moi, pendant cette période de l'Occupation vécue à Pigalle, au milieu des trafics, du marché noir, des règlements de comptes passionnels, de l'adultère et de tout ce qui est lié à la Collaboration, la Résistance et l'épuration" (*Le Cinéma selon François Truffaut,* 142).

2. "C'était peut-être ambitieux de faire un film de vieillard, mais ce recul m'a fasciné qui me permettait d'arriver à un certain détachement" (ibid., 129).

3. François Truffaut, *Journal de tournage de Fahrenheit 451,* Cinéma 2000 (Paris: Seqhers, 1974).

4. "Je ne suis absolument pas sensible à la nature. Si on me demandait quels sont les lieux que j'ai le plus aimés dans ma vie, je dirais que c'est la campagne dans *L'Aurore* de Murnau ou la ville du même

film, mais je ne citerais pas un endroit que j'ai réellement visité, car je ne visite jamais rien. J'ai conscience que c'est un peu anormal, mais c'est ainsi. Je n'aime pas les paysages ni les choses; j'aime les gens, je m'intéresse aus idées et aux sentiments" (*Le Cinéma selon François Truffaut,* 262).

5. "Il fallait constamment intégrer la nature, l'environnement, d'où tous ces panoramiques à 360 degrés. Pas question de montrer le chalet sans montrer la prairie, ni la prairie sans la forêt." (ibid., 231).

6. "Je ne suis jamais conscient de l'aspect global du sujet quand je le sélectionne et quand je le traite. D'habitude je le comprends longtemps après avoir fait le film. J'avais une relation très difficile avec ma famille, en particulier avec ma mère, et j'ai compris il y a seulement quelques années que j'ai fait *Jules et Jim* pour lui plaire et obtenir son approbation. L'amour jouait un grand rôle dans sa vie, et comme *Les 400 Coups* était pour elle comme un coup de couteau dans le dos, j'ai fait *Jules et Jim* dans l'espoir de lui montrer que je la comprenais" (*Le Cinéma selon François Truffaut,* 144).

7. "un hymne à la vie et à la mort, une démonstration par la joie et la tristesse de l'impossibilité de toute combinaison amoureuse en dehors du couple" (*Correspondance,* 172).

8. On the substance of this discussion, see Chapters 4, 5, and 6 of the book by Mohammed Masud Raza Khan, *Le Soi caché* (Paris: Gallimard, 1976).

9. In contrast to a clock, whose movement is irreversible, an hourglass is an indicator of time that perfectly evokes the idea of "starting all over again."

10. "J'ai voulu éviter le vieillissement physique, les cheveux qui blanchissent. Gruault a trouvé une chose qui m'a beaucoup plu, pour marquer le temps qui s'écoule, c'était de placer dans les décors les toiles ma^tresses de Picasso. On a vraiment une graduation, on verra arriver l'impressionnisme, l'époque cubiste, les papiers collés" (*Le Cinéma selon François Truffaut,* 129).

11. Ibid., 142.

12. "deux natures de récit: ce qui dit et ce qui se dit, le présent et l'imparfait" (Philippe Carcassonne, "Truffaut le narrateur," *Cinématographe* 32 [November 1977]: 15–17).

13. This text reprints, in part, an article by Anne Gillain, "Fantasme originaire: le plaisir narratif," *CinémAction* 50 (1989): 60–67.

14. Peter Brooks, *Reading for the Plot* (New York: Vintage, 1984).

15. Ibid., 124.

16. For these concepts, see Guy Rosolato, *Essais sur le symbolique* (Paris: Gallimard, 1969), 36–96.

17. "J'ai filmé, pour justifier le titre et pour obtenir deux ou trois articulations dans le récit, quelques plans de métro, mais ne puis en garder aucun, car ils sont désespérément modernes; éclairage néon, stations remodelées et toujours trop de lumière ambiante . . . J'avais gardé un souvenir très fort de votre film *La Première Nuit,* et je viens de le revoir avec la même admiration. J'ai noté dans les dix premières minutes trois ou quatre plans – au total moins de trente secondes – qui conviendraient parfaitement si vous me permettiez de les utiliser." (*Correspondance,* 588).

18. "souvenir infantile se caractérisant à la fois par sa netteté particulière et l'apparente insignifiance de son contenu." (J. Laplanche and J. B. Pontalis, *Vocabulaire de la psychanalyse* [Paris: PUF, 1967], 450).

19. *Le Cinéma selon François Truffaut,* 394.

20. "C'est curieux parce que dans *Le Dernier Métro,* on ne voit pas que l'enfant a un petit rôle en réalité. Mais pourtant je suis persuadé que c'est une vision de l'Occupation qui est ma vision enfantine. Moi, J'avais donc huit ans au début

de la guerre et douze ans à la fin. Mais quelqu'un qui était adulte pendant la guerre ne ferait pas le même scénario. Il ferait peut-être la même histoire, mais il n'aurait pas retenu les mêmes détails. Je l'ai rempli des détails qui frappaient l'enfant que j'étais" (ibid., 399).

21. "J'avais onze ans. Lachenay m'a dit qu'on pouvait dormir dans les stations de métro les plus profondes transformées en abri. J'y suis allé. C'était noir de monde. On nous donnait une couverture, mais on nous réveillait à 5 heures pour laisser le métro marcher. A ce moment, on donnait un litre de vin contre 125 grammes de cuivre, alors on volait des boutons de portes ou des trucs comme ça, et on vendait le vin" (*Le Cinéma selon François Truffaut*, 22).

22. Guy Rosolato, "Souvenir-écran," *Communications* 23 (1975): 79–87.

23. "Je garde de cette époque une grande angoisse, et les films sont liés à une angoisse, à une idée de clandestinité" (*Le Cinéma selon François Truffaut*, 16).

24. "J'ai peut-être appris cent cinquante mots de vocabulaire que je ne connaissais pas . . . il y avait des choses sur l'amour qui me semblaient – je ne peux pas dire nouvelles parce que je n'avais pas beaucoup d'expérience – en tout cas originales" (ibid., 20).

25. "l'occasion d'une séduction indirecte entre parents et enfants et plus exactement, comme la plupart des cas le montrent à partir de la mère." (Rosolato, "Souvenir-écran," 82).

26. "En écrivant pour la collection 10/18 une préface aux premiers articles d'André Bazin, réunis sous le titre *Le Cinéma de l'Occupation*, je dus faire travailler ma mémoire de jeune spectateur et, aussitôt, des souvenirs de cette époque me revinrent en masse, me détermianant à concrétiser mon plus vieux rêve" (François Truffaut, "Pourquoi et comment *Le Dernier Métro?*," *L'Avant-Scène Cinéma* 303–304 [mars 1983]: 4–5).

27. *Le Cinéma selon François Truffaut*, 398. Truffaut made it clear, moreover, that in doing this he was going against historical truth, given that the light lasted until very late at that time, because France was on German daylight-saving time: "I preferred to sacrifice historical truth and create an aesthetic truth, shall we say, so that my story could be more plausible" (J'ai préféré sacrificier la vérité historique et avoir une vérité esthétique, disons, afin que mon histoire soit plus plausible). It needed an "affective" truth that was more realistic.

28. The use that Truffaut makes of period songs in the film arises, in a very simple way, from the same desire to "plug" the spectator into affective memory by short-circuiting the rational.

29. "C'était la première fois que je présentais des personnages si peu approfondis, des personnages que je ne considérais pas comme très forts et qui me changeaient d'un personnage comme celui d'*Adèle H.*" (*Le Cinéma selon François Truffaut*, 399).

30. With regard to the theme of delinquency, it is significant that the different attempts at theft suffered by members of the troupe (thefts of a bicycle, burglary of the lodge, the usurpation of the position of director by Daxiat) are all defused and played down as a result of Marion's benevolent authority. She refuses to exact reprisals in order to protect the creative activity of the troupe and to assure the security of her husband.

31. *L'Avant-Scène Cinéma* 303–304 [mars 1983]: 4.

32. Truffaut originally planned to make Bernard die in a tank, which would have confirmed the importance of Lucas but would have deprived the film of its epilogue.

33. Marc Chevrie, "L'Amour à l'imparfait," *Cahiers du cinéma* 369 (mars 1985): 8–11.

4. SENTIMENTAL EDUCATIONS

1. "J'ai failli abandonner *Baisers volés* quinze jours avant, tellement j'avais honte, je me sentais inconfortable. J'avais déjà le script de *L'Enfant sauvage* et celui de *La Sirène du Mississipi.* Je me disais: quand même, j'ai deux bons scripts à tourner; il y a des romans magnifiques et je vais tourner dans quinze jours un film où on ne raconte rien du tout! Jétais consterné" (*Le Cinéma selon François Truffaut,* 193).

2. "Les huit ou dix personnes qui l'ont déjà vus . . . pensent que c'est le plus beau de mes films, grâce à la photo. Je suis du même avis . . . Le montage actuel, presque définitif, est de 2 heures 13 minutes, et il semble qu'on ne s'ennuie pas" (*Correspondance,* 403).

3. François Truffaut, *Hitchcock* (New York: Simon & Schuster, 1984), 327.

4. "une double vie de cinéaste et de militant" (*Le Cinéma selon François Truffaut,* 195).

5. "En vérité, dans *Baisers volés,* chaque spectateur 'amenait' son sujet, pour les uns c'était *L'Education sentimentale,* pour d'autres l'initiation, d'autres encore pensaient à des aventures picaresques. Chacun apportait ce qu'il voulait, mais il est vrai que c'était dedans. On avait bourré le film de toutes sortes de choses liées au thème que Balzac appelle 'Un début dans la vie'" (ibid., 204).

6. "Je n'ai pas d'antenne pour ce qui est moderne. Je ne marche que par sensations, par choses déjà éprouvées. C'est un peu pour ça que mes films sont pleins de souvenirs de jeunesse. En faisant la préparation de celui-ci, je me suis d'ailleurs aperçu que tout avait changé, les calots des soldats, le mont-de-piété, tout. A ce moment-là, j'ai décidé de tricher, de faire du vieux, mais dans le Paris d'aujourd'hui. *Baisers volés,* c'est un peu comme si on faisait un film en 45, mais sans le dire" (ibid., 198).

7. Jeunesses Musicales International (JMI) is an organization created in Brussels in 1945 for the purpose of encouraging young people to develop through music across all boundaries.

8. "Je me souviens d'avoir improvisé une scène à cause du décor parce que la façade du pavillon des parents avait deux issues . . . Cette scène contredisait complètement la psychologie des personnages. On voyait Jean-Pierre arriver chez les parents de la fille; la mère sur le pas de la porte lui disait que Christine était partie, mais elle insistait pour qu'Antoine entre dans la maison; sur la droite de l'image, on voyait la porte de la cave s'ouvrir, Claude Jade en sortir et passer en se baissant devant les fenêtres. Cette saynète inexpliquée n'était reliée à rien; elle sous-entendait une complicité entre la mère et la fille, qu'Antoine n'est pas toujour bien vu dans cette maison, que Christine a une autre vie que lui . . . Bref, c'était une fausse piste" (ibid., 204).

9. *Antoine and Colette* is a short film made for the anthology collection *Love at Twenty* (1962), which includes segments by a number of directors, including, besides Truffaut, Shintarô Ishihara, Marcel Ophüls, Renzo Rossellini, and Andrzej Wajda.

10. "Lorsque Jean-Pierre Léaud répète des dizaines de fois son nom devant la glace, c'est très impudique, mais il le fallait" ("Truffaut par Truffaut," *Le Nouvel Observateur,* September 9, 1968).

11. Ibid.

12. "Avec les années qui passent, je crois que cette dernière scène de *Baisers volés,* qui a été faite avec beaucoup d'innocence sans savoir moi-même ce qu'elle voulait dire, devient comme une clef pour presque toutes les histoires que je raconte" (*Le Cinéma selon François Truffaut,* 205).

13. "L'observation, je le crois profondément, est une souffrance" (ibid., 274).

14. "on ne voit pas une histoire d'amour, mais on assiste à son *récit*"

(Chevrie, "L'Amour à l'imparfait," *Cahiers du cinéma* 369 [March 1985]: 11).

15. "Dans la production romanesque et cinématographique, la plupart des histories d'amour sont des histoires d'amour empêchés, mais ici les empêchements ne sont presque jamais extérieurs: ils sont intérieurs, et même mentaux" (*Le Cinéma selon François Truffaut,* 281).

16. François Truffaut, "Mes Deux Anglaises, mon onzième film," *L'Avant-Scène Cinéma* 121 (January 1972): 11.

17. See Jean Collet, *Le Cinéma de François Truffaut* (Paris: Lherminier, 1977), 144.

18. Aristides Maillol (1861–1944) was a French Catalan sculptor and painter, whose mature work focuses on the representation of the female body.

19. Michel Duran, *Le Canard enchaîné,* December 1, 1971.

20. Louis Chauvet, *Le Figaro,* November 29, 1971.

21. Jean de Baroncelli, *Le Monde,* November 25,1971.

22. "festival de psychologie subtile avec méandres et délicatesses furtives" (*Le Nouvel Observateur,* November 29, 1971).

23. Referring to Marcel Proust's *À la recherche du temps perdu* (*In Search of Lost Time*), a novel in seven volumes published between 1913 and 1927.

24. Referring to the film directed by Jean Renoir, *La Règle du jeu* (1939), which is widely considered to be Renoir's masterpiece.

25. *Hitchcock,* 327.

26. Ibid., 278.

27. Roché's diary has been published by Editions André Dimanche.

28. "Dans son roman, Roché idéalise, il atténue la souffrance des femmes. Dans le journal, au contraire, il ne craint aucune vérité et cela fourmille de détails intimes, parfois d'une grande cruauté" (*Le Cinéma selon François Truffaut,* 282).

29. "J'ai commencé ce film dans un mauvais état moral qui s'est amélioré au fur et à mesure du tournage. Ce qui m'a fait suffler cette phrase à Claude (il vient d'achever son premier roman): 'Je suis mieux à présent, j'ai l'impression que ce sont les personnages du livre qui vont souffrir à ma place'" (ibid., 287).

30. Ibid., 285.

31. Chevrie, "L'Amour à l'imparfait," 11.

32. Ibid.

33. Jean Gruault, "Le Secret perdu," *Cahiers du cinéma,,* Supplément 366: *Le Roman de François Truffaut* – Numéro spécial (December 1984): 59–62.

5. CRIMINAL WOMEN

1. "Les hommes que rencontre Jeanne Moreau sont les mistons qui ont grandi" (*Le Cinéma selon François Truffaut,* 186).

2. "*La Mariée* peut paraître simpliste et mécanique à quiconque refuserait qu'un film adult puisse commencer par 'Il était une fois'" (ibid., 187).

3. "son effort constant de simplification et de stylisation" (ibid.).

4. "Si vous regardez les images de *La Mariée,* vous voyez une femme qui va d'un endroit à l'autre, qui rencontre des hommes et qui les tue. Si on écoute la bande sonore, on entend des conversations sur l'amour, sur la façon dont les hommes regardent les femmes. Il n'est jamais question de tuer" (ibid., 186).

5. "In all fairy stories, the tale is based on enumeration. Goldilocks goes into the house of the three bears. She sees the three bowls. The gruel of the father bear is too hot. That of the mother bear is too cold. That of the baby is just right. It is a narrative strategy that I greatly like" ("Dans tous les contes, le récit est fondé sur l'énumération. Boucle d'Or s'introduit dans la maison des trois ours. Elle voit les trois bols. La bouillie de papa ours est rop chaude. Celle de maman ourse est trop froide. Celle de bébé est tout juste bien. C'est un principe de narration qui me plaît

beaucoup.") (*Le Cinéma selon François Truffaut,* 190).

6. "Avec ses quatre cents plans, c'est mon film le moins découpé. Je l'ai senti comme cela. La forme d'un film se présente généralement à votre esprit en même temps que l'idée. Il y a de nombreux plans-sequences, car chacun des personnages masculins du film ne dispose que d'un quart d'heure de projection pour exister devant nous" (ibid., 189).

7. "Rien n'est plus satisfiant pour le public que le spectacle d'un personnage qui va jusqu'au bout. Et ce trajet en droite ligne, nous avons convenu avec elle qu'il devait s'effectuer sans artifices, sans coquetterie, à la fois gravement et légèrement. Je souhaite que Jeanne Moreau, dans *La Mariée,* fasse moins penser à la déesse de la vengeance qu'à une personne obstinée et compétente" (ibid., 188).

8. "Mon rêve, c'est la persuasion clandestine. Je voudrais que les gens aient vu des plans qui ne sont pas là, qu'ils repensent à leur passé, qu'ils fassent une plongée dans leur passé. Je voudrais provoquer des associations d'idées, faire surgir des hasards, favoriser des rencontres plus ou moins concertées" (ibid., 190).

9. Georges Charensol, *Les Nouvelles littéraires,* 18–24, September 1972.

10. Michel Mohrt, *Carrefour,* 13, September 1972.

11. "Je ne considère aucun de mes films comme un cas à part, même *Une belle fille comme* moi qui est peut-être plus maîtrisé, cohérent et complémentaire des autres. Je lui trouve une grande logique, une vraie raison d'être. Il y a des erreurs dedans, mais je ne vois pas du tout ce film comme une parenthèse ou une concession à quoi que ce soit" (Le *Cinéma selon François Truffaut,* 295).

12. "Dans Les Deux Anglaises . . . j'essayais de détruire le romantisme en étant très physique, d'où cette insistance sur la maladie, la fièvre, les vomissements, etc. *Une belle fille comme moi* était la continuation de cette destruction: c'est la dérision de l'amour romantique, c'est l'affirmation de la réalité brutale, de la lutte pour la vie . . . " (ibid., 291).

13. "Elle lutte pour la vie tout au long de ce film et les notions de sympathie ou d'antipathie ne me préoccupent absolument pas, et quand les gens sont venus me dire que c'était une vraie garce, j'étais très étonné. Je me dis qu'ils ont mal regardé le film" (ibid., 295).

14. "C'est un film cruel sans une once de sentiment, un comique de la dérision où tout est bafoué, mais j'espère que c'est trop gai pour être amer" (ibid., 292).

15. Cited by Gilles Cahoreau in *François Truffaut,* 383.

16. D. W. Winnicott, "The Antisocial Tendency," in *Collected Papers,* 311.

17. Ibid., 309.

18. "Dans *Une belle fille,* la construction s'organisait à partir du magnétophone. Tout partait de là et y revenait" (*Le Cinéma selon François Truffaut,* 318).

19. "C'est Bernadette la sauvage, et cette fois on est contre l'éducateur qui n'a rien compris à la vie" (ibid., 294).

20. "C'était seulement une autre forme littéraire qui m'attirait: après la belle langue de Roché, faite de phrases courtes, d'une préciosité incroyablement raffinée, je m'attachais à un langage complètement inventé, un argot très grossier, certes, mais aussi peu vulgaire que le Queneau des *Aventures de Sally Mara*" (ibid., 291). Truffaut is referring to *Le Journal intime de Sally Mara* (1950) by the French poet and novelist Raymond Queneau (1903–1976).

21. "Le film a été vu comme méprisant, c'est une erreur car on ne se méprise pas soi-même. Le film a été fait *contre moi,* c'est cela qui n'a pas été compris. Le film est ambigu dans le sens où il est secrètement mais pas moins autobiographique que mes autres films. Dans *Une belle fille comme moi,* je suis les deux personnages: Camille

Bliss et Stanislas, le sociologue. Je me moque de quelqu'un qui s'obstine à voir la vie d'une façon romantique: je donne raison à la fille qui est une espèce de voyou, qui a appris à se méfier de tout le monde et à lutter pour survivre. Je les oppose l'un à l'autre, mais je les aime tous les deux" (*Le Cinéma selon François Truffaut,* 296).

22. Quoted by Gilles Cahoreau in *François Truffaut,* 283.

23. "Si j'avais été une femme, j'aurais ete comme elle" (*Le Cinéma selon François Truffaut,* 282).

24. "En multipliant la vitalité de Bernadette Lafont, j'ai tenté avec *Une belle fille* une expérience de vitalité cinématographique" (extract from the press kit).

25. "Au fond, il ne prenait dans ce que vous lui apportiez que ce qu'il avait déjà dans la tête" (Gruault, "Le Secret perdu," 60).

6. IN SEARCH OF THE FATHER

1. Truffaut, *Hitchcock,* 17.

2. "Les scènes de dialogue seront serrées, et je me fais une règle de ne pas raccourcir les 'moments privilégiés,' c'est-à-dire les scènes purement visuelles: allées et venues des pompiers, départs en alerte, incendies et diverses bizarreries" (François Truffaut, *Journal de tournage de Fahrenheit 451,* [Paris: Cinéma 2000/Seghers, 1974]).

3. François Truffaut, *Correspondance* (Paris: Hatier, 1988), 316.

4. "Si je recommençais le film à zéro, je dirais au décorateur, au costumier et à l'opérateur en guise d'instructions: faisons un film sur la vie comme la voient les enfants, les pompiers seront des soldats de plomb, la caserne un superbe jouet, etc." (Truffaut, *Journal de tournage de Fahrenheit 451,* 185).

5. The problematic of the false self is evident here, of course. The society of *Fahrenheit 451* imposes on its members a depersonalization that excludes any kind of creative approach to reality. The internal world is denied and invaded by a particularly constraining external reality.

6. "asexuer Clarisse pour ne pas l'immiscer, ni Montag, dans une situation adultérine . . . Ni maîtresse, ni girl-scout, ni girl-friend, Clarisse n'est qu'une petite fille questionneuse et raisonneuse" (Truffaut, *Journal de tournage de Fahrenheit 451,* 190).

7. Ibid.

8. "Je tente d'évoquer un square où jouent des enfants. Les pompiers 'ratissent' le square et fouille les gens: vieillards, nurses, etc. Montag en fouillant un vieil homme sent la présence d'un livre sous le pardessus, et cependant il le laisse filer. En quittant le square, le capitaine, pour s'amuser, fouille un bébé d'un an, trouve dans une petite poche de sa layette un livre miniscule du genre 'Pensées chinoises,' et le confisque" (ibid., 198).

9. "J'ai choisi deux jumeaux pou être 'Jane Austen's *Pride and Prejudice.*' Alors Montag leur demande: 'Vous êtes le même livre tous les deux?' et ils répondent: '*My brother is volume one. – My brother is volume two.*'" (ibid., 216).

10. "Depuis quelques jours, je sentais qu'il manquait quelque chose dans le scénario de *Fahrenheit 451,* une idée pouvant s'exprimer visuellement par des détails différents que l'on placerait ici ou là. Je me suis décidé pour le narcissisme . . . Dans les séquences du métro suspendu, je montrerai un voyageur qui se caresse la joue avec son poignet comme une petite fille qui s'endort, un autre embrassant son reflet sur la vitre. Linda, dans sa cuisine, se caressera la poitrine, bref, il n'y a que l'embarras du choix avec cette idée qui peut réellement travailler à travers le film" (ibid., 171).

11. "Pour *Fahrenheit 451,* j'ai été influencé par certains articles qu'écrivait Roger Caillois dans la NRF sur les livres

et la lecture. Il disait que les livres ont une valeur différente selon les individus. Il parlait des gens – plutôt les universitaires – qui s'intéressent au contenu, et des autres – plutôt des autodidactes – qui considèrent le livre comme un objet avec tout ce que ça comporte de souvenirs et de sentimentalité. Dans ce contexte, qui est celui de mon film, le livre devient un objet que l'on chérit de plus en plus. Même la reliure, la couverture, l'odeur des pages, acquièrent une grande valeur sentimentale" (*Le Cinéma selon François Truffaut,* 172).

12. "Je me suis aperçu aujourd'hui seulement que laisser des livres tomber hors du cadre est impossible dans ce film. Je dois accompagner leur chute jusqu'au sol. Les livres, ici, sont des personnages, et couper dans leur trajet equivaut à décadrer la tête d'un comédien" (Truffaut, *Journal de tournage,* 182).

13. "Un autre plan 'magique': tentative pour filmer au ralenti une pile de livres qui tombent sans raison. Pour obtenir le plan de mes rêves, il faudrait lui consacrer deux jours. Pour en finir avec la magie, nous tentons de faire voler un livre, comme une mouette, dans un décor vide, afin d'insérer cette image dans un cauchemar que fera Montag, malade" (ibid., 177).

14. "Clarisse prend ses vêtements, les jette sur l'armoire, installe un tabouret sur son lit, grimpe dessus, soulève une lucarne, récupère ses vêtements, les lance sur le toit et se hisse dehors. Nous continuons à la voir en pyjama au-dessus du toit, passant entre deux cheminées devant le ciel étoilé" (ibid., 189).

15. "Vous savez, les gens vont voir des tas de grandes idées dans *Fahrenheit*.. On va dire que c'est un film sur la culture et la liberté, une critique sociale ou peut-être même une diatribe contre les pays où l'on brûle des livres. Mais je m'en fiche, ça ne m'intéresse pas personnellement à ces grandes idées, à ce côté solennel . . . Moi, je ne peux faire un film qu'à partir d'idées qui me sont personnelles" (*Le Cinéma selon François Truffaut,* 177).

16. "en pensant constamment à la Résistance et à l'Occupation" (Truffaut, *Journal de tournage,* 184).

17. "un type de la Gestapo qui s'intéresserait à la Résistance" (ibid., 175).

18. *Le Cinéma selon François Truffaut,* 267.

19. "Je ne suis pas contre la violence par idéalisme, par adhésion à l'idée de non-violence. Je suis contre parce que la violence signifie un affrontement . . . J'ai gardé cela de l'enfance, justement. Pour moi, ce qui remplace la violence, c'est la fuite, non pas la fuite devant l'essentiel, mais la fuite pour obtenir l'essentiel. Je crois avoir illustré cela dans *Fahrenheit.* C'est un aspect du film qui a échappé à tout le monde et qui, pour moi, est le plus important: c'est l'apologie de la ruse. 'Ah bon! Les livres sont interdits? Très bien, on va les apprendre par coeur!' C'est la ruse suprême. On ne me fera pas signer avec des amis cinéastes un papier contre la censure parce que je considère qu'il y a cinquante façons de ruser, de triompher de la censure" (ibid., 179).

20. "le seul grand artiste qui se soit déclaré favorable à toutes les formes de censure" (ibid., 173).

21. "Ma mère ne supportait pas le bruit et me demandait de rester sans bouger, sans parler, des heures et des heures. Donc, je lisais, c'était la seule occupation que je pouvais adopter sans l'agacer. J'ai lu énormément pendant la période de l'Occupation" (ibid., 30).

22. "J'ai toujours préféré le reflet de la vie à la vie elle-même. Si j'ai choisi le livre et le cinéma, dès l'âge de onze ou douze ans, c'est bien parce que j'ai préféré voir la vie à travers le livre ou le cinéma" (ibid., 262).

23. *Correspondance,* 465.

24. "Truffaut, Chabrol, Demy, Rohmer se sont fait ramasser par le système" (ibid., 464).

25. Ibid., 469.

26. "Bons ou mauvais, mes films sont ceux que j'ai voulu faire et *seulement* ceux-là" (ibid., 467).

27. "Je me suis rassemblé et réconcilié avec moi-même grâce à *La Nuit américaine* qui concerne simplement ma raison de vivre. (Vous adorez votre mère, je hais la mienne, même morte, comment pourrions-nous avoir deux idées en commun?" (ibid.).

28. "Bon, à part ça, ma mère est morte; vous vous en foutez? Moi aussi, mais tout de même je dois participer plus ou moins aux salamalecs finaux" (Gilles Cahoreau, *François Truffaut,* 256).

29. "La mort de sa mère ne l'avait pas beaucoup ébranlé" (ibid).

30. "Le scénario de *La Nuit américaine* était illisible: c'était une suite de sketches . . . On avait l'impression que Truffaut comprenait de mieux en mieux son propre film au fur et à mesure de nos séances. Il lui devenait clair que ce n'était pas un film sur des histoires d'amour entre gens du cinéma, dans les coulisses d'un tournage, mais un film sur le cinéma, à la gloire du travail de cinéma. J'ai l'impression que la métamorphose a eu lieu pendant la finition du film" (*Le Roman de François Truffaut,* 92).

31. Winnicott, *Playing and Reality,* 87.

32. "la créativité est un fait sans lequel il n'ya pas de vie psychique, mais seulement une survie, pas d'existence, mais une habitude qui s'entretient de ses automatismes, indifférente à la vie comme à la morte" (André Green, "La Royauté appartient à l'enfant," *D. W. Winnicott, L'Arc* no. 69 [1977], 11).

33. Winnicott, *Playing and Reality,* 142.

34. Ibid., 91.

35. "Je crois qu'on rit davantage pendant la première partie, qui est descriptive, moins dans la seconde, qui est plus narrative. La coupure se fait à peu près lors du premier départ, celui de Dani" (*Le Cinéma selon François Truffaut,* 305).

36. "le metteur en scène est un voleur" (ibid., 306). Ferrand, moreover, steals a vase from the hotel to put it in the decor of the film, and will also steal the despairing phrases the Julie utters during her nervous breakdown, so that he can incorporate them in his screenplay.

37. Obviously, Truffaut also chose this film because of its artistic importance and its formative role in shaping his cinematic sensibility. But one can guarantee that with him every important detail is overdetermined.

38. "Depuis la scripte qui est enceinte sans qu'on sache de qui, jusqu'à l'actrice Julie Baker qui a épousé (dans la vie) un médecin qui pourrait être son père et qui s'en va (dans le film) avec son beau-père, en passant par Léaud qui tue son père, Valentina Cortese qui boit parce que son fils est leucémique . . . Tout cela m'a sidéré après coup, lorsque je m'en suis aperçu en cours de montage" (*Le Cinéma selon François Truffaut,* 301).

39. Jean Maurice Eugène Clément Cocteau (1889–1963) was a French poet, novelist, dramatist, designer, playwright, artist and filmmaker greatly admired by Truffaut. Édouard Dermithe [born Édouard Dermit] (1925–1995), Cocteau's lover, as well as his adopted son, was a French actor and painter who was famous for having played the role of Paul in *Les Enfants terribles* (dir. Jean-Pierre Melville, 1950), based on a novel by Cocteau. For further comment on Cocteau's influence on Truffaut, see Annette Insdorf, *François Truffaut,* 195–196.

40. Jean Collet, *Le Cinéma de François Truffaut,* 244.

41. *Le Roman de François Truffaut,* 100.

42. François Truffaut, *The Films in My Life,* trans. Leonard Mayhew (New York: Da Capo Press, 1994), 208.

43. "A travers le jeune acteur interprété par Jean-Pierre Léaud, je tourne toujours autour de la question qui me tourmente

depuis plus de trente ans: le cinéma est-il plus important que la vie? Ci qui n'est peut-être guère plus intelligent que de demander: 'Préfères-tu ton père ou ta mère?' Mais je pense au cinéma un si grand nombre d'heures chaque jour et depuis un si grand nombre d'années que je ne puis m'empêcher de mettre en concurrence la vie et les films et de reprocher à la vie de ne pas être aussi bien agencée, intéressante, dense, intense que les images que nous organisons. 'Il n'ya pas d'embouteillages dans les films, dit Ferrand à Jean-Pierre Léaud, pas de creux, pas de temps morts. Les films avancent comme des trains dans la nuit" (*Le Cinéma selon François Truffaut*, 304).

7. MARRIAGES

1. "Je me classe parmi cette série de réalisateurs pour qui le cinéma est un prolongement de la jeunesse, celui des enfants qu'on a envoyés s'amuser dans un coin, qui refaisaient le monde avec des jouets et qui continuent les jeux à l'âge adulte à travers les films. C'est ce que j'appelle le 'cinéma de la chambre du fond,' avec le refus de la vie telle qu'elle est, du monde dans son état réel et, en réaction, le besoin de recréer quelque chose qui participe un peu du conte de fées, un peu de ce cinéma américain qui nous a fait rêver étant jeunes" (*Le Cinéma selon François Truffaut*, 269).

2. "Il y avait les vendeuses, et de voir cet homme acheter des bas, cela les faisait sourire, et voilà. C'était une scène de rien du tout, mais c'était difficile à faire" (ibid., 164).

3. D. W. Winnicott, "The Concept of a Healthy Individual," in *Home is Where We Start From*, 31.

4. "*La Sirène*,c'est finalement l'histoire d'un type qui épouse une femme qui est exactement le contraire de ce qu'il voulait. Mais l'amour est apparu et il l'accepte telle qu'elle est" (*Le Cinéma selon François Truffaut*, 248).

5. *The New York Times*, April 11, 1970.

6. A tribute to Cocteau: Heurtebise is the guardian angel in Cocteau's film *Orpheus* (1950).

7. *Monorail* is the title of a novel by Jacques Audiberti. In the film, Truffaut locates this hotel in a square bearing the name of the writer. The idea of an airborne daydream implicit in the title is reinforced by the ascending movement of Louis when he climbs the facade of the hotel to meet up with Marion.

8. "Il n'y a pas de deuxième homme ou de deuxième femme et j'ai pu entièrement me concentrer sur l'intimité d'un couple" (*Le Cinéma selon Françoit Truffaut*, 247).

9. "C'est *La Femme et le Pantin, L'Ange bleu, La Chienne*... Ce thème de la femme fatale, de la vamp subjuguant un honnête homme au point d'en faire un pantin, tous les cinéastes que j'admire l'ont traité. Je me suis dit: il faut le faire... Et puis je m'aperçois que je ne peux pas" (*Le Cinéma selon Françoit Truffaut*, 246).

10. "un film sincère, qui tenterait cependant de ressembler à un roman-photo... J'ai cherché à introduire dans la même séquence à la fois un 'cliché' et une émotion; les spectateurs ont vu surtout les 'clichés,' ils ont moins perçu la sincérité" (ibid., 248).

11. Ibid., 248.

12. "Un parti pris secret m'animait dans mon travail lorsque j'ai fait ce film: pour moi, Catherine était un garçon, un voyou qui en avait vu de toutes les couleurs, et Jean-Paul, une petite jeune fille qui attend tout de son mariage" (ibid., 250).

13. To take one small detail among many: Louis reads Balzac; Marion, *Détective*. Truffaut read both.

14. Winnicott, *Playing and Reality*, 109.

15. Ibid., 114.

16. "la mère qui "est" moins qu'elle ne "fait" induit chez l'enfant une identité qui est celle de quelqu'un *qui fait comme*"

(André Green, "La Royauté appartient à l'enfant," *L'Arc* no. 69, 11).

17. "Comme d'habitude, c'est l'héroine qui prend les initiatives; comme d'habitude l'histoire . . . est ressentie par le héros" (*Le Cinéma selon Françoit Truffaut*, 247).

18. It should be noted that dissociation of the female element precludes the practice of homosexuality. This practice, in fact, establishes masculinity, that which prohibits the split off feminine element (Winnicott, *Playing and Reality*, 105).

19. "Depuis quelques années, je suis influencé par Lubitsch, dont je regarde les films de très près, étant passionné par cette forme d'esprit très particulière qui se perd après avoir eu une énorme importance à l'iépoque, sur Leo McCarey notamment et Hitchcock. Cela consiste à arriver aux choses d'une façon détournée, à se demander: étant donné que l'on a telle situation à faire comprendre au public, quelle sera la manière la plus indirecte, la plus détournée, de la présenter?" (*Le Cinéma selon François Truffaut*, 268).

20. "Lubitsch ne cherche pas à ce qu'on croie à l'histoire. Il nous prend par la main et démonte systématiquement tous les mécanismes qu'il met en branle. Il nous raconte une histoire et fait une blague toutes les deux minutes pour nous montrer quil raconte une histoire" (ibid., 321).

21. "J'ai une grande propension à parler de moi et une très grande répugnance à le faire directement. Pour cette raison, j'ai l'impression d'être plus intime et plus sincère à travers des sujets empruntés – *La Sirène du Mississipi, L'Enfant sauvage, Les Deux Anglaises* – qu'à travers les Doinel, où je redoutais constamment l'identification entre Jean-Pierre Léaud et moi" (ibid., 287).

22. "Elle est dans *Tirez sur le pianiste, La Peau douce* et, si on peut l'intégrer dans un rêve, dans *Fahrenheit*. Je crois que j'ai toujours filmé le même personnage principal et qu j'ai demandé à tout le monde de jouer comme Léaud. Je crois même qu'il est le personnage de *La Sirène*" (ibid., 267).

23. "A cause du fait que les gens étaient amoureux de *Jules et Jim*, re ressentais une espèce d'irritation et je me disais que c'était de ma faute car je n'avais pas fait le film assez pessimiste, pas assez dur; alors j'ai voulu faire *La Peau douce* pour montrer que l'amour est quelque chose de beaucoup moins euphorique, exaltant" (ibid., 274).

24. Ibid.

25. "Et puis finalement *Domicile conjugal* a été terminé et, à ce moment-là, j'ai trouvé qu'il était triste lui aussi . . . Quand on touche à l'adultère, ce n'est pas gai et, pour en faire une chose gaie, il faut mentir comme dans certaines comédies américaines" (ibid., 275).

26. Insdorf, *François Truffaut: le cinéma est-il magique?* (Paris: Ramsay, 1989), 203; see also Insdorf, *François Truffaut* (Cambridge: Cambridge University Press, 1994), 82–84.

27. "J'avais une fin heureuse, mais l'on voit que Jean-Pierre Léaud se comporte comme se comportait avant le chanteur d'opéra, c'est-à-dire qu'il prend le manteau et le sac à main de sa femme et les jette dans l'escalier; il est devenu un mari comme celui-ci. Mais je ne veux pas non plus finir là-dessus, je montre le chanteur qui fait la grimace, qui dément ce que dit sa femme, c'est-à-dire que chaque plan contredit celui d'avant dans cette fin où l'on montre successivement deux indices heureux et deux indices malheureux" (*Le Cinéma selon François Truffaut*, 275).

8. WORDS AND THINGS

1. "Cette biographie m'a beaucoup ému, peut-être parce qu'elle présente l'envers de la médaille de *L'Enfant sauvage*. Comme l'enfant de l'Aveyron, Adèle a un problème d'identité, mais ici c'est l'inverse puisqu'elle est la fille de l'homme le plus célèbre du monde." (*Le Cinéma selon François Truffaut*, 329).

2. "Cet enfant a grandi à l'écart de la civilisation, si bien que tout ce qu'il fait dans le film, il le fait pour la première fois" (François Truffaut, "Comment j'ai tourné *L'Enfant sauvage,*" *L'Avant-Scène Cinéma* 107 [October 1970]: 10).

3. *Aline Desjardins s'entretient avec François Truffaut* (Paris: Ramsay, 1987), 62.

4. One from 1801, the other from 1806. In the film, Truffaut transforms them into a diary.

5. *Le Cinéma selon François Truffaut,* 329.

6. "Du jour où j'ai décidé de jouer Itard, le film a pris pour moi une raison d'être complète et définitive." (ibid., 256).

7. *Correspondance,* 374.

8. "l'un des plus grands chefs opérateurs du monde" (Truffaut, "Preface" to Nestor Almendros, *Un homme à la caméra* [Paris: Hatier, 1991], 4).

9. "*L'Enfant sauvage* est un hommage à la photo des films muets . . . Leur style, sans fard, avait cette précision d'épure aujourd'hui disparue . . . Les techniques du cinéma muet sont parvenues à un degré exceptionnel de raffinement, mais ses secrets disparaîtront avec la mort de ses créateurs. Il faut redécouvrir ces techniques" (ibid., 57).

10. Ibid.

11. Renata Gaddini, "Le Déni de la séparation," *L'Arc* 69 (1977): 79.

12. Truffaut himself was in the habit of doing this when a news item caught his attention and seemed to contain matter that he could use in a film.

13. "Pendant que je tournais le film, je revivais un peu le tournage des *400 Coups* pendant lequel j'initiais Jean-Pierre Léaud au cinéma" (Aline Desjardins, 62).

14. "J'ai réussi à faire de l'antidocumentaire avec une chose extrêmement vraie." (*Le Cinéma selon François Truffaut,* 320).

15. "*Tout,* dans ce film, est obligatoirement 'composé' (nous ne vivons pas en 1798, et 'Victor' n'existe pas): à la fois mis en scène et joué. Tout faux parti 'documentaire,' tout principe de tournage fondé sur le 'pris sur le vif' (ou voulant en donner l'illusion) serait un mensonge, donc une faute . . . Ce qui commande, me semble-t-il, une mise en scène très apparente, explicite . . . une re-constitution de phénomènes et d'attitudes précis: 'fabrication' logique, *donc* poétique" (Archives des Films du Carosse).

16. Truffaut, *Hitchcock,* 240.

17. "C'est un travail de rigueur très grisant . . . comme un électricien, je dénude les fils, je réduis le nombre d'éléments." (*Le Cinéma selon François Truffaut,* 332).

18. Truffaut had wanted to adapt this story, and it was when Arthur Penn beat him to it that he decided to make *The Wild Child.*

19. "progrès spectaculaires . . . son acquisition d'un certain vocabulaire écrit" (Aline Desjardins, 64).

20. Octave Mannoni, "Itard et son sauvage," in *Clefs pour l'imaginaire ou l'autre scène* (Paris: Seuil, 1969), 184–201.

21. An excellent thesis by Anne Gabbay studies Itard's methods: *L'Enfant sauvage: La Genèse du problème de l'humanisation à travers l'approche différenciée du docteur Itard et de François Truffaut,* Mémoire de D.E.A. de Politiques Comparées sous la direction de M. le Professeur Robin. Année 89–90.

22. Étienne Bonnot de Condillac (1715–1780), a French philosopher and epistemologist.

23. "blessure . . . irréparable" (*Le Cinéma selon François Truffaut,* 258).

24. "Il y a pourtant une scène que je m'étais représentée à la lecture des *Rapports* et qui m'a déterminé à faire le film. C'est d'ailleurs la seule scène dramatique: la punition injuste infligée par Itard à son élève afin de le faire se révolter." (ibid., 254).

25. As Mannoni explains (*Clefs pour l'imaginaire,* 184–201), this language is not

really a true one because, in contrast to the sign language of deaf people, it does not involve a combination of signs. The language of the deaf appears in many of Truffaut's films: *A Gorgeous Girl Like Me, Small Change, The Man Who Loved Women, The Green Room*. In *Day for Night,* Ferrand wears a hearing aid. As his sojourn in the Institute shows, Victor is still more deprived than they are.

26. In this regard, *The Green Room* continues the meditation begun in *The Wild Child* by focusing on an adult character, Davenne (played by Truffaut), who, like Itard, is surrounded by a housekeeper and a child deprived of language. The law of the mother reigns in this film, in a blaze of candles.

27. Natasa Durovicová, "Biograph as Biography," *Wide Angle* 7:1 and 2 (1985): 3–17.

28. *Le Cinéma de François Truffaut,* 256.

29. Dès le début, je montre que c'est foutu: jamais le lieutenant n'aimera Adèle." (*Le Cinéma selon François Truffaut,* 325).

30. On this subject, Marie-France Pisier writes: "He was fascinated by unconscious wordplay. I suspect that he had read a lot of Freud and even a little Lacan. I remember his shy laugh when I asked him that question" (*Le Roman de François Truffaut,* 129).

31. Truffaut first became interested in the story in 1969 when he read in *Le Nouvel Observateur* a critique by Henri Guillemin of Adèle's diary, which an American academic, Frances Vernor Guille had decoded – Adèle wrote in an encrypted language.

32. "Je ne voulais plus entendre parler du soleil dans un film d'époque, ni du ciel. Le film *Adèle* est devenu de plus en plus serré, claustrophobe, l'histoire d'un visage." (*Le Cinéma de François Truffaut,* 329).

33. Maurice Jaubert (1900–1940) was a French composer of incidental music for stage and screen who collaborated with earlier filmmakers such as René Clair, Julien Duvivier, and Marcel Carné.

34. *Le Cinéma selon François Truffaut,* 329.

35. "Dans la mesure où j'avais le sentiment en tournant *L'Histoire d'Adèle H.* de faire un film sans tenir compte des préoccupations d'aujourd'hui, ça me plaisait d'utiliser une musique de 1930–1940" (ibid., 333).

36. *Le Roman de François Truffaut,* 87.

37. Maurice Jaubert composed, for example, the music for *L'Atalante, Quai des Brumes,* and *Hôtel du Nord.*

38. "Depuis quelques années, on étudie plus sérieusement le cas d'enfants qui ont grandi dans la détresse morale, physique ou matérielle, et les spécialistes décrivent l'autisme comme un mécanisme de défense. Or, on le verra clairement à travers les exemples puisés par Bazin dans l'oeuvre de Chaplin, tout est mécanisme de défense dans les faits et gestes de Charlot" (Truffaut, *Le Plaisir des yeux,* 68).

39. The first versions of the screenplay for *Adèle H.* clearly depict a female figure who has emerged from childhood as the original source of trauma. In the nightmare scenes, we see the small Adèle shut in a cupboard in which she is suffocating, while in the salon an "old woman dressed in black" is playing grotesque music that is terrifying the child.

40. D. W. Winnicott, "Fear of Breakdown," *The International Review of Psycho-Analysis* 1 (1974): 103–107.

41. Ibid.

42. Elizabeth Bonnafons, in her book *François Truffaut* (Lausanne: L'Age d'Homme, 1981), studies the same concept under the term (which is that used by Bettelheim) "extreme situation."

43. J.-B. Pontalis, "Preface" to Winnicott, *Jeu et Réalité,* xi.

44. Truffaut was happy at having achieved, in this scene, the visual erasure

of an unimportant character. Filmed through a half-opened door, only Pinson can be seen, listening to the colonel, whose presence is merely revealed by his voice.

45. "J'ai délibérément tourné *L'Enfant sauvage, L'Histoire d'Adèle H.*, et *La Chambre verte* pour les faire ressembler à des objets et même, au fond de moi, à des oeufs en ivoire qu'on pourrait voir, toucher mais pas entamer" ("Entretien avec François Truffaut," *Cinématographe* 44 [February 1979]: 60).

46. Claude Lévi-Strauss, *The Jealous Potter*, trans. Bénédicte Chorier (Chicago and London: University of Chicago Press, 1988), 197.

9. THE CHILD KING

1. Dominique Rabourdin, *Truffaut par Truffaut* (Paris: Editions du Chêne, 1985, 135).

2. "On croit y perdre un temps fou. Et dès que la caméra est dans l'hélicoptère, on gagne un temps immense. On filme trente kilomètres en dix minutes." (*Le Cinéma selon François Truffaut*, 335).

3. "J'ai compris que la jeunesse est bénie, qu'elle est un risque à courir, mais que ce risque même est béni" (ibid., 343).

4. "Les adultes sont montrés plutôt faibles, quelquefois un peu démissionnaires ou handicapés par quelque chose, comme cet infirme, le père de Patrick, mais ils ne sont pas montrés negativement, méchamment. Absolument pas" (ibid., 348).

5. "Le film n'est pas autobiographique parce que je ne suis pas précisément un des personnages" (ibid., 341).

6. By Victor Hugo. See Daney and others, "Entretien avec François Truffaut," *Cahiers du cinéma* 316 (October 1980): 33.

7. Gilles Cahoreau, 250.

8. "Fall" is the appropriate word because these objects are found under a merry-go-round formed of little suspended airplanes.

9. Winnicott, *Collected Papers*, 313.

10. Daney and others, "Entretien avec François Truffaut," *Cahiers du cinéma* 316 (October 1980): 35.

11. Bruno Bettelheim, *The Uses of Enchantment: The Meaning and Importance of Fairy Tales* (New York: Vintage, 1977).

12. "Les enfants sont les spectateurs privilégiés de ce film." (*Le Cinéma selon François Truffaut*, 348).

13. Dominique Rabourdin, *Truffaut par Truffaut*, 171.

14. *Le Cinéma selon François Truffaut*, 383. The series is composed of *The 400 Blows*, the short film *Love at Twenty:* "Antoine and Colette," *Stolen Kisses*, and *Bed and Board*.

15. Eugène de Rastignac is a fictional character from *La Comédie humaine*, a series of novels by Honoré de Balzac.

16. Serge Daney, "*L'Amour en fuite*," *Cahiers du cinéma* 298 (March 1979): 57.

17. Paul Léautaud (1872–1956) was a French novelist, critic, and essayist who was an illegitimate child abandoned soon after his birth by his mother, an actress, and lived a lonely and melancholy childhood. His novelistic writing involves a search for his own identity.

18. "J'aimerais citer la phrase de Scott Fitzgerald: 'Toute vie est un processus de démolition.' Nous savons que la view ne va pas vers quelque chose d'exaltant et d'ascendant. Vous trouverez toujours plus de fraîcheur sur un visage d'enfant." (*Le Cinéma selon François Truffaut*, 384).

19. *Le Roman de François Truffaut*, 78.

10. FETISHISM AND MOURNING

1. Truffaut reported that the technicians working on *The Green Room* called this film "The Man who Loved Flames."

2. Truffaut, *The Films in My Life*, 268.

3. "J'ai envie depuis longtemps de montrer dans un film tout ce qui arrive à un livre: le livre s'écrit, puis il est com-

posé, imprimé, on vous donne les épreuves à corriger, on choisit la couverture, et puis le livre est là, fini, comme un objet" (*Le Cinéma selon François Truffaut,* 360).

4. "Les jambes des femmes sont des compas qui arpentent en tous sens le globe terrestre, lui donnant son équilibre et son harmonie" (François Truffaut, *L'Homme qui aimait les femmes* [Paris: Flammarion, 1977], 42).

5. "Que le fétiche ne puisse fonctionner comme tel, et la décompensation qui s'ensuit prendra la forme d'une dépression, raison pour laquelle le patient viendra consulter" (Guy Rosolato, *Le Désir et la Perversion* [Paris: Seuil, 1967], 23).

6. "Le meilleur de ce livre, ce sont les pages où Bertrand Morane raconte son enfance, surtout ce qu'il nous fait entrevoir de sa mère. Malheureusement cela occupe seulement un chapitre: pour moi il est passé à côté du vrai sujet" (Truffaut, *L'Homme qui aimait les femmes,* 96).

7. "l'émergence irrépressible de la vérité" (Marc Vernet, *Lectures du film,* coauthored with Jean Collet, Michel Marie, Daniel Percheron, and Jean-Paul Simon [Paris: Albatros, 1977], 98).

8. "La mésaventure de cet enfant sacrifié me reportait loin en arrière, à la période la plus lamentable de ma propre jeunesse, lorsque ma mère me laissait seul plusieurs jours de suite pour aller refoindre ses amants" (Truffaut, *L'Homme qui aimait les femmes,* 54).

9. We should recall that it was at about the same age that Truffaut discovered, in rummaging through a wardrobe, that, like Adèle H., he was "born of an unknown father."

10. "Une fois pour toutes, elle m'avait interdit de jouer, de bouger ou même d'éternuer. Je ne devais pas quitter la chaise qui m'était allouée, mais par contre je pouvais lire à volonté à condition de tourner les pages sans faire de bruit" (Truffaut, *L'Homme qui aimait les femmes,* 83).

11. "Ma mère avait pris l'habitude de se promener à demi nue devant moi, non pas pour me provoquer évidemment, mais plutôt, je suppose, pour se confirmer à elle-même que je n'existais pas" (ibid.).

12. "à la fréquentation précoce et familière de la réalité dans la promiscuité de non-pudeur de la mère" (Guy Rosolato, *Le Désir et la Perversion,* 45).

13. "Je sais bien [que les femmes n'ont pas de pénis] . . . mais quand même" (Mannoni, *Clefs pour l'imaginaire,* 9–33).

14. A crime thriller by Clinton Seeley published under the title *Storm Fear* in 1954, translated from the English by Marcel Duhamel and published in the Série Noire collection by Gallimard in 1955. It had been reissued by Gallimard in the Poche Noire series in 1970.

15. "Le pervers fétichiste se définit par le fait qu'il n'est jamais sorti du désir de la mère, qui a fait de lui le substitut de ce qui lui manquait. Phallus vivant de la mère, tout le travail du sujet pervers consiste à s'installer dans ce mirage de lui-même et à y trouver l'accomplissement de son désir" (Jean Baudrillard, *L'Echange symbolique et la Mort* (Paris: Gallimard, 1976), 156). The standard English edition gives a different translation of this passage: "fetishistic perversion is defined by the fact that it has never gotten over the desire for the mother, making the fetish the replacement for what the fetishist lacked. All the labour of the perverse subject consists in settling into the mirage of himself as the living phallus of the mother so as to find a fulfillment of desire there" (Baudrillard, *Symbolic Exchange and Death,* trans. Iain Hamilton Grant, introduction by Mike Gane [London and Thousand Oaks, CA: Sage, 1993], 113).

16. ". . . Ses jambes se dessinent avec la précision d'ombres chinoises sur la blancheur de la blouse . . . Lui qui ne devait faire aucun mouvement se redresse et tend le bras vers ces jambes qui

l'attirent comme un aimant, comme le crucifix en or attirait l'avare Grandet agonisant" (*L'Homme qui aimait les femmes,* 122). The miser Grandet is a character in *Eugénie Grandet,* one of the novels by Honoré de Balzac in his cycle *La Comédie humaine.*

17. D. W. Winnicott, "The Capacity to be Alone," *The International Journal of Psychoanalysis* 39 (1958): 416–420.

18. Ibid., 418.

19. "Je m'aperçus qu'il n'y a pas de règle, que chaque livre est différent et exprime la personnalité de son auteur. Chaque page, chaque phrase de n'importe quel écrivain lui appartient en propre: son écriture lui est aussi personnelle que ses empreintes digitales" (*L'Homme qui aimait les femmes,* 91).

20. *Forbidden Games* is a film directed by René Clément, released in 1952.

21. Insdorf, *François Truffaut: Le cinéma est-il magique?,* 274.

22. "on doit constamment délaisser des lois psychologiques pour des lois musicales." (*Le Cinéma selon François Truffaut,* 364).

23. Lévi-Strauss, *The Raw and the Cooked,* 16.

24. This role is played by Truffaut.

25. *Le Cinéma selon François Truffaut,* 325.

26. "Je crois à l'émotion retenue, à l'émotion non par paroxysme mais par accumulation. Je voudrais qu l'on regarde *La Chambre verte* la couche ouverte, qu'on aille d'étonnement en étonnement, et que l'émotion ne nous étreigne qu'à la fin, grâce au seul lyrisme de la musique de Jaubert." (ibid., 376).

27. His behaviour also recalls that of the "madman" with the raincoat in *Stolen Kisses.* Like him, he pursues his obsession right to the end.

28. "Le film repose sur l'idée classique de faire quelque chose avec presque rien" (*Le Cinéma selon François Truffaut,* 376).

29. Almendros, *Un homme à la caméra,* 150.

30. *The Altar of the Dead* (1895), *The Beast in the Jungle* (1903), and *The Friends of the Friends* (1896).

31. *Le Cinéma selon François Truffaut,* 374.

32. The actress who lent her features for Julie in the photographs also did so for the mannequin in this scene. Its open eyes are painted over closed eyelids, exactly in the process used by Cocteau in *Le Testament d'Orphée.*

33. As with a palimpsest, the character of Massigny is complex. He certainly represents the Idealized Father involved in the Oedipal rebellion, just like the captain of the firemen in *Fahrenheit 451;* however, the description of his conflict with him that Davenne offers seems to refer to Truffaut's relationship with Godard.

34. *Le Cinéma selon François Truffaut,* 344.

11. THE ROLE OF PLAY

1. *813* was the title of a novel by Maurice Leblanc, a French crime writer who created the character of Arsène Lupin, sometimes regarded as a French counterpart to Arthur Conan Doyle's detective, Sherlock Holmes.

2. Jacques Becker (1906–1960), a French director whose gangster film *Touchez pas au grisbi* (1954) exerted considerable influence on subsequent crime thrillers.

3. Alluding to Jean Cocteau's comment on his visit to the deathbed of Marcel Proust: "That pile of paper on his left side went on living like the watch on a dead soldier's wrist" (quoted in Edmund White, "Cocteau: The Great Enchanter," *Vogue* (May 1984).

4. *La vie est un roman* (literally, "Life is a Novel") (dir. Alain Renais,1983).

5. *Corréspondance,* 626.

6. "un film du samedi soir conçu pour le plaisir" (*Le Cinéma selon François Truffaut*, 421).

7. "Je vois le cinéma comme un art classique. Surtout, il était magique. Et il a un peu cessé de l'être à cause de la télévision. Mon travail est d'essayer de retrouver cette magie" (ibid., 424).

8. "J'ai envie que mon public soit constamment captivé, envouté. Qu'il sorte de la salle de cinéma hébété, étonné d'être sur le trottoir. Je voudrais qu'il oublie l'heure, le lieu où il se trouve, comme Proust, plongé dans la lecture de Combray. Je souhaite avant tout l'émotion" (ibid., 415).

9. "la haine du documentaire . . . [qui] donne a voir les choses ou les êtres sans l'amorce d'une fiction" (ibid., 418).

10. "tout ce qui ressemble à de l'interview, tout ce qui ressemble à de l'improvisation. Tout ce que nous montre le journal télévisé du soir" (ibid., 425).

11. "L'imprevisible, le bizarre se faufilent toujours avec l'impair" (ibid., 417).

12. "J'ai toujours pensé que les histoires, les récits ne pouvaient se bâtir qu'autour d'une femme, car les femmes – et c'est également vrai pour la littérature – véhiculent l'histoire plus naturellement que les hommes . . . L'action appartient aux femmes" (ibid., 419). This remark is consistent with the view of another writer of fiction, Patrick Modiano: "In a novel, it is much more effective to take a woman as a point of identification! A novel that takes a woman as its subject is more romantic, more interesting" (C'est beaucoup plus for, dans un roman, de prendre une femme comme point d'identification! Un roman fait à partir d'une femme est beaucoup plus romanesque, et plus intéressant"); see Gabrielle Rolin, "Patrick Modiano le dernier enfant du siècle," *Lire* 120 (1985):63.

13. "On a été obligé d'inventer tout le milieu du film pour avoir du visuel à l'écran" (*Le Cinéma selon François Truffaut*, 422).

14. Jean Aurel, "Le Jeu avec le spectateur," *Le Roman de François Truffaut*, 94.

15. Referring to the ball of red fleece thread, in Greek myth, that Ariadne gave Theseus, so that he could find his way out of the Minotaur's labyrinth.

16. Meaning "in trouble" in English, a play on the verbal echo of "Barbara" in "l'embarras."

17. "L'idée de sincérité est une idée importante au début . . . Après, il y a la notion de carrière. La sincérité ne suffit plus. Il faut une certaine habileté. On se forge des lois. On y obéit" (*Le Cinéma selon François Truffaut*, 425).

18. "Le plaisir doit être plus fort que l'analyse. Lubitsch, par exemple, s'amuse beaucoup à faire croire au public qu'il a deviné ce qui va se passer. Et à la fin de la scène, c'est la surprise. Il se passe autre chose. C'est un jeu" (ibid., 423).

19. Bruno Bettelheim, *The Empty Fortress: Infantile Autism and the Birth of the Self* (New York: The Free Press, 1972), 387.

CONCLUSION

1. "L'âge d'or est derrière nous . . . dans le travail des réalisateurs qui ont commencé sous le muet, il y a un aspect décisif qui a été irrémédiablement perdu par la suite" (Daney and others, "Entretien avec François Truffaut, *Cahiers du cinéma* 316 [October 1980]: 26).

2. "la solution la plus radicale" (ibid.).

3. François Truffaut, "Les Extrêmes me touchent," *Cahiers du cinéma*, no. 21, March 1953, 62. Truffaut is referring to Raymond Radiguet (1903–1923), a French author known chiefly for his novel *Le Diable au corps* (1923).

4. Anne Gillain, "Reconciling Irreconcilables: An Interview with François Truffaut," *Wide Angle* 4:4 (1981): 35.

5. Pinchas Noy, "Symbolism and Mental Representation," *Annual of Psychoanalysis* 1 (1973): 125–158.

6. Ibid., 156.

7. " Ce qui fait le plus de mal dans la vie, c'est le manque d'imagination et l'incapacité de classer les informations dans le bon ordre" (*Cahiers du cinéma* 316 [October 1980]: 35).

8. J. Laplanche and J-B. Pontalis, *Vocabulaire de la psychanalyse,* 159.

9. Anton Ehrenzweig, *The Hidden Order of Art: A Study in the Psychology of Artistic Imagination* (Berkeley and Los Angeles: University of California Press, 1967), 127.

10. "cette région d'indécidabilité entre le fantasmatique et le secondaire" (Jean-François Lyotard, "Par-delà représentation," preface to Anton Ehrenzweig, *L'Ordre caché de l'art* [Paris: Gallimard, 1974], 20).

11. Pinchas Noy, "A Theory of Art and Aesthetic Experience," *Psychoanalytic Review* 55 (1968–1969): 623–645, esp. 640–641.

12. Lévi-Strauss, *The Raw and the Cooked,* 17.

13. "récuperer . . . les structures de la pensée mythique" (Claude Lévi-Strauss and Didier Eribon, *De près de loin* [Paris: Odile Jacob], 243).

14. Lévi-Strauss, *The Raw and the Cooked,* 26.

15. "A cause de son déroulement ininterrompu, le film peut se comparer à une pièce de musique jouée dans une salle de concert, mais à rien d'autre et surtout pas à une visite de musée ni à la lecture d'une livre" (Truffaut, *Le Plaisir des yeux,* 26).

16. "Le cinéma est un art qui a beaucoup plus de dimensions que la peinture ou la littérature et qui, de ce point de vue, ne me paraît commensurable quà las musique" (Michel Delahaye and Jacques Rivette, "Entretien avec Claude Lévi-Strauss," *Cahiers du cinéma,* no. 156 [June 1964], 25).

17. *The Naked Man* is the fourth and final volume of Claude Lévi-Strauss's *Mythologiques.*

18. "J'ai appris qu'il existait désormais des livres imprimés en gros caractères pour les gens qui commencent à avoir une mauvaise vue. J'ai commandé ces livres, ne serait-ce que pour les avoir sous la main et non parce que j'ai une mauvaise vue. La mienne est bonne. Mais ces livres, je voudrais les toucher parce qu'ils représentent ce que je veux faire" (*Le Cinéma selon François Truffaut,* 374).

19. Lévi-Strauss, *The Jealous Potter,* 206.

20. Truffaut, *The Films in my Life,* 76.

Filmography

Les Mistons, 1957
Director: François Truffaut
Screenplay: François Truffaut, after the novel by Maurice Pons, published in *Virginales* (Julliard). (AF: Check spelling of Julliard)
Cinematographer: Jean Malige
Production Company: Les Films du Carrosse
Cast (chief characters): Bernadette Lafont, Gérard Blain.

The 400 Blows (*Les 400 Coups*), 1959
Director: François Truffaut
Screenplay: François Truffaut
Cinematographer: Henri Decae
Music: Jean Constantin
Production Company: Les Films du Carrosse, Sédif Productions
Cast (chief characters): Jean-Pierre Léaud (Antoine Doinel), Albert Rémy (the father), Claire Maurier (the mother), Patrick Auffay (René Bigey), Robert Beauvais (the headmaster of the school), Pierre Repp (the English teacher).

Shoot the Piano Player (*Tirez sur le pianiste*), 1960
Director: François Truffaut
Screenplay: François Truffaut and Marcel Moussy after the novel by David Goodis, *Down There.*
Cinematographer: Raoul Coutard
Music: Georges Delerue
Production Company: Les Films de la Pléiade
Cast (chief characters): Charles Aznavour (Charlie Kohler), Marie Dubois (Léna), Nicole Berger (Théresa), Michèle Mercier (Clarisse), Albert Rémy (Chico), Serge Davri (Plyne).

Jules and Jim (*Jules et Jim*), 1962
Director: François Truffaut
Screenplay: François Truffaut and Jean Gruault
Cinematographer: Raoul Coutard
Music: Georges Delerue
Production Company: Les Films du Carrosse, Sédif Productions
Cast (chief characters): Jeanne Moreau (Catherine), Oskar Werner (Jules), Henri Serre (Jim), Marie Dubois (Thérèse), Boris Bassiak (Albert), Sabine Haudepin (Sabine).

Antoine & Colette, 1962
First sketch for the film *Love at Twenty,* comprising five episodes by François Truffaut (France), Renzo Rossellini (Italy), Marcel Ophuls (Germany), Andrzej Wajda (Poland), and Shintaro Ishihara (Japan).
Director: François Truffaut
Screenplay: François Truffaut
Cinematographer: Raoul Coutard
Music: Georges Delerue

Production Company: Les Films du Carrosse
Cast (chief characters): Jean-Pierre Léaud (Antoine Doinel), Marie-France Pisier (Colette), Patrick Auffay (René), Rosy Varte (Colette's mother), François Darbon (Colette's stepfather).

The Soft Skin (*La Peau douce*), 1964
Director: François Truffaut
Screenplay: François Truffaut and Jean-Louis Richard
Cinematographer: Raoul Coutard
Music: Georges Delerue
Production Company: Les Films du Carrosse, Sédif Productions, Simar Films
Cast (chief characters): Françoise Dorleac (Nicole), Jean Desailly (Pierre Lachenay), Nelly Benedetti (Franca), Daniel Ceccaldi (Clément), Sabine Haudepin (Sabine).

Fahrenheit 451 1966
Director: François Truffaut
Screenplay: François Truffaut and Jean-Louis Richard
Cinematographer: Nicholas Roeg
Music: Bernard Herrmann
Production Company: Anglo Enterprises, Vineyard Films Ltd.
Cast (chief characters): Julie Christie (Linda Montag and Clarisse), Oskar Werner (Montag), Cyril Cusack (the captain).

The Bride Wore Black (*La Mariée etait en noir*), 1967
Director: François Truffaut
Screenplay: François Truffaut and Jean-Louis Richard
Cinematographer: Raoul Coutard
Music: Bernard Herrmann
Production Company: Les Films du Carrosse, Les Productions Artistes Associés, Dino de Laurentiis Cinematografica
Cast (chief characters): Jeanne Moreau (Julie Kohler), Claude Rich (Bliss), Jean-Claude Brialy (Corey), Michel Bouquet (Coral), Michael Lonsdale (Morane), Charles Denner (Fergus), Alexandra Stewart (Mademoiselle Becker).

Stolen Kisses (*Baisers volés*), 1968
Director: François Truffaut
Screenplay: François Truffaut, Claude de Givray, Bernard Revon
Cinematographer: Denys Clerval
Music: Antoine Duhamel
Production Company: Les Films du Carrosse, Les Productions Artistes Associés
Cast (chief characters): Jean-Pierre Léaud (Antoine Doinel), Claude Jade (Christine), Daniel Ceccaldi (Monsieur Darbon), Claire Duhamel (Madame Darbon), Delphine Seyric (Fabienne Tabard), Michael Lonsdale (Monsieur Tabard), André Falcon (Monsieur Blady).

Mississippi Mermaid (*La Sirène du Missisipi*), 1969
Director: François Truffaut
Screenplay: François Truffaut, after the novel by William Irish.
Cinematographer: Denys Clerval
Music: Antoine Duhamel
Production Company: Les Films du Carrosse, Les Productions Artistes Associés, Produzioni Associate Delphos
Cast (chief characters): Catherine Deneuve (Marion), Jean-Paul Belmondo (Louis Mahé), Michel Bouquet (Comolli), Marcel Berbert (Jardine).

The Wild Child (*L'Enfant sauvage*), 1970
Director: François Truffaut
Screenplay: François Truffaut and Jean Gruault, after Jean Itard, *Mémoire et Rapport sur Vicor de l'Aveyron* (1806)
Cinematographer: Nestor Almendros

Music: Antonio Vivaldi
Production Company: Les Artistes Associés, Les Films du Carrosse, Les Productions Artistes Associés
Cast (chief characters): Jean-Pierre Cargol (Victor de l'Aveyron), François Truffaut (Doctor Jean Itard), Françoise Seigner (Madame Guérin), Jean Dasté (Philippe Pinel).

Bed and Board (*Domicile conjugal*), 1970
Director: François Truffaut
Screenplay: François Truffaut, Claude de Givray, Bernard Revon
Cinematographer: Nestor Almendros
Music: Antoine Duhamel
Production Company: Les Films du Carrosse, Valoria Films, Fida Conematografica
Cast (chief characters): Jean-Pierre Léaud (Antoine Doinel), Claude Jade (Christine), Daniel Ceccaldi (Lucien Darbon), Claire Duhamel (Madame Darbon), Hiroko Berghauer (Kyoko), Claude Vega (the strangler).

Two English Girls (*Les Deux Anglaises*), 1971
Director: François Truffaut
Screenplay: François Truffaut and Jean Gruault, after the novel by Henri-Pierre Roché
Cinematographer: Nestor Almendros
Music: Georges Delerue
Production Company: Les Films du Carrosse, Cinetel
Cast (chief characters): Jean-Pierre Léaud (Claude Roc), Kika Markham (Anne), Stacey Tendeter (Muriel), Sylvia Marriott (Mrs. Brown), Marie Mansart (Claire Roc), Philippe Léotard (Diurka), Annie Miller (Monique de Montferrand), Mark Peterson (Mr. Flint).

A Gorgeous Girl Like Me (*Une belle fille comme moi*), 1972
Director: François Truffaut
Screenplay: François Truffaut and Jean-Loup Dabadie, after the novel by Henry Farrell
Cinematographer: Pierre-William Glenn
Music: Georges Delerue
Production Company: Les Films du Carrosse, Columbia Films
Cast (chief characters): Bernadette Lafont (Camille Bliss), Claude Brasseur (Mr Murène), Charles Denner (Arthur), Guy Marchand (Sam Golden), André Dusollier (Stanislas Previne), Philippe Léotard (Clovis Bliss).

Day for Night (*La Nuit Américaine*), 1973
Director: François Truffaut
Screenplay: François Truffaut, Jean-Louis Richard, Suzanne Schiffman
Cinematographer: Pierre-William Glenn
Music: Georges Delerue
Production Company: Les Films du Carrosse, PECF, Produzione Intercontinentale Cinematografica
Cast (chief characters): François Truffaut (Ferrand, the director), Jacqueline Bisset (Julie Baker/Nelson – Paméla), Valentina Cortese (Séverine), Alexandra Stewart (Stacey), Jean-Pierre Aumont (Alexandre), Jean-Pierre Léaud (Alphonse), Nathalie Baye (Joëlle), Jean Champion (Bertrand, the producer), David Markham (Doctor Nelson), Dani (Liliane).

The Story of Adèle H. (*L'Histoire d'Adèle H.*), 1975
Director: François Truffaut
Screenplay: François Truffaut, Jean Gruault, Suzanne Schiffman
Cinematographer: Nestor Almendros
Music: Maurice Jaubert
Production Company: Les Artistes Associés, Les Films du Carrosse, Les Productions Artistes Associés

Cast (chief characters): Isabelle Adjani (Adèle Hugo), Bruce Robinson (Lieutenant Pinson), Sylvia Marriott (Mrs. Saunders), Joseph Blatchley (Whistler, the bookseller).

Small Change (*L'Argent de poche*) 1976
Director: François Truffaut
Screenplay: François Truffaut and Suzanne Schiffman
Cinematographer: Pierre-William Glenn
Music: Maurice Jaubert
Production Company: Les Films du Carrosse, Les Productions Artistes Associés
Cast (chief characters): Geory Desmouceaux (Patrick Desmouceaux), Philippe Goldmann (Julien Leclou), Sylvie Grezel (Sylvie), Claudio and Franck Deluca (Mathieu and Franck Deluca), Richard Golfier (Richard Golfier), Ewa Truffaut (Patricia), Laura Truffaut (Madeleine Doinel), Jean-François Stévinin (the teacher), Tania Torrens (Madame Riffle).

The Man Who Loved Women (*L'Homme qui aimait les femmes*), 1977
Director: François Truffaut
Screenplay: François Truffaut, Michel Fermaud, Suzanne Schiffman
Cinematographer: Nestor Almendros
Music: Maurice Jaubert
Production Company: Les Films du Carrosse
Cast (chief characters): Charles Denner (Bertrand Morane), Brigitte Fossey (Geneviève Bigey, the editor), Nelly Borgeaud (Delphine Grezel), Geneviève Fonanel (Hélène, the lingerie seller), Nathalie Baye (Martine Desdoits), Leslie Caron (Véra, the ex).

The Green Room (*La Chambre verte*), 1978
Director: François Truffaut
Screenplay: François Truffaut and Jean Gruault, after themes by Henry James
Cinematographer: Nestor Almendros
Music: Maurice Jaubert
Production Company: Les Films du Carrosse, Les Productions Artistes Associés
Cast (chief characters): François Truffaut (Julien Davenne), Nathalie Baye (Cécilia Mandel), Jean Dasté (Bernard Humbert, editor of *The Globe*), Jean-Pierre Moulin (Gérard Mazet), Jane Lobre (Madame Rambaud, the housekeeper), Patrick Maléon, young Georges), Annie Miller (Genviève Mazet), Nathan Miller (her son).

Love on the Run (*L'Amour en fuite*), 1979
Director: François Truffaut
Screenplay: François Truffaut, Marie-France Pisier, Jean Aurel, Suzanne Schiffman
Cinematographer: Nestor Almendros
Music: Georges Delerue
Production Company: Les Films du Carrosse
Cast (chief characters): Jean-Pierre Léaud (Antoine Doinel), Marie-France Pisier (Colette), Claude Jade (Christine), Julien Bertheau (Monsieur Lucien), Dani (Liliane), Dorothee (Sabine), Marie Henriau (the divorce judge).

The Last Metro (*Le dernier métro*), 1980
Director: François Truffaut
Screenplay: François Truffaut and Suzanne Schiffman
Cinematographer: Nestor Almendros
Music: Georges Delerue
Production Company: Les Films du Carrosse, Sédif Productions
Cast (chief characters): Catherine Deneuve (Marion Steiner), Gérard Depardieu (Bernard Granger), Jean Poiret (Jean-Loup Cottins), Heinz Bennent (Lucas Steiner), Jean-Louis Richard (Daxiat), Marcel Berbert (Merlin).

The Woman Next Door (*La Femme d'à côté*), 1981
Director: François Truffaut
Screenplay: François Truffaut, Suzanne Schiffman, Jean Aurel
Cinematographer: William Lubtchansky
Music: Georges Delerue
Production Company: Les Films du Carrosse, TFI Films Production
Cast (chief characters): Gérard Depardieu (Bernard Coudray), Fanny Ardant (Matthilde Bauchard), Henri Garcin (Philippe Bauchard), Michèle Baumgartner (Arlette Coudray), Véronique Silver (Madame Jouve).

Confidentially Yours (*Vivement dimanche!*), 1983
Director: François Truffaut
Screenplay: François Truffaut, Suzanne Schiffman, Jean Aurel, after the novel by Charles Williams
Cinematographer: Nestor Almendros
Music: Georges Delerue
Production Company: Films A2, Les Films du Carrosse, Soprofilms
Cast (chief characters): Fanny Ardant (Barbara Becker), Jean-Louis Trintignant (Julien Vercel), Philippe Laudenbach (Clément, the lawyer), Caroline Sihol (Marie-Christine Vercel), Phiippe Morier-Genoud (Superintendent Santelli), Jean-Pierre Kalfon (Jacques Massoulier), Anik Belaubre (the cashier at the Eden theater), Jean-Louis Richard (Louison), Georges Koulouris (detective Lablache).

Bibliography

Almendros, Nestor. *Un Homme à la caméra*. Paris: Hatier, 1980.

Argentieri, Simona. "Truffaut and the Failure of Introjection." In Glen Gabbard, ed. *Psychoanalysis and Film*. London and New York: Karnac, 2001, 107–113.

Baecque, Antoine de, and Serge Toubiana. *Francois Truffaut*. [Paris]: Gallimard, 1996.

———. *Truffaut*. Berkeley: University of California Press, 2000.

Barthes, Roland. *Image/Music/Text*. New York: Hill and Wang, 1977.

Bashevis-Singer, Isaac. *Contes*. Trans. Marie-Pierre Bay. Paris: Stock, 1985.

Baudrillard, Jean. *L' Échange symbolique et la mort*. [Paris]: Gallimard, 1976. Print.

———. *Symbolic Exchange and Death*. London; Thousand Oaks: Sage Publications, 1993.

Bellour, Raymond. *L'Analyse du film*. Paris: Éditions Albatros, 1980.

———. *The Analysis of Film*. Bloomington: Indiana University Press, 2000.

———. *Le Corps du cinéma: Hypnoses, émotions, animalités*. Paris: P.O.L, 2009.

Bertolucci, Bernardo, and Andrea Sabbadini, "Psychoanalysis: The 11th Muse (A Conversation), *Psychoanalytic Inquiry* 27:4 (2007): 381–394.

Bettelheim, Bruno. *The Empty Fortress: Infantile Autism and the Birth of the Self*. New York: The Free Press, 1972.

———. *The Uses of Enchantment: The Meaning and Importance of Fairy Tales*. New York: Knopf, 1976.

———. *The Uses of Enchantment: The Meaning and Importance of Fairy Tales*. New York: Vintage Books, 1977.

Bonnafons, Elizabeth. *François Truffaut*. Lausanne: L'Age d'Homme, 1981.

Brooks, Peter. *Reading for the Plot: Design and Intention in Narrative*. New York: Knopf, 1984.

Cahoreau, Gilles. *François Truffaut 1932–1984*. Paris: Julliard, 1989.

Carcassonne, Philippe. "Truffaut le narrateu," *Cinématographe* 32 (November 1977): 15–17.

Campion, Jane. "Director's Commentary." *Sweetie*. DVD Directed by Jane Campion. Irvington, NY: Criterion Collection, 2006.

Chevrie, Marc. "L'amour à l'imparfait." *Cahiers du cinéma* 369 (1985): 8–11.

Clough, Patricia Ticineto. *The Affective Turn: Theorizing the Social*. Durham and London: Duke University Press, 2007.

Collet, Jean. *Le Cinéma de François Truffaut*. Paris: L'Herminier, 1977.

———. *Lectures Du Film*. Paris: Éditions Albatros, 1977.

Corrigan, Timothy. *A Cinema Without Walls: Movies and Culture After Vietnam*. New Brunswick, N. J.: Rutgers University Press, 1991.

Crittenden, Roger. *La Nuit Americaine.* London: British Film Institute, 1998.

DalMolin, Eliane. "A Voice in the Dark: Feminine Figuration in Truffaut's 'Jules and Jim.'" *Literature Film Quarterly* 22:4 (1994): 238–245.

Damasio, Antonio. *Self Comes to Mind: Constructing the Conscious Brain.* New York: Pantheon, 2010.

Daney, Serge. " L'amour en Fuite." *Cahiers du cinéma.*298 (1979): 55–57.

Daney, Serge; Narboni, Jean; Toubiana, Serge. "Entretien avec François Truffaut." *Cahiers du cinéma* 316 (1980): 21–35.

de Lauretis, Teresa. *Alice Doesn't: Feminism, Semiotics, Cinema.* Bloomington: Indiana University Press, 1984.

Delahaye, Michel and Jacques Rivette. "Entretien avec Claude Lévi-Straus." *Cahiers du cinéma.*156 (June 1964): 19–29.

Desjardins, Aline, and François Truffaut. *Aline Desjardins s'entretient avec François Truffaut.* Paris: Ramsay, 1987.

Doane, Mary Anne. *The Desire to Desire: The Woman's Film of the 1940s.* Bloomington: Indiana University Press, 1987.

Durovicová, Natasa. "Biograph as Biography." *Wide Angle* 7.1 and 2 (1985): 3–17.

D. W. Winnicott. L'Arc; 69. [2]. ed. Aix-en-Provence: L'Arc, 1977.

Ehrenzweig, Anton. *The Hidden Order of Art; a Study in the Psychology of Artistic Imagination.* Berkeley: University of California Press, 1967.

Foucault, Michel. "What is an Author?" Trans. Donald F. Bouchard and Sherry Simon. In *Language, Counter-Memory, Practice.* Ed. Donald F. Bouchard. Ithaca, NY: Cornell University Press, 1977, 124–127.

Fox, Alistair. *Jane Campion: Authorship and Personal Cinema.* Bloomington: Indiana University Press, 2011.

Freud, Sigmund. *Le Mot d'esprit et Ses Rapports avec l'inconscient.* Paris: Gallimard, 1978.

Gabbard, Glen, ed. *Psychoanalysis and Film.* London and New York: Karnac, 2001.

Gaddini, Renata. "Le Déni de la séparation." *L'Arc* 69 (1977): 77–83.

Gerstner, David A., and Janet Staiger, eds. *Authorship and Film.* New York: Routledge, 2003.

Gillain, Anne. "Fantasme originaire: le plaisir narratif," *CinémAction* 50 (1989): 60–67.

———. *François Truffaut: le secret perdu.* Paris: Hatier, 1991.

———. "Reconciling Irreconcilables: An Interview with François Truffaut." *Wide Angle* 4.4 (1981): 26–37.

———. "La Scène de l'audition," *L'Avant-Scène Cinéma* 362–363: 69–75.

Graham, Peter John, and Ginette Vincendeau. *The French New Wave: Critical Landmarks.* London: Palgrave Macmillan, 2009.

Grant, Barry Keith, ed. *Auteurs and Authorship: A Film Reader.* Maldon, MA: Blackwell Publishing, 2008.

Green, André. "La Royauté appartient à l'enfant." *L'Arc* 69 (1977): 4–12.

Gruault, Jean. "Le Secret Perdu." *Cahiers du cinéma,* Supplément 366. *Le Roman de François Truffaut*--Numéro spécial (1984): 59–62.

Hayward, Susan, and Ginette Vincendeau. *French Film: Texts and Contexts.* London; New York: Routledge, 2000.

Holmes, Diana, and Robert Ingram. *François Truffaut.* Manchester; New York: Manchester University Press, 1998.

Ingram, Robert. *François Truffaut: Film Author 1932–1984.* London: Taschen, 2003.

Insdorf, Annette. *Francois Truffaut.* Cambridge; New York: Cambridge University Press, 1994.

Insdorf, Annette, Bruno Joliet, and Yves Coleman. *François Truffaut: le cinéma est-il magique ?* Paris: Ramsay, 1989.

Kané, Pascal. "Qui y a-t-il sous les jupes des femmes?" *Cahiers du cinéma* 329 (1981): 51–52.

Kehr, David. "A Poet of Darkness Who Longs for the Light." *The New York Times*, 16 May 1999.

Khan, Mohammed Masud Raza, et al. *Le Soi caché*. Paris: Gallimard, 1976.

Klein, Melanie. *Love, Guilt and Reparation: And Other Works 1921–1945*. New York: The Free Press, 1975.

Kline, Thomas Jefferson. "Cinema and/as Dream: Truffaut's "Royal Road" to *Adèle H.*" In *Unraveling French Cinema: From L'Atlante to Caché*. Chichester: Wiley, 2010. 109–131.

Kofman, Sarah. *Pourquoi rit-on ? Freud et le mot d'esprit*. Paris: Galilée, 1985. Print.

Kohn, Max. *Mot d'esprit et événement*. Paris: Éd. l'Harmattan, 1991.

Laplanche, Jean, and J. B. Pontalis. *Vocabulaire de la psychanalyse*. Paris: Presses Universitaires de France, 1967.

Le Berre, Carole. *François Truffaut*. Paris: Editions de l'Etoile/Cahiers du cinéma, 1993. Print.

———. *François Truffaut at Work*. London; New York: Phaidon Press, 2005.

Lévi-Strauss, Claude. *The Jealous Potter*. Trans. Chorier, Bénédicte. Chicago: University of Chicago Press, 1988.

———. *The Raw and the Cooked: Introduction to a Science of Mythology: I*. Trans. Weightman, John and Doreen. Harmondsworth: Penguin, 1986.

Lévi-Strauss, Claude, and Didier Eribon. *De près et de loin*. Paris: O. Jacob, 1988.

Mackillop, Ian Duncan. *Free Spirits Henri Pierre Roché, François Truffaut and the Two English Girls*. London: Bloomsbury, 2000.

Mannoni, Octave. *Clefs pour l'imaginaire; ou, l'autre scène*. Paris,: Èditions du Seuil, 1969.

Marie, Michel. *The French New Wave: An Artistic School*. Trans. Richard John Neupert. Malden, MA: Blackwell, 2003.

Mulvey, Laura. *Visual and Other Pleasures*. Bloomington: Indiana University Press, 1988.

Neyrat, Cyril, and others. "François Truffaut." *Collection Grands cinéastes* 2. Paris: "Cahiers du cinéma," "Le Monde," 2007. 2 vol. (95, 35).

Nicholls, David. *Francois Truffaut*. London: B.T. Batsford, 1993.

Noy, Pinchas. "Symbolism and Mental Representation." *Annual of Psychoanalysis* 1 (1973): 125–158.

———. "A Theory of Art and Aesthetic Experience," *Psychoanalytic Review* 55 (1968–1969): 623–645.

Rabourdin, Dominique. *Truffaut par Truffaut*. Paris: Éditions du Chêne, 1985.

Rivette, Jacques. "Notes sur une révolution," *Cahiers du cinéma* 54 (Christmas 1955), 18–19.

Rolin, Gabrielle. "Patrick Modiano le dernier enfant du siècle," *Lire* 120 (1985):63.

Le Roman De François Truffaut. Paris: Cahiers du cinéma, Éditions de l'Étoile, 1985.

Rosolato, Guy. *Le Désir et la perversion*. Paris: Seuil, 1967.

———. *Essais sur le symbolique*. Paris: Gallimard, 1969.

———. "Souvenir-Écran." *Communications* 23 (1975): 79–87.

Sabbadini, Andrea. "Cameras, Mirrors, and the Bridge Space: A Winnicottian Lens on Cinema," *Projections* 5:1 (Summer 2011): 17–30.

———, ed. *The Couch and the Silver Screen: Psychoanalytic Reflections on European Cinema*. Hove and New York: Brunner-Routledge, 2003.

Silverman, Kaja. *The Acoustic Mirror: The Female Voice in Psychoanalysis and Cinema*. Bloomington: Indiana University Press, 1988.

Stam, Robert. *François Truffaut and Friends: Modernism, Sexuality, and Film*

Adaptation. New Brunswick, N.J.: Rutgers University Press, 2006.
Téchiné, André. "D'une distance l'autre," *Cahiers du cinéma* 157 (July 1964): 50–51.
Truffaut, François. *Le Cinéma Selon François Truffaut*. Ed. Anne Gillain. Paris: Flammarion, 1988.
———. *Correspondance. Lettres recueillies par Gilles Jacob et Claude de Givray. Notes de Gilles Jacob*. Paris: Hatier, 1988
———. "Comment j'ai tourné *l'Enfant sauvage*," *L'Avant-Scène Cinéma* (1970).
———. "Les Extrêmes me touchent," *Cahiers du cinéma* 21 (March 1953): 61–63.
———. "Entretien avec Georges Franju," *Cahiers du cinéma* 101 (November 1959): 1–12. Print.
———. "Entretien avec François Truffaut," *Cinématographe* 44 (February 1979): 59–63.
———. *Les Films de ma vie*. [Paris]: Flammarion, 1975.
———. *The Films in My Life*. New York: Da Capo Press, 1994.
———. *L' Homme qui aimait les femmes cinéroman*. [Paris]: Flammarion, 1977.
———. "Mes Deux Anglaises, mon onzième Film." *L'Avant-Scène Cinéma* no. 121 (January 1972): 11.
———. *Le Plaisir Des Yeux. Écrits sur le cinéma*. Ed. Jean Narboni and Serge Toubiana. Paris: "Cahiers du cinéma," 2000.
———. "Pourquoi et comment *Le Dernier Metro*," *L'Avant-Scène Cinéma* 303–304 (March 1982): 5.
———, Mirella Jona Affron, and Elliot Rubinstein. *The Last Metro: François Truffaut, Director*. New Brunswick, N.J.: Rutgers University Press, 1985.
———, and Alfred Hitchcock. *Hitchcock*. New York: Simon and Schuster, 1984.
———, Dominique Rabourdin, and Robert Erich Wolf. *Truffaut by Truffaut Transl. from the French by Robert Erich Wolf*. New York: H. N. Abrams, 1987. Print.
———, Helen G. Scott, and Alfred Hitchcock. *Hitchcock*. Rev. ed. London: Paladin, 1986.
Tsai Ming Liang. "On the Uses and Misuses of Cinema," *Senses of Cinema* 58 (March, 2011) http://www.sensesofcinema.com/2011/feature-articles/on-the-uses-and-misuses-of-cinema/. Accessed November 9, 2011.
Vanoye, Francis. *L'Adaptation littéraire au cinéma*. Paris: Armand Colin, 2011.
Verhoeven, Deb. *Jane Campion*. New York: Routledge, 2009.
Walz, Eugene P. *Francois Truffaut: A Guide to References and Resources*. Boston, Mass.: G.K. Hall, 1982.
Wexman, Virginia Wright, ed. *Film and Authorship*. New Brunswick, N.J.: Rutgers University Press, 2003.
Winnicott, D. W. *The Child and the Outside World: Studies in Developing Relationships*. New York: Basic Books, 1957.
———. *Collected Papers: Through Paediatrics to Psycho-Analysis*. London: Tavistock, 1958.
———. "Fear of Breakdown," *The International Review of Psycho-Analysis* 1: 103–07.
———. *Home Is Where We Start From: Essays by a Psychoanalyst* Clare Winnicott, Ray Shepherd, Madeleine Davis ed. Harmondsworth: Penguin, 1986.
———. *The Maturational Processes and the Facilitating Environment: Studies in the Theory of Emotional Development*. International Psycho-Analytical Library, No. 64. London: Hogarth, 1965.
———. *Playing and Reality*. London; New York: Routledge, 2005.
———, and Janet Hardenberg. *The Child and the Outside World: Studies in Developing Relationships*. London: Tavistock, 1957.
———, and others. *Deprivation and Delinquency*. London; New York: Tavistock Publications, 1984.

Index

ANNE GILLAIN is Professor Emerita at Wellesley College and is known for her work in French cinema, particularly the films of François Truffaut. She is the author of *Le Cinéma selon François Truffaut* and *The 400 Blows.*

ALISTAIR FOX is Professor of English at the University of Otago. He is the author of *Jane Campion: Authorship and Personal Cinema* (IU Press, 2011).